The *Sams Teach Yourself in 24 Hours* Series

Sams Teach Yourself in 24 Hours books provide quick and easy answers in a proven step-by-step approach that works for you. In just 24 sessions of one hour or less, you will tackle every task you need to get the results you want. Let our experienced authors present the most accurate information to get you reliable answers—fast!

D1449877

MAINTAIN AN ERROR-FREE CHECKBOOK—HOUR 6

SET UP ONLINE ACCOUNT SERVICE—HOUR 4 AND HOUR 15

CREATE A PLAN TO ELIMINATE CREDIT CARD DEBT—HOUR 9

AVOID CREDIT CARD OVERCHARGES—HOUR 9

CREATE A PLAN FOR A DEBT-FREE AND PROSPEROUS FUTURE THAT REALLY WORKS—HOUR 13 AND HOUR 14

SET UP A PRUDENT BUDGET YOU CAN ACTUALLY LIVE WITH—HOUR 13

DETERMINE THE TRUE COSTS OF A LOAN OR MORTGAGE—HOUR 10

OBTAIN ANY INFORMATION ABOUT YOUR FINANCES AT A GLANCE—HOUR 7

NEVER AGAIN LOOSE TRACK OF MONEY YOU'VE BEEN PAID—HOUR 8

AUTOMATE BILL PAYMENTS—HOUR 11

DETERMINE UPCOMING BILLS AT A GLANCE—HOUR 11

PLAN FOR A MORTGAGE YOU CAN LIVE WITH, BUT STILL MAINTAIN THE HIGHEST TAX ADVANTAGE—HOUR 10

INSTANTLY LOCATE AND TRACK ANY CHECK YOU'VE WRITTEN—HOUR 6

INSTANTLY CREATE ANY TYPE OF ACCOUNT—HOUR 4

TRANSFER MONEY BETWEEN ACCOUNTS—HOUR 4

CREATE AN ADVANTAGEOUS BILL-PAYING STRATEGY—HOUR 11

QUICKLY LOCATE ANY FEATURE IN MONEY 99—HOUR 3

GET INSTANT HELP—HOUR 3

DIVIDE ALL YOUR EXPENSES INTO HELPFUL CATEGORIES—HOUR 5

TRACK AND CATEGORIZE INCOME SOURCES—HOUR 5

continues

SAMS

Teach You

Microsoft
Money 99

in 24
Hours

PRINT PROFESSIONAL LOOKING CHECKS—HOUR 12

PRINT HIGHLY ACCURATE AND SOPHISTICATED FINANCIAL REPORTS—HOUR 12

MAP OUT YOUR FINANCIAL FUTURE WITH REVEALING CHARTS AND GRAPHS—HOUR 12 AND 17

CREATE A FINANCIAL SELF-PORTRAIT—HOUR 1

INSTANTLY DETERMINE HOW MUCH MONEY YOU'VE PAID ANYONE, AND WHEN—HOUR 8

SET UP AUTOMATIC MORTGAGE AND LOAN PAYMENTS—HOUR 10

LEARN WHICH TYPE OF MORTGAGE IS THE MOST BENEFICIAL TO YOU—HOUR 10

PAINLESSLY PAY OFF COSTLY MORTGAGES AND LOANS—HOUR 10

SET UP AUTOMATED CREDIT CARD PAYMENTS WITH AN ONLINE ACCOUNT—HOUR 9

KEEP BETTER TRACK OF CREDIT CARD SPENDING—HOUR 9

SAMS

Winston Steward with
David Karlins

SAMS
Teach Yourself

Microsoft® Money 99

in 24 Hours

SAMS

A Division of Macmillan Computer Publishing
201 West 103rd St., Indianapolis, Indiana, 46290 USA

Sams Teach Yourself Microsoft® Money 99 in 24 Hours

Copyright © *1999* by *Sams*

International Standard Book Number: 0-672-31367-7

Library of Congress Catalog Card Number: 98-85628

Printed in the United States of America

First Printing: *November 1998*

00   99   98   1   4   3   2   1

Interpretation of the printing code: The rightmost double-digit number is the year of the book's printing; the rightmost single-digit, the number of the book's printing. For example, a printing code of 98-1 shows that the first printing of the book occurred in 1998.

Trademarks

EXECUTIVE EDITOR
Angela Wethington

ACQUISITIONS EDITOR
Stephanie J. McComb

DEVELOPMENT EDITORS
John Gosney
Valerie Perry

MANAGING EDITOR
Thomas F. Hayes

TECHNICAL EDITOR
Debra King

PROJECT EDITOR
Sossity Smith

COPY EDITOR
Julie McNamee

INDEXER
Becky Hornyak

PROOFREADER
Lynne Miles-Morillo

LAYOUT TECHNICIAN
Steve Geiselman

Overview

Introduction   xxi

PART I THE FIRST STEPS   **1**

Hour 1   Money 99—Before You Begin   3
      2   Getting Started   19
      3   A First Look Around Money 99   37
      4   Setting Up Accounts   59
      5   Dividing Expenses into Categories   85
      6   Writing Checks   115

II MONEY 99 DAY TO DAY   **131**

Hour 7   Using the Register   133
      8   Tracking Payees   151
      9   Setting Up and Tracking Credit and Debit Cards   169
     10   Setting Up and Tracking Loans and Mortgages   197
     11   Paychecks, Bills, and Other Recurring Transactions   229

III THE BIGGER PICTURE   **251**

Hour 12   Printing Checks and Other Forms   253
     13   Creating a Budget   271
     14   Long-term Planning and Goals   299
     15   Money Online   325
     16   Money Reports   349
     17   Charts and the Chart Gallery   367
     18   Money and Taxes   383

IV ADVANCED TOOLS   **395**

Hour 19   Money as an Investment Tool   397
     20   Money and Your Small Business   413
     21   Regular Tasks   427
     22   Backing Up and Archiving Your Data   439
     23   Customizing Money   449
     24   Converting from Quicken   461

Contents

INTRODUCTION XXI

PART I THE FIRST STEPS   1

HOUR 1 MONEY 99—BEFORE YOU BEGIN   3

Creating a Financial Self-Portrait 4
Choosing a Start Date 4
    Pick the Earliest Date Possible 5
    Why Go to the Trouble? 6
Financial Records Checklist 7
    Regular Income Sources and Expenses...7
    Infrequent or Irregular Income Sources and Expenses 7
Prepare a List of Assets 8
How to Approach Money 99 9
    Information Is King...9
    Explorer Anyone? 10
What Is an Account?...10
Thinking in Categories 11
    Be Patient with the Data Entry 11
Installing Microsoft Money 99 12
Browser Wars and Money 99 12
Changing the Installation Folder 12
Installing and Setting Up Online Options 13
    Opting for Online Registration 13
    Problems with Installation?..14
Setting Up Your Internet Connection 15
    To Do: Making Money 99 Aware of Your Internet Connection 15
Internet Access and Choosing a Browser 16
Summary 16
Q&A..16

HOUR 2 GETTING STARTED   19

Starting Money 19
Creating a Desktop Shortcut 20
    To Do: Creating a Shortcut on the Desktop 20
What You See When You Start Money 21
What Is a Money File? 24
    Create More than One Money File? 24
Your Money at a Glance 25
    The Bills Area...26
    The Accounts Area 27

The Monthly Report 27

    The Chart of the Day 28

Money Home's Articles, Connections, and Tips 30

    The Advisor FYI 30

    The Decisions Center 31

    Money 99 Investor 32

Updating Money Home 32

    To Do: Updating Money Home 32

Exiting Money 33

Summary 34

Q&A 35

HOUR 3 A FIRST LOOK AROUND MONEY 99   **37**

The Navigation Bar...37

The Money Menu 39

    The File Menu 39

    The Edit Menu 39

    The Go Menu 39

    The Favorites Menu 39

    The Tools Menu 40

Money "Channel Guides"..41

    What's Down Below? 41

Money 99 Wizards 43

Money 99 Access Tips 44

    Right-Click for Additional Options...44

    Drop-Down Lists 44

    "The Mouse Cursor Just Changed!" 46

What Are Active Features? 47

    To Do: Understanding Active Features 47

    Single- and Double-Clicking..47

Money's Help System..48

    The Help Topics Channel Bar 48

    Exploring Links to Related Topics 49

    Performing a Keyword Search 50

    Money 99 Context-Sensitive Help 51

    "What's This?" 52

    Navigation Bar Help Tool 53

Internet-Based Help for Money 99 53

    Microsoft Money Home Page 54

    Frequently Asked Questions 54

    Online Support...55

    Help for Quicken Users...55

Calling Microsoft Technical Support 56

    To Do: Locating Your Computer's System Information 56

Summary 57

Q&A 57

HOUR 4 SETTING UP ACCOUNTS   **59**

Understanding Accounts 59

What Kinds of Accounts Are There? 60

Determining an Account's Purpose 61

Creating Accounts 61

To Do: Creating an Account 63

Organizing Your Accounts with a "Getting Started" Account Checklist 65

To Do: Creating an Account Checklist 66

Understanding Account Balances 67

Navigating Your Accounts 67

Viewing All Your Accounts 67

Viewing Your Accounts 68

Using the Account Registry View 68

Using the Account History View 70

Using the Details View 70

Editing Account Transactions 72

To Do: Editing a Transaction You've Already Entered 72

Closing and Deleting an Account 73

Quickly Accessing an Account 74

Setting Up an Account Online 75

Where's My Bank? 76

Getting Started with Online Banking 76

To Do: Choosing and Setting Up an Online Banking Service 76

Adjusting Your Money 99 Start Date 80

To Do: Setting a Money 99 Start Date 80

To Do: Entering Older Transactions into Money's Accounts 81

To Do: Correcting for an Initial Balance 81

Summary 82

Q&A 82

HOUR 5 DIVIDING EXPENSES INTO CATEGORIES   **85**

Exploring the Categories & Payees Screen 86

Why Use Categories? 88

Why Use Classifications? 88

Categories and Concepts 88

Viewing a Category Close-Up 88

Where Do Payees Come In? 90

Creating a New Category or Subcategory 90

To Do: Creating a Category or Subcategory 91

Deleting Categories..93

Restoring Money 99's Standard Categories 94

Categories at Work 94

    Assigning a Category to a Transaction 95

    Creating a New "Instant" Category..98

    Viewing and Editing Transactions in a Category 98

    Creating a Subcategory On-The-Fly 98

Viewing and Editing Category Details 99

    To Do: Modifying Category Details 99

    The Category Bar Graph 101

    The Category Transaction List 101

    The Category Budget Link 101

Assigning Transactions to a New Category 102

    To Do: Reassigning Categories to a Group of Transactions..................102

Tracking Tax Information with Categories...104

Working with Classifications 105

What Happens When You Create Classifications?.....................................105

    How Classifications Work 106

    Using and Applying Classifications 108

How to Create Classifications...110

    To Do: Creating a Classification 110

    A Classification Is Just a Label...111

    Applying Classifications to Transactions 112

    Creating a Second Classification...112

Q&A 113

HOUR 6 WRITING CHECKS   **115**

Getting Ready to Write Checks 115

Writing a Check 117

The Automatic Fill-In Feature 120

Avoid Crossing Category Types 120

Putting the Memo Feature to Good Use..121

Editing a Transaction 121

    To Do: Editing a Check 122

Editing Reconciled and Cleared Transactions 123

Voiding and Deleting Checks 124

    To Do: Voiding and Deleting a Check...125

    To Do: Restoring a Voided Check 125

Depositing Funds to an Account...125

    To Do: Making a Deposit 125

Transferring Funds Between Accounts..126

    To Do: Transferring Funds 127

Summary 128
Q&A 128

PART II MONEY 99 DAY TO DAY   131

HOUR 7 USING THE REGISTER   133
Changing the Way Transactions Are Listed 134
Working with the Register 136
Creating a Split Transaction 137
    Two Examples of Split Accounts 138
    How to Create a Split Transaction 139
Making a Cash Withdrawal 141
    Should You Create a Cash Account? 141
Balancing an Account 144
    How to Balance Bank and Credit Card Accounts 144
    When the Account Doesn't Balance..148
    Balancing an Asset Account 149
Summary 149
Q&A 150

HOUR 8 TRACKING PAYEES   151
Opening the Payees list 152
Adding a Payee..155
    To Do: Directly Adding a Payee 155
    When You Have More than One Payee at a Company 155
    Locating and Replacing Payees and Transactions 157
Finding a Specific Transaction in a Large List....................................158
    To Do: Finding a Specific Transaction 159
Viewing and Editing Payee Information 160
How Transactions Are Listed 163
Editing Transactions from the Payee Details List 164
Viewing All Payments to a Single Payee 165
    To Do: Changing a Payee Report Date Range 165
Summary 166
Q&A 167

HOUR 9 SETTING UP AND TRACKING CREDIT AND DEBIT CARDS   169
How Credit Card Accounts Differ from Other Accounts 170
How Money 99 Credit Accounts Work 171
A Safeguard to Free Credit Card Spending 171
Setting Up a Credit Card Account 171
    To Do: Creating a Credit Card Account 172
    Entering Credit Card Transactions 174

How to Itemize Credit Card Purchases 175

Transferring Credit Card Funds to Another Account 176

Recording a Credit or Refund 177

Refund Considerations 177

To Do: Voiding a Credit Card Transaction 178

To Do: Crediting a Partial Refund or Return 178

To Do: Issuing a Simple Credit to Your Credit Card Account 180

Assigning the Right Category to a Credit 180

To Do: Categorizing a Credit to Your Credit Card Account 180

Changing Credit Card Options 181

To Do: Viewing Credit Card Account Details 181

Paying a Monthly Credit Card Bill 183

To Do: Paying a Credit Card Bill with AutoBalance 184

Why Not Disable AutoBalance Permanently? 186

Itemizing Purchase Categories with Your Payment 186

To Do: Paying Your Credit Card Bill with a Split Transaction 186

Balancing Your Credit Card Account 188

To Do: Balancing Your Credit Card Account 189

Credit Cards and Your Future 192

To Do: Including a Credit Card in Your Debt Reduction Plan 192

Summary 194

Q&A 195

HOUR 10 TRACKING MORTGAGES, LOANS, AND ASSETS   **197**

Tools for Getting Started 198

When to Use the New Loan Wizard 199

Determining How Much You Can Borrow 200

To Do: Learning How Much You Should Borrow 200

Setting Up a Mortgage Account 206

To Do: Creating a Mortgage or Long-Term Loan Account 206

Making Payments on Your Mortgage 210

Automating Your Mortgage or Loan Payment 212

Balancing Your Mortgage Account 213

Making an Extra Mortgage Payment 214

Moving Between Your Related Accounts 215

Updating Loan Details 217

Changing Specific Loan Information 218

Updating Your Interest Rate 219

Refinancing Your Mortgage or Long-Term Loan 219

To Do: Exploring Refinancing with the Loan Worksheet 220

Where Do I Put My Loan Company's Contact Information? 222

To Do: Storing Information About Your Loan Company 222

Asset Accounts 222

Recording Changes in an Asset Account's Value 223

The Home Inventory Worksheet 223

    To Do: Tracking Valuables with the Home Inventory Worksheet 224

Creating an Account to Manage Home Inventory Items 225

    To Do: Creating a Home Inventory Asset Account 226

Summary 226

Q&A 226

HOUR 11 PAYCHECKS, BILLS, AND OTHER RECURRING TRANSACTIONS   **229**

Money and Planning 229

Not Only Bills 230

A Quick Tour of the Bills Screens 230

Setting Up an Online Transaction 232

    To Do: Setting Up a Recurring Deposit or Bill 232

Itemizing Your Scheduled Paycheck 237

Special Issues for Scheduling Bills 239

Paying Bills 240

    To Do: Paying Bills 240

Navigating Between Bills, Payees, Categories, and Accounts 241

Working with the Bill Calendar 242

The Balance Forecast 243

Picking a Balance Forecast Date Range 244

Using the Chart to Show Daily Balance Changes 246

    To Do: Viewing Changing Account Balances on a Chart Line 246

Selecting Which Account to View in the Forecast 247

    How to Interpret the Forecast 247

    Viewing the Budget Forecast 247

Summary 248

Q&A 249

PART III THE BIGGER PICTURE   **251**

HOUR 12 PRINTING CHECKS AND OTHER FORMS   **253**

Printing Checks 253

Ordering Checks from Microsoft 254

    Check Styles 255

Proceed with Patience 255

What Starting Number Should I Pick? 255

Getting Ready to Print 256

    A Page of Checks 256

    What Does Money 99 Print on Each Check? 257

Getting Ready to Print Checks 257

To Do: Preparing for Check Printing 258

Designating a Check For Printing 258

Printing Checks..260

To Do: Printing the Checks 260

Printing Other Money Documents 263

Getting Ready to Print Reports..264

Printing a Report 265

Exporting a Report to a Spreadsheet 265

To Do: Exporting a Money Report to a Spreadsheet 265

Printing Documents Linked to an Article..267

To Do: Printing Linked Documents 267

To Do: Printing Everything on Your Money 99 Screen 268

Fixing Printer Problems 268

Summary 269

Q&A 270

HOUR 13 CREATING A BUDGET   **271**

Overview...271

Motivation 271

Information 272

Examination...272

Creative Change 272

Initial Budgeting Steps 272

Take Money's Budget Self-Tests...273

Where I Am and Where I Want to Be 274

The Debt Reduction Planner..276

Making a Budget..280

Including Income Sources in Your Budget 280

Adding a Category..283

Including Savings in Your Budget Plan...285

Editing Long-Term Saving Source Accounts 287

Taking the Longer View 287

Setting Aside Money for Occasional Expenses 288

Including Debts and Loans in Your Budget 289

Viewing Your Expenses..290

Creating an AutoBudget 291

Extra Money? 291

Adjusting Savings Amounts 292

Looking Ahead 292

Reducing Monthly Obligations..294

Answers to your Financial Questions 295
    To Do: Search "Ask The Experts"...295
Summary 296
Q&A 296

Hour 14 Long-Term Planning and Goals   299

Viewing the Lifetime Planner 299
    How The Lifetime Planner Is Organized 300
    Telling Money About Yourself 301
    Looking at Savings and Investments..302
    Managing Profitable Accounts 303
    Projecting with Various Return Rates 304
    Adding a New Investment Account 306
    Modifying an Account via the Lifetime Planner 306
Planning a Long Range Goal 309
    The Lifetime Planner...309
    Using the Lifetime Planner to Create ìWhat Ifs?î 309
More Ways to Learn About Your Plan 312
    Identifying Problems in Your Plan 312
    The Bottom Line 313
    Assumptions 315
    Snapshots 316
    The Action Plan 317
    Viewing Forecasts that Include Your Goals 317
    To Do: Viewing Forecasts 317
    To Do: Forecasting Your Future Income 317
    To Do: Printing Your Complete Financial Plan............................319
Using the Decisions Centers...319
    Savings 320
    Automobile 320
    Calculator Tools and Worksheets 320
Summary 322
Q&A 322

Hour 15 Money Online   325

Getting Online 325
    Installing Explorer...326
    Choosing an Internet Connection 326
    Electronic Payments, Transfers, Automatic Payments, Electronic Bills........328
Choosing a Bank with Online Services 329
    To Do: Setting Up Money 99's Online Services............................330
    Paying Bills Online 330
    Updating Your Balance Online 333
    Reading Your Statements 334

Transferring Money Between Accounts Online 335
Emailing Your Bank 337
Statements & Balances Area 338
Payments in Progress..338
Bill Paying Information...340
Standing Orders..340
If Your Bank Does Not Offer Online Service 341
To Do: Third-Party Providers 341
Special Online Situations 342
Canceling a Transaction Online 342
Following Up on an Online Payment 343
Canceling an Online Automatic Payment 344
Canceling Your Online Banking 345
Cancel Web Financial Services 346
What If I Change Banks 346
Summary..347
Q&A 347

HOUR 16 MONEY REPORTS   349

Where Money Gets Its Data 350
Adding Helpful Data 350
Paying Attention to the Scope of the Report...350
Choosing a Date Range 350
How Reports Work 350
Harnessing Helpful Information 350
Navigation Through a Report 351
Making a Report a Favorite 353
Exporting Reports 353
A Report Versus a Chart 355
Knowing the Most Helpful Way to View Information 355
Switching Between Reports and Charts 356
Editing a Chart in a Report 358
Opening a Report 359
Loan Reports 359
Working with Reports..360
Creating a Favorite 360
Customizing Reports 361
Printing a Report 361
Resetting Reports You've Customized 362
The Monthly Report 362
The Report Categories 362
How to Use the Information 363
Viewing Transactions 364

Summary 365
Q&A 365

HOUR 17 CHARTS AND THE CHART GALLERY   367

Tracking Your Money with Charts 367
Selecting the Chart of the Day 368
    To Do: Define Chart of the Day Display 368
    Changing Chart Display 369
    Locating and Opening Charts 370
    Opening a Transaction from a Chart 371
Customizing Charts 373
Changing Date Ranges 373
Switching Between Chart Types 375
    Renaming a Chart 375
    Defining Chart Display 376
    Defining Rows Versus Columns 377
    Creating a Favorite Chart 380
    Resetting Customized Charts 380
Printing a Chart 380
Exporting a Chart 381
Summary 381
Q&A 382

HOUR 18 MONEY AND TAXES   383

How Money Helps You with Your Taxes 383
Preparing for Taxes 384
    Viewing Categories with Tax-Associated Information 384
    Assigning Tax-Related Information to Categories 385
    Reviewing Money Insider's "Taxes" Articles 386
Filling Out the Tax Worksheet 387
    To Do: Filling Out the Tax Worksheet 387
Preparing Tax Forms 389
Exporting Information to Money and Tax Software 392
    To Do: Exporting Money 99 Files to *txf Format 392
Summary 393
Q&A 393

PART IV ADVANCED TOOLS   299

HOUR 19 MONEY AS AN INVESTMENT TOOL   397

Defining Your Investments for Money 398
    Setting Up an Investment Account 398
    Associating Securities with an Account and Getting Online Quotes
        from Investor 400

Setting Up an Account for a Single Investment 404

Working with Mutual Funds 404

Maintaining Investment Accounts 405

Tracking Stock Prices 405

Buying Additional Stocks 405

Selling Stocks 406

Transfer Money to an Investment Account 406

Viewing Investment Information 407

Total Portfolio Value 407

Viewing Investment Account Details 407

Retirement Planning 408

Viewing Investments in Graphs...408

Summary..412

Q&A 412

HOUR 20 MONEY AND YOUR SMALL BUSINESS   413

Starting Your Business 413

To Do: Create a New Small Business Account..414

How Money Can Help Your Business 414

Tracking Expenses and Liabilities 415

Monitoring Large Numbers of Transactions..416

Tracking Expenses...418

Keeping Up-to-Date 420

What Money Does Not Do 420

Managing Payroll 420

Creating Special Payroll Accounts 420

Creating Subcategories for Deductions and Contributions...........................421

Creating a Subcategory for Net Income 421

Issuing Paychecks 422

Information for Tax Forms 424

To Do: Generate an Annual Report of All Payroll Deductions for

One Employee..424

Summary..425

Q&A 425

HOUR 21 REGULAR TASKS   427

Daily Chores 428

Keeping Track of Receipts 428

Recording Credit Card Transactions as They Are Made..............................429

Thinking "Category" 430

What's New at Money's Home Page? 430

To Do: Get Investment Information Online 432

Weekly Tasks 432

Monthly Tasks 433
Create and Back Up a Money Archive 434
Delete Regular Bills that No Longer Apply 434
Deleting Outdated Payees 434
Closing or Deleting Old Accounts 435
Quarterly Tasks 436
Near the End of the Tax Year 436
Summary 436
Q&A 436

Hour 22 Backing Up and Archiving Your Data   **439**

Backing Up Your Money File 440
Backing Up Files Manually..440
Other Ways to Back Up Your Files 441
Changing Backup Preferences..441
Restoring Files from a Backup 443
To Do: Restore a Backed Up File 443
Archiving Your Data 444
Archiving Strategies 444
How to Archive Your Money Accounts...444
Opening an Archive File 446
Summary 446
Q&A 447

Hour 23 Customizing Money   **449**

Customizing at a Glance...449
Changing Billing Options 450
To Do: Customize Bill Reminder Features 450
Automating Data Entry 450
Choosing How Aggressively the Planner Tracks Income 453
Changing Categories, Investment Options, and Currencies 454
Defining Expense Category Rules 454
Defining Investment Tracking and Currency Rates 455
Specifying How Checks Are Printed 456
To Do: Define a Check Form 457
Setting Up Internet Connection Preferences 457
Specifying Tax Filing Status and Rates 458
Setting Options for Downloaded Statements 458
Summary 459
Q&A 459

hour 24 Converting from Quicken   **461**

Allowing Money to Convert Your Quicken Files 462

    To Do: Import Quicken Files 462
    Importing Quicken Data After Installation 464
    Importing Other Quicken Files 464
    Quicken Elements Lost in Conversion 465
Special Assistance for Quicken Users 466
    To Do: Print Quicken Checks with Money 99 466
    Resolving Account Balance Differences.......................................466
    Noting Similar Commands 467
Summary..467
Q&A 468

INDEX   469

About the Author

Winston Steward is a freelance writer and designer. He has authored and coauthored many books, including *Using QuickBooks and QuickBooks Pro Version 6.0*, *Teach Yourself TurboTax in 24 Hours*, and *The Comprehensive Guide to WordPerfect 8*. He is a community college instructor, teaching weekend classes on Excel and Word 97, and he appears regularly on the National Public Radio program "Insight," fielding software-related questions from all over the United States.

David Karlins is a computer book author and also trains at corporations, community colleges, and commercial training centers. His most recent books include *Teach Yourself CorelDRAW 8 in 24 Hours*, *Teach Yourself FrontPage 98 in a Week*, *Wild Web Graphics with Microsoft Image Composer*, and *Create a Web Site for Free*. David is also a co-author of the *FrontPage 2000 Bible*. Visit David anytime at `www.ppinet.com`.

For everyone who reads this: To a life less anxious. — W.S.

Acknowledgments

"Thanks to friends and family, and Margot Malley, Agent Extraordinaire, and to Stephanie Mccomb and Sossity Smith for thoughtful and patient editing, and especially my buddy Maria: "I've got a backstage pass to my next dream that says I'm not alone.""

Tell Us What You Think!

As the reader of this book, *you* are our most important critic and commentator. We value your opinion and want to know what we're doing right, what we could do better, what areas you'd like to see us publish in, and any other words of wisdom you're willing to pass our way.

As the Executive Editor for the General Desktop Applications team at Macmillan Computer Publishing, I welcome your comments. You can fax, email, or write me directly to let me know what you did or didn't like about this book—as well as what we can do to make our books stronger.

Please note that I cannot help you with technical problems related to the topic of this book, and that due to the high volume of mail I receive, I might not be able to reply to every message.

When you write, please be sure to include this book's title and author as well as your name and phone or fax number. I will carefully review your comments and share them with the author and editors who worked on the book.

Fax: 317-817-7448

Email: office@mcp.com

Mail: Executive Editor
          General Desktop Applications
          Macmillan Computer Publishing
          201 West 103rd Street
          Indianapolis, IN 46290 USA

Introduction

Have you ever been driving down the freeway and wondered how much money slips through your fingers in a lifetime, doing the calculations in your mind, multiplying that monthly paycheck by twelve for each year of your working life? Yes, it's an astounding amount of money, all told. Then the obvious question arises: "Where does it all go?" The big items take much of the money, to be sure—the mortgage, the car payments, children's education, perhaps a major vacation or two, and fixing up the house before reselling it. But that doesn't account for all of it. What about the rest?

If you're a spontaneous person, an impulse buyer, you may tend to spend rather freely. When you think about the big sums of money you make over the years, you may start to wonder what could be possible if those nickels and dimes were minded a bit more intentionally. If you add all that spare change up, you think of opportunities missed.

Microsoft Money can help automate and make sense of all your financial transactions. You can micromanage every expense down to the gum you chew, or just let Money manage the bigger expenses. Money can function as an electronic checkbook, but it also analyzes purchasing power by pointing out where there is some flexibility and where a little fiscal sanity can be restored. Then it draws a chart showing how impressive the results can be, if dollars are managed a little differently.

Your experience with Money 99 is about to begin. Like other financial programs, Money plays accountant for you, but it also shows how some of your favorite "what ifs" are not merely daydreams. After you see what corners to cut, it's truly remarkable when Money draws up the long-term results. You'll learn that even small expenditures make a substantial difference, over the long haul. Because you have the software ready to go and this book in your hand, there's never a better time to start than right now.

A Quick Glance at What's New

To emphasize what's new in this version, let's indulge in a quick overview of some of Money 99's most remarkable features. Consider this a quick walk-through of some of the nicest points in this program.

Day to Day with Money 99

Money 99 helps manage your finances, keeping you in touch with how your money is being spent and giving you tools to make better spending decisions. To get started, you let Money know about all your bills and income sources. You can then schedule regular bill payments and check deposits, so Money automatically stays on top of your spending and earning. Because the program handles redundant tasks like paycheck deposits and monthly bills, you can spend more time charting financial goals, rather than fretting over the checkbook. And to help you with your goals, Money 99 makes budgeting suggestions, both short-term and long-term.

The Most Common Money 99 Tools

Some of the most common tools you'll be working with in Money 99 are described in the following sections.

Setting Bill Payments and Deposits, and Writing Checks

The screen for entering bill and deposit information is shown in Figure I.1. To enter payments or deposits, just follow the onscreen instructions. Bills and Deposits are covered in Hour 11, "Paychecks, Bills, and Other Recurring Transactions."

FIGURE I.1.

Let Money 99 know about your bills and deposits. Just enter the information when prompted.

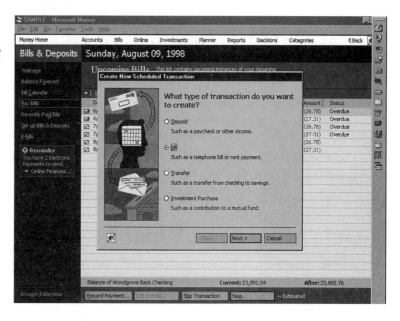

The Check Register window is shown in Figure I.2. As you can see, making out a check in Money 99 is similar to using your paper checkbook: just type in an amount, date, and payee. The program keeps track of check numbers and helps you organize your payments into categories, using that information to your advantage when you create a budget. Writing Checks is covered in Hour 6, "Writing Checks."

FIGURE I.2.

Making a check in Money 99 is similar to filling out a standard paper check register.

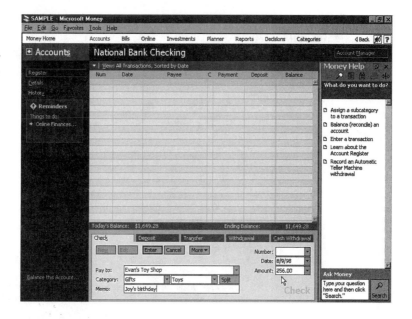

Knowing Where Your Money Goes

Figure I.3 shows the Payee's List. Every time you write a check to someone, their name and information is recorded here. Click any name in this list to find out how much you've paid this payee in the last month or year. If you made a check out to someone, perhaps even two years ago, and there's some question about it, you can easily locate that check in Money. The Payees list is covered in Hour 8, "Tracking Payees."

Creating Accounts

You create accounts and move between them in the Account Manager (see Figure I.4). In Money 99, accounts are not merely where the bank keeps your money. Accounts are Money 99's way of setting aside money for various purposes, all with a view towards building your financial goals. Accounts are covered in Hour 4, "Setting Up Accounts."

Setting Up Categories

The Categories list is shown in Figure I.5. When you assign income and spending to categories, Money 99 uses that information to map out everything you need to know about improving your financial picture. Any time you write or deposit a check, it is assigned to a category. You can also create your own categories. Working with categories is covered in Hour 5, "Dividing Expenses into Categories."

FIGURE I.3.

Every time you write a check to someone, an entry is created in the Payee's List.

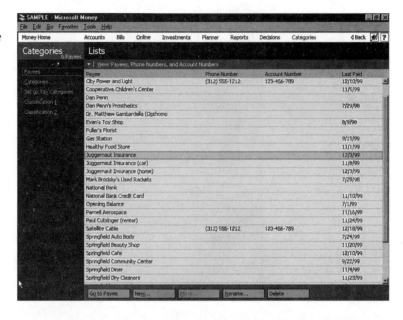

FIGURE I.4.

In the Account Manager you create new accounts and move between them.

FIGURE I.5.

*Money 99 creates
income and expense
categories. This
information makes
the reports and fore-
casts more accurate.*

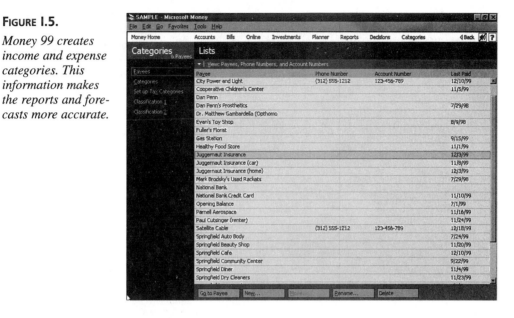

Those are some of the features you'll work with most often in Money 99. Let's briefly
review what you can do with Money 99 Online.

Money 99 Online

You can sign up through Money 99 with any one of dozens of lending institutions to gain
instant online access to your funds. You can write checks, automate deposits and bill-
paying, and transfer money online, using Money's own secure connection. These transactions do not occur over the World Wide Web, where anyone else can see them. Figure I.6
shows upcoming online bill payments through the Woodgrove Bank. Notice that you can
also download bank statements, and cancel upcoming online bill payments.

After you've signed up for online banking, you can pay many bills by selecting Epay in
the Check Number area of your Check Register, as shown in Figure I.7. Or, Money can
conduct banking business without your even being at the computer by scheduling payments and deposits in advance, as long as your Internet connection is open. Money
Online is covered in Hour 15, "Money Online."

FIGURE I.6.

Many types of transactions can be carried out online. As shown here, you can download a bank statement, cancel a payment, and pay a bill.

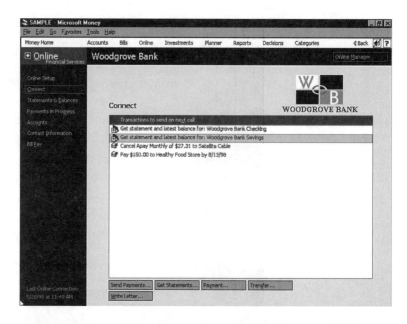

FIGURE I.7.

To pay a bill online, select Epay in the area where you normally type a check number.

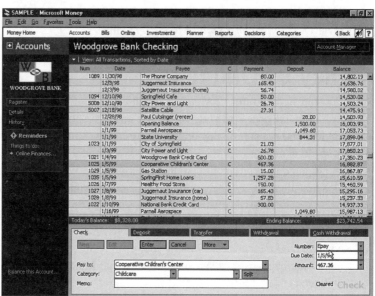

If you own stocks, use Money 99 to get instant quotes online by opening your Internet connection and clicking the Online Quotes button at the bottom of the Investments to Watch page, as shown in Figure I.8. Investing with Money 99 is covered in Hour 19, "Money as an Investment Tool."

FIGURE I.8.

To obtain instant stock quote information, open your Internet connection and click Online Quotes on the Investments page.

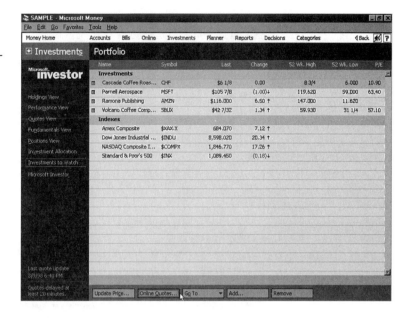

Money 99's Reports

Take a glance at some of Money 99's reports and charts. Reports and charts inform you of specific trends in your spending and earning that you ought to be aware of.

Figure I.9 shows a chart reporting how much money has been in a checking account during the last 12 months. Information such as this will be at your fingertips soon. Click the Report icon at the bottom left of the screen to see the same results expressed in a written report, rather than in a chart.

Reports can inform you of big financial trends or specific minutiae. In Figure I.10, you see a report detailing all the trips to the hair salon during the current year. To see more details about one particular visit, click its line in the list. A screen appears, providing more information. Reports are covered in Hour 16, "Money Reports."

The Planners

Three strategic features are the Planners. The Lifetime, Debt Reduction, and Budget Planners draw from your financial data, prompt you to select or create a goal, and present you with changes in your spending patterns required to reach those goals. You are then given an opportunity to adjust those plans, and after they are in place, Money 99 keeps you informed about your goal's status from month to month.

FIGURE I.9.

To view chart data as a report, just click the Report icon at the bottom left of the page.

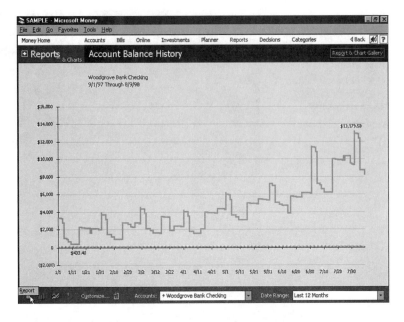

FIGURE I.10.

Reports can cover specific transactions, not just global trends that involve all your finances.

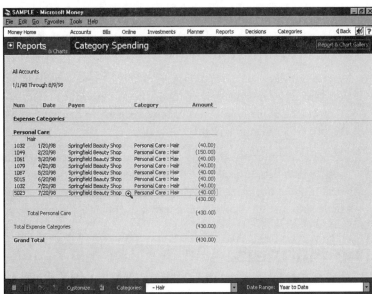

Figure I.11 shows a screen from the Lifetime Planner. The question at the top: "What expenses will I have?" is answered in the graph below. (Notice the plan extends to the year 2053).

FIGURE I.11.

The Lifetime Planner can answer a wide range of common questions involving financial forecasts.

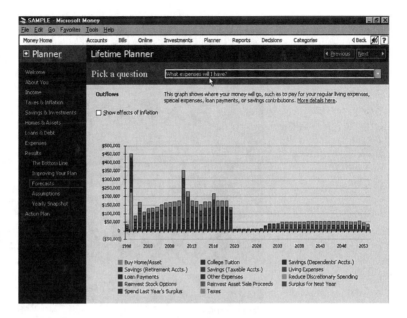

Here is a brief synopsis of each of the planners:

- Money's Lifetime Planner guides you towards a credible plan for achieving long-term financial goals, such as saving for tuition, or retirement.

- The Budget Planner draws from your income and spending levels and suggests budget plans that will gradually increase your savings. Before too long, you'll have a decent amount of money saved, without undo deprivation.

- The Debt Reduction Planner takes a look at all your debts and guides you towards a plan for paying them off. Choose a payment amount and a timeline for becoming debt-free, making adjustments using sliders. Creating a plan to become debt-free this way is kind of fun, and more intuitive than you might expect from a machine.

Staying Informed

When contemplating a financial decision, turn to the Decisions Center, a collection of special calculators like Debt Ratio and Tax Deduction Finder, worksheets for helping you choose one loan over another or compare mortgage rates, as well as articles of financial interest.

Pictured in Figure I.12 is the Education page of the Decisions Center. Here you can learn how to plan for your children's higher education, and make strategic investment decisions that especially benefit your kids. Notice there are links to informative Web sites like Money Insider and Microsoft Investor. The Decisions Center is covered in Hour 15.

FIGURE I.12.

The Education page of the Decisions Center contains articles and special calculators regarding your children's college funds.

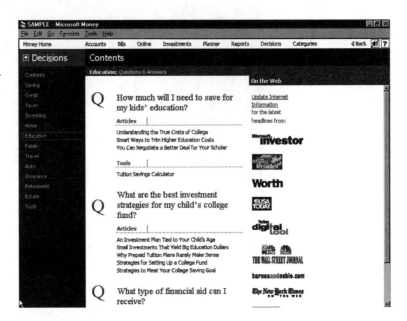

Customizing the Opening Screen

Before starting in Hour 1, please note that you can change what you see when you first turn on the program. By default, Money 99 opens to the Money Home Page. You'll see reminders of important dates, articles to read, and a Monthly Spending Progress graph right in the middle of your screen.

However, you can change what is shown when Money 99 first starts. If you want, specify that a different chart appear or let Money know that only certain kinds of articles interest you. Or, set aside the Money Home Page all together and have the program start up with for example, your Checking Account or Bills screen.

To customize what you see when you first start Money, click Customize, as shown in Figure I.13, or, click "Personalize your Financial Home Page" at the bottom left of the screen.

FIGURE I.13.

Customize the Money Home screen so it shows only the information you want.

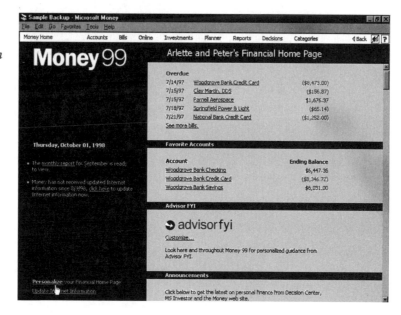

PART I
The First Steps

Hour

1 Money 99—Before You Begin

2 Getting Started

3 A First Look Around Money 99

4 Setting Up Accounts

5 Dividing Expenses into Categories

6 Writing Checks

Hour 1

Money 99—Before You Begin

If you bought this program to automate many of your financial *transactions* and to get a bird's-eye view of your overall financial picture, you are in luck. However, there's a little work to do first. Money 99 depends on you to provide a lot of initial information, such as paycheck stubs, and routine and irregular deposits and bills. In this first hour, you'll learn how to easily track down the type of documents Money wants to keep records of. You'll soon see why this is so important.

NEW TERM   **Transaction**—In Money 99, a *transaction* is the movement of funds. It is the act of paying, getting paid, or transferring money. The term is also used to describe buying or selling merchandise or shares.

You'll then take a quick look at how Money 99 approaches your finances along with the wisdom it provides. You'll soon see that the more you tell Money about yourself, the better feedback you'll get.

Finally, you'll learn about what to expect when you install the program. The process is automated, but there are a couple "curve balls" in the installation process that you should know about.

Creating a Financial Self-Portrait

To get going with Microsoft Money, you are required to enter the following information:

- Bank account information
- Regular bills you pay
- Income you receive
- Yearly or biannual expenses, such as property tax
- Irregular income such as an inheritance, and other windfalls

So after loading the software, you drag out your checkbook, a pile of pending bills, a couple of manila folders that contain bills you don't have to look at quite so often, records of work bonuses, and any extra checks you received.

Throughout this book, you'll learn step by step how to enter all this information into Microsoft Money. The purpose, of course, is to let Money know all about you, your spending and earning habits, what happens to the lion's share of your discretionary income, and who gets the dribs and drabs. Money can then produce reports that highlight spending patterns and suggest how to better maximize your net worth.

Choosing a Start Date

So, you want to bring Money up to speed with your finances, but when it's time to start typing, you question how far back into your records to reach? Does Money care only about this month's, this week's, or this fiscal year's figures? Yes, you should enter your current bank balance, but what led up to that current balance? Should you start with a new month? Or go back to when your bank accounts were brand new? This is called choosing a Start Date for Money.

NEW TERM **Start Date**—Your Money 99 *start date* is the date that Money should start tracking your finances. You can choose a date from the past, or start now.

You might be thinking, why not make it easy on yourself, and start with your current account balances, your current pile of bills, and begin fresh? After all, it's a new software program, a new day, why not just start over?

But remember, the purpose of Microsoft Money is not merely to automate your bill paying and check writing but to shed light into those old dark corners, and perhaps teach you how to manage your money a bit better. That takes data, lots of it, even old data. Microsoft Money excels at pointing out long and short-term trends. The best way for it to do its job is if you give it as many numbers to work with as possible. For example, you can generate the report shown in Figure 1.1, and then ask Money to crunch the numbers in slightly different ways to learn entirely new facts about your spending and earning patterns. To see this report, click the word Reports near the top of the screen on the Navigation Bar. When a new screen appears, click Where the Money Goes at the far right.

FIGURE 1.1.

The Where The Money Goes report has been customized to show all the spending for a year. The percentage pie is color-coded, matching the legend shown at the right. Click a pie slice to learn more about that spending item.

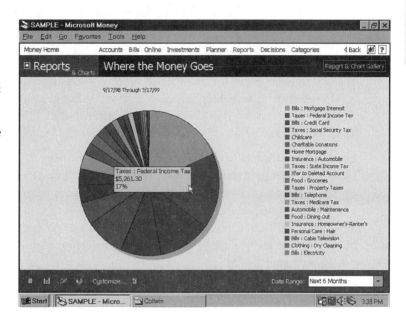

Pick the Earliest Date Possible

Based on the previous discussion, you should not only grab your checkbook and current bills, but also open the closet and dig up financial records going back to the beginning of the year, or as far back as you have reliable records. If you have several months' worth of paycheck stubs, rummage around and find them, especially if there are irregularities such as overtime, vacation, or extra shifts worked. If you have phone bills dating back a ways, bring those out too, and enter them, date by date. Quarterly insurance payments, one-time medical bills, even bank accounts that are no longer open are helpful in providing Money with an accurate financial profile.

Well, then, what date do you start with? Was there a particular month that you started judiciously saving check stubs, credit card receipts, invoices from the plumber and such? Look through this pile of financial records and see when they began to become regular.

At long last, here is the basic rule: Choose the date that you began seriously keeping hard copies of your financial transactions as your Money Start Date. It's okay if there are occasional gaps, some missing receipts and such.

Microsoft Money's charts, forecasts and reports can still be revealing even if there are a few holes in the data.

Why Go to the Trouble?

The benefit of choosing an early start date is that you can see Money work its magic before you even begin adding your daily expenses. After completing Hour 16, "Money Reports," you can view your past spending patterns in several formats and shed light on how you may want to do things differently in the future.

Looking at past spending can be revealing. Sometimes, memory and perception tell a different story than the numbers do (see Figure 1.2). Periods that bring to mind huge extravagance may not actually be as over-the-top as they appear, because perhaps some corners were cut subconsciously in other spending. Also, people tend to unwittingly spend a lot after a long period of deprivation, because they feel they have it coming. Microsoft Money helps to remove that subjective edge to budgeting, and reveal what is really happening with one's wealth.

To see the report shown in Figure 1.2, click the word Reports on the Navigation Bar and then, at the far right of the screen, click Spending Habits and How I'm doing on my Budget. Reports are covered in Hour 16. You'll learn about making budgets in Hour 13, "Creating a Budget."

FIGURE 1.2.

In the Budget/Actuals report, each spending item shows two bars. The first bar indicates how much you spent on that item. The second shows how much you had budgeted for it.

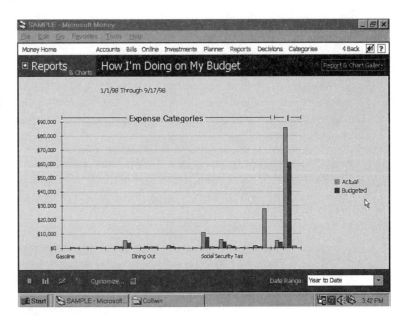

Financial Records Checklist

Here is a quick checklist of some of the common income and expense sources that Money would like to know about. It may help bring to mind some financial transactions you'd forgotten about completely. All you need to do now is locate and gather them. As you move through the book, it will be clear how to enter them into Money's database.

Regular Income Sources and Expenses

Money can make use of the following regular income and expense information:

Paychecks	Bank fees
Stock dividends	Monthly retirement contributions
Capital gains	Personal loan repayment
Advances	Insurance
Proceeds from sales	Living expenses
Monthly bills	Discretionary income/entertainment expenses

Infrequent or Irregular Income Sources and Expenses

Money can make use of the following irregular income and expense information as well:

Inheritance	One-time contributions to retirement plans or tax shelters
Work bonuses	Legal settlements or expenses/IRS settlements
Profit-sharing payouts	Major purchases, such as auto
Tax returns	Out-of-pocket medical expenses
Monetary gifts	Vacations
Stock windfall	Unexpected licensor fees and expenses
Year-end business profits	Remodeling/home repair
Royalties	Tuition
Stock purchases	

The subject of donations and charitable contributions deserves a special mention here. Don't forget to tell Money about any cash donations you've made since your Start Date. You may be surprised how they add up. They can be a remarkable tax advantage. When you give that money away, charitable contributions can at least help you choose who will get it.

Prepare a List of Assets

*Asset*s are an important part of your net worth. Having a list of physical assets helps you collect in cases of theft or fire, and Microsoft Money helps track the depreciation of physical assets, giving you a more accurate picture of what each major item is really worth.

NEW TERM **Asset**—In Money 99, an Asset is anything that has a value worth tracking. A house or boat is an asset, because you would use Money 99 to keep track of how it increases or decreases in value. Items that diminish rapidly in value (such as electronic equipment) are often not considered assets, unless you imagine they'll be worth something over time.

Keep in mind that right now, you are merely preparing a list of these physical assets and determining, as best you can, their current value. Later, you'll learn how to enter them into Money's database.

So, what should you consider an asset, worthy of mention in your records? That's entirely up to you. When determining your assets, try to be knowledgeable about how quickly it devalues. Here are some examples and rules of thumb:

- Electronic goods devalue rapidly, no matter how expensive they are originally, but custom furniture and jewelry do not.

- Assets are considered more valuable if they are important to your livelihood. Photography equipment would be considered a very valuable asset to a journalist, although the same equipment would only amount to its dollar value for a casual user.

- Items of personal, rather than monetary, value should be named as assets only if they are insured.

- Items like compact discs or baseball cards may be considered assets if you feel they have collector's value, or if you have them in very large numbers. Consider ascribing a single monetary value to collections of this sort, rather than itemizing each piece.

How to Approach Money 99

As you begin to explore Money 99, keep the following information in mind to help you get your bearings. In the following hours, you'll move through each of Money's features step-by-step.

Information Is King

The Microsoft Money Home screen shows your account information front and center, flanked on the left by reminders and upcoming financial events. To the right is Money's Help system, which can be closed by clicking the small Close (X) button in the Help system's upper-right corner. Below your personal account information are financial articles and advice (see Figure 1.3). Use the scroll button at the right of the screen to glance at links to articles by small business owners and financial experts with a wealth of information to share, as well as a never-ending stream of up-to-the-minute financial news. Although it's possible to navigate around Money and never investigate this material, some of it might be of interest to you, at least occasionally. Most of the links are geared toward people who are "starting small." Non-billionaires will not feel left out.

FIGURE 1.3.

In the center of the opening screen are account balances and upcoming bills. To the right is the Money Help system. To the left are important reminders.

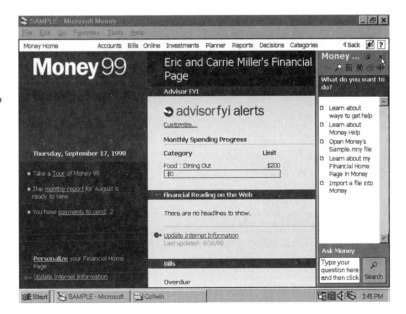

> You can change what is shown on the Money Home screen by opening the Tools menu and selecting Options (click Tools at the top of the screen). When a box with 13 tabs appears, click Money Home.

If you don't want to read through this collection of money managing tips and free-flowing advice, later in the book, you'll learn how to change the opening screen to look more like your checkbook or portfolio.

Why does Money continually push this information? Money 99's viewpoint is that even minor adjustments in spending patterns can have major results down the road. You'll always be encouraged to learn how to maximize that extra edge and again, not just fritter away financial opportunities.

Explorer Anyone?

Money's opening screen resembles Internet Explorer, and many menu options will be recognized by Explorer-based Web surfers. Here are some examples:

- The Favorites list, except that in Money 99, you track your favorite accounts and reports in your Favorites list, rather than Internet addresses.
- The Home and Back buttons, for returning to the opening screen or retracing your steps.
- The Navigation bar, found directly beneath the main menu at the top of the screen.
- Many features have an Update button. While online, click this button to automatically download the latest information pertinent to that feature.
- The "channel" guide on the left is a narrow strip of links that changes what you see to the right.

What Is an Account?

First you need to know how Microsoft Money uses the word "account."

A big part of your Money setup process is taking the numbers in your checking and savings accounts and entering them into Money. You create accounts in Money that parallel the accounts you have at your banks. Later, when you write a check, you enter the sum in Money and debit the appropriate account.

However, you can also create an account in Money that does not parallel an account you have at a bank. Such an account is really a bookkeeping method to help manage a savings goal, a budget, or an ongoing expense. Here are some examples of how accounts are used to track important items or goals:

- Create an account for your car, so you can keep tabs on how much money is spent on upkeep.
- Likewise, create an account for your home, for keeping track of repair expenses and such.
- Create an entertainment account and place a certain amount—perhaps $300—in it each month, assuring that you do not spend more than that sum on entertainment.

In Hour 4, "Setting Up Accounts" you'll learn step-by-step how to set up accounts. You'll learn the eight different types of accounts that Money 99 can set up and manage.

Thinking in Categories

As you assemble your financial portrait, grouping together expenses and income sources, look for natural *categories*. Microsoft Money creates many categories for financial transactions and uses them to generate helpful reports and graphs. However, you can also add your own and make a habit of entering your financial transactions into the categories you create.

NEW TERM   **Category**—In Money 99, a *category* is a group of related expenses or income sources. Buying groceries and eating out can both be categorized as food expenses. Stock windfalls and patent earnings can both be categorized as irregular sources of income.

What can you use as your own category? Anything that makes sense to you. Categories like Gasoline, Cable TV, Charitable Donations, Dry Cleaning, and Dining Out are already set up for you by Money. But say you have a Monday and Thursday Bowling Night that seems to eat away at the pocketbook more than it should. Go ahead and create a category just for that. Want to track those compact disc splurges, trips to Starbucks, power tool binges, or other nearly obsessive-compulsive financial behavior? Go ahead and make a category for it, if you dare! Later, when Money generates reports, you'll find the results more illuminating than if you had simply used the built-in category "Entertainment" or "Household Expenses."

Be Patient with the Data Entry

Finally, you might think that some of the numbers that Microsoft Money asks you for may not seem necessary at first, and they might seem a lot of bother. At first, it'll seem like you are spending much more time typing than you did when you paid bills "the hard way."

After Money has set up your regular and reoccurring transactions, you'll open Money only to initiate these routine payments and deposits, or implement occasional new ones. With some planning, you'll have to spend dreary hours doing data entry just once.

Next, you'll learn how to install Money 99.

Installing Microsoft Money 99

When you place the Money 99 CD-ROM in your CD-ROM drive, Microsoft Money begins installation. You are prompted to enter your name, instructed to close any open programs, and to write down the Product ID number that appears on the screen.

Money then checks for previously installed components (such as other Microsoft products that share the same files) and necessary disk space to continue installation. If you have adequate disk space and available RAM, installation continues.

Browser Wars and Money 99

Money will not proceed with installation unless it determines you have the latest version of the Internet Explorer browser on your computer. Happily, the Money 99 CD comes with Internet Explorer 4.1, so you are immediately prompted to install it. After doing so, you can begin Installing Money 99 again.

If you use Netscape Navigator, Opera, or some other browser, allow Internet Explorer to be installed, then afterwards, set up your favorite browser as the default again, and all Money's Internet activity will use that browser.

Changing the Installation Folder

You are prompted to accept Microsoft Money's choices for installation (see Figure 1.4). Files are installed in the C:\Program Files\Microsoft Money folder), or you can choose your own folder for installation.

If you decide to install Money 99 in another folder, click the Change Folder button, and type a folder name and path into the Path text box. If that folder doesn't exist, Money creates it for you.

There are few situations in which you will need to change setup folder information, but there might be some. For example, if you are going to be accessing Money across a network, some network setups do not work well with long filenames. In such a case, you might want to install Money 99 in a folder titled C:\Money99, or something similar.

FIGURE 1.4.

You can choose to install Money 99 in a different folder.

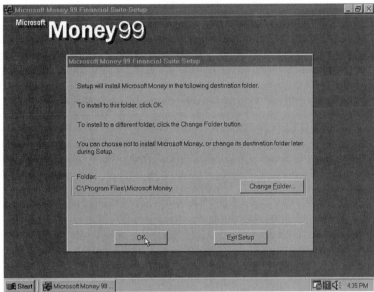

Installing and Setting Up Online Options

Other than file location, there are really no customized setup options for Money 99. Just read the licensing agreement, click past the prompts, and allow the program to begin installation.

A blue bar expanding from left to right indicates your setup progress, and shows the completed installation percentage (see Figure 1.5).

When Money 99 finishes copying and installing the files, you are asked if you want to set up the Online Banking option. If you choose not to install these files, you need to have your Money 99 CD handy in case you ever decide to pursue online banking.

Because this process involves locating modem and network drivers, you may be prompted to insert your Windows 95 or 98 setup disks. Money 99 installs a few extra files at this time to accommodate Online Banking later. You won't be asked to choose a bank, or to answer any other questions that you may not want to answer at this point.

Opting for Online Registration

After you're asked about online banking, you'll have the opportunity to choose Online Registration if you like. If you have an open Internet connection at the moment, Money 99 opens the Microsoft Web site, and presents you with an online form for you to fill out with the required registration information.

FIGURE 1.5.

As files are being copied, the advancing blue bar marks Money 99's installation progress.

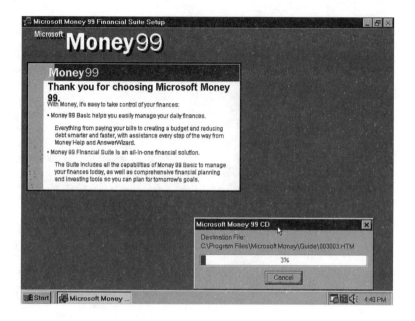

Problems with Installation?

If something goes wrong with your installation, just place the Money 99 CD in your CD-ROM drive, click past the prompts and choose "Reinstall" when that option is offered. Money then reinstalls all the files missing from the previous installation attempt.

If you finish installing Money 99 and an error occurs when the program starts, it's best to remove the program first, then reinstall.

To Do: Uninstalling and Reinstalling Money 99

1. From the Windows Start menu, click Settings, then Control Panel.
2. Choose Add/Remove Programs.
3. Scroll down and choose Money 99 from the list.
4. Click Uninstall and follow the onscreen instructions.
5. At the end of the uninstall process, Money asks to restart your computer. Close all programs and allow Money to restart your computer.
6. Then you can install Money again and hope things go well.
7. If you find further problems, check out this Web Site:
   `http://support.microsoft.com/support/c.asp?FR=0`

   Or

   `http://support.microsoft.com/support/`

Setting Up Your Internet Connection

If you plan to use any of Money 99's Online features, you need to make Money aware of your Internet connection. Money does not require any special type of Internet service provider to work correctly. Any connection you normally access the Internet through will work just fine when Money 99 accesses the Internet to retrieve data for your file or to show you the newest online financial news.

To Do: Making Money 99 Aware of Your Internet Connection

1. Determine how you access the Internet—perhaps a dialup connection through Earthlink, or some other Internet service provider, such as America Online or Prodigy.

2. Open Money 99. Click the Tools menu, and choose Options.

3. The Options dialog box appears. You'll see 13 tabs. Click the Connection tab.

4. In the Internet Connection window, click Internet Connection Settings. This is where you tell Money 99 how you connect to the Internet.

5. A dialog box appears giving you three choices:

   - If you have any other Internet service provider besides AOL or Prodigy, click the first option: Have Money connect to the Internet Using My Internet Service Provider from the List Below. Choose your connection type from the drop-down list.

   - If you connect to the Internet through work, and your connection pretty much never turns off, you probably have what is called a Local Area Network connection to the Internet. In this case select the second option: Access the Internet via a Local Area Network.

   - If you have a commercial online service such as AOL 3.0 or higher, choose the third option: Manual. Use this option if your Internet connection is not listed previously.

All you're doing is choosing the dialup connection you selected when you first signed up with your ISP. There may only be one option, and it probably will read "My Connection," just as it does in the example.

Internet Access and Choosing a Browser

If you are new to the Internet, allow me to clarify a couple of terms. When you open your Internet connection, you are ready for Internet activity. You are online. But to do anything, you'll need a browser to search around and locate the Internet content you might be looking for.

Money 99 does not require that you open your browser (for example, click your Netscape icon) to go online with Money. Save yourself a few mouse-clicks, because when you click an Internet link in Money 99, Money opens your browser for you and then proceeds. You don't have to open the browser yourself.

However, if you access the Internet through America Online, for example (or some other commercial online service), you'll have to log on to AOL *before* you click an Internet link in Money. When accessing a Money 99 Internet link with AOL, you'll be asked to click to confirm that you are logged on before proceeding.

 As mentioned earlier, Money 99 requires that you install Internet Explorer before you can even put Money on your computer. After you have the program up and running, however you can go ahead and use Netscape Navigator to access Money's Internet links if you want to.

Summary

Before you first use Money 99, take the time to gather all the recent financial information about yourself that you can find. Money 99 provides more helpful analysis and reporting as a result. As you explore Money, you'll see links to articles and advice about every aspect of personal financial well-being. You'll also find that the program looks a lot like Internet Explorer, which makes sense, because Money always seeks to update itself with information from the World Wide Web. Also, when you first install Money 99, the program insists on installing the most recent version of Internet Explorer as well.

Q&A

Q Before I start writing checks and making deposits with Money 99, what do I have to do first?

A The more financial information you provide money with, the better it can help you. Money 99 provides the type of sophisticated budget analysis that people gladly pay a lot of money for, but it needs data to analyze. So your first job is to locate financial records about yourself going as far back as the beginning of the year, if you have them.

Q What types of financial information should I provide Money with?

A Bills, paycheck stubs, payments or financial obligations and liabilities of any kind—Money 99 can make rich use of all this type of information.

Q When I first started Money 99, it asked me 18 questions about me and my family. Why were those questions important?

A Age-related information is helpful for assessing a time frame for your children's college education and your own retirement. The number of children helps determine how much money to sock away for their college, if that is a goal of yours. Spouse information helps with tax planning and determining if financial records are going to be kept in common.

Q Why might it be a good idea to enter previous bills and income into Money's database? Why not just start from scratch now?

A Because if Money 99 can detect patterns in spending and income, it can already be of great use to you. You can read reports and learn from Money 99 even before you enter a single current daily transaction.

Hour **2**

Getting Started

In this hour, you'll learn how to start Money 99 and what to expect when the program first opens. You'll learn about the Personal Profile screen and the *money file*, which holds all your financial data. Then you'll explore the opening Money Home screen, which you can customize in a number of ways. Finally, you'll see the significance of backing up your files as the program closes and of making a copy of your Money data on a floppy disk.

Starting Money

You can start Money 99 by clicking the Windows Start menu, choosing Programs, and then choosing Microsoft Money, as shown in Figure 2.1. You don't have to open a Program Group, just scroll near the bottom of the Start menu and click the icon.

FIGURE 2.1.

*You can start Money
99 by scrolling down
near the bottom of
your Windows Start
menu.*

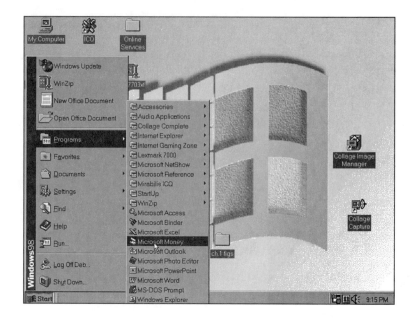

Creating a Desktop Shortcut

If your Start menu is a bit large and unwieldy, you might like to make a shortcut to
Money 99 on the Windows desktop.

To Do: Creating a Shortcut on the Desktop

1. With at least a portion of the Windows desktop clearly visible, right-click the
   Windows Start menu and select Explore.

2. Double-click the Program Group icon.

3. While pressing the Ctrl key, scroll down or across and locate the Money 99 icon.

4. Drag the icon onto the desktop (see Figure 2.2).

FIGURE 2.2.

Create a shortcut to Money on your desktop by opening the Start menu in Explorer and dragging the icon.

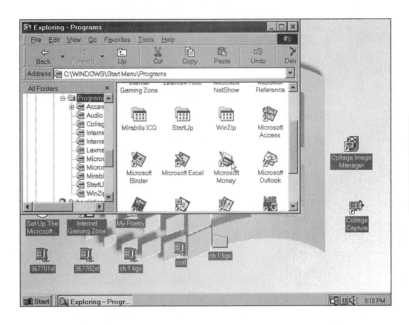

You can then start Money 99 by clicking the desktop icon.

What You See When You Start Money

When you click the Money icon and the program opens, you may see the Product Tour screen (see Figure 2.3). Click the appropriate button to view a video tour of Money, the Quicken User Overview, or special tips for users of previous Money versions.

You'll see a video tour made up of bite-sized animated descriptive overviews of Money's general features. To watch this video tour, your Money 99 CD must be in the drive. If you do not see this video tour when Money opens and it somehow intrigues you, you can view it later by selecting Product Tour from the Help menu.

Alternatively, you can begin building your Personal Profile. When Money 99 starts, you are prompted to answer basic questions Money needs to know to begin building your financial picture. (It's a series of 18 questions about such things as the number of family members, home ownership, and marital status.)

Upon answering these questions, the File Required dialog box may appear, as shown in Figure 2.4. Money needs a data file to get started. Click the Open button. From that point, you can do one of the following things:

- Create a new Money file from scratch (do this to immediately start entering your own account data).

- Open an existing Money or Quicken file, allowing you to see Money 99 in action and view active accounts and reports. (If you would like to play with a "dry run," experiment with creating accounts and writing checks before building your own Money data, then open the Sample Money file.)

- Restore a backup file.

For most of this book, the Sample data is used to show you Money's features. It's perfectly fine to follow along with this book's steps by using the Sample data. When you create accounts, you'll be adding additional accounts to the Sample data, simply as a learning exercise for yourself. But when you "get serious" and want to begin entering real account data, you'll have to create a new Money file from scratch.

You may find that the transactions shown from the Sample file used in this book differs from yours. However, the meaning of each example still applies.

FIGURE 2.3.

The Product Tour screen may appear the first time you start Money 99.

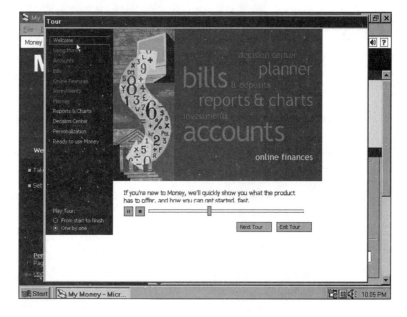

After clicking the Open button, the Open dialog box appears. To create your own Money file, type a name in the File Name text box and click New as shown in Figure 2.5. You'll then see an additional dialog box called New. It explains that you really don't need to make a new file if you've already made one. Because this is your first Money 99 data file, just ignore what it says and click OK.

FIGURE 2.4.

When you first start Money, you are prompted either to create a new file from scratch, or to open the Sample.

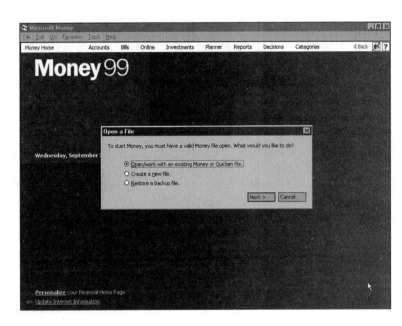

FIGURE 2.5.

When you first start Money 99, you can either create a new file as shown or learn how Money works by opening the Sample.MNY file.

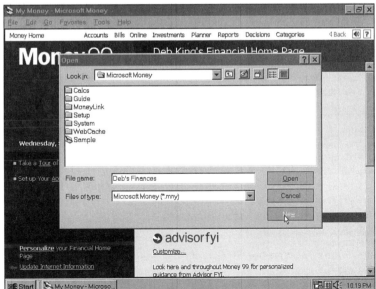

A Create New File progress bar appears, and you'll hear your computer clicking away momentarily while Money prepares your new data file. When it's done, the Money Home screen appears. Off to the left you'll see the command Set Up Your Accounts (see Figure 2.6), which you'll do in Hour 4, "Setting Up Accounts."

FIGURE 2.6.

After creating a new money data file, the Money Home screen appears. There is no Sample data filling the center anymore, only a command to Set Up Your Accounts.

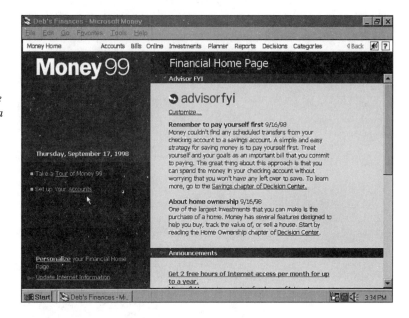

What Is a Money File?

Money files hold all your financial data, accounts, transactions, program preferences, and other settings. It is saved in your Money folder, and has a .MNY file extension. You need only make one. After creating a Money file, it opens automatically each time Money starts. You automatically add to this file each time you create new accounts or conduct transactions.

Create More than One Money File?

Here are two instances in which you'd make more than one Money file:

- If you have a small business that you run separately from your personal finances
- If you are in charge of a charity, and you need to keep that money totally separate from your own

Information is not shared between Money files. If, for whatever reason, you have two files, reports, budget, and goal advice will not draw from both of your files—only the file that is currently open.

Your Money at a Glance

You have control over how your opening Money screen looks, and if you want the screen to reflect more about your financial status and less about the world of money at large, that can be easily arranged. You'll learn how later in this hour, but for now, you need to know what appears on the screen by default.

By default, Money 99 opens to the Money Home screen (see Figure 2.7). As mentioned previously, this screen presents a glance at your most pertinent financial data. Scroll down and you'll see regularly updated financial commentary. Click Customize to change what you see when the program first starts.

After viewing the Money Home screen, you'll most likely navigate elsewhere to actually conduct financial transactions. Return to the Money Home screen at any time by clicking Money Home on the Navigation Bar.

Think of the Money Home screen as a launching pad from which you jump into the financial transactions of any given day. Take the time to look around before you get started. Click Personalize at the bottom left to change how the Home screen looks when you start the program.

FIGURE 2.7.

Click Personalize at the bottom left to customize what is shown when the program first starts.

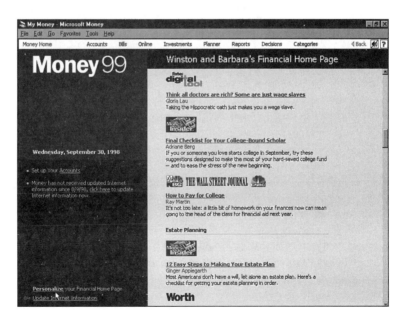

The main area of the opening screen offers three types of financial data, drawn from your accounts. Depending on how you customize it, you can open straight to a list of upcoming bills, or your checking register. Or, you can wake up to screen financial charts that track your financial dealings.

The Bills Area

Whenever you view the Money Home screen, you're reminded of bills that are due in the next 10 days. You can adjust that reminder period, putting off the bad news until the last possible minute, or apprising yourself even a month in advance, if you like. Choose Tools, Options on the Navigation Bar at the top of the screen. Then select the Bills tab, as shown in Figure 2.8. (In Hour 23, "Customizing Money" you'll explore how to customize Money 99 to your liking.) The Money Home screen's Bills list places overdue bills nearer to the top of the page.

FIGURE 2.8.

To change how far in advance you get news of impending bills, click the Bills tab in the Options dialog box. Type in the number of days.

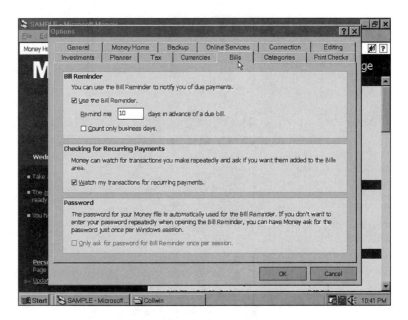

Hover your mouse over an individual bill reminder, and the mouse becomes a hand. Click the line of text (see Figure 2.9), and a more complete list of Bills opens giving you a comprehensive view of what you have to pay out this month and to whom.

FIGURE 2.9.

To see a more detailed list of upcoming bills, click any due bill. When your mouse cursor turns into a hand, clicking takes you to a new screen.

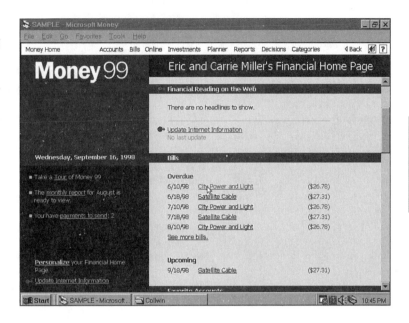

The Accounts Area

Below the Bill area is Accounts. This area shows the current value of all the accounts you have in your Favorites List. (In Hour 4, you'll learn how to turn an account into a Favorite and the reasons why you might do that.) Click any account shown to open that account's register.

Please note that the purpose of Money 99's Home screen is to inform. You'll be able to glean lots of financial information at a glance, but there are more direct ways to actually pay the bills and make account adjustments. (Those tasks are described in detail in Hours 4 and 11.) You can always change Money's opening screen to show, perhaps, your checking account, or lists of upcoming bills.

The Monthly Report

Near the end of each month, Money 99 produces a thorough financial health report based on the *previous* month's data. Money announces this report's availability in white letters at the center left of the Money Home screen (see Figure 2.10). This report makes observations about your current worth, suggests plans of action and details where you stand at the moment, compared to previous months.

FIGURE 2.10.

Near the end of any month, look for this message, which indicates that a full financial report on the previous month is now ready for viewing.

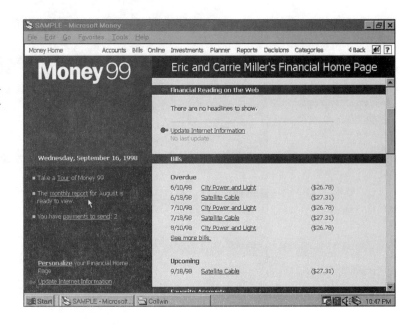

To view the previous month's Monthly Reports, click Reports on the Navigation Bar at the top of the screen. When the Gallery of Reports and Charts opens, select Monthly Reports at the far left (see Figure 2.11). (You'll learn about reports and their uses in Hour 16, "Money Reports.") You can also click here to view this month's report, even if Money 99 says it's not quite ready yet. Just click Monthly Reports, then select the current month from the drop-down list.

The Chart of the Day

If you like, you can direct Money 99 to display the chart of the day (see Figure 2.12), displayed near the bottom of the Money Home screen. This is a quick little "insight bubble" that lets you get a glimpse of your finances in a certain light.

To alter what the Money 99 Home screen displays, choose Tools, Options. Choose the Money Home tab and place a check by features you want visible. Other buttons on the tab let you choose the type of articles or charts displayed on startup.

Figure 2.11.

After viewing this month's report, snoop around and compare your fiscal health to your status in the previous months.

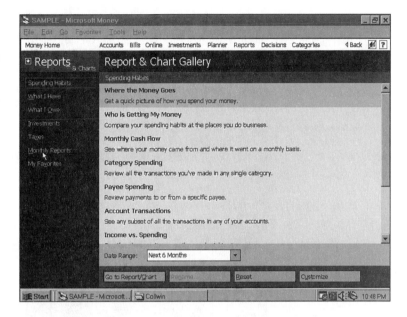

Figure 2.12.

Scroll down the Money Home screen to see the Chart of the Day.

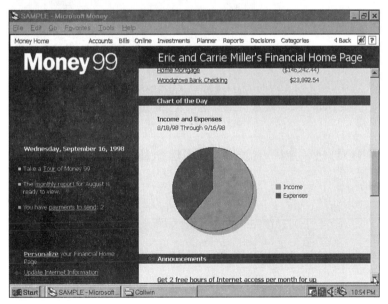

By default, this chart shows your current liabilities (the major categories of how much money you currently owe). It's a simple pie chart. Hover your mouse over one slice of the pie or the other. The dollar amount, name, and percentage of that particular liability appears. You can change which chart appears by choosing Tools, Options from the menu bar at the top of the Money 99 screen. Click the Money Home tab, and then click the Chart of the Day button as shown in Figure 2.13. You can see, for example, all your current assets, income, and expenses side-by-side or all your bills from last month.

FIGURE 2.13.

The Money Home tab of the Options menu lets you change the chart of the day.

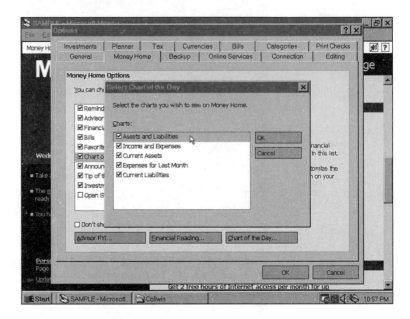

Also, note the buttons for changing the type of Financial Readings Money 99 provides for you, as well as the contents of the Advisor FYI area.

Money Home's Articles, Connections, and Tips

Still working with Money's opening screen, your personal financial data is in the center of the screen. On either side are financial articles of interest, tips for improving your financial picture, and connections to relevant Web sites. These articles are placed here with a good deal of forethought, based on time of year and where the chips seem to be falling for you at this particular moment. More often than not, what ends up in these slots is worth taking a glance at on a regular basis. Here's a look at the articles and Internet links you'll see on Money Home.

The Advisor FYI

The Advisor FYI sort of peaks over your shoulder, helping you set priorities and prevent common financial mistakes. Advisor FYI comments are usually no more than a paragraph or two, and they are displayed in the margin of articles you read in the Decisions Center, pointing out specifically how this article applies to your financial situation. The longer you work with Money 99, the more specifically geared for you Advisor FYI's advice becomes. Money 99's Home screen displays the last three Advisor FYIs you've seen for seven days and then begins "collecting" new ones for that view. The Monthly Report also includes all the Advisor FYIs you've seen during that month.

The Decisions Center

The Decisions Center is a collection of articles and worksheets available by clicking Decisions on the Navigation Bar, to the upper right of your screen. You'll see links to Money Insider, which is a Web page featuring articles on all kinds of financial topics, including Home Ownership, Tuition, Travel, Family, and Simple Living (see Figure 2.14). They're written by noteworthy authors whose names are familiar to those who read syndicated financial articles in their local paper. The Decisions Center tools include Renting versus Buying, Mortgage Comparison, and Tuition Saving calculators.

FIGURE 2.14.

The Money Insider Web site complements The Decision Center's articles in Money 99.

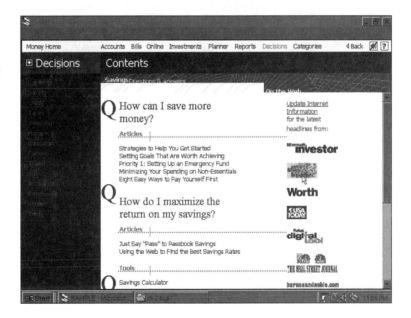

If you enjoy exploring Money 99's online offerings, Money Insider also features a drop-down list to other Microsoft sites of interest such as MSNBC (rich channel content for specific types of news viewing), Expedia Maps for navigating to any destination in the United States, and Microsoft CarPoint, for getting deals on cars and insurance and such. Click any link in this drop-down list to visit that new site.

Money 99 Investor

Investor is a Microsoft Web page of investment tips and advice that does a good job of staying abreast of the newest trends in stocks, bonds, and mutual funds (see Figure 2.15). Brief introductions to Money 99 Investor articles appear at the lower-left of the Money Home screen. With your Internet connection open, click the hyperlink at the beginning of any article "teaser," to view the whole document. There are specialty workshops, interviews, trend analysis, and a complete index of all the Investor articles that have appeared in the last two months.

FIGURE 2.15.

Get investment information and advice on the Microsoft Investor Web page.

Updating Money Home

Money 99's opening page features articles that change several times a week. This is done by establishing your online connection (connecting to the Internet) and clicking the Update Internet Information icon at the bottom right of Money Home.

To Do: Updating Money Home

1. Log on to the Internet.

2. Click the Update Internet Information icon on the Money Home page.

3. You'll see a prompt asking you to open your Internet connection, which you've already done, so click OK.

▼ 4. The Connecting dialog box appears to indicate that your information is being updated (see Figure 2.16). Money actually retrieves information from four locations, so this may take a few minutes. Be patient.

FIGURE **2.16.**

You'll see this screen animate when Money 99 is updating Money Home and other information.

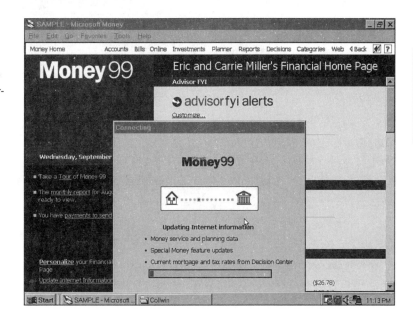

5. When Money has retrieved all available online information, you'll see the Call Summary window, indicating that all has gone well.

6. If Money found new information on any site that wasn't previously on your computer, you'll see links to those articles on your Money Home screen now. If your
▲ page was already up-to-date, then you'll see nothing new on your screen.

Exiting Money

After you've completed all your Money 99 transactions, click the Close (X) button in the upper-right corner of the screen. Before entirely closing, Money backs up your data automatically. This process creates an alternate money file that the program can rebuild your data from, should anything happen to this file (backing up and archiving your data is covered in Hour 22). Money then asks if you want to back up your data to a floppy disk (see Figure 2.17).

FIGURE 2.17.

Money 99 offers to back up your Money file before the program actually closes.

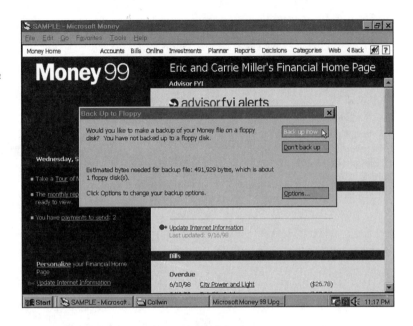

You are informed how large the backup file will be. To back up the data to another location, perhaps a Zip drive or other removable media, click the Options button.

To start a backup, click the Back Up Now button. To close the program, click Don't Back Up.

> Your backed up file will have an .mbf file extension, should you ever need to restore from it.

Click the Backup button. If you want to save the file in another location, perhaps on a floppy disk, click the Browse button, change directories and then click OK, which saves the backup file to that new location. After Money creates the backup file, the program automatically closes.

Summary

You can start Money from the Windows Start menu or by placing a shortcut on the desktop. When you first start the program, you'll be prompted to provide Money with enough personal information to start building your financial picture. Then you'll have to create a *Money File*, which holds all your money data. Then you'll see the opening Money Home screen, which you can customize as you like. When closing Money, you'll be asked to back up your data onto a floppy disk, which is a good idea to do about once a month.

Q&A

Q How do you start Money 99?

A Money 99 automatically places a shortcut on the Windows Start menu, although it's no trouble at all to make a shortcut on your desktop as well.

Q Where does Money 99 store all my financial information?

A In a Money file, which is a data file that you name and back up from time to time. It has a .MNY file extension. It is found in the same folder as the Money 99 program itself. You should also take pains to save it onto a floppy disk or Zip disk and to back it up when prompted.

Q: Will I ever need to create more than one Money 99 file?

A: Only if you have a reason to keep certain financial dealings of yours away from your personal finances. For example, if you run a small business or if you are in charge of maintaining money for a charitable activity.

Q: Whenever I open this program, the Home screen shows updated articles to read, and new Web links to follow. Why is that so important to me?

A: Money 99's point of view is that good spending and saving habits are augmented by staying informed of any financial trends that could even indirectly affect your net worth.

HOUR 3

A First Look Around Money 99

In this hour, you'll become familiar with the "look and feel" of Money 99. You'll see how Money's features are arranged in predictable placements around the screen. For example, you'll learn that the controls to create anything "new," (such as a new account, category, or investment) are usually found at the bottom of the screen. Also, you can click a drop-down arrow below a feature title to immediately change to a related feature.

A quick tour of the Navigation Bar—the Money 99 menus—will familiarize you with other ways Money has provided to navigate the program. You'll also explore ways to get help with features that are unclear.

The Navigation Bar

The Navigation Bar is your main tool for moving around Money 99. With it, you can quickly switch to any of Money's main views. The Navigation Bar is the row of ten phrases near the top of the screen, beginning with Money Home, at the far left, and ending with the red question mark, off to the right (see Figure 3.1). Here, the Navigation Bar is pictured above the Decisions Screen. Click any word on the Navigation Bar to access that page. Here are some common Money tasks that begin with the Navigation Bar:

- **Accounts**—To create and edit accounts, click Accounts. You'll see picture representations of each of your accounts. Click any of them and get to work.

- **Bills**—To pay a bill, delete a regular bill, or see when a bill is due (even months from now), click Bills. Also, click Bills to see how much money you'll have over the next couple months (all things being equal).

- **Planner**—To set Lifetime Financial Goals, create a workable budget, and devise a Get Out of Debt plan, click Planner.

FIGURE 3.1.

The Navigation Bar takes you almost anywhere you want to go in Money 99. It is pictured here open to the Decisions screen.

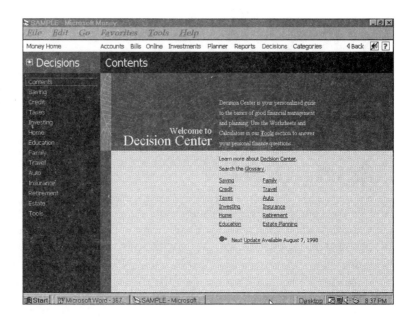

NEW TERM **Links**—Clickable words or buttons that move you to a new location in Money. Some links open a Web site or page rather than a new Money 99 screen.

Three Navigation Bar links that deserve special mention are

- **Money Home**—This link returns you to Money's opening screen, which contains the Help question mark that answers most questions about what you are doing in Money at that moment.

- **Decisions**—This is your link to dozens of unique tools, articles, question-and-answer sessions, and regularly updated commentaries on everything to do with personal finance. Tools worth mentioning (although there are 21 of these, and they are all great) are the Tax Bite and Tax Relief Act Calculator, the Retirement Income Calculator, and the Debt Ratio Calculator.

- **Back**—The Back feature returns you to the screen you were most recently viewing. Keep this convenience in mind. Using the Back button lets you quickly retrace your steps.

Each of Money's features are explained in due course, but for now, understand that when you need to go somewhere in Money 99, the Navigation Bar takes you there. If not exactly there, it will take you very close.

The Money Menu

At the upper left of the Money 99 screen is the menu bar, which should appear familiar to you if you've used other Windows programs. From left to right, you'll read these menu labels: File, Edit, Go, Favorites, Tools, and Help. Click any menu label to reveal a drop-down list of options.

Now you need to take a quick look at what each menu contains. This is only a fast glance at what's inside each menu. Each Money 99 feature referred to in a menu is covered in full later.

The File Menu

Click the File menu to create a new Money file, import or export Money data to another program, create passwords, print reports and checks, and back up Money files (see Figure 3.2).

The Edit Menu

The Edit menu changes depending on which feature you are working with. Sometimes, if you are working with a Money feature and the task you need to accomplish is not obviously in front of you, the command you need can be found in the Edit menu. The Edit menu contains special commands for the Investment Portfolio, Bills, and Categories.

The Go Menu

The Go menu contains the exact same options that appear on the Navigation Bar.

The Favorites Menu

The Favorites menu lets you store accounts or reports that you use often, much like you'd bookmark a link using Internet Explorer. After you assign an account or report as a Favorite, it is always just one click away.

FIGURE 3.2.

Use the File menu to print Money data, create Passwords, back up and import files, and carry out other tasks.

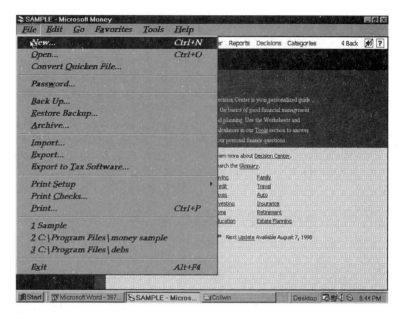

The Tools Menu

The Tools menu contains a helpful Find and Replace feature. Use it to locate any transaction. For example, if you wrote a check a while back for $49.99, and it just cleared the bank and you cannot remember who you wrote it to, use Find and Replace to locate that check (see Figure 3.3). Also in the Tools menu, click Options for fine-tuning how your version of Money looks and runs. Click Set Up Tax Categories to assign selected expenses and income sources to specific *tax lines* on your tax forms (Money 99 and taxes are covered in Hour 18, "Money and Taxes"). Click the Important Records Organizer to store policy numbers, insurance account numbers, or any kind of documentation that you need to avoid losing. Finally, If you want to change the basic information Money knows about you (such as if you get married or have another child or change jobs), click Personal Profile. To change the information you see on the Money Home screen, click Customize Advisor FYI options.

NEW TERM **Tax Line**—The IRS and other tax agencies calculate the deductibility of certain expenses according to where they are listed on a particular form, or what "line" they are recorded on.

Later in this hour, you'll learn about the Help menu.

FIGURE 3.3.

Use the Find and Replace feature to locate any transaction based on Text, Account, Date, Amount, Category, Payee, or Details.

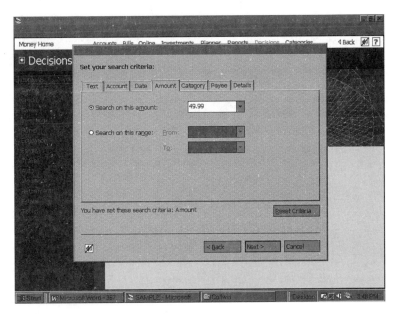

Money "Channel Guides"

Often in Money 99, what you click on the left changes what you see on the right. In features such as Investments, Decisions Center, and Online, Money sets aside a small strip of clickable links on the left side of the screen as a "channel flipper," changing what you see towards the right. Figure 3.4 shows the Accounts screen, with a home mortgage account visible. Click any of the three phrases (options) on the upper left, in the black area, and the main screen content changes. For example, click Register to see an account as it would appear in your checkbook. Again on the left, click Payment Terms, and the right side of screen shows the new information you are looking for.

What's Down Below?

When you want to create something new, such as an investment, account, category, or bill, the options for doing this will be at the bottom of the screen. (Figure 3.5 shows the bottom strip of the Category screen.) Also down along this strip of controls are tools for editing and deleting. For example, if you want to delete a bill or category, at the appropriate screen, use the Delete button.

FIGURE 3.4.

In any account, click an option on the left to change what you see in the main screen.

FIGURE 3.5.

In many Money 99 screens, a row of buttons at the bottom of the screen contains tools to create and edit items.

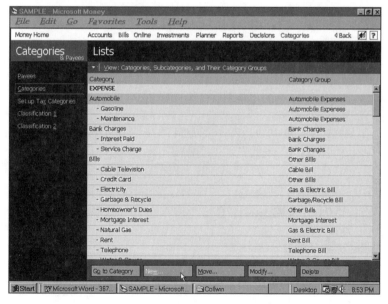

Money 99 Wizards

When Money 99 needs to learn your preferences or specifications about a particular transaction or task, a *wizard* is used. For example, Money uses wizards to gather information about opening a new account, setting up a loan, or planning a long-term goal. You'll know you are working with a wizard when Money presents you with a screen with two or three questions, usually requiring you to select answers from a list of options. At the bottom of wizard screens are Next and Back buttons (see Figure 3.6). When you are finished answering a set of questions on the screen, click Next.

> When working with a wizard, if you change your mind about a particular answer from a previous screen, click the Back button, and specify a new answer.

3

FIGURE 3.6.

The New Category creator is a typical Money 99 Wizard that walks you through the entire process of creating a useful tool.

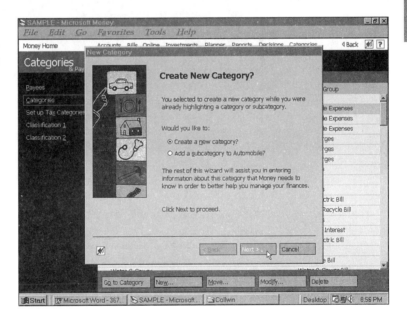

Finally, after answering perhaps five or six screens of the wizard's questions, you'll see an OK button. Click OK when you are happy with all your answers. Money then records your data, and the chore is finished.

Money 99 Access Tips

Here are some quick ways to get around in Money that can save you from having to hunt for a feature that you would think should be right in front of you (it probably is, if you know how to access it).

Right-Click for Additional Options

Often, when you right-click a transaction, account, or report item, you'll find a menu of options that lets you get right to the task at hand. In Figure 3.7, the user is right-clicking an account transaction. A menu appears for editing and deleting that transaction, moving it to another account, or changing its status from unreconciled to reconciled.

FIGURE 3.7.

Right-click any trans-action to reveal a list of options.

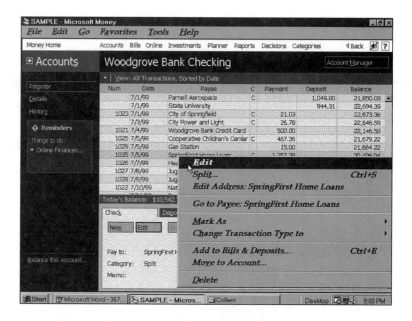

In Figure 3.8, you can see after right-clicking a chart that it's easy to customize, print, change styles, and add the chart to your Favorites menu. As you'll see later in this hour, if you don't understand a feature, you can right-click it for a brief description of how it works.

Drop-Down Lists

On some Money features, such as accounts and reports, you'll notice a down-facing arrow next to the title. Click the title to reveal a list of locations related to what you are currently viewing. Sometimes mini-arrows appear next to submenus, allowing you to view your data in a slightly different format. Figure 3.9 shows what happens when you click <u>V</u>iew in the Bills & Deposits screen. Two additional options appear. You can view your bills by payee or by date due.

FIGURE 3.8.

Right-click a chart to change it from a pie to a bar or line-style chart or add it to your list of Favorites.

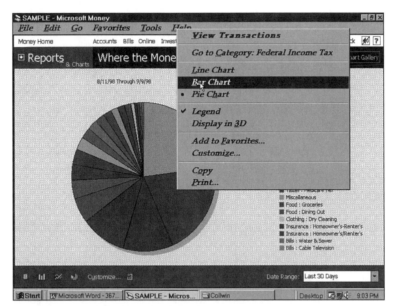

FIGURE 3.9.

To change the way bills are sorted for viewing, click the <u>V</u>iew drop-down list in the Bills & Deposits screen.

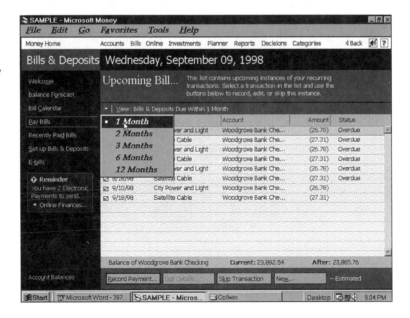

In Figure 3.9, a bit lower on the screen, notice the mini-arrow next to the phrase "Balance Forecast." The graph on display here shows all account balances over a given month. However, it's confusing to see them overlapping. So to view one account at a time, click the down-facing arrow, next to the word View, and choose which account to view.

"The Mouse Cursor Just Changed!"

If you've poked around Money a little bit on your own, you've perhaps noticed that in some instances, the mouse cursor transforms when you move it into certain positions. You'll notice this in two situations:

- On the Money Home Page, hold your mouse over the title of an article, and the mouse cursor changes into a hand. When you see this, click the mouse, and the article opens. You'll notice this in any Money 99 location where there are hyper-links.

- Hold the mouse over any portion of a chart (see Figure 3.10), and the cursor changes to a magnifying glass. Data also appears, showing you the numbers associated with that exact portion of the chart. In the example shown, the mouse cursor is positioned over a line graph representing World Wide Importers stock. You can quickly learn that on a particular date, AT&T cost $55.43 per share, before leveling off again at $33.14.

FIGURE 3.10.

Hold your mouse over part of a line graph, and it changes into a magnifying glass.

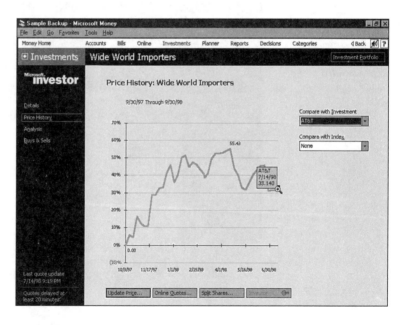

What Are Active Features?

In many instances, holding your mouse over a feature causes the feature's label to change color. If the label changes color, that means if you click the mouse, something will happen. That feature is *active*.

To Do: Understanding Active Features

1. Click Accounts on the Navigation Bar, and the Account Manager opens. Click an icon for a Checking Account.

2. The Register opens for that account. Near the bottom, hold your mouse over the New label. Nothing happens, indicating that you can't make anything New.

3. Again, hold your mouse over the Edit label. Nothing happens, because there's nothing yet to edit. Both those controls are currently *inactive*.

4. Finally, hold your mouse over the word Enter. It lights up, indicating that If you click it, something will happen. That control is *active*.

5. Again, hold your mouse over the label Cancel, and you'll see it change color, meaning that you are allowed to cancel this transaction at this time.

6. Poke around, and you'll find that almost all of Money 99's controls change color when they are active, and remain "gray" when not available.

Single- and Double-Clicking

Money 99 features behave differently depending on whether they are clicked once or twice. For example, you'll find that clicking once on a transaction will *select* it (meaning that it's ready for editing, or to be examined more closely), while double-clicking actually opens that transaction. You'll notice this especially when you want to edit a particular account or some other transaction.

To Do: Selecting a Transaction for Editing

Try this action in which single-clicking selects a bill in a list, and double-clicking opens it for editing:

1. If you have the money Sample data loaded, click Bills on the Navigation Bar. The Bills screen appears.

2. Click any line once. Pick a line that has data on it. Notice it turns yellow, indicating it is *selected*, and ready for action.

3. Now double-click any line, picking a line with data on it. A dialog box opens, allowing you to make changes to that transaction.

4. Without making any changes, go ahead and click Cancel to leave the transaction.

▼ Please note that quite often, features accessed from the left side of the screen need only
to be clicked once to be effective. While you are viewing the Bill screen, click any date
on the calendar. As soon as you click a date, any transaction related to that date is
▲ selected.

Money's Help System

Money provides several methods of obtaining help and an additional set of help tools for
Quicken users. The following sections show you where to turn when you want more
information on Money 99 or one of its features.

The Help Topics Channel Bar

As you may have noticed, a step-by-step onscreen Help system is always available (see
Figure 3.11). It appears in the form of a Channel Bar at the far right. You may close it by
clicking the Close (X) button in the corner of the bar itself. (Notice in Figure 3.11 that
the mouse is hovering over that X, and a ToolTip is displayed: "Close Money Help.")

 Tooltip—Perhaps you've noticed that when you leave your mouse over an icon
or a command for a couple seconds, a short phrase appears. This is a Tooltip,
simply a word or two explaining what that command will do.

FIGURE 3.11.

*Money Help displays
step-by-step instruc-
tions on any topic.*

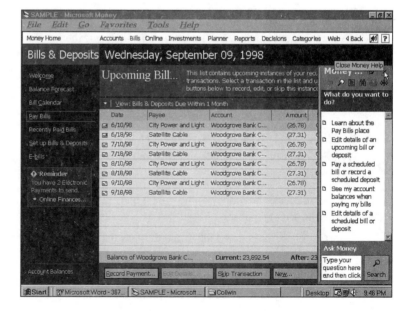

The key to the Money Help channel bar lies at the bottom right in the Ask Money text box. Click in the white area (text box) below the phrase Ask Money and type in a question. Then click the Search icon to the right of the question area, as shown in Figure 3.12. Money displays possible answers to your questions in the area above the Search icon. Click the answer that seems likely to be the most helpful. A step-by-step solution to your question appears.

FIGURE 3.12.

After typing in a question, click Search, and a step-by-step solution appears in the Help Channel Bar.

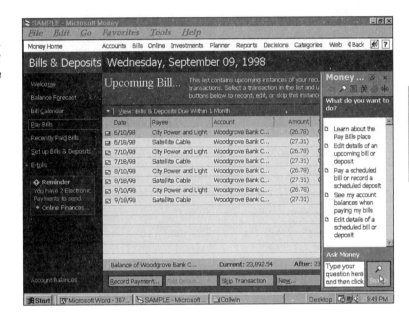

To expand the Money Help Channel, click the double arrow at the far upper-right. Hold your mouse over it momentarily, and it will read "Resize Money Help." Click, and the Channel bar expands to fill about one-third of the screen.

Exploring Links to Related Topics

If the initial step-by-step instructions that Money Help displays do not suffice, notice how along with the step-by-step, more questions appear. Click any of these questions to open an entirely new set of answers and step-by-steps.

Following a Help Topic Link

1. Make sure the Money Help Channel Bar is displayed. If not, click the Help menu, and choose Help Topics.

2. At the top of the Money Help Channel Bar (which should now appear as a rectangle at the right of the screen), click the small magnifying glass icon. (If you hold your mouse over the rectangle momentarily, it may read New Search.)

3. Locate the Ask Money text box at the bottom of the Help Channel. Money provides this area for you to type in a natural-language question.

NEW TERM **Natural-language question**—When you type a question into the Money Help area, just use the same language as you would if you were addressing a friend. Money 99's Help System understands normal language vocabulary usage.

4. Click the Search icon to the right of the question area at the bottom of the Help Channel Bar.

5. The main area of the Help Channel Bar returns with a list of topics. One or more of these topics should address your question. Clicking any of these topics opens a specific step-by-step answer.

6. Click the topic that seems the most helpful to your current search.

7. Follow the steps provided to carry out the task you had in mind. If this answer did not quite hit the spot, locate the scroll button to the far right of the Help Channel Bar and scroll to the bottom of the step-by-step answers that appear. You'll see a list of several related topics. Each is a link to another set of step-by-step answers to related questions.

8. To view a new set of step-by-step solutions, click one of those topics at the bottom of the Help Channel.

> If you've branched out a bit from your original search, you may want to retrace your steps and find the set of answers you were originally viewing. To do so, click the right-facing arrow at the upper-left of the Help Channel Bar.

Performing a Keyword Search

Sometimes asking a natural-language question does not provide specific enough answers. It could be more helpful to search for instances of a particular word. If you want, the Money 99 Help System will show you all the articles that contain a certain word or phrase. Here's how it's done.

To Do: Viewing All Articles with Particular Words

1. On the Money Help Channel Bar, click the Binoculars icon at the top middle of the bar. A Type Words to Search text box appears.

2. Where the blinking cursor appears, type in a word or phrase, or use the one of the available keywords. Right below where you type your phrase, you'll see a list of hundreds of keywords (in the Or Choose Keywords area). A scroll button is provided, if your word is not immediately visible on that list.

> As you begin to type in your own phrase or word for searching, the Or Choose Keywords area changes to show phrases that might be what you are looking for.

3. As you type in phrases or select keywords from the list, the bottom area of the Money Help Channel Bar begins to show topics. These topics are the results of your search. The Help system does not wait for you to press Enter or even finish typing. As soon as it thinks it knows what you want, the Topics area at the bottom starts to display step-by-step solutions for you to click.

4. Click any topic at the bottom of the Help Channel to view it. If you need more screen room to read the results or carry out the steps, click the double arrow at the top of the Help Channel Bar.

5. Some articles or step-by-step solutions display certain phrases in green. These are links. Click any green phrase or word to open the article or step-by-step suggested by that clickable phrase.

6. If you've found a solution that you'd like to keep track of for later, print it out. Do this by clicking the Printer icon at the top of the Money Help Channel Bar.

> Unlike traditional Windows Help systems, you cannot make a bookmark to easily locate a particular Help article later. Your best bet is to copy the text you want to a word processor and save it that way. To do so, use your mouse to select the text you want to save, right-click, and select Copy. Now open your word processor and choose Edit, Paste. Save this Help document text in your word processor by choosing File, Save.

Money 99 Context-Sensitive Help

What's This? and the Navigation Bar help tool are Money 99 Help systems that understand what your question might be, based on the task you are trying to accomplish. As you work with Money, access either of these help systems when you have a question about an immediate task.

> For a one- or two-word description of a feature, hold your mouse over any button momentarily, a ToolTip may appear, defining that feature in a word or two.

"What's This?"

Sometimes all you need is a brief description of a feature to point you in the right direction. It would be nice to read a couple sentences about a particular tool at hand and not have to search through a list of topics first. Money 99 offers the "What's This?" feature to make this possible. Right-click any menu label or any option within one of the Money screens, and you'll get a brief description as to its purpose. In Figure 3.13, the user has right-clicked the Get Out of Debt Goal Planner. A pop-up label "What's This?" appears. Click the "What's This?" and you'll see the description you seek.

FIGURE 3.13.

Right-click a feature for a brief description.

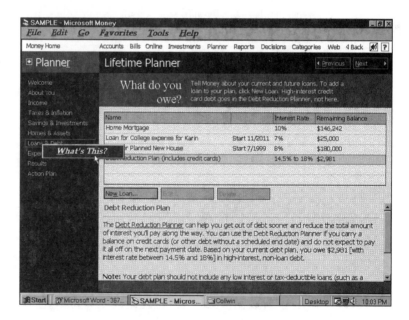

"What's This?" help is not always available, because for some features right-clicking invokes another submenu, as was explained previously in the "Single- and Double-Clicking" section. For example, if you right-click one of the Decisions Center titles, such as Car Buying or the Tax Worksheet, you'll see an extended feature menu, but no "What's This?" tip.

> You can always right-click for a "What's This?" on any Navigation Bar label
> or main menu label.

Navigation Bar Help Tool

When you'd like something more in-depth than what the "What's This?" tool can provide, just click the feature you have questions regarding, and then click the red question mark in the upper-right corner of the Navigation Bar. The Help System opens a sheet of links to answers to common questions about the feature you just accessed (see Figure 3.14). The answers to questions usually begin as an overview with general commentary and move towards more task-oriented solutions, as you click further down the menu of links.

3

FIGURE 3.14.

When a question arises about something you're working on, click the red question mark in the upper-right corner of the screen.

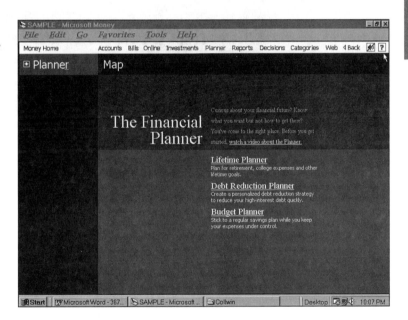

Internet-Based Help for Money 99

Money 99 provides lots of online help options, some of a technical support nature, and some that give general answers to common questions about Money. For example, Money 99's Online Support feature lets you type your question in natural language, searching a database far larger than what's available on your own computer. To access this expanded Online Help menu, click <u>H</u>elp on the menu bar, then scroll down to Microsoft on the <u>W</u>eb (see Figure 3.15). You'll see several online options.

To access any feature in this segment, you must have your Internet connection open.

FIGURE 3.15.

Viewing the Microsoft on the Web submenu.

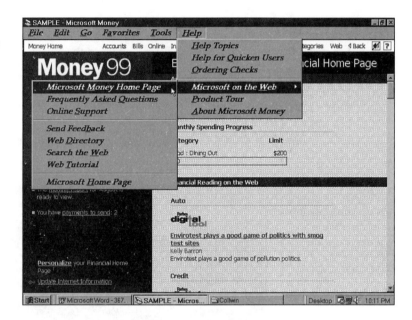

Microsoft Money Home Page

Select Microsoft Money Home Page from the Microsoft on the Web submenu, and you'll have access to a lot of supplemental information about Money 99 (see Figure 3.16), articles about Online banking and financial fitness, and extra add-on tools such as a small program that lets you back up Money files in a single step.

Don't confuse the Microsoft Money Home Page with the Money Home screen that appears when you start the program.

Frequently Asked Questions

Sometimes a question you have about Money might be very similar to someone else's. To obtain answers to Frequently Asked Questions (or FAQs, pronounced "facks"), click Microsoft On the Web from the Help menu, then click Frequently Asked Questions. You'll see a special segment of the Microsoft Support Online Web site that has been set aside for answering these questions. You'll see a set of "starter questions" that are very general. Click a question and answer set that appears closest to what you want to know. Each new group that appears is more specific in nature and may eventually show you the information you need.

FIGURE 3.16.

Microsoft's Money Home page on the Web.

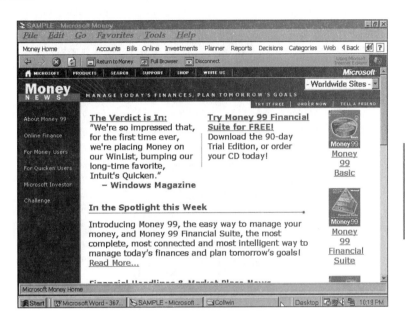

Online Support

Microsoft provides a Web site for specific queries related to Money 99. You can type in a question, using any wording you like, and Microsoft searches its Online Help database for the answer. To open it, click Microsoft on the Web from the Tools menu, and then select Online Support (see Figure 3.17).

1. First, use the My Search Is About drop-down list to select which Microsoft product you are inquiring about.

2. Then type your question in the text box labeled My Question Is. If you like, use the other options available to refine your search.

3. Finally, click the Find button, and be patient while Microsoft searches the database for your answer.

Help for Quicken Users

If you are switching from Quicken, Money 99 provides an entire menu of questions and answers to make your transition easier. From the Help menu, click Help for Quicken

Users, and a list of articles with further questions and answers appears. Topics covered include Preparing a Quicken File for Conversion to Money, Resolving Account Differences after Converting From Quicken, and Using Quicken Checks with Money. Use the Help system's Back button to navigate between articles.

FIGURE 3.17.

The Money Help menu offers a number of online options, supplementing the program's own Help resources.

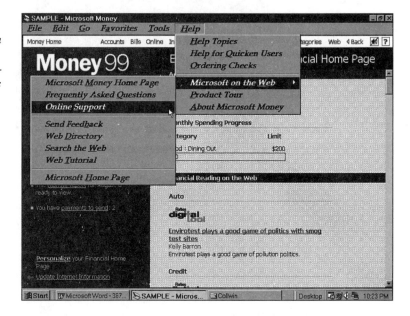

Calling Microsoft Technical Support

You can ring up a Microsoft Technical Engineer to help you with your Money 99 question by calling 425-635-7131. You will not be charged anything beyond the cost of the telephone toll charge itself (which could be substantial, because you will be put on hold before being able to ask your question).

When the Microsoft Engineer appears on the phone, she will ask you specific questions about your computer system first. These questions can reach beyond the knowledge of the average computer user very quickly. To answer them accurately, do the following:

To Do: Locating Your Computer's System Information

1. Select Help from the Money 99 Navigation Bar, then choose About Microsoft Money.

2. First note the serial number, which the technical person will ask you for.

3. Click the System Info button. You'll see a screen containing all kinds of data about your computer and the programs currently running.

▼ 4. If these numbers make no sense to you, don't worry. The Tech Engineer will tell
       you where to click, and what she needs to know to be of the most help.

   5. However, you do want to go make a sandwich or something before calling these
▲   people because you *will* be on hold for at least a few minutes.

Summary

The best way to switch between Money 99's main features is the Navigation Bar. It contains controls that move you to Money's most important screens in a single mouse-click.
Above the Navigation Bar is the menu bar. The File and Tools menu provide submenus
that you'll find invaluable. And if a particular option does not seem immediately available, try right-clicking a main feature screen. You'll find lots of shortcuts there. If any
features are unclear, Money's help system, always available at the right of the main
screen, can provide guidance.

3

Q&A

Q In a nutshell, what's the best way to navigate around Money 99?

A Use the Navigation Bar, located at the top of the screen, under the menu bar. Most
   features not accessed on the Navigation Bar can be found in the menu bar above it.
   The Money Home button brings you to the opening screen, and the Back button
   helps you retrace your steps.

**Q If there is a task or chore I want to complete and I don't see an obvious tool in
front of me, what should I do?**

A Right-click the feature, and you may see an extended menu of options (called a
   shortcut menu) that could help you on your way.

Q What are some other rules of thumb for locating Money 99 features?

A Often at the bottom of the screen are controls for creating, editing, or deleting any
   items you may be working with at the moment, such as checks, categories, or other
   transactions. Also, sometimes along the left side of the screen are channel controls
   that change what appears in the main area on the right.

Q How can I get help with Money 99?

A Click Help at the upper-right of the menu bar, and you'll see Money 99 topical
   help, as well as links to many Web pages that are frequently updated with newer
   concerns. Also, right-click any feature and you may see a label: "What's this?"
   Click it for a one or two-sentence description of the features.

Hour 4

Setting Up Accounts

In this hour, you'll learn about the different types of accounts and their various uses. You'll explore the three main account views and take a brief look at how to set up an online account. You'll also learn how to determine a good starting date for an account.

Understanding Accounts

We tend to think of accounts as bank accounts—a place to store our money. However, in Money 99, an account is a method for tracking money, or anything valuable, really. While maintaining perhaps only two bank accounts, such as checking and savings, in Money 99 you'll be setting up multiple accounts to help allocate portions of that money toward various ends. Certain funds, like those earmarked for retirement, ought to be placed in high-interest accounts that have the potential to earn well for you over time. However, you can create accounts here in Money 99 that do not parallel "real-world" bank accounts.

What Kinds of Accounts Are There?

You'll see that creating accounts in Money 99 takes only a few mouse-clicks, so before we go over it step by step, let's take a look at the types of accounts Money can create for you.

Asset accounts—Create an asset account to track valuable personal property and money that is owed to you. If the money owed to you is in the form of an amortized loan, create a loan account to track that instead. When creating an asset account, you are asked if you borrowed money to acquire this asset. If the answer is yes, then a loan account is automatically set up as well.

Savings accounts—Savings accounts are associated with a particular lending institution. When you create a new savings account, you'll be asked to provide an account balance, account number, and to specify a start date.

Checking accounts—Like savings accounts, be prepared to provide an account number, current balance, and start date for this account. Checking accounts tend to have the most fluid balances of all your accounts, because presumably you use them to pay bills with, and write the bulk of your checks. You'll find that the *check register* that you work with in Money 99 is similar to the one you use when you are out and about.

Cash accounts—Think of cash accounts as a way to keep a lid on your petty-cash spending. Create a cash account here in Money 99, type in a balance, and then mentally set aside that same amount from a checking account you keep at a bank. Then, when you make a withdrawal from this cash account, you must also enter that same transaction in your checking account. Why do this "double work"? Because Money can create much more detailed reports and offer you more thorough advice if it knows how much cash slips through your fingers every month.

Credit Card accounts—If you have a line of credit, a credit card, or charge card, create a credit card account to manage this debt. Money can keep track of an introductory interest rate, as well as when the higher rate "kicks in." Do not use this type of account to keep track of debit cards, because those cards are not associated with monthly payments.

Investment accounts—Create investment accounts to track securities, which would include all the following: stocks, bonds, money markets, mutual funds, T-bills, and Certificates of Deposit (CDs).

Liability accounts—Create a liability account to track any nonamortized loan or purchase that you make regular payments on. For example, insurance premiums, furniture that you are paying for "in six E-Z payments," big-screen TVs that you don't even have to start paying for until next year, and tax settlements or alimony that you pay monthly or quarterly.

Loan accounts—Loan accounts include home mortgages, car loans, loans for college, or any amortized amount that you either owe or are lending. Tell Money the interest rate, payment schedule, date the final amount is due, and any balloon payment associated with the loan, and Money provides many tips for managing this loan to your advantage.

Retirement accounts—Create retirement accounts to track tax-deferred retirement plans, which would include 401(k)s, IRAs, 403(b)s, Keoghs, SEPs, and RRSPs. Even if you intend to withdraw and spend these accounts before retirement (perhaps to purchase a second home, start a business, or adopt children), for the sake of accurate reports and interest accumulation, use Money's retirement accounts to track them.

Determining an Account's Purpose

When creating cash, checking, or savings accounts, Money asks you whether this account is primarily used for Spending Money, Short-Term Savings, or Long-Term Savings. When Money sees how much you plan to set aside for savings, or for "rainy day" expenses, monthly reports are tailored for your allocations. For example, if, for the time being, you decide that saving is just not your thing, and you set aside a lot of money for daily expenses, Money's monthly reports will reflect this priority. Before creating accounts, load Money's Sample data and look at some of the monthly reports, scrolling down to see the suggestions near the bottom of the report. You'll see, for example, a timetable for getting out of debt, or if your savings goal is realistically within sight. Consider how your own data would fare in such an evaluation.

Creating Accounts

Before you actually create a new account, you should know that some account types such as investment and liability prompt you for many account preferences and answers to questions. Others, such as asset and house, require little input from you. After creating an account, its icon appears in the Account Manager (see Figure 4.1). Later, double-click that icon to open that account's *Register,* which looks similar to what you see in Figure 4.2.

FIGURE 4.1.

A New Account icon appears in the Account Manager.

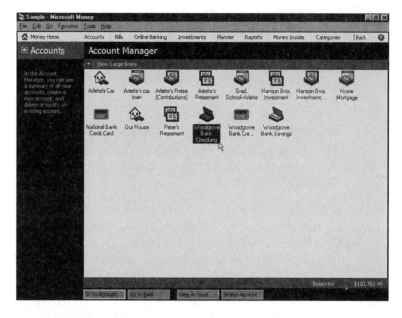

FIGURE 4.2.

The Account Register parallels your check-book in many ways. The mouse cursor highlights a command to print a check. Notice the Print Checks reminder to the left.

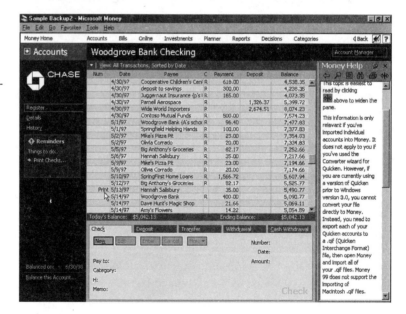

The register is used to do three things:

- Ascribe expenses to that account (write checks from it, or spend the money you've assigned to that account)

- Increase the account's value (make deposits, or make a purchase that increases an asset's net worth, such as adding to your Civil War-era stamp collection)

- Enter a new dollar amount, reflecting a change in your account's net worth (For example, if your house is worth more because of changes in the market, open your asset account called Our House, and type in the new market value.)

Now you're ready to do the work of creating an account.

To Do: Creating an Account

1. Click Accounts on the Navigation Bar.

2. Right-click anywhere on the white area of the screen and select New Account, or click the New Account button at the bottom of the screen. The New Account Wizard appears.

3. The first screen of the wizard asks whether this account is associated with a lending institution (see Figure 4.3). If so, type in the name. If you have multiple accounts at this bank or institution, you have to type in the name only once. Remember, not all accounts have to be associated with lending institutions.

▼ To Do

4

FIGURE 4.3.

The first screen of the New Account Wizard prompts you to specify a financial institution.

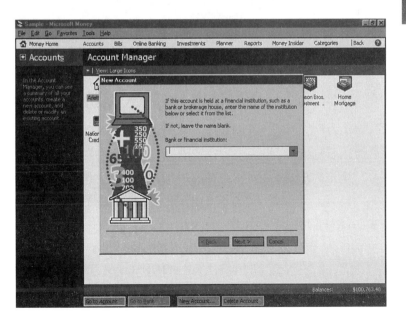

> After entering an account name the first time, it appears on the Bank or Lending Institution drop-down menu.

> Keeping in mind what was mentioned in Hour 1, "Before You Begin," about choosing an early Money 99 start date, you might want to read the final section of this hour, "Adjusting Your Money 99 Start Date," before actually conducting online transactions. It takes a little extra work, but it may be worth it.

4. After typing in a bank name (or choosing to leave this area blank), click the Next button, and you are asked to choose the *type of account* you are creating (see Figure 4.4). After clicking an account type, read the description that appears in the gray box to the right of the list.

FIGURE 4.4.

In the New Account Wizard, specify what type of account you are creating.

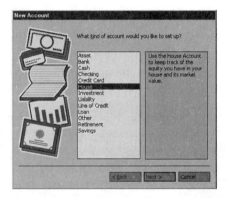

5. Click Next again. Name your new account as prompted. Click Next once more.

6. At this point, the course the wizard takes you on varies greatly depending on the type of account you are creating. Here are some examples of what to expect:

   • When creating a checking or savings bank account, be prepared to provide the account number and an accurate current (or opening) balance.

   • If you are creating an account to track the value of your home, Money 99 asks whether you want to associate this account with a loan (see Figure 4.5). Likewise, asset and liability accounts prompt Money to offer to track a related loan, as well.

▼ FIGURE 4.5.

Some accounts ask whether you'd like to associate them with a particular loan. Answering Yes opens the Loan Wizard.

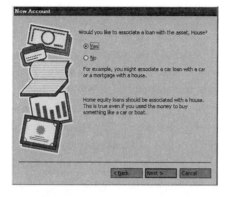

FIGURE 4.6.

Most investment accounts have cash accounts associated with them.

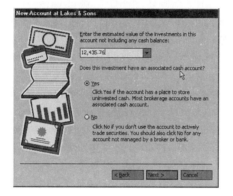

4

- Choosing investment account prompts Money to ask about the tax-deferred status of this account, its value, and whether you want to create an associated cash account along with it (see Figure 4.6). You then must choose a start date for this investment account, and retrace your steps from that date to the present by adding shares in the account register.

- Credit cards and line of credit accounts require you to provide the interest rate, total amount due, and monthly payment requirements.

Organizing Your Accounts with a "Getting Started" Account Checklist

Here's a checklist to help organize accounts in Money 99. Included are special tips for getting an accurate "starting picture" of each account.

To Do: Creating an Account Checklist

1. First, create a savings and checking account that reflects your current balances in your "real life" bank accounts. Call your bank to find out checks that have not yet cleared. You can record uncleared checks in Money 99, marking them as such. Later, when they do clear the bank, it's easy to let Money know about them.

2. Create credit card and line of credit accounts, making sure you know the current balance and interest rate. Make note of any charges that have not yet appeared on your current statement, and be prepared to record those in Money 99 when they finally do clear.

3. Create a cash account to help rein in how much petty cash is spent each month. For the account balance, start with the amount of cash you have on hand at the moment. Try to keep a record of each time you run to the ATM, or get "cash back" from paying with a check at the grocery store. Make sure each time you enter an amount into this cash account that you deduct the same amount from your checking account.

4. Go grab your most recent mortgage statement and create an account reflecting what it tells you. You may name it "Our Home," or something similar. When Money 99 creates reports, it will make thorough use of information such as remaining loan balance, amortization and interest rate, balloon payments, and so on. If the information on your current statement from your lending company is not complete, call the institution to find out what's missing.

5. Make Money aware of any retirement accounts you have, including their current value, accrual rate, and such. When creating retirement accounts in Money, make sure to take into consideration your employer's matching contribution, if there is one. You might have to make a couple of telephone calls to learn your correct current balance.

6. If you have investments, all you need immediately to create this account is knowledge of its current dollar value. If you like, contact your broker and find out exact share numbers and individual share value, if applicable. If you have records of your history of share purchases and sales, follow Money 99's directions on how to input that information. If you go to this trouble, Money can generate a current report on your fund's performance.

▼

    7. If you have an idea on how much you'd to set aside for events, such as vacations, children's education, rainy-day funds, or adding on to your home, create accounts for each of those purposes. You may start with a zero balance if you like, and then, direct money to set aside monthly totals for each of those savings goals. In Hour 13, "Creating a Budget," you'll learn about Money's Budget and Savings Goal fea-

▲   ture.

Understanding Account Balances

In Money 99, it's important to point out that an increase in an account balance does not always mean you have more money. That would depend on the type of account that showed an increase. For checking, savings and investment accounts, an increased account balance indicates a rise in your net worth. However, a higher loan, credit card, or mortgage account balance would mean you owed more money.

Navigating Your Accounts

In later hours, you'll learn the specifics for setting up loans, mortgages, investments and credit cards. For now, let's move on to learn how to navigate around your accounts, and conduct and organize basic transactions.

4

Viewing All Your Accounts

To see your accounts at any time, do the following:

1. Click Accounts on the Navigation Bar.

2. After clicking Accounts, you'll see one of two views:

    • The details of one particular account that you were previously working with.

    • The Account Manager "bird's-eye" view of all your accounts.

3. If Account Manager is not visible, click the Account Manager button at the upper-right corner of the Account screen. You'll see all the accounts you created. Account Manager presents each account as an icon, lined up with the others.

4. To access various views of any account, right-click its icon. The result of this operation is shown in Figure 4.7.

▼

▼ **Figure 4.7.**

Right-click any account, and you'll be able to view it and edit it in a number of ways.

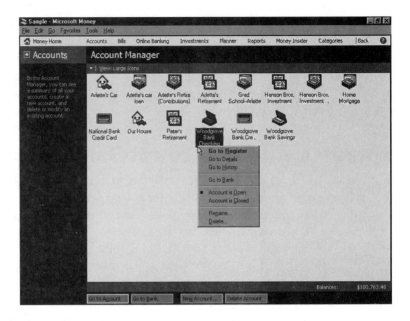

▲

Viewing Your Accounts

From Account Manager, double-click any account icon. On the left, you'll see links to three account views: Registry, Details, and History. Let's take a brief look at working with your account with each of those views.

Using the Account Registry View

Every account has a registry, which, you may notice, resembles your checkbook. Each transaction is shown line by line, and starting from left to right, you'll notice this information recorded about each transaction:

- Date.
- Payee.
- Transaction status (Reconciled or unreconciled: The "R" signifies that transaction matches your bank's own records. "C" means that the transaction has been cleared.)
- Payment or deposit amount.
- Resulting balance after the transaction was recorded.

In Hour 7, "Using the Register," you'll thoroughly explore working with the Account Register. For now, this is simply an introduction.

> Negative account balance numbers appear in red, in parentheses. If a negative balance occurs in an account after conducting a transaction, be sure to "cover it" by transferring money from a less emaciated savings or checking account, bringing the balance above zero. To facilitate a quick exchange of funds, Money 99 provides a Transfer tab at the bottom of the Account Registry screen.

How Accounts Work with the Register

Notice, near the left corner of the Registry View, the word View appears. Click it and you'll see that Money has provided a number of ways to view your transactions here. At times, you won't want to see each and every one of them, lined up as such. Changing your view helps you quickly locate a transaction you may need to edit. You'll learn more about the various Registry Views in Hour 7.

The lower section of the Register is called the check-writing area, or transaction area. Look down there, and you'll see five tabs:

- Check
- Deposit
- Transfer
- Withdrawal
- Cash Withdrawal

Most of your day-to-day business with an account in Money 99 involves these five tabs. Most often, you'll come here to write a check, transfer money between accounts, or create a record of a credit card payment or some other transaction. The best way to acquaint you with how the Transaction Area basically works is to briefly walk through how to write a check. You'll find that most transactions are fairly similar. Writing checks is covered in Hour 6, "Writing Checks," but for now, here's a little preview.

To Do: Getting Started with Check Writing

1. Take a look at the bottom of the register, where checks, deposits, and transfers are conducted.
2. Type in the name of a payee or use the drop-down arrow to select one.
3. Select a category (covered in Hour 5, "Dividing Expenses into Categories").
4. Money automatically includes a check number based on the sequence of previous checks, or you may type in your own.
5. Money includes the current date, but if you want to postdate this check, or let Money know about an earlier check you've written, you can type in a new date.

4

▼ To Do

▼   6. Type in an amount for your transaction. You need not type in commas or dollar
        signs.

     7. Click the Enter button (notice the row of buttons: New, Edit, Enter, and Cancel),
        and your new transaction appears in the register. The total account balance is
▲   adjusted as well.

> When you create a transaction, Money assumes that transaction should be
> effective on the current date. To quickly change a date, make sure your
> mouse cursor is in the Date field, and use your keyboard's plus (+) key to
> move the date forward and minus (-) key to move back.

> The account controls we just examined at the bottom-left of the registry
> vary, depending on the type of account you are working with at the
> moment. You'll find tools to balance your account, update interest rates,
> make extra payments, and many other features.

Using the Account History View

To instantly view a two-month history of most account types, right-click the account icon
in the Account Manager, and select History. If you happen to be viewing that account's
register at the moment, click the History control at the left of the screen.

Your account's history appears as a *line chart*. Move your mouse along the line, over a
transaction date, and a magnifying glass appears, illuminating the date and amount of
that particular transaction (see Figure 4.8). Notice on this chart that dollar amounts
appear at the first day of every month. You can do a lot with this chart. The Chart Gallery
is covered thoroughly in Hour 17, "Charts and the Chart Gallery."

Using the Details View

In the Details View, you can change the name of an account, alter its net worth or opening balance, and manipulate other details. For example, depending on the type of account
you are working with, you can also specify a new minimum balance for an account,
change the account number or interest rate, and access Online Setup for that account.

To view and edit an account's details, right-click the account's icon in the Account
Manager and choose Details.

What you see on the Details screen depends on the type of account you are working
with. If the account is an asset, it may be associated with a certain loan. For example, a

car or home is usually set up as an asset account, associated with a loan you took on to pay for it. If you change lending companies or consolidate all your loans, you'll need to change that asset's *Associated Loan* information. This is done in the account's Details View (see Figure 4.9). Loans, mortgages, and assets are thoroughly covered in Hour 10, "Setting Up and Tracking Loans and Mortgages."

FIGURE 4.8.

When viewing an account chart, hover your mouse cursor over any segment, and a magnifying glass appears.

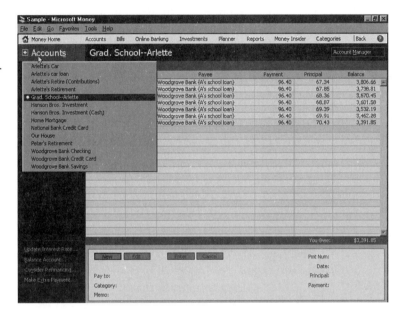

FIGURE 4.9.

In the Account Details View, you can change some basic features of your account.

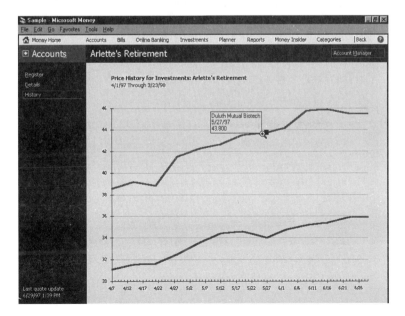

A basic rule of thumb: Use the Details View to change the "front porch" information of an account, meaning what you see first—the name, account number, value, and associated features.

Let's move on to learn how to edit *transactions within an account*, such as checks you've written, or purchases you've made with a credit card.

Editing Account Transactions

Even after a transaction is entered, you may want to edit it. Here are two examples of why you may want to edit a transaction that you've already entered:

- If you entered a credit card purchase, and then realize you entered the wrong date.
- If you want to change the payee of a check to an organization's parent company, rather than the person you initially sent it to.

Here are examples of the types of information you can edit, even after creating a transaction:

- Dollar amount or amount of shares
- Account name
- Balance
- Payee name, or name of investment company
- Check number (or credit card transaction number)
- Category

To Do: Editing a Transaction You've Already Entered

1. Locate the account you want to edit in the Account Manager.
2. Right-click the account icon, and select Register.
3. In the list, locate the transaction you want to edit. To make locating your transaction easier, use the <u>V</u>iew drop-down menu at the upper-left to rearrange the order, if you like.
4. Double-click the transaction. It now appears in the Transaction Area (below the main Register View), ready to edit (see Figure 4.10).
5. Determine which field you want to edit, such as name, transaction amount, or check number.
6. Click your mouse once in that field. The text in that field appears shaded in blue.

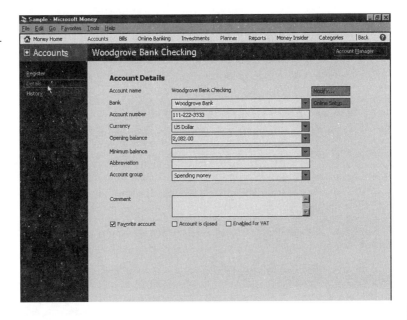

▼ FIGURE 4.10.

Double-click any transaction, and it appears again in the Transaction Area, ready to edit.

7. Type in the new name, amount, or identification number.

8. You can edit more than one field if you like. When you're happy with the edited transaction, click the Enter button.

9. Your edited transaction appears in proper order with the others. Changes you made to the account balance are immediately effective. If you changed the name of the payee, the entry is realphabetized into the list.

Procedures such as reconciling transactions, moving transactions between accounts, and marking them as cleared are covered in Hour 7.

Closing and Deleting an Account

Before deleting or closing an account, make sure all funds have been removed or transferred, and anything that used to be in that account has been accounted for and reconciled.

To delete or close an account, right-click its icon in the Account Manger View, and select Account is Closed, or Delete.

The differences between a closed and deleted account are the following:

- When an account is closed, it is not removed from the Account Manager View. A red X appears on its icon. A closed account means that its future activity will not be considered as part of Money's reports, forecasts, budgeting, or debt-reduction goals. A closed account can be reopened by right-clicking its icon in the Account Manager View, and selecting Account is Open.

- A deleted account no longer exists and its data is not retrievable. You cannot use the Edit, Undo menu command to restore a deleted account.

Quickly Accessing an Account

To get to your accounts in a hurry, do one of the following:

- The fastest way to access all your accounts at once is to open Account Manager. Do this by clicking the Accounts button on the Navigation Bar. If Account Manger is not visible, click the Account Manager button on the upper-right area of the screen.

- To switch between accounts, click Accounts at the upper-left corner of any account view and a drop-down list appears (see Figure 4.11). Choose your account from the list.

FIGURE 4.11.

To switch between accounts, click Accounts on any account screen.

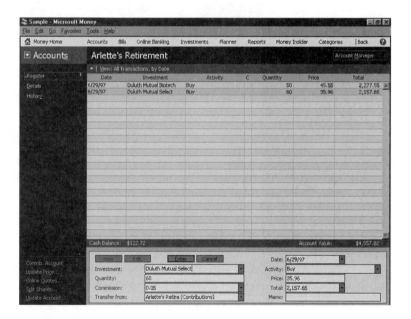

- For the accounts you use most frequently, make them Favorites. A Favorite account is always available from the Favorites list, making it one click away, no matter what view you are in. To make an account a Favorite, do the following:

  1. Double-click its icon in the Account Manager.

2. Click Favorites on the Money 99 menu (if you are already in the Account Register, Details or History View, you don't need to click Account Manager; just click Favorites on the menu).

3. Now scroll down and select Add to Favorites. From now on, you'll see it in that same menu.

Setting Up an Account Online

This section details what is involved in setting up an account online. Money 99 has a special Online Banking screen for carrying out all these tasks outlined here:

1. First, you must determine whether your bank provides online services. They may provide online account management, which allows you to check balances and transfer funds from your computer, and they may also provide online bill-paying. With online bill-paying, you can write checks from your account online to your payees, without ever leaving your computer. You don't have to mail a thing.

2. If your current financial institution does not offer online banking, you can search from a list in Money 99 for one that does, and set up an account with that company.

3. While Online, you must download the terms and agreement document from a bank of your choosing.

4. After reviewing the terms, you can submit your application online, or over a phone call to an account manager from that institution.

5. You must then sit on your hands and wait for that institution to provide a bit of paperwork for you to sign, with password, account number, and routing number information. This usually has to come through the mail, and can take about 10 days.

6. After you have all the account information from your bank and can get started, you can return again to the Money 99 Online Banking area. Click Step 5: Set Up Direct Services, and finish setting up the online components to your accounts.

To get an overview of Online Banking, take the Online Banking Tour. To do this, place the Money 99 CD-ROM in your CD-ROM drive, select Online Banking on the Navigation Bar, and then click Take a Tour.

Where's My Bank?

The list of financial institutions that supports online banking with Money 99 is more than 100 entries long. By browsing through this list, you may succumb to the notion that your bank (or a bank near you) has got to be on this list somewhere. And yes, it may be on that list. However, in many cases, after walking through the Online Banking Wizard, you'll discover that the institution you are signing up for online banking with is *not your own*, but rather, a company called Check Free, which charges $9.95 per month to pay a total of 15 monthly bills on your behalf.

Getting Started with Online Banking

With that overview out of the way, here's how to get started.

To Do: Choosing and Setting Up an Online Banking Service

1. If you are inclined to stay with your current bank, it might be faster just to call them up and find out what online options they truly offer.

2. Verify whether your bank offers online banking via Money 99.

   • If they do, get them to send you an Online Setup Kit, which includes documents you must sign agreeing to their terms of service.

   • If they do not offer Online Banking, or, if you were not able to get a clear answer to your questions from that branch, then proceed through the following steps:

3. Open your Internet connection, because much of what you'll be doing during this session is online.

4. From the Navigation Bar, click Online Banking.

   • If you have an idea of which bank you'd like to investigate first, set up an account with them, using the New Account at the bottom of screen, and type in the name of the account. Then go see what they have to offer online.

   • If you are browsing banks right now, and seeing what's available, then click New Account, and then, the Financial Institutions button. Locate and click the name of a bank you'd like to check out. Then see what they have to offer online.

5. The New Account At dialog box appears. Select the type of account you want to set up. In the next screen, choose a name for this account. You need not use the name they specify. Click Next.

6. Walk through the Online Banking Wizard screens, clicking Next after filling out the requested information. You'll see screens for verifying your account number and balance. You can always go back and add these later in the Account details section.

7. At the end, you can finish creating this account, or create another account at this same institution. Please note that even if this is only an exploratory walk-through for you, you still must go through the motions of setting up an account to go online and get informed.

8. When the Account Created! dialog box appears (see Figure 4.12), make sure the Go to Online Setup For... box is checked, and click Finish.

FIGURE 4.12.

To continue with Online setup, check the Go to Online Setup For... check box.

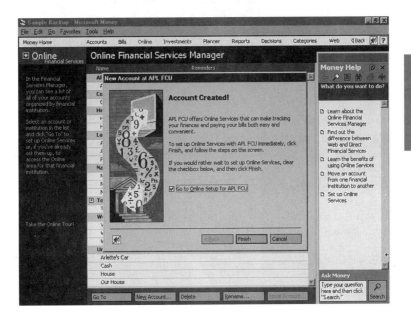

9. The Online Financial Services screen may appear at this point. To continue, click Step #2: Investigate offerings.

10. You'll find yourself at the Online Financial Services screen for the account you've created. The Direct Services Setup For... dialog box is open, and ready for your click of the mouse to go online and search (see Figure 4.13).

Money 99 is ready to search the Internet for the bank you specified.

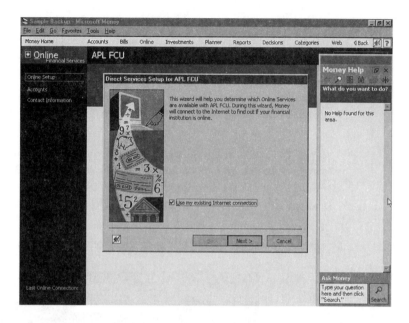

11. Click Next, and Money 99 searches online momentarily and returns with a bank option that most closely matches what you indicated (see Figure 4.14). If you are happy with Money's choice, click Next, and online info from that institution is downloaded to your computer.

FIGURE 4.14.

After searching, Money returns with any institutions that match what you requested. There may be more than one, and you have to choose which to work with.

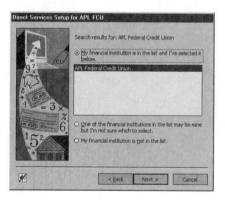

12. Money 99 informs you that Web financial services or Direct financial services are available from your chosen institution (or both kinds of service, as shown in Figure 4.15). Click Next through the following screens, watching the videos provided to learn about the differences between these types of services.

▼

▼ FIGURE 4.15.

Money 99 informs you if Web or Direct banking services are available from the institution you selected. Both may be provided.

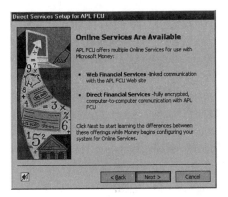

13. After reviewing these distinctions, you'll be informed that you are finished with Step #2. The Online Financial screen returns to view. Click Step #3: Review Service Details.

14. Continue with the wizard that tells you all about Check Free's Online Bill Paying service, walk through all the wizard screens and finally, click Finish.

15. You should walk through all the wizard screens even if you have no intention of using Check Free, because if you don't, then Step #5: Set up Direct Services does not become available. This is an advertisement for Check Free that everyone gets to click past, or read thoroughly.

16. If your chosen bank has secured Web access for conducting bank business, you'll notice a new option at the far left of the Online Financial Services screen: Connect (see Figure 4.16). To get more information straight from the bank you've chosen, click Connect, then, toward the right, click the Get Statements button.

17. After you've filled out your online application, or phoned the bank and finally received your passwords and account numbers in the mail, then return to this same screen: Online Financial Services. Click Step Five: Set up Direct Services, to input your password information and get started downloading statements, or, click Connect, then Get Statements, as outlined.

18. After completing this final step, you'll be able to use Online Banking options from the account register. To carry out online banking transactions, download your Online Statements periodically, and, instead of printing checks from your check register, select online payment options instead. These steps are covered in detail in Hour 7, and Hour 15.

▼

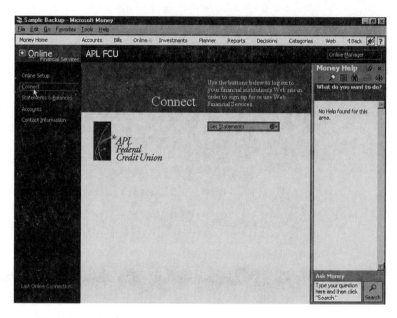

After you've finished Step #4, the Connect Feature for your chosen institution may be available, if they have a secure Web site for doing banking online.

Adjusting Your Money 99 Start Date

In Hour 1, we discussed why it might be a good idea to take the time to enter older transactions, especially in your checking and savings accounts, to help Money 99 get a good picture of your spending patterns up until now. The following instructions mostly apply to checking, credit card, and savings accounts. First, you'll determine a good start date. Then, you'll enter all relevant prior transactions into Money 99's records. Finally, you'll make sure your Money 99's records match your bank balances.

To Do: Setting a Money 99 Start Date

1. First, you must determine the best starting date for your Money 99 records to choose the month that you began to seriously save paycheck stubs, credit card statements, and other financial records. Or, as far back toward the beginning of the year that you care to go.

2. To help determine that date, locate the earliest transaction you want Money 99 to begin tracking from. Thumb through your checkbook register and find the earliest transaction, perhaps a bill paid near the beginning of the year, or your first paycheck of the year. Whatever the balance was at that date, make that your current balance.

Now we have to let Money know about those prior transactions, building up from your chosen start date. Here's how that is done:

To Do: Entering Older Transactions into Money's Accounts

▲ To Do ▼

1. For each account, locate those older transaction you want to include.

2. Open the account (if you need to, review the earlier section "Navigating Your Accounts"), click the New button, and enter that earliest transaction. Make sure you include a payee, check number (or transaction number), amount, and a date.

3. Click the Enter button.

4. Notice that when you include an earlier date, you've also told Money 99 to begin tracking transactions from that earlier time period. You've essentially moved your starting date to that earliest transaction you've just entered.

5. There, of course, now exists this huge gap between the first transaction you entered and the current date. Move through your paper checkbook and add all the transactions, taking care to keep your balance correct. Don't forget, if you skip transactions, it affects your balance.

6. With each account, use the New button to record all those past transactions, paychecks you received, bills you paid, credit card transactions, and others.

7. Call your bank (or credit card company) and verify your current balance.

   If you've kept good bookkeeping all these months, the ending balance you've arrived at by including all your payments and deposits should match what the bank tells you on the phone.

   If this is so, you can put up your feet and begin your new life with Money 99 and your true account balances perfectly reconciled.

   If there are discrepancies between what the bank tells you and the account balance you've arrived at by adding all your transactions, then move to the following to-do

▲   section: "Correcting for an Initial Balance."

To Do: Correcting for an Initial Balance

▲ To Do ▼

1. Call the banks and find out which checks are outstanding or deposits not credited yet.

2. If a credit card purchase is creating an imbalance, call the credit card company and see whether a patron you visited has yet to charge your credit card.

3. Enter the amount of the missing checks, deposits, or purchases and see whether this sum reconciles your account. If not, then move on to the next step.

4. Carefully go through your checkbook and statements and make sure each transaction is accounted for. If your balances still do not match, then you can perform a manual Reconciliation, which is covered in Hour 7, in the "Balancing an

▲   Account" section.

4

Before you enter any current transactions in Money 99, it's imperative that Money 99 and your bank balances are synchronized.

Summary

In Money 99, accounts are more than places to bank your money. They help you organize and group your finances to meet a particular savings goal. Accounts are a basic part of Money 99. Use accounts to write checks, track your home equity, and keep an eye on savings. But before you start using an account day-to-day, you must determine the best start date for your accounts. In the next hour, we'll learn about dividing your income sources and expenses into categories and classifications.

Q&A

Q In Money 99, what is an account?

A Money 99 creates accounts that parallel those that exist at your bank or other lending institution, but also, accounts can be created to help you save money or keep track of spending. In that sense, a Money 99 account can be a tool to help you establish spending and saving priorities.

Q What are some basic account types?

A Just for a few examples, there are checking and savings accounts, pension and investment accounts, liability accounts, which are like credit card debts without interest, really, and asset accounts.

Q What does an account in Money 99 look like?

A Most often, it resembles a check register, with transactions recorded at the top, and a check-writing area near the bottom. Investment and retirement accounts include details about shares and bonds and funds, and asset accounts help keep track of the total value of your assets.

Q In Money 99, what are some of the ways you can view accounts?

A The most familiar view is the Register, which resembles your checkbook. Even investment and retirement accounts have a Register View. Also, the Details View lets you change fundamental features of your account, such as its name and current balance. The History View is a bar graph showing the account's fluctuations over time.

Q **Is it easy to set up an online account or make my current account active online?**

A If your current account is one of the banks that has chosen to smoothly integrate with Money 99, then setting up online banking for you is a snap. Also, if you are open to the idea of changing banks to one that is particularly Money 99-friendly, then you should have no problem. If you want to keep your current bank regardless, then you should read about your online options very thoroughly, and make sure you know what you are getting.

4

Hour 5

Dividing Expenses into Categories

Money 99 uses categories to track your income and spending, determining with high accuracy where your money comes from and where it goes. When you assign income and expenses to categories, Money 99 sifts through them and generates reports that are more than just general commentary. When you write a check, make a deposit, or conduct almost any transaction in Money 99, assigning a category is automatic. Whether you accept Money's chosen categories for transactions or create your own, you'll appreciate the extra feedback Money provides, both when reports are generated and at tax time. (Reports are covered thoroughly in Hour 16, "Money Reports," and taxes are covered in Hour 18, "Money and Taxes.")

Classifications are another way for you to organize what you spend and earn. If you are especially curious about some aspect of your income or expenses, try creating classifications in Money 99 that make sense to you and applying transactions appropriately. You'll probably learn something about your finances.

Exploring the Categories & Payees Screen

Categories appear in a list, looking something like an account register. But instead of each line in the Register representing a particular transaction, each line is a category for an expense or income source. Viewing your category list is always one click away—just click Categories on the Navigation Bar.

After you've opened the Categories & Payees screen, you'll find that lists of all your Payees (people or institutions you owe money to) are now one click away. You can learn a lot by moving quickly between viewing who you owe money to and a list elaborating why you owe it to them. Payees are covered in Hour 8, "Tracking Payees." For now, let's explore categories and classifications.

Here's a quick walk-through of the Categories & Payees screen.

From the Navigation Bar, click Categories and see the categories that Money provides (see Figure 5.1).

FIGURE 5.1.

The Categories & Payees screen opens by default showing a scrollable list of categories.

Notice how detailed the entries are—most categories are also broken down into subcategories. Don't worry, you won't be working that often with categories in this unwieldy list. When you write a check or deposit money, you'll use a drop-down list that's found on the check itself, selecting a category to associate that transaction with.

Below the small label Categories on the left, you'll see two Classification options. These provide yet another way to organize spending and income in ways that make sense to you. We'll learn how to work with them later in this hour.

At the bottom of the Categories and Payees screen are option buttons for modifying, deleting, and creating new categories. Just click the appropriate button to start the activity.

You don't have to use all of Money 99's categories. Create your own to fit your own earning or spending patterns. Here are two useful examples:

- If you spend money every week on food for a girl scout troop and you'd like to keep tabs on the totals, create a special category.
- If you receive income from royalties, patent rights, or some other source that Money 99 does not account for with its built-in categories, create your own.

You can also create subcategories to better break down your spending:

- If you have two cars and would like to know which one eats more gas, create a subcategory under "Fuel," one for each car.
- If you'd like to know how much gas gets guzzled on the weekend, as opposed to your drive to work and back, create two subcategories under "Fuel" as well.

You can also modify and rename Money's existing categories, rather than create new ones. For example, Figure 5.2 shows the Money 99 category Leisure, broken down into eight subcategories. If your leisure spending is not represented well in this breakdown, rename the subcategory by clicking the Modify button at the bottom of the Categories & Payees screen.

FIGURE 5.2.

The category Leisure has eight subcategories beneath it.

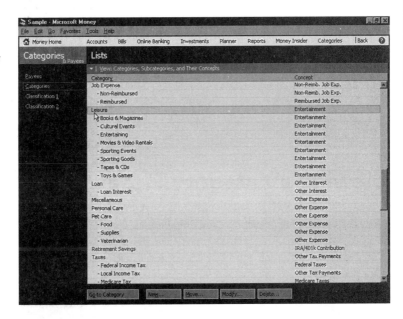

5

Why Use Categories?

By allowing you to be specific about how your money is spent, Money 99 can offer you more tools for getting a handle on spending, and doing a better job of saving. If you use Money 99's Budget Creator, Goal Planner, or Debt Reduction Planner, Money uses data from categories to help devise a workable plan. Also, Money's reports track spending and earning by category over time, suggesting various factors that could contribute to unhealthy fluctuations in income and expenses. That's why when you create categories and subcategories a wizard appears, asking you a number of questions along the way.

Why Use Classifications?

Money 99 also provides *classifications*, which are another way to track earnings and expenses. For example, if you train dogs and take them to shows, you can create a category of income called Dog Shows and within it, create classifications for each animal you enter. Or, if you sell girl scout cookies, create classifications for each type of cookie, so you'll know how many to pre-order next time. Classifications are great for keeping track of how much money you spend on clothing for each child and tracking which household pet still needs to go back to the vet to get its round of shots.

Categories and Concepts

Money 99 places categories within larger groups called *concepts*. Concepts help you get an accurate picture of your spending by, for example, keeping your interest on your car loan separate from interest on your house payment or credit card.

Under the Grocery Costs concept, Money 99 has created two categories: Groceries and Dining Out. If you wanted to keep track of how much of your eating out was fast food and how much constituted a genuinely social activity, rather than simple convenience, you could create two such categories under the category Dining Out. Creating categories and then faithfully assigning expenses to them can clear up a lot of assumptions about spending.

Viewing a Category Close-Up

Let's look closely at one familiar category that most everyone is likely to use. Figure 5.3 shows what happens when you double-click the category Automobile, from the Categories & Payees list.

FIGURE 5.3.

Double-click any category, and it opens in the Details View.

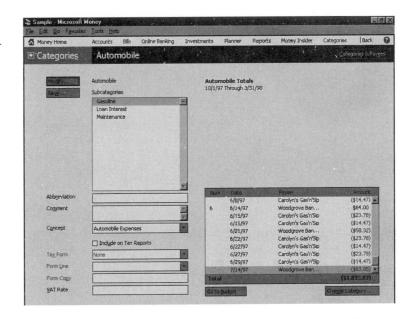

Starting with the left, you'll see that within the category Automobile, there are three subcategories: Gasoline, Loan Interest, and Maintenance. This is where you can edit categories and subcategories, and see how much money was spent on this category as a whole. However, notice that the Automobile category falls under the *concept* Automobile Expenses. That's because driving a car incurs much more expense than buying the car itself. The Automobile Expense *concept* creates an umbrella to quickly examine all the hidden costs of driving.

If you are wondering why automobile insurance isn't listed here, that's because Money 99 creates an entire category called Insurance, and beneath that are the subcategories Home, Life, and Auto Insurance.

The bottom-right window of this same screen shows a list of specific transactions that fall under the chosen Automobile category. (Scroll down to see more of the list.) Double-click a transaction, and it appears in a Check Register View, ready for you to edit (see Figure 5.4). This specific transaction is a gasoline purchase. Notice the Category line shows Automobile as the category and Gasoline as the subcategory.

FIGURE 5.4.

In the Category Details view, click a specific transaction to open it for editing or closer inspection.

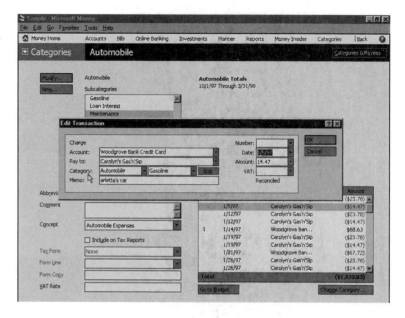

Where Do Payees Come In?

When you work with categories, you can see your payees as well. That way you can see *who* is getting your money, as well as *why*. Creating new payees from this list is not very efficient, but there are reasons why listing your payees here is helpful:

- As you use your checking account to pay regular bills, you'll also assign categories to each payee as you go along.

- Each payee appears on the Payee list right here, along with its associated categories.

- Later, click a payee to see what categories are associated with it and how much money each payment category has cost you.

Creating a New Category or Subcategory

There are three paths for accessing the New Category Wizard. You may want to know each, so that when the need for a new category arises, getting started will only be a click away.

You can start the New Category Wizard by:

- Right-clicking the categories list (the result is shown in Figure 5.5). Using this starting point is helpful because it allows you to see how your new category will fit in with all the others.

FIGURE 5.5.

To create a new category, right-click the Categories & Payees list, and select New.

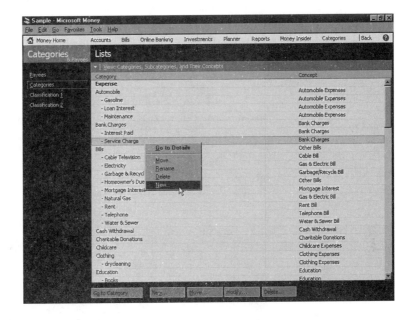

- Typing in a new category name while filling out a transaction. This is helpful if a need for a new category suddenly occurs to you while writing a check or making a deposit. You won't have to stop what you are doing, create your category, then try to retrace your steps back to your Check Register.

- Clicking the New button from any Category Details View, as discussed in the "Viewing and Editing Category Details" section later in this Hour. This last method only lets you create a subcategory. If you want to create a subcategory under *any category* of your choosing, use this method.

To Do: Creating a Category or Subcategory

1. After choosing any of the above paths, the New Category Wizard appears, as shown in Figure 5.6.

2. First click either the Create a New Category or Add a Subcategory check box:

   - When the New Category window appears, type in a category (or subcategory) name. When prompted, indicate the *category type*.

   - When creating a new subcategory, Money 99 assumes you want to create a subcategory under the category you were just working with.

   - If you want to choose which category to create a subcategory *for*, then click Go to Category at the bottom of the Categories & Payees list. Now click the New Category button at the left. You can then choose your parent category

▼

from the Subcategory For drop-down list (see Figure 5.7). Please note that if you select New Category from the bottom of the Categories & Payees list, you won't be able to choose your parent category.

FIGURE 5.6.

The New Category Wizard steps you through the process.

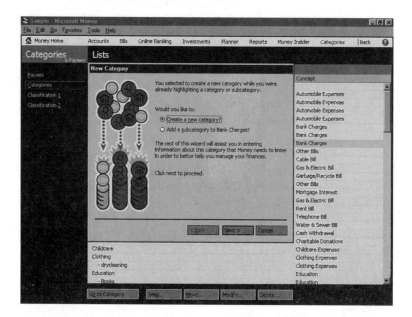

FIGURE 5.7.

If, while creating a transaction, you type a name in the Subcategory field, the New Category Wizard appears.

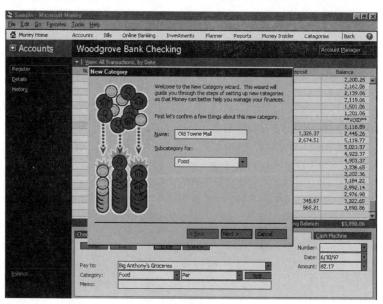

▼

▼   3. After typing in a category name, choose a concept from the drop-down list (see
         Figure 5.8). Money places your categories in these groupings to create a more
         accurate picture of your finances.

FIGURE 5.8.

*You must choose a
concept for your new
category.*

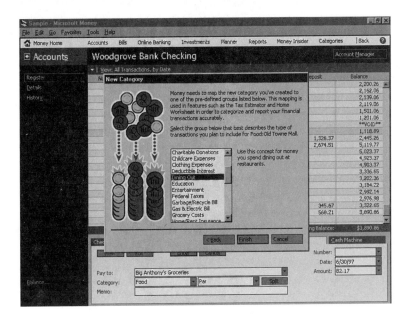

▲

     4. After choosing a concept, click Finish, and your category is included in the cate-
         gory list.

Deleting Categories

To delete a category, right-click it in the Category list and choose Delete from the pop-up
menu. Here are three points to remember when deleting categories:

- If you are deleting a category that has subcategories beneath it, you'll be warned
  that the subcategories will be erased as well.

- If you attempt to delete a category or subcategory that has transactions assigned to
  it, a Delete Category dialog box appears (see Figure 5.9), prompting you to pick or
  create a new category for those transactions.

- To leave the transactions unassigned, make sure the Category field of the Delete
  Category dialog box remains blank.

FIGURE 5.9.

When deleting a category, you'll be prompted to do something with the transactions assigned to it.

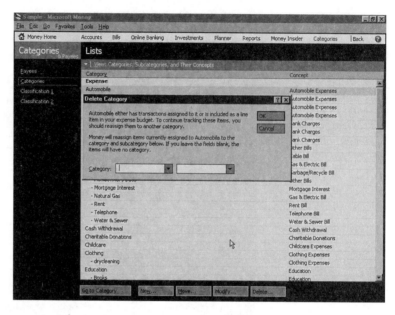

You cannot undelete deleted categories, except as outlined in the next section.

Restoring Money 99's Standard Categories

If you find your experimenting with Money 99's categories has taken a turn for the worse, restore the original set of categories and subcategories by selecting Options from the Tools menu (the menu at the top of the Money 99 screen) and clicking the Categories tab. Now click the Restore Standard Categories button. This feature does not remove categories you have created. Rather, it restores Money's original categories to their default positions and undeletes those you've deleted.

Categories at Work

To see how valuable categories are, let's look at a sample monthly report (see Figure 5.10). Here we are only seeing a small portion of the entire report, but notice how specific the data is. Spending and Earning categories are broken down in dollar amounts and percentages. Reports such as Spending Habits and What I Owe graph this data over time, so the trends you are creating can be seen more clearly. Reports are covered in Hour 16.

Next, let's explore how easy it is to work with and create categories and subcategories. Classifications are covered at the end of this hour.

FIGURE 5.10.

Monthly reports make thorough use of categories.

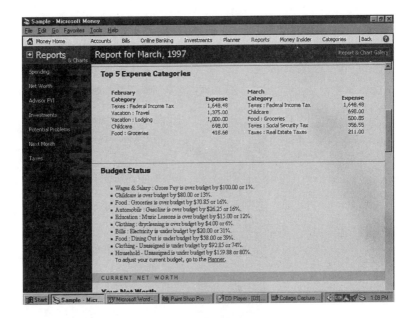

Assigning a Category to a Transaction

You've not learned yet the entire process of writing a check with Money 99, but you will in Hour 6, "Writing Checks." For now, however, let's open up a typical check book Register and add categories to individual transactions, such as paying bills and making deposits.

Whether you are working with the Sample data provided with Money 99 or have begun adding your own accounts transactions, the procedure here is the same. Here's how it's done:

To Do: Viewing a Category in an Existing Transaction

First, let's look at how a category was applied to a previous transaction:

1. Click Accounts from the Navigation Bar, and select a checking account. You may have to click the Account Manager button to get the best view of all your accounts. For this task, make sure you are viewing the Register View of your checking account.

2. Double-click any existing transaction in the Check Register, and look in the Categories field.

3. What appears in the first drop-down list is the transaction's category. Click the arrow, and you can see what some of the choices are.

▲ To Do

5

▼   4. Scroll up to the top of the list, then down. You'll notice Expense categories are at
        the top of the list, followed by Income categories, which are followed by Special
        categories (see Figure 5.11).

FIGURE 5.11.

The Category drop-down list is large, with three unique segments. The top of the Expense category list is not shown here.

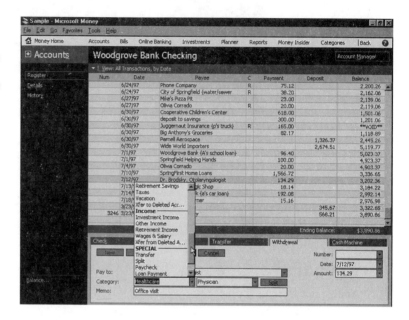

5. Click any category to apply it to this transaction in place of the category that existed
   there before.

6. To make sure you don't really record this change in the account, click the Cancel
   button, near the bottom middle of the screen.

▲

Now let's learn how to assign a category to a transaction from scratch. Most types of
transactions, for example, payments, deposits, and cash withdrawals, should have categories assigned to them. In fact, if you attempt to enter a transaction without a category,
you'll be prompted to add one.

Let's create a transaction with a category. Using Money 99 Sample data, we'll make out
a check to Amy's Flowers for $24.38, categorized as a Gift.

To Do: Creating a Transaction with a Category

1. Make sure you are looking at the registry of a checking account, as explained
   earlier.

2. Let's assign a payee. If you're following along with the Sample data, Amy's
   Flowers may be one of the regular payees that appears when you click the Payee
   drop-down list (see Figure 5.12). (The Sample data may vary.)

▼ **FIGURE 5.12.**

Assign Amy's Flowers as a payee for this transaction.

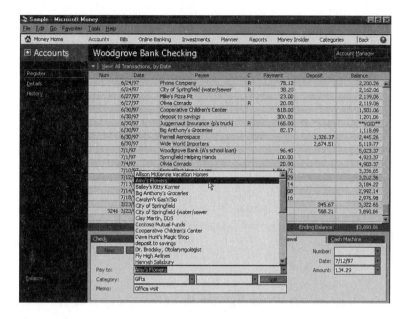

3. Because Amy's Flowers is a regular payee, an amount automatically appears in the Amount field. You can override this sum by typing in any number you want.

4. A check number and date is provided automatically. Since you will be deleting this transaction after evaluating it, don't concern yourself with those values.

5. You may notice that when you selected Amy's Flowers from the drop-down list, Gifts was automatically provided as the category. The category chosen for the previous transaction involving Amy's Flowers is automatically provided here.

If you had previously chosen the Household category for a check to Amy's Flowers, then Household will again appear in this new transaction. Override this automatic choice by choosing a different category, if you want.

6. To the right of the category you chose is the subcategory field. It also has a drop-down list of choices. If you want this transaction to apply to a subcategory as well as a category, select one from the menu.

7. To finalize the transaction, click Enter, and the transaction appears in the Register. The account's total balance immediately reflects the new transaction.

▲

5

Creating a New "Instant" Category

You can create a new category on-the-fly right here, while completing a transaction. This can be handy because if, while making a deposit or filling out a check, some useful categorization suddenly occurs to you, then you don't have to close and open a bunch of menus to make it happen.

To Do: Creating a New Category While Completing a Transaction

1. When creating a category, don't click the Category drop-down list.

2. Instead, type in the name of your new category, and press Enter on your keyboard.

3. The New Category Wizard appears, asks you a handful of questions, and then implements your category.

In a moment, you'll walk through the New Category Wizard, and see how easy it is to create new, effective categories.

Viewing and Editing Transactions in a Category

First, see how your new transaction with its category information is integrated into Money 99's record-keeping.

To Do: Seeing Your New Transaction in a Category List

1. Complete your transaction in your account Register, keeping in mind the category name.

2. Click Categories on the Navigation Bar.

3. From the list of categories that appears, double-click the category you used for this new transaction. The Category Details screen appears.

4. In the scrollable menu that appears at the lower-right section of the screen, scroll down and you'll see your transaction among those listed under this category. You can see how much money you spent on this category as a whole.

5. Double-click it inside this list, and the transaction appears in the Edit Transaction dialog box.

6. You can now alter the payee, check number, amount, category, and subcategory.

Creating a Subcategory On-The-Fly

To create a new subcategory while filling out a transaction, just type in whatever you want to call your new subcategory in the field to the right of the Category field. Type in a subcategory name rather than using the drop-down list to choose one. The New Category Wizard appears and walks you through creating your new subcategory.

After you get the hang of using categories, you'll discover that some subdivision of your main category naturally occurs to you while writing a check or making a deposit.

Categories and subcategories that you create on-the-fly as explained here appear with all the others in the Categories & Payees list.

Viewing and Editing Category Details

You can find out how much money was spent or earned in a particular category and change category details by double-clicking any category in the Category & Payees list. This opens the Category Details screen (see Figure 5.13). From here you can modify its subcategories as well.

FIGURE 5.13.

The Category Details screen enables you to match spending or earning patterns to a particular category.

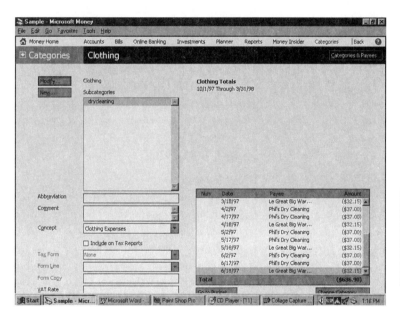

Use this area to change certain category features—such as adding a comment to a category—and to convert a category from an expense to an income.

To Do: Modifying Category Details

1. Click Categories on the Navigation Bar. The Categories list appears.
2. Scroll down the list and locate the category or subcategory you want more information about or want to modify.

▼   3. Double-click it, and the Category Details screen appears.

▲   4. At the upper-left you'll see the category name, with its subcategories beneath it.

Let's start by working with the "form" area on the left side of the screen.

To Do: Modifying Category Properties

1. To change the name of the category, or to alter the category type (Expense to Income, or Income to Expense, as shown in Figure 5.14), click the Modify button.

FIGURE 5.14.

Click the Modify button to change an Expense category to an Income category, or the reverse.

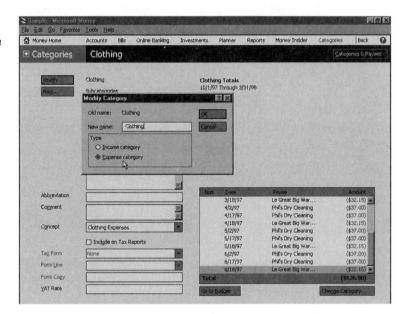

2. To create a new subcategory or category, click the New button. You'll learn how to create new categories later in the "Assigning New Categories to Transactions" section.

3. Moving along the form area on the left side of the screen, you can assign an Abbreviation to a category. This creates a typing shortcut. After choosing an Abbreviation, type it anywhere in Money 99, and the full name of the category appears instead.

4. Type a comment for your own reference in the Comment area. That comment only appears in the Details screen.

   Money places all categories into broad groups called Concepts. These groups are
▼   used to prepare your Tax Worksheet in Money Insider, as well as regular reports.

Use the **Concept** drop-down list to reassign a category to a new concept. (If Money 99 has already chosen a concept for your category, use caution when reassigning it.)

5. Click the Include on Tax Reports check box if you want this category included on Money 99's preparations for tax forms and schedules.

Money 99 automatically assigns many categories and subcategories to the appropriate tax documentation. Before you click the **Include** on Tax Reports check box and assign a form to this category, make sure you've got a clear understanding of tax rules in this regard.

The Category Bar Graph

To the right of the form for modifying category details is a bar graph. This graph shows all the financial activity for this category for the last six months. Each bar represents one month. Move your mouse over any bar to show dollar amounts and percentages for that month. Right-click the chart to display a menu of viewing, copying, and printing options (charts will be covered thoroughly in Hour 17, "Charts and the Chart Gallery").

The Category Transaction List

Below the bar graph is a Category Transaction list of every transaction with this category assigned to it. Scroll through the list, if necessary, to view all the entries.

Double-clicking any transaction brings up the Edit Transaction dialog box.

Here you can alter just about any transaction's feature, such as the payee, the amount, check number, and assigned account. If you double-click a transaction that has been reconciled, you'll be warned that changing its information can unbalance your account.

The Category Budget Link

While reviewing a category of spending, you might want to get the big picture. Click the Budget button at the bottom-left of the Transaction list. The Budget screen that appears (see Figure 5.15) does not deal specifically with that category, however, so click the Income Details button to show a screen that allows you to add or remove categories. Budgets and forecasts are covered in Hour 14, "Long-term Planning and Goals."

5

FIGURE 5.15.

The Budget button at the bottom of the Category Details screen opens this Budget View.

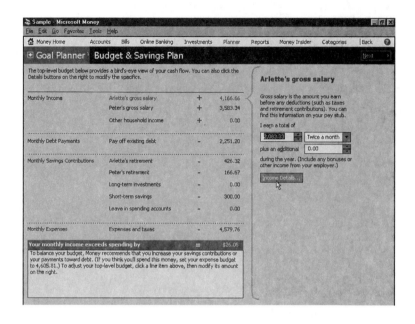

 Remember, you can always return to the Categories & Payees list by clicking Categories on the Navigation Bar.

Assigning Transactions to a New Category

Until now, you've mostly worked with assigning a category to a transaction. As you fill out a check or deposit, you've used the Category drop-down list to select a category, which is then applied to that transaction. But you can work with the Details screen of the Categories & Payees list and move transactions to a different category. You'll want to do this if you suddenly decide that certain transactions can be more accurately accounted for in some other category. For example, perhaps certain trips to the service station really belong under the category Automobile: Maintenance, rather than Automobile: Gasoline. Luckily, you can change an entire group of similar transactions' categories in a single procedure.

To Do: Reassigning Categories to a Group of Transactions

There's an easy way to reassign groups of transactions to new categories, rather than moving one at a time.

1. Click Categories on the Navigation Bar.

▼ 2. Determine the category that all these transactions are currently assigned to. Using the previous example, locate transactions assigned to the Automobile category and the Gasoline subcategory.

3. Scroll down the Category list and double-click the Gasoline subcategory within the Automobile category. This brings up all transactions that fall into that category/subcategory grouping.

4. A screen appears showing details related to those transactions (see Figure 5.16). A bar graph shows Gasoline Totals for the previous six-month period and, below that bar graph, a scrollable list of all Gasoline transactions.

FIGURE 5.16.

Get a closer look at how automobile expenses are broken down.

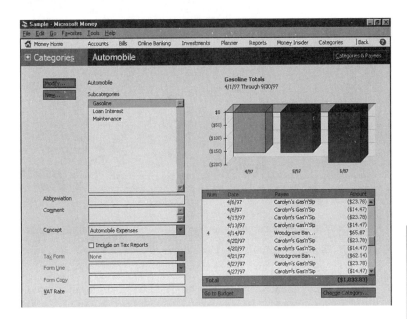

Let's stop and examine these transactions for a moment: If you are following along using the Sample data, you can see that a lot of money went to pay for Gasoline. From this view, you can't tell whether the payee was paid by cash, check, or credit card; only the amounts of each transaction are visible. Perhaps you've determined that the more expensive transactions shown were for an oil change rather than just buying gas.

In this example, you select each transaction totaling $23.78, and leave out those totaling $14.47. Then you change all the more expensive transactions with one ▼ procedure.

▼   Let's continue selecting all the more expensive transactions in this list.

5. Press the Ctrl key and select each target transaction with your mouse (see Figure 5.17).

FIGURE 5.17.

Make a category change to a group of transactions, rather than one at a time.

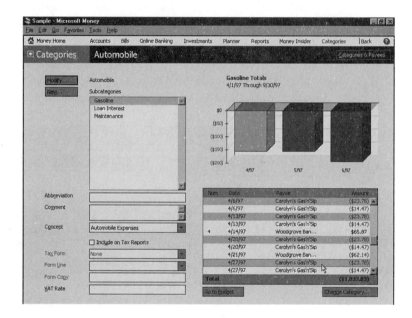

6. Click the Change Category button, and the Change Category dialog box appears.

7. Scroll down this list and choose the new category and subcategory you want applied to these selected transactions.

8. Click the OK button, and all those transactions are altered. Money 99 uses these new category assignments in its forecasts: tax planning, budget goals, and regular reports.

▲

Tracking Tax Information with Categories

Categories organize transactions not only for good logical sense, but to make taxes easier to compute. Many categories represent deductible expenses or income that applies to your base tax rate. You can assign categories to certain tax forms and tax lines by opening the Categories & Payees list and clicking Set up Tax Categories. The Details screen appears, which includes check boxes and drop-down lists for choosing tax assignments that Money 99 has already designed. Money 99 and taxes are thoroughly covered in Hour 18.

Working with Classifications

At times you may want to experiment around with grouping certain types of expenses and income without disrupting the pristine organization that Money provides.

Without changing categories or altering the concept groups that Money places transactions in, you can still create your own private "shorthand" classifications for seeing things lined up the way that makes sense to you:

- If you buy lots of auto parts, but the parts are more for fun and really don't fall under the category of Automobile Maintenance, you can classify such purchases as Auto Parts, keeping track of expenses without having to rethink spending categories just yet.
- Or, let's say you shop at two different supermarkets, and you want to know how much you spend at each but don't feel that this distinction warrants a new category. You can create classifications instead.
- If you get paid every two weeks, some months will be "three-paycheck" months. Often, you can afford to do something special with that third paycheck. It's nice to have a way to mark that third paycheck as extra without creating another account or a new income category, which would be a little excessive.

Classifications are yours to play with, without messing with the books in a big way.

What Happens When You Create Classifications?

When you create a classification, a new field appears on every transaction. You can ignore the field if you like, but because it appears in the "check window" of every account you work with, you should probably only create a classification if you plan to use it regularly.

You can experiment with classifications by assigning transactions to them. If you delete those classifications, Money prompts you to reassign the transactions you created while using them.

 Don't worry about deleting Money's record of your transactions when you delete a classification. Money won't delete any transactions associated with it.

It is easy to get creative with classifications When you rename a classification, every transaction that used it will show the new name of the classification in its records. This makes it painless to experiment.

Figure 5.18 shows my experiment with classifications. I wanted to organize music equipment purchases according to where the equipment would be used. Some would be at a
home studio. Some would be at a more full-featured recording studio.

FIGURE 5.18.

*Creating classifications
to sort out a goal.*

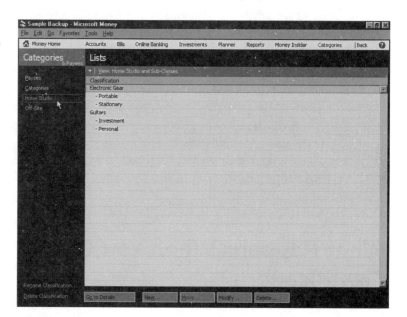

I was playing around with the idea of actually opening a recording studio at a location
other than my musty garage.

By creating classifications, I could see at what point it would make financial sense to
actually do this. Beforehand, I never really thought to set up different accounts for music
equipment purchases, so I didn't want to create new categories yet and risk changing
how things looked "tax-wise." I just wanted to see what the numbers would look like and
not "break anything" in the process.

How Classifications Work

Let's look at the details of the previous figure to understand why the classifications are
organized the way they are. There are two Classifications: Home Studio and Production.
Home Studio is currently selected.

Within the Classification Electronic Gear, two subitems were created: Portable and Stationary. This was easy to do, because as I looked over my equipment purchases I just figured out a helpful way to classify them. I could then see how much music equipment I could count on moving around from place to place.

Beneath Electronic Gear is a Classification called Guitars. Again, just looking at a list of guitar purchases, I could see some were only for personal use, while others were more like collector's items or for investment.

Figure 5.19 shows the third major classification: Off-Site. This classification would show the equipment I could reasonably expect to live without at home, and would be somewhat profitable in a studio situation.

FIGURE 5.19.

My third classification, Off-Site, helped me sort out equipment that I didn't need at home.

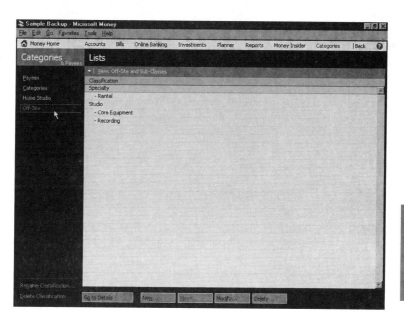

One subitem, Speciality, would show how much money I could make renting specialty guitars, or collector's guitars.

The other subitem in this classification, Recording, would track how much money I made renting out the recording studio.

Notice how classifications can freely swing between tracking expenses and tracking income sources.

Using and Applying Classifications

These classifications can be applied immediately to purchases, past and future. Figure 5.20 shows a transaction in the Account View—a purchase of a musical instrument. It makes full use of the classifications just discussed.

FIGURE 5.20.

Applying the new classifications to a purchase.

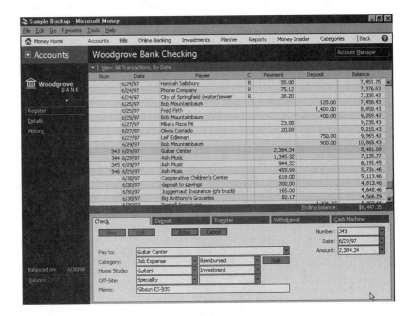

To use classifications, continue to apply them to purchases you make, or go back, re-open transactions, and apply them to purchases or deposits from prior dates.

You Must Create Subitems

After creating a classification, you'll notice that every transaction now has a field for including it. Look closely at the previous figure, and you'll learn that creating a classification does no good unless you create *subitems* of that classification that can be applied to a transaction.

As you can see, Home Studio is merely a label, the title of a classification. Within Home Studio are two subitems—Electronic Gear and Guitars. The Home Studio category drop-down list contains other subitem choices as well.

Create subitems on-the-fly by typing a name into the Classification field when you conduct any transaction. (Whenever you create a classification, Money 99 automatically adds a field for it on every transaction form, such as a check or deposit). As soon as you type a subitem name into a classification field that Money has not seen before, Money opens the New Classification Wizard, and allows you to finish creating this subitem, before letting you finish your transaction. Money 99 then begins tracking that subitem immediately, beginning with the transaction you are currently completing. This is efficient because you are likely to think of subitem groupings as you are making a purchase or organizing past purchases.

To Do: Applying a Classification to an Existing Transaction

To apply a new classification or subitem to a past transaction (a purchase, a deposit, or whatever you like), do the following:

1. Double-click its name in the Register. That transaction opens, ready for editing. You'll notice new fields now exist, containing subitems of the categories you've created.

2. Use the drop-down list to locate the subitem you want to apply, or type in new ones. Notice that when you create a classification (shown here are two classifications: Home Studio and Off-Site), fields for two subitems appear to the right of the classification title.

3. You need not use two, but remember, you can add them on-the-fly just by typing in their names.

4. When finished, click OK, and the edited transaction appears again in the account list.

Viewing All the Transactions in a Classification

After you've applied classifications to more than a handful of transactions, you can view all the transactions that use these classifications.

To Do: Viewing Your Transactions According to Classification

View your transactions this way so you can see any pattern in spending or earning that may emerge from your classifying.

1. Click Categories on the Navigation Bar.

2. On the far left, below Categories & Payees, click the name of one of the classifications you've created.

3. The screen to the right changes to show the subitems you've created along with those classifications (see Figure 5.21). Double-click the subitem that you want to examine first.

4. A Subitem Details screen appears. Just like the Categories Details screen, you can view a bar graph showing the results of that classification's transactions. Below that bar graph is a list showing those transactions line by line.

5. On the left, click any subitem to change the view on the right. The bar graph and list changes to show the details of the subitem you've selected.

▼ FIGURE 5.21.

*To break down spend-
ing and income into
more detail, click a
subitem under a
Classification, and view
the results on the right.*

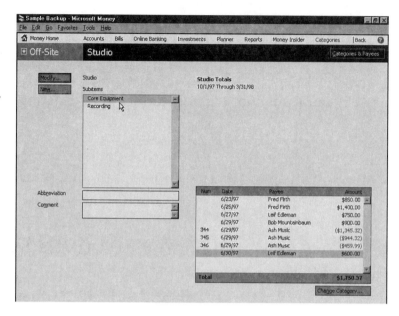

▲

How to Create Classifications

The instructions for creating classifications appear in the following section. Remember
that creating a classification will not "mess up" your categories, or move your financial
data around and make it hard to locate with your usual methods. Categories can simply
serve for your own enlightenment.

To Do: Creating a Classification

1. Click the Classification 1 control at the far left of the Categories & Payees list. The
   Add Classification dialog box appears (see Figure 5.22).

2. Six classification paths are suggested, but if you select one of these, Money creates
   a classification title only.

3. Select one of Money's classifications or type in your own in the space provided.

4. You'll see your new classification appear on the left side of the screen. What
   you've created here is a Classification *label.* You still need to create at least one
   subitem that you can select and apply to transactions from your accounts.

5. To add subitems to your classification, click the classification name at the left, and
   then select the New button at the bottom. You are prompted to type a name for a
   New Class or Subclass that will appear beneath your classification.

▼ 6. Type in a name, and select OK.

▼ **FIGURE 5.22.**

Click Classification 2, and the Add Classification dialog box appears.

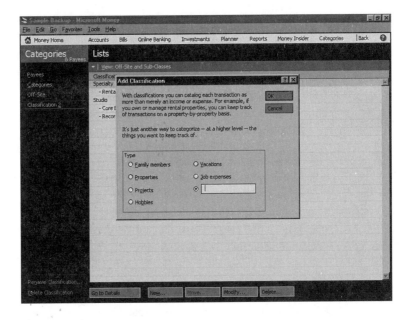

7. The new subitem (or subclass) appears to the right of the classification name.

   Stop for a moment and see what you've done so far. You've created a classification, a label for your subitems, and one subitem that will appear on a drop-down list, available for every transaction.

8. Let's create another subitem: Think again about what other distinctions are suggested by this classification, click the Classification name at the left of the screen, and select the New button. You are creating another subitem.

9. When prompted, type in a name for a new subitem and select OK.

▲ 10. You'll see this new subitem appear beneath the first.

A Classification Is Just a Label

You must create the subitems that will be applied to your transactions. For example, if you select Vacations in the Add Classification dialog box, Money 99 replaces the title *Classification 1* with the title *Vacations*. Then you could do any of the following:

- Create subitems that set money-saving goals (airfare, hotel, food)
- Create subitems that emphasize information gathering (bookstores, travel agencies, international tourist bureaus)

Even if you select Money 99's option, the content of these classifications is still up to you to determine.

Applying Classifications to Transactions

Let's look at how to apply classifications to transactions.

To Do: Applying Your Classifications and Subitems

1. Click the Accounts button on the Navigation Bar, and choose a checking account. Double-click it to open that account in the Register View.

2. Click the New button in the Checkbook area (below the Register). Your new classification is below the Category field.

3. Click the Classification drop-down list, and you'll see the subitems you created. Selecting one applies it to the transaction.

4. If you want to create another set of subitems that can be applied along with the ones you've just created, just name them on-the-fly in the field to the right of the one filled with your current subitems.

> These new subitems provide another way to break down your data. For example, you could now create a classification group: Vacations-France-Paris; Vacations-France-Lyon; and Vacations-England-London; Vacations-England-Liverpool, rather than lumping everything under one country.

> You can add subitems beneath subitems by clicking a subitem in the Categories & Payees list and selecting the New button. Yet another subitem group would make the following transaction tracking possible: Vacations-France-Paris-Eiffel Tower, and Vacations-England-London-Covent Gardens.

Creating a Second Classification

You've just learned how to create one classification, with two subitem groups beneath it. However, Money 99 allows you to have two classifications. To make a second classification, just click the label Classification 2 on the Categories & Payees list. Repeat the steps you carried out with the first classification. To use the same examples, adding that second classification allows you to create a set of transactions involving Relocation-England-London, rather than simply Vacations-England-London.

Q&A

Q What are categories?

A Categories are the method Money 99 uses to group your expenses and income into meaningful distinctions. These groupings make it possible for Money to examine your finances in great detail and make recommendations. Categories are used by Money 99's reports to shed light on your spending and earning patterns.

Q What are concepts?

A Concepts are the over-arching groups that each category is placed into. Concepts are used directly by Money for developing your Tax and Home Worksheets.

Q Can you create your own categories?

A Yes. In fact, you should. Feel free to group your income and spending into categories that make sense to you. Assigning each category to a concept assures that your new category will be every bit as useful as those created by default.

Q What is a classification?

A A classification is like a category, but a little more free-wheeling. You can experiment more casually with classifications, coming up with ways to group your financial activity that makes sense to you.

Q Does Money come with any preset classifications?

A If you decide to use classifications, Money offers a few to choose from, but it's very easy to create your own.

5

HOUR 6

Writing Checks

When writing checks or making deposits in Money 99, think of your own checkbook. Now imagine a checkbook that thinks it already knows what you are going to say, and you're about 90% there. Checking and depositing in Money 99 is like having a friend who insists on finishing your sentences for you.

Money 99 checkbook transactions lend themselves to the notion that the check you wrote to someone last month will look very similar to the one you are writing now. That's why, as soon as you select a payee for your transaction, the details of their previous transaction fill the checkbook area. Money 99 has several time-saving features that, after you get used to them, cut the time you spend writing and depositing checks to a fraction. Never is Money 99's convenience so evident as when you finally get to sit down and enter those monthly transactions.

Getting Ready to Write Checks

To open your Money checkbook, open an account. You'll most often write checks from your checking account, but Money 99 allows you to write checks from any account that has a positive balance.

Access your account by clicking Accounts on the Navigation Bar, and selecting Account Manager. From this view, choose the account you want to work with. There are two reasons you may want to approach your accounts this way:

- It's nice to look over Account Manager before conducting large numbers of transactions, because visiting here jogs your memory about any new accounts you may have recently created. It is helpful to have this recollection *before* you get started writing checks and making deposits, rather than after it is all said and done.

- When you open your accounts from Account Manager, the Account Register always opens, which is where check-writing takes place.

The Account Register is covered thoroughly in Hour 7, "Using the Register," but for now, let's look at a checkbook Account Register, and you can see all your previous transactions in the top part of the screen, although the bottom portion is where you create and edit transactions (see Figure 6.1). This bottom portion is where you write checks, make deposits, transfer funds, and withdraw cash.

FIGURE 6.1.

The checkbook Account Register shows you all the checks you've written on this account.

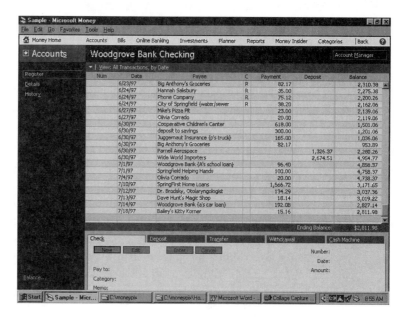

Along the bottom, there are five tabs (see Figure 6.2). For now, let's deal with the first three: Check, Deposit, and Transfer. Withdrawal and Cash Machine features are covered in Hour 7.

FIGURE 6.2.

The bottom section of the checkbook Register is for check-writing.

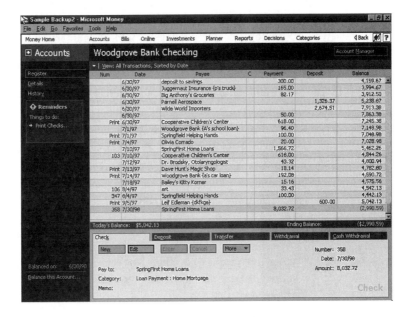

Writing a Check

Writing a check is one of the most universal activities in personal finance, alas, more common than making deposits.

To begin, choose your transaction by clicking the Check tab, and clicking New. After clicking the New button, the following text boxes appear: Pay to, Category, Split Transaction, Memo, Check Number, Date, and Amount.

1. Type in who is to receive this check in the Pay to text box. If this is a payee familiar to Money 99, click the Payee drop-down list, and select their name from the list.

> You can move through transaction text boxes by pressing the tab button.

2. When you've typed in or chosen the name, click the Category text box, and the drop-down list of category choices opens. Select a category from the list, or type in a new one. Categories were covered in Hour 5, "Dividing Expenses into Categories."

3. After choosing a category, click the drop-down menu to the right, and see if a sub-category exists that could help further distinguish this expense from others. If none

6

exists, jog your brain for a moment and see if you can think of one. For example, if you are writing a check to a physician for immunization shots for your children, a category exists called Health Care, but why not add a new subcategory called Immunizations on-the-fly, because those records are timely and important.

4. The Split Transaction feature allows you to assign an expense or income source to two categories. For example, a mortgage payment is always considered a split transaction, because part of it goes to the Interest category, and part is assigned to Principal. (The Split Transaction feature is covered in Hour 7.)

5. In the Memo area, you can leave a note to yourself on any transaction. This memo can be more than 100 characters, and only appears in the check area of the Register. It does not appear in reports.

6. Regarding the check number area (labeled Number), here are some points to keep in mind:

   • When you create an account, you specify your starting check number. Every subsequent check follows this sequence. You need not type the number, Money does that for you.

   • If, for some reason, you break sequence and type in a specific number for a check, Money thereafter follows the new sequence.

   • You can advance or decrease the check number by using the plus or minus keys on your keyboard. (First, make sure your mouse cursor is in the Number text box.)

   These three points apply only to checks that will be printed out. For online transactions, use the Number drop-down list to specify Electronic Payments, Electronic Transfers, and Print this Transaction (see Figure 6.3). Online payment and deposits are covered in Hour 15, "Money Online."

7. Money automatically fills in the transaction with the current date. Use your keyboard's plus or minus keys to alter the date one day at a time, or type in a new one, using the forward slash key as a separator. Click the arrow next to the date, and a calendar appears (see Figure 6.4). Choose a date by clicking it on the calendar. Select a new month by clicking the forward and back arrows next to the month name.

8. If you've ever written this payee a check before, Money 99 automatically uses that most recent sum in the Amount text box. To change the amount, type in a new number, or click the arrow next to the Amount text box to reveal a pop-up calculator. To make a number negative, press the minus key while holding down the Ctrl key.

FIGURE 6.3.

The check Number drop-down list shows Automatic and Electronic payment options.

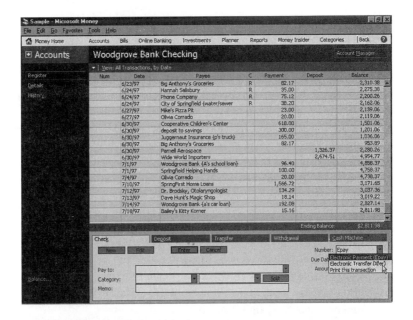

FIGURE 6.4.

Click the arrow next to the Due Date list, and a calendar appears. Use this calendar to choose your date and month.

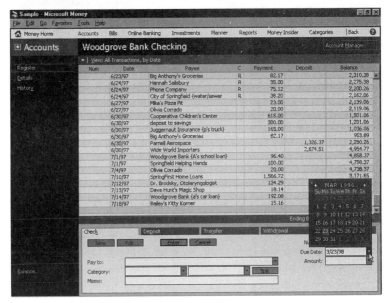

To finalize your transaction, click the Enter button at the top middle of the check-writing area. The check appears in proper sequence with the others (click the View drop-down list in the Register to change the sequence that transactions appear in). The account balance automatically reflects the new check you wrote. Printing checks is covered in Hour 12, "Printing Checks and Other Forms."

The Automatic Fill-In Feature

If you've used Money 99 to write this payee a check before, you'll notice that the payee's entire name appears as soon as you type in the first couple of letters of their name. This can be convenient, but sometimes, it's hard to remember to stop typing. This immediacy takes a little getting used to. As soon as the name appears, just click with the mouse in the Category text box. That way you won't accidentally erase what Money 99 has typed in for you.

This automatic fill-in feature of Money 99 can be a little confusing if you have several payees with similar lettering. Here's an example: If your regular payees include Springfield Helping Hands, Springfield Savings & Loan, and Springfield Water & Power, this is what will happen when you begin to type in any three of those names: As soon as you type the keys: "Spr," Money 99 fills in Springfield Helping Hands, because that name occurs first alphabetically.

Now what if you want to type in Springfield Water & Power? Well, it's tempting to stop typing and just erase what Money 99 has incorrectly filled in. But it doesn't work that way. Just continue to type in Springfield Water & Power. As soon as you type the "W" in "Water," Money 99 will fill in the rest, because it now knows that you couldn't possibly mean to type Savings & Loan or Helping Hands, because you've typed a "W."

The rule is this: When you have payees with similar names, just continue to type all the letters, no matter what Money 99 puts in that text box. As soon as you type in a letter that rules out any other similar name, then the entire name appears. This takes some getting used to, before it seems like that much of a convenience.

Avoid Crossing Category Types

When you are selecting a category from the drop-down list to apply to your check, it's easy to forget that this drop-down list is divided into *Category Types*. Some are Expense, some are Income, and some are Special categories. Make sure that when you are writing a check, you specify an Expense category (Figure 6.5 shows a portion of the Category drop-down list, just to jog your memory). If you try to apply an Income category to a check you are writing, you'll be warned that doing so will make Money 99's reports less accurate. This can happen, for example, if you are paying somebody to mow your lawn with a check, and you scroll down to select Wages and Salary. In this example, you've selected a category that is a *source of income to you*, and tried to apply it when writing a check to someone else. In this case, you should use the Household Expense category, and create a subcategory, such as Exterior.

FIGURE 6.5.

Scroll up and down the Category list to see that it has three segments. Don't confuse them when choosing a category.

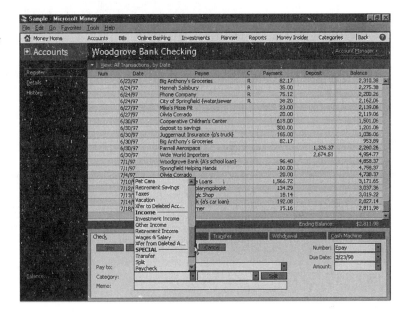

Putting the Memo Feature to Good Use

After typing a memo in a transaction, you can type that same memo in similar transactions, and later, use Money 99's Find feature (from the Tools menu, click Find and Replace) to list all transactions that included it.

For example, you could type a memo "Concert Tickets for Greek Theatre" in several checks throughout the year. At the end of the year, search for that memo text (see Figure 6.6) to see how much you spent on tickets to that locale. A memo is great for this use, because the phrase "Concert Tickets for Greek Theatre" is too long for a category entry.

6

Editing a Transaction

When you edit a transaction, you replace the transaction you are editing with a new one. There remains no record of the previous transaction. There is no Undo feature for restoring an edited transaction.

FIGURE 6.6.

Use the Memo text for a helpful search, when a text string is too long for a category.

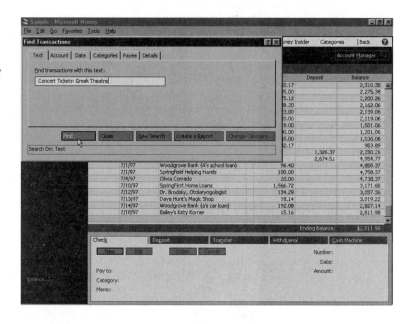

To Do: Editing a Check

The instructions here apply directly to checks, but features for other transactions operate in a similar way.

1. To edit a check, double-click it in the Register. The check appears in the check-writing area.

2. Click any text box to change its contents. You can replace the payee, add a memo, change the category, add a subcategory, or change the check number, sum, or date.

3. Changes you make in this check aren't effective until you click the Enter button. Before doing so, review your changes to ensure accuracy.

4. After clicking the Enter button, your new check again appears in the Register. It may show up in a different sequence than before, depending on the information you altered.

Money 99 provides no way to retrace your steps if you altered a check (or any other transaction) in error. If it turns out your adjustment is incorrect, you must delete that adjusted transaction and make a new one, or edit the transaction to return it to the way it was.

Editing Reconciled and Cleared Transactions

In Hour 7, you'll learn everything you need to know about reconciling and clearing transactions. But for now, let's get briefly acquainted with this important process.

At least once a month, you should go through your Check Register and compare those entries to your bank's records, and see if they match. This process is called *reconciling your account.* Money 99 can't be a very good oracle of the future if the data it's working with is flawed. Money has several tools for matching your records.

Part of the reconciling process is marking which transactions have cleared the bank. Then you can deduct any outstanding checks that might be wreaking havoc with your numbers. Just as a sneak preview, to reconcile or clear a transaction, right-click an individual transaction in the Register, and select either Cleared or Reconciled from the menu that appears. (A check that has both *cleared* the bank and accurately appears in your Money 99 Register is *reconciled.*)

Bear in mind that if you try to edit a transaction that has been reconciled in your account, Money 99 warns you of this (see Figure 6.7).

FIGURE 6.7.

Take care in editing a transaction that has been reconciled, or has cleared the bank.

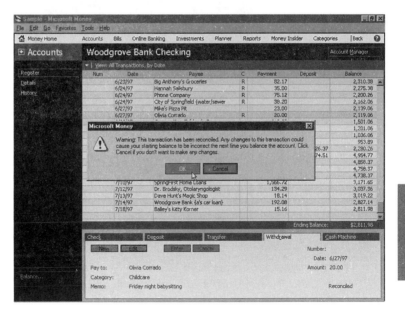

However, if you try to edit a transaction that has cleared the bank, you will not be warned.

If you incorrectly change check amounts, check numbers, and payees of checks that have already cleared the bank, you'll have no way of learning you've made an error, other than painstakingly looking over each and every transaction in both your bank's records and Money 99's Register.

Voiding and Deleting Checks

When you void a check, the sums involved are restored to the affected accounts, and are paid out, should an attempt be made to collect them. However, the account still shows the transaction, but not as a dollar amount. Rather, VOID appears in the Balance area of that transaction's line (see Figure 6.8). Also, in Money 99, you can restore a voided check just as easily as you voided it to begin with.

FIGURE 6.8.

In the Account Register, VOID appears at the far right of a voided transaction.

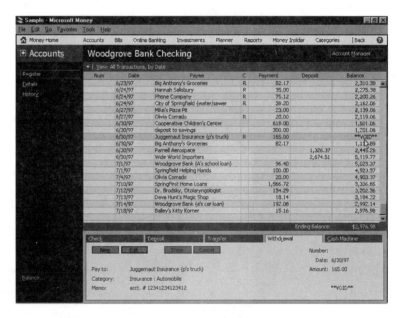

But when you delete a check, its record is gone. The sum of the transaction is restored to the accounts involved, and there is no trace that anything ever happened.

Deleting transactions, unless they arose from an error in procedure, is considered somewhat sloppy bookkeeping. You cannot use Undo from the Edit menu to restore a deleted check.

To Do: Voiding and Deleting a Check

This process is similar for other transactions as well, such as deposits and cash withdrawals.

1. To void a check, in the Account Register, right-click the transaction you want to void.

2. Select Mark As from the menu. Select Void from the submenu that appears.

3. The account balance reflects this reversed transaction, and the word Void appears on the transaction line, to the far right.

4. To delete a check, right-click the transaction in the Register, and select Delete from the menu. A warning appears asking you if you are sure you want to delete this transaction. If you answer OK, the transaction is removed irrevocably.

To Do: Restoring a Voided Check

1. Right-click it in the Register, scroll down to the Mark As menu.

2. You'll notice that a check appears next to the word Void. Click it to remove the check.

The transaction is restored.

Depositing Funds to an Account

Depositing works the same way as writing a check—just move through the fields, identifying the payer, check number, amount, deposit date, category, and any memo you may want to add.

To Do: Making a Deposit

1. Identify the account you want to deposit to, as outlined earlier in the introduction to this hour.

2. At the bottom of the Account Register, click the Deposit tab (see Figure 6.9).

3. In the From text box, type in or choose a payer, the source for this deposit. Previous payers appear in the drop-down list when you click the arrow next to the From text box. Type in a name familiar to Money 99, and the name is filled in for you.

4. Fill out the rest of the fields, using the drop-down lists and plus and minus keys to enter the data more conveniently. Don't forget the Date drop-down list has a calendar available by clicking the drop-down arrow, just as the Amount text box has a calculator.

6

FIGURE 6.9.

In the Account Register, the Deposit tab is just to the right of the Check tab.

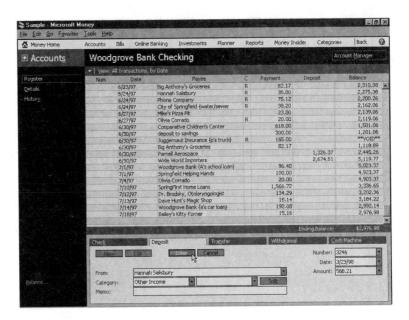

5. Use the date text box to your advantage to post-date your deposit, so you don't spend it before the amount has really cleared the bank.

6. Finally, click the Enter button and the deposit appears in sequence with the rest of the transactions.

Transferring Funds Between Accounts

You can use Money 99 to transfer funds between any accounts. Most often, people think of transferring funds from a savings account to a checking account of the same bank, but because Money 99's accounts have so many uses, this Transfer Funds feature is more powerful than it initially appears. Remember that in Money 99, accounts are not limited to mirroring bank accounts that you hold at lending institutions. You can create accounts to reflect your saving priorities, such as creating a special account for vacations savings. Although this money is actually held in your savings account at your bank, you can set aside a certain amount of money from that account, and in Money 99, create a Vacation account for it.

So sometimes, in Money 99, transferring money between accounts just reflects a change in your saving priorities, perhaps putting more money in a House Repair account, and less in a Vacation Savings account.

Please keep in mind that, for your "transfer orders" to immediately affect the money that sits in your lending institution, you'd have to work online, and be using two online accounts. They must also be at the same bank. Otherwise, there is nothing instantaneous about transferring money between accounts in Money 99. You must still contact any banks involved in this transfer, and let them know what you want to do. Money 99's end of the deal, however, is quick and painless.

To Do: Transferring Funds

1. Access the Register of any account. You do not need to be at the Register of any particular account for this procedure.

2. In the check-writing area of the Register, click the Transfer tab (see Figure 6.10).

FIGURE 6.10.

Use the Transfer tab to move funds from one account to another.

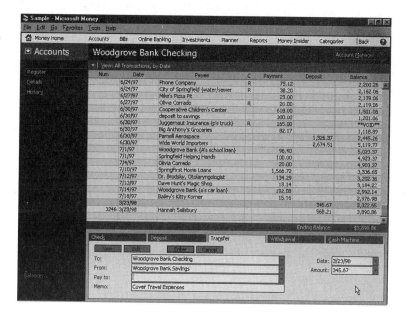

3. Click the To drop-down list and choose the account that should receive these funds.

4. Click the From drop-down list to select the account you want to transfer funds from.

5. If the account to receive these funds requires a special payee, include that name in the Pay to text box.

6. Type in a memo if one would be helpful. You might want to include here your bank's transaction number, if you are transferring funds between two accounts at the same bank.

7. Regarding the check number, transfers between two accounts at the same bank do not require one, nor do transfers from personal accounts that exist only in

6

▼   Money 99. A check number is required only if you will be sending a check from
     one financial institution to another. Email payments and transfers are covered in
     Hour 15.

  8. Type in an amount, using the pop-up calculator if you like.

▲ 9. Click the Enter button to finalize your transaction.

If you want to double-check the transfer, locate the target account and see if the sum you
transferred appears there.

Now, as a variation on the joke "How can I be overdrawn? I still have checks left," please
keep in mind that you still must deal with the lending institutions named in your transfer.
What you did here in Money 99 will not automatically happen downtown at your bank,
unless this was an online transfer. If this was an online transfer, however, then you are
done.

Summary

Money 99 makes it easy to write checks, keeping track of account balances and individual transaction status with ease. It's also easy to void checks if you like, and, well, a little
too easy to delete them. By taking care to reconcile and account for cleared transactions,
your checking account balance can be accurate and reliable.

Q&A

Q What happens in Money 99 when I write a check or make a deposit?

A The amount of your transaction is automatically reflected in the account balance,
     and the new financial activity in that category will be noted in Money 99's reports.

**Q Why is it that when I write a check, Money 99 automatically fills the area with
     an amount and a category?**

A When you begin a transaction, Money 99 looks at the payee or payer, and recalls
     the most recent transaction with them. Money then automatically fills in that same
     amount and category you most previously used. Override this choice by typing in a
     new amount and category.

Q Why do I get a warning when I try to assign a category to my transaction?

A When writing a check, you must take care to assign an Expense category, not an
     Income category. The reverse is true for making a deposit. The Category drop-
     down list is divided into three segments. You'll have to scroll up and down to see
     them all.

Q Can I go back and edit a transaction I already made?

A Yes, you can. Use caution in changing the amount or payee of a transaction that has already cleared the bank or been reconciled in your account, but there are several instances in which you may want to alter a check or deposit that you've already recorded. Money allows you to do so.

6

PART II
Money 99 Day to Day

Hour

7 Using the Register

8 Tracking Payees

9 Setting Up and Tracking Credit and Debit Cards

10 Tracking Mortgages, Loans and Assets

11 Paychecks, Bills, and Other Recurring Transactions

Hour 7

Using the Register

The Register shows your account activity line by line, transaction by transaction. The Register is like your checkbook: You write in every deposit or withdrawal on its own line. You've already become acquainted with the Register, so you know that as soon as you complete a transaction, such as writing a check, the results are posted immediately in the list of transactions. In this hour, you'll see what the Register does in other accounts, such as Credit Cards and Investments. You'll learn how to quickly gather all the information you want about any account, clear transactions, reconcile and balance your accounts, and move transactions from one account to another. You'll also learn about split transactions and using Money 99's Cash Withdrawal feature.

As you've seen in previous hours, you access the Account Register by clicking Account on the Navigation Bar and then clicking any account icon. This automatically opens that account's Register. To switch quickly between accounts, click the word Account at the far left of the screen, and a drop-down list appears. Select any account, and it opens in the Register View.

Changing the Way Transactions Are Listed

When viewing your transactions, they are normally listed in date order, one line apiece. Click the View menu, as shown in Figure 7.1, and you see a number of viewing options. Rather than only in date order, transactions can be listed

- **In the order you entered them**—Most often, this is the same as date order, but not always, because there will be times you may want to go in and change a transaction date.

- **According to check or transaction number**—This is a helpful view if you are looking for missing checks or checks written out of sequence.

- **By unreconciled transactions**—At times, you may want to pay special attention to transactions that have not cleared the bank yet or are unreconciled. To view only unreconciled transactions, click the View menu and choose Unreconciled Transactions.

FIGURE 7.1.

Click View on the Account Register to change the order of the transactions. This View menu works similarly for all types of Account Registers.

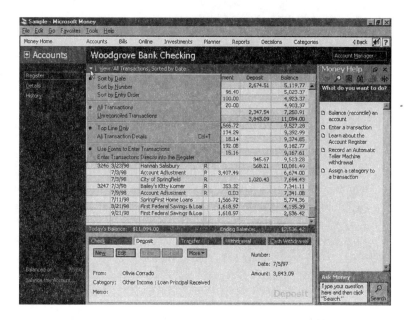

By default, Money 99 shows only the amount of a transaction's detail that will fit on one line. You can make the Register show each transaction in a higher level of detail by selecting All Transaction Details from the View drop-down list menu (see Figure 7.2). This view requires three lines per transaction and greatly reduces the number of transactions you can see at one time without scrolling.

FIGURE 7.2.

To see more details of each transaction, click All Transaction Details from the View menu.

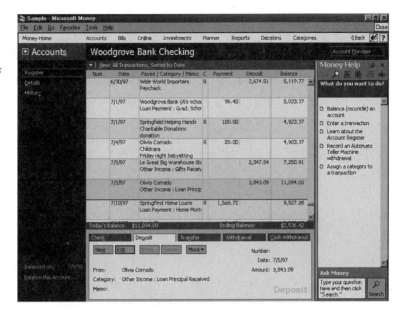

So far, you've always seen the Register showing a list of transactions above, with a check-writing area below, where you actually create or edit transactions. You can dispense with the check-writing area and enter transactions directly into the Register, as shown in Figure 7.3. In this view, the bottom line of the Register is reserved for creating a new transaction. Previous transactions are listed above. To work with this view, select Enter Transactions Directly into Register from the View drop-down list. To restore the default view, showing the check-writing area, click Use Forms to Enter Transactions from that same menu.

> Not all Account Registers offer the same view options. For example, loan and mortgage accounts show transactions only in date order. Investment accounts provide a special view, listing transactions by Investment name or type of activity.

7

FIGURE 7.3.

You can get rid of the check-writing (transaction) area and enter transactions directly into the Register.

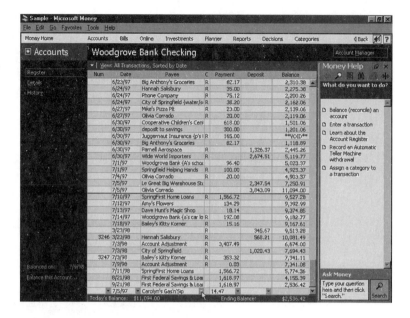

Working with the Register

Although you've actually used the Register quite a bit in previous hours, you can now explore the types of activities that can be initiated from the Register:

- **View all transactions in any account**—The Register shows the list of every accounts transactions.

- **Creating and deleting transactions**—This includes any type of transaction, from depositing funds to purchasing stocks and bonds and changing investment fund allocations.

- **Make extra loan payments**—Most often, you'll automate regular loan payments, allowing Money to deduct funds, create the checks, or transfer the funds without you having to make the effort. However, if you want to double up payments on a home mortgage, for example, you can use the Account Register to make that extra payment.

- **Edit previous transactions**—Click any transaction in the Register to edit its contents, changing, for example, the date, amount, and check number.

- **Balance accounts**—Money provides a wizard walk-through for balancing every type of account. Look for the Balance this Account option in the lower-left corner of the Register.

- **Reconcile and clear transactions**—Most accounts require you to sit down with your bank statement and square each transaction with your Money 99 records. With online accounts, this process is a bit more automated, but still you must regularly take the time to match what your bank says about your account with Money's info. Reconciling and clearing transactions occurs at the Account Register.

- **Moving transactions from one account to another**—If you decide that particular transactions should be tracked in an account other than the one in which you created it, just move those transactions to a new account. This is also done in the Account Register.

- **Creating split transactions**—Certain transactions pertain to more than one account or category. For example, as an artist, if you purchased art supplies at an art store but also bought picture frames as gifts, you can split that transaction. One portion is a job expense, but the other is not.

- **Exploring refinancing an account**—When viewing a loan or mortgage account, you may at times want to consider refinancing. These accounts have a Consider Refinancing feature, at the lower-left corner of the Register.

- **Updating interest rates**—Loan accounts also have a feature for updating your account interest rate, especially important for Adjustable Rate mortgage accounts. This feature, when available, is found at the lower-left corner of the Register screen.

Creating a Split Transaction

Certain transactions may not fall neatly into one category if you want to track spending or income accurately. For example, when you pay your mortgage, a portion of the payment is assigned to an Interest category, although the rest is assigned to the mortgage's loan, reducing the amount you owe on the principal.

When you create a *split transaction*, you select a payee or payer as usual, and a total amount, then you click the Split button (see Figure 7.4). The dialog box for that split transaction appears (see Figure 7.5). Each row represents one of the target categories for your transaction. As you can see by the number of rows, you can assign your transaction to many categories, not just two. Each line requires you to assign an amount, and a category. Type in a description if you like.

7

FIGURE 7.4.

Click the Split button to assign a transaction to more than one category.

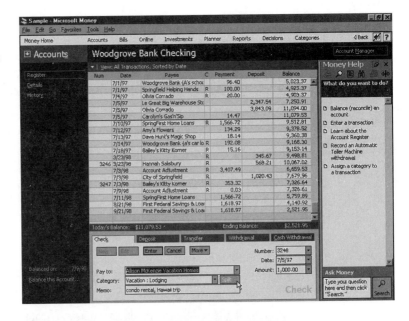

FIGURE 7.5.

Type in details about your transaction, and assign it to as many extra categories as you like.

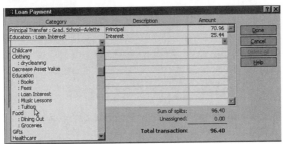

Two Examples of Split Accounts

Figure 7.6 shows a car loan payment. In the Loan Payment split transaction dialog box, you see how the payment, $192.08, is split into two categories: Principal Payment and Interest. Notice the interest, $64.94, is shown in parentheses because it reduces how much you are really contributing to paying off your car. The remainder at the bottom, $127.14, is the principal after that interest is deducted. Notice at the bottom that the principle, $127.14, is called the Total, rather than the $192.08 payment.

FIGURE 7.6.

A car loan payment is a good example of a split transaction.

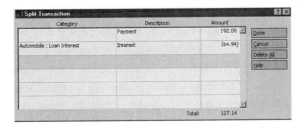

Figure 7.7 shows a split view of a Mortgage payment. The total payment is $1,566.72. That sum is divided among four categories: Principal, Loan Interest, Property Tax for Escrow, and Insurance Payments for Escrow. Notice that the principal is $270.69.

FIGURE 7.7.

A single mortgage payment is divided into several categories.

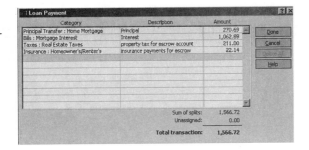

The split feature does not assign transactions to multiple *accounts*, but only multiple categories.

How to Create a Split Transaction

Split transactions are created in the Account Register and are usually seen in checking, savings, loan, and liability accounts.

To Do: Assigning a Transaction to More than One Category

1. Open the account you want to work with, in the Register View.

2. Create a new transaction. (You can do this by right-clicking a blank area of the Register and selecting New, or by clicking the New button at the bottom left of the screen.)

3. The check-writing area of the Register appears with blank text boxes, ready for creating a new transaction.

4. Assign a Payee or Payer to your transaction and a total amount, as well as a check number, if needed.

To Do

7

▼   5. Click the Split Button. The split transaction dialog box appears, as shown in the
          previous figures. Notice that at the bottom of the dialog box, the total dollar
          amount of that transaction is shown. As you add categories and their corresponding
          amounts, you'll see this sum divided into Assigned and Unassigned portions.

       6. Click the first line to assign the first category for this transaction. Each line is
          divided into three segments: Category, Description, and Amount.

       7. Choose a category from the drop-down list that appears. In the Amount area, type
          in a dollar amount, a portion of the total transaction that should be assigned to this
          category.

       8. Click the line below the line you've been working on, and the sum of the first
          Category appears, as shown in Figure 7.8. That amount is labeled "Sum of Splits."

FIGURE 7.8.

When you add a cate-
gory and assign an
amount to it, that
amount contributes to
the total transaction.

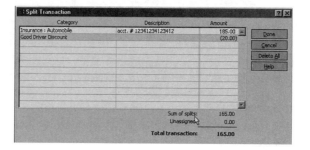

       9. Using that second line you just clicked, include a second category, description, and
          amount. If you've not yet assigned the entire dollar amount of the transaction, then
          click the third line.

      10. As soon as you click the third line, the "Sum of Splits" total grows, reflecting how
          much money you assigned to that second category.

      11. Look at the dollar amount that is still "Unassigned." Keep adding categories and
          amounts until this is zero. In a split transaction, the sum of the category amounts
          must equal the total amount of the transaction.

      12. If you try to close the split transaction dialog box without assigning all the money
          specified in the total transaction amount, you are prompted either to reduce the
          transaction amount and assign the remainder proportionally among all the cate-
▲   gories you choose, or to go back and add more categories (see Figure 7.9).

FIGURE 7.9.

Here are your options for making a Split transaction "even out." A remainder can't be left over.

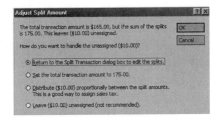

When working with a mortgage loan, you need not assign part of the amount to the principal and part to interest. When creating a split transaction, any amount unassigned to interest or some other fee is automatically assigned to the principal payment.

Making a Cash Withdrawal

Money has several features to help you track spending money, especially those trips to the ATM.

- Using your regular checking Account Register, just use the Cash Withdrawal tab to track each visit to the ATM. Money just follows your cash spending as part of your overall checking account activity.

- Create a special account called "Cash." Each time you go to the ATM or get cash back from a check you write, just transfer funds from your checking account (or whatever account is the true source of that cash) to that cash account.

Should You Create a Cash Account?

Using your regular checking account to track cash is fast and easy. Just click the Cash Withdrawal tab of the Account Register, type in an amount and a category, and Money 99 treats that withdrawal as if it were a trip to the ATM. When money generates its reports, it takes how much spending cash you use and what you use it on into consideration (that's why you assign the ATM withdrawal to a category). Money makes recommendations on how to cut down on these extra cash withdrawals, if applicable.

When you use the Cash Withdrawal option, pulling cash out of your regular checking account, there is no account called "Cash." Thus, you cannot quickly get a birds-eye view of how much cash you use (which you could if you created a cash account). You must wait for the next report to get the whole scoop on cash spending.

7

Working with a dedicated cash account is a little more involved. You must create the cash account then, and each time you go to the ATM in real life, rush back home and transfer funds *from* your checking account *to* this cash account in Money 99. However, if you create your own cash account, Money provides more detailed and useful reports. Plus, creating a cash account lets you assign a payee to your ATM visits, rather than just a category. Assigning payees *and* categories allows more specific accountability.

To Do: Managing Cash from Your Checking Account

To keep tabs on your ATM cash withdrawals without setting up a special cash account, follow these steps:

1. Locate all recent ATM withdrawal receipts, going back to your most recent bank statement.

2. In Money 99, open the account that you use at your bank for funding ATM withdrawals. Open this account to the Register View. Most often, this is your checking account.

3. Click the Cash Withdrawal tab (see Figure 7.10) at the lower-right of the screen.

FIGURE 7.10.

Let your checking account know about a visit to the ATM.

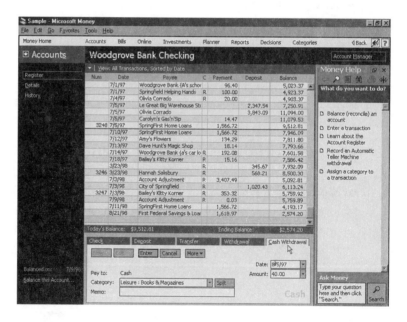

4. Enter an account transaction for each recent cash withdrawal. Each visit to the ATM to take out $40 (or whatever amount) should be entered as a separate transaction.

5. Type in an amount and a category for each transaction. Feel free to create categories to help illuminate where this money goes.

▼   6. Use the Date feature to indicate the dates of each withdrawal.

    7. From now on, make it a habit to enter ATM cash withdrawals into Money 99 soon after you actually withdraw the money from the bank. This practice helps keep your balance current. Also, the more recent a transaction is, the easier it is to assign
▲   it to a meaningful category.

If you create a separate account to monitor ATM cash flow, you can see a graph tracking how much cash slips through your fingers in a given month. Money 99 also generates thorough reports on cash usage in its projections and forecasts.

To Do: Creating a Cash Account

To Do ▼

To create a separate account for your cash usage, and monitor it regularly, do the following:

    1. From Account Manager, right-click the screen, and choose New from the menu. (You can also press Alt+F, and then "N")

    2. The New Account Wizard appears. Walk through the steps to create a cash account (see Figure 7.11). Most often, a cash account is linked to your checking account, because that is the account you are most likely to use for ATM withdrawals.

FIGURE 7.11.

Money 99 lets you create a specific cash account for tracking ATM visits.

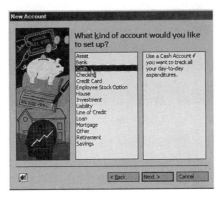

	What kind of account would you like to set up?	
	Asset	Use a Cash Account if you want to track all your day-to-day expenditures.
	Bank	
	Cash	
	Checking	
	Credit Card	
	Employee Stock Option	
	House	
	Investment	
	Liability	
	Line of Credit	
	Loan	
	Mortgage	
	Other	
	Retirement	
	Savings	

< Back   Next >   Cancel

You can create an account at your bank that you use especially for ATM withdrawals. However, it's not necessary to create a separate bank account to use Money 99's ATM Withdrawal feature.

7

    3. For the opening balance, start with the amount of cash you have in your wallet or
▼   purse at the moment.

▼   4. Each time you go to the ATM (or obtain cash back from a check you write for a
          purchase, such as at a grocery store), keep the receipts or make a note of the
          amount.

       5. Open Money 99, and transfer the amount of each ATM withdrawal from your
          checking account to your cash account. Please note that your cash account balance
          rises with every cash withdrawal. It's your checking account balance that diminish-
▲   es when you withdraw cash.

> Do not confuse the cash account being discussed here with an associated
> cash account, which Money offers to set up when you create an investment
> account.

Balancing an Account

In Money 99, balancing an account is the process of matching your Money 99 account
records with the regular statements you receive from the bank.

Checking, savings, mortgage, loan, credit card and asset accounts can all be balanced.
Investment and retirement accounts do not require such an option.

Balancing checking, savings, and any type of loan account involves sitting down with
your bank statement and Money 99, checking off all transactions that match until the
difference between them reaches zero. In the event that there remains a discrepancy
between Money 99's records and your bank statement, you must then scour Money 99's
Account Register for math errors and missed or duplicated transactions. (If it appears
that the bank is at fault, you can call them and get help on their end.)

Balancing an asset account works differently from the rest. See "Balancing an Asset
Account" later in this hour.

How to Balance Bank and Credit Card Accounts

Money 99 provides a Balancing Wizard for balancing accounts.

To Do: Balancing Your Most Common Accounts

The procedure that follows applies to your month-to-month balancing of checking, savings, and credit card accounts.

       1. Open any bank or credit card account and click the <u>B</u>alance this Account option,
          found at the lower-left corner of the Register.

▼   2. A wizard appears, with the instruction "Enter the following information from your statement." The key phrase here is "from your statement." Money 99 wants to begin comparing its own information with that from the bank (see Figure 7.12).

FIGURE 7.12.

Use the Balance Wizard to compare your bank's statement to Money 99's records.

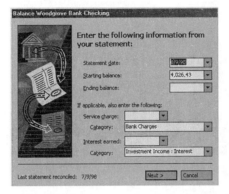

3. As shown in the figure, enter the statement date (the statement shows all the checks that have cleared the bank up through that date).

4. Now enter the opening and ending balance from that statement, not from Money 99.

5. Type in the service charge and account interest earned for that period. This information, if applicable, should be right there on the statement.

6. Apply Money 99 categories to both the service charge and the interest earned. Money 99 suggests categories for tracking these items.

If you choose your own category, make sure you assign an *expense category* to the service change, and an *income category* to the interest earned.

7. Click Next at the bottom of the wizard, and you are returned to the Register screen. The left side of the screen shows a worksheet for checking off cleared checks.

▼   8. Look up and down the columns of your bank statement. As you see cleared checks that match a Money 99 entry, click the "C" column of that transaction, as shown in Figure 7.13.

7

FIGURE 7.13.

Click the "C" column by each transaction that appears in both Money 99's records and your bank statement.

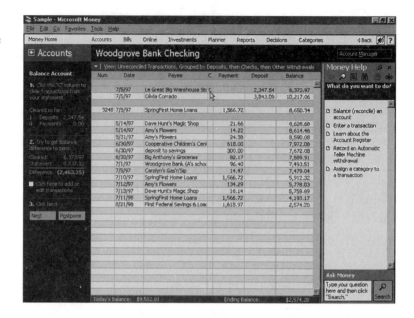

9. A "C" signifies that a transaction has been cleared. As soon as you click the "C" column in any transaction, the difference between your Money 99 account records and your bank statement is adjusted by that amount. While this balance procedure is in process, try clicking the "C" column of a transaction, while keeping your eye on the line that reads "Difference" (the line that the mouse cursor is highlighting in Figure 7.14).

Notice that the difference between your balance moves up and down depending on whether you just cleared a deposit or wrote a check. Note also, that the Balance transactions worksheet, is divided numerically:

- Shows how many Deposits and Payments have cleared so far. Each time you click a "C" by a transaction, the number of cleared deposits and payments increases appropriately.

- Compares the sum of transactions that have cleared the bank according to Money 99 with your bank statement balance. The "Difference" line moves closer to zero as you clear more and more transactions.

FIGURE 7.14.

The "Difference" figure should be ever-shrinking, as more transactions match both records.

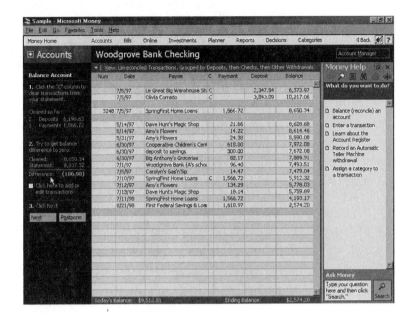

10. As you clear all the transactions for the current statement period, you should find that difference reduced to zero. Regarding missing transactions, here are some points to consider:

    - If a check appears in your Money 99 Account but not on your statement, perhaps it has not yet cleared the bank.

    - If a check appears in your bank statement that is missing from Money 99, perhaps you forgot to enter it or perhaps you entered it into another Money 99 account.

11. If you suddenly remember a check or deposit that was not entered into Money 99, note that the Register Balance worksheet lets you add transactions on-the-fly. To make a change in an amount, or create a new transaction that helps balance your account, click the Click Here to Add or Edit Transactions check box, as shown in Figure 7.15.

7

FIGURE 7.15.

Click here to jump back in and add or edit transactions that help balance this account.

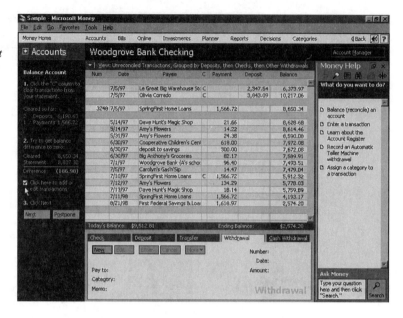

When the Account Doesn't Balance

If after clearing all transactions, your Money 99 account does not match your bank statement, here's a checklist to help isolate the problem.

- Try to see whether the difference between your records is the same as a particular transaction that has not cleared the bank yet or that you forgot to include in Money 99.

- Check for math errors, especially transposed numbers (Entering $33.45 instead of $33.54). If the difference between Money 99's record and your bank statement is divisible by 9, then you probably transposed numbers.

- Perhaps a very old transaction from before this statement period finally cleared the bank. Check your older records to see if a transaction missing from back then is the same amount as your current discrepancy.

- ATM visits are easy to lose track of. If the difference between the two account records is an even amount, such as $20 or $40 dollars, then perhaps you forgot to let Money know about an ATM withdrawal.

- A transaction may have been entered into Money 99 twice. See whether the difference between your account records is the same as one particular transaction. If the list of transactions in the Account Register is long and it's not easy to spot a duplicate, use Money's Find and Replace feature (see Figure 7.16) to search for a suspected transaction's exact sum. If the same exact transaction turns up twice, then you know you entered it twice.

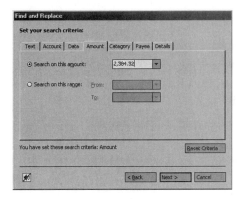

FIGURE 7.16.

Money 99's Find and Replace feature lets you track down single transactions that may be causing trouble with your account.

- Maybe you typed in the wrong ending statement balance. In the first step of the Account Balance Wizard, you were asked to type in your bank statement's ending balance. Double-check that you entered it correctly. While you're there, make sure you entered the correct Earned Interest and Service Charge amounts as well.

Balancing an Asset Account

In Money 99, balancing an asset account, (such as a car, valuables of some sort, or business assets), really amounts to *adjusting the value of the asset*. All you are really doing in such a case is typing in a new dollar value for that asset. This is important for maintaining an asset account that represents your home. As the value of your home rises over time, you want to make note of that increase in value in your Money 99 home asset account, but you don't want to increase the value of your loan taken out on that house, only the house value itself. So, in Money 99's terminology "balancing" your asset account value is not the same thing as balancing the loan you took out to pay for that asset.

Summary

In Money 99, you'll probably end up spending a great deal of time working with the Register. It operates similarly to your checkbook. Here you balance accounts, enter transactions, and move transactions from one account to another, among other tasks. In the next hour, you'll learn how to keep track of the people you owe money to, called Payees.

7

Q&A

Q I'd like to view more than just one line of a transaction. That's not enough information for me. What can I do?

A In the Register, click the <u>V</u>iew drop-down list at the upper-left, and choose All Transaction Details.

Q Why would I create a split transaction?

A If you wanted to assign one expense to two categories, such as a car payment, one portion for principal and another for interest.

Q Why would I want to make a separate account called "Cash?" Why not just manage cash from my checking account?

A Because when expenses are assigned to their own accounts, Money 99 can generate detailed and informative reports, illumining your spending patterns.

Q What's involved in balancing an account?

A Mostly just looking over transactions that appear on your bank statement and matching them with those in your Money 99 records of that same account. If they are not the same, you have choices to make to get them to reconcile.

HOUR **8**

Tracking Payees

Often in Money 99, you are viewing the same set of transactions, but listed in different ways. So far in these lessons, you've explored how to manage money according to accounts and categories. You've worked with listing your expenses and income sources as they appear in various accounts and in categories such as Dining Out or Home Maintenance. There are other ways to view financial patterns as well. For example you can

- See a list of your largest year-to-date expenses.
- Find out what method of payment you most frequently use.
- Look at spending totals per quarter. Perhaps there is one quarter of the year where money always runs short, and you'd like to find out why.

In this hour, you will learn how to work with your Payees list. In Money 99, you can quickly see a list of everybody you owe money to, or have made payments to since you began to use the program. (To view the Payees list, click Categories on the Navigation Bar, and choose Payees, at the upper left.) This information can be important in the following instances:

- A payee is claiming that a payment was not received.

- You need to total how much you've paid to a particular payee.

- You need to retrieve information that won't show up on your monthly records. For example, payments that are made quarterly, biannually, or someone whom you pay irregularly.

- You need to investigate tax advantages based on certain payment totals. For example, according to current law, if medical bills exceed 7% of your income, they are tax deductible.

- Some payees give you discounts if you pay them larger sums at once. You may be able to arrange such a discount if you have a good idea of how much you generally pay this company, and if you can arrange, larger, less frequent payments at a discount.

Opening the Payees list

To open the Payees list, click Categories on the Navigation Bar and choose Payees. An alphabetical list appears of every individual or company you've used Money 99 to make a payment to (see Figure 8.1).

FIGURE 8.1.

The Payees list is found under the same menu as the Categories list.

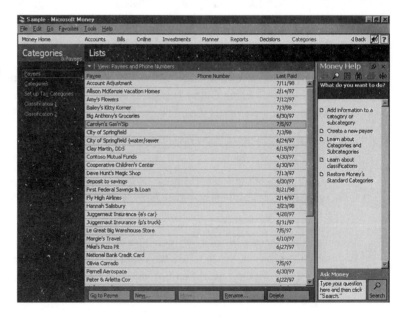

Notable features of this Payees list screen include the following:

- By default, the list shows names of payees, their phone numbers, and the date of your last payment to them.

> When you create a new payee, you are given a chance to provide address, phone number, account number, and contact information. If you didn't set up that information at first, you can always go back and add it.

- By clicking the View drop-down arrow, you can change the payee list to include account numbers or to show only the names of the payees, and last payment dates (see Figure 8.2).

FIGURE 8.2.

Click the View drop-down list to change the details of your view.

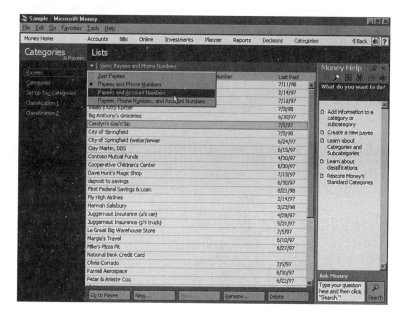

- Even if you don't see the payee immediately on the list, type the first letter of the payee's name. The first payee beginning with that letter is highlighted. (For example, Payees beginning with the letter "S" may not appear on the screen, because they are too far down the list. Type an S and the first payee beginning with "S" is highlighted. Type "S" repeatedly to scroll through all payees beginning with "S.")

You cannot change the date range of the Payee list. It always shows a list of everyone you've ever paid money to using Money 99. You can exclude payees from the list by deleting their names. If you want to create a list of payees using a particular date range, it's easy to customize a report for that purpose. Reports are covered in Hour 16, "Money Reports."

- You can switch back and forth between Payees, Categories, and Classifications by clicking the options on the left side of the screen. You can also access tax categories set up in that same menu. Because payment totals of certain items are sometimes important for establishing taxable income, this grouping can be convenient for you at tax time.

- To view details of any payee, double-click the payee name or anywhere on that line. You'll learn more about the Payee Details screen momentarily.

- At the bottom of the Payee screen are controls for creating a new payee and for deleting or renaming an existing payee. Access that same set of options by right-clicking the Payee list (see Figure 8.3).

FIGURE 8.3.

Right-click the Payee list for a menu of options.

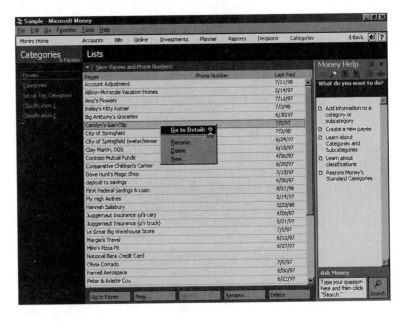

When you delete a payee, no transactions are affected. Deleting a payee does not delete checks you've written to that payee. You've only removed the payee's name from the list.

Adding a Payee

You may never have occasion to add a payee to your payee list directly. Most often, you probably think in terms of the checks you write, not the people you pay. You're more apt to open a checkbook and fill it out than add someone to whom you owe money on this ever-growing intimidating list. Therefore, when you fill out a check in Money 99, the payee of that check is placed on the Payee list automatically. You don't need to add it separately. You can add payees directly to the Payee list by doing the following:

To Do: Directly Adding a Payee

1. Click Category on the Navigation Bar. The Category list appears.

2. On the far left, click the Payees option. The Payee list appears.

3. At the bottom, click the New button. The Create New Payee dialog box appears (see Figure 8.4).

FIGURE 8.4.

The Create New Payee dialog box lets you add payees directly to this list.

4. Type in a name for your new payee, and click OK. The payee appears on the Payee list, as well as on the Payee drop-down list that appears when you write a check.

5. This procedure only adds a payee name. To have an adequate record, you should fill it out with contact information, and you should assign a category to the payee. To do that, double-click the payee's name in the Payees list itself, and the Details screen appears. (You'll learn allabout the details screen in the "Viewing Payee Details" section.)

When You Have More than One Payee at a Company

Sometimes, you'll make several payment types to the same institution, at the same address. In such cases, it may not be clear from the Payee information (or the check information) what specifically this payment is for. Money 99 provides a way of typing "invisible information" right on the payee line that you can read, but will not be printed on the check. This can help if, for example, you and your spouse both have a credit card with the same lending institution.

You could include identifying information on the check memo, but it's more convenient to glance at the payee name and know exactly which payee a particular payment is going towards. In a nutshell, type anything you want in the payee line and enclose it in curly brackets ({ }). Any words you include inside those curly brackets will not be printed onto the check itself. Let's look at it step by step:

To Do: Including "Hidden" Information on a Payee Line

Your goal is to be able to take care of two different bills, even though they both go to the same payee. One payee line will read something like: "Visa Card {Susan's}," and the other will read "Visa Card: {Arnie's}."

Here's how to include identifying information on the payee line that helps with your record-keeping but does not appear on the printed check.

1. In the Register of your checking account, select the payee that you want to duplicate in the Payee drop-down list.

2. Type the "hidden text" inside the curly brackets, for example: "Pacific L & P {Guest House}."

3. Continue to fill out the check for that account, including the amount and check number.

4. Click Enter to finalize the transaction. When you mail this check only "Pacific L & P" appears. But when you see the Payee in the list, {Guest House} also appears (see Figure 8.5).

FIGURE 8.5.

Part of this payee line will not be visible on the printed check.

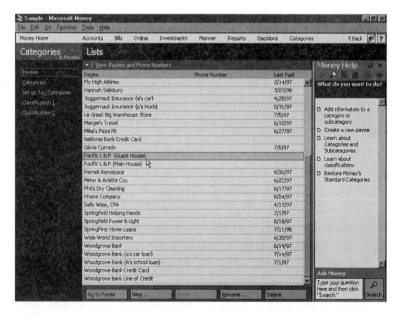

▼ 5. Still working inside your checkbook, click the New button to begin a new transaction.

6. Click the Payee drop-down list and select the payee you just created, with the hidden text.

7. Change the text inside the curly parenthesis, perhaps to {Main House}.

8. Fill out the check, including the amount for this second bill. What appears in the Payee list is "Pacific L & P {Main House}."

9. Click Enter to finalize the transaction. Again, the check itself will only read "Pacific Light and Power."

10. From now on, your Payee list will include that payee twice, with the single address, to take care of two separate bills (see Figure 8.6).

FIGURE 8.6.

The checking account shows two entries, each going to the same payee, but for different accounts.

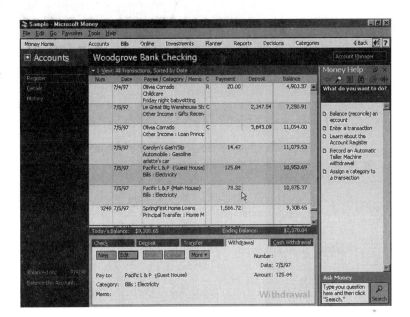

Locating and Replacing Payees and Transactions

There are times when it won't be very helpful to view a list of all your payees or even every payee in a certain category. If you are busy trying to reconcile your accounts, it might be nice to quickly see a list of everyone you've paid money to recently whose check hasn't cleared the bank yet or everybody you've paid over a certain dollar amount.

To create a list of payees that fits a certain criteria, choose Tools, Find and Replace on the Money 99 menu, at the top of the screen. (Another way to open the Find and Replace menu is to press Alt + T, then the "F" key.) The Find and Replace dialog box appears. Click the Advanced Search checkbox, then Next. You'll see a row of seven tabs.

Each of those tabs plays a role in helping you list specific groupings of transactions or payees (see Figure 8.7). This can help you zero in on just the transactions or payees you were looking for without scrolling through a whole list.

FIGURE 8.7.

The Find and Replace dialog box has seven tabs for narrowing down your search for specific transactions.

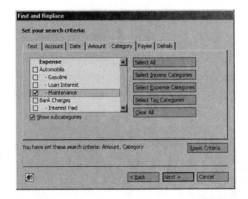

Finding a Specific Transaction in a Large List

Let's use the Find and Replace dialog box to create a list of all unreconciled transactions to all local city agencies above $200 dollars within the last three months. By doing this exercise, you'll be able to set your own search criteria and locate any payee and transaction you need to find just by narrowing down your search with this tool. While you're locating the criteria that fits with this exercise, take a minute to look at the other drop-down lists in the different tabs. You can narrow your search to only deposits or only outstanding online payments, or even select a handful of totally unrelated payees, and search for payments that meet that criteria in one single procedure.

> To use these detailed search mechanisms, click Advanced Search when the Find and Replace dialog box first appears (before you see the seven tabs).

For this particular example search, you need to do four things:

- Set a Date Range criteria (the last three months).
- Narrow our search to unreconciled transactions only.
- Search only for payees that include the city name.
- Narrow the search to include only transactions with amounts below $200.

To Do: Finding a Specific Transaction

1. In the main menu at the top of the Money 99 screen, choose Tools, Find and Replace (Or press Alt + T, then the "F" key). Then, check Advanced Search, and click the Next button.

2. Click the Date tab, and using the Range drop-down list, select Last 3 Months (see Figure 8.8).

FIGURE 8.8.

Select a date range by using the Range drop-down list on the Date tab.

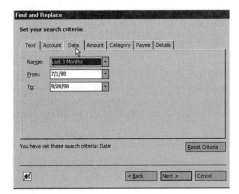

3. Click the Amount tab, and check the Search on this Range button. In the From drop-down list, type the numeral 0. In the To drop-down list, type 199.

4. Click the Payee tab, and then select the Clear All button. Now scroll through the list and locate all payees with the name "Springfield" in the title (see Figure 8.9).

FIGURE 8.9.

Use the Payee tab to search for a transaction from a certain payee.

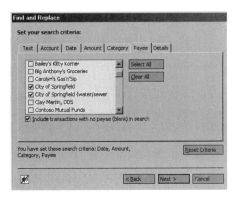

5. Finally, click the Details tab, and use the Status drop-down list to select Unreconciled Transactions.

▼   6. Click the Next button, and you'll see a list of all transactions that meet your crite-
          ria. You can generate a report on your results by clicking the Create Report button.
▲   Or, double-click any transaction to edit it directly.

Viewing and Editing Payee Information

To open the Payee Details screen (see Figure 8.10), double-click any payee in the Payees
list. You can change a payee's address information, view a graph or report on a specific
payee, and see total amounts paid to any payee. You can also edit specific transactions,
changing assigned categories and such.

FIGURE 8.10.

*The Payee Details
screen shows contact
information and much
more.*

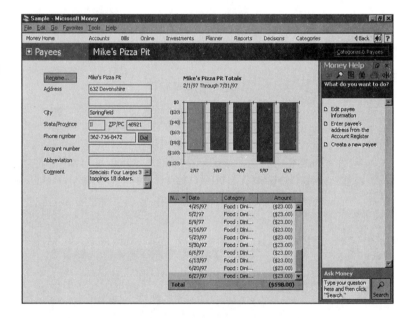

You may recognize a similar screen from working with accounts and categories.
Highlights of the three main segments include the following:

- The left side of the screen provides address and contact information on the payee.
  This can be edited at any time. For example, if you just now found out this payee's
  fax number, type it here in the Comments text box. There is no Enter or OK button
  to click to finalize information you type here. As soon as you type it, the new
  information is part of the payee's record.

Just as a reminder, the Abbreviation text box is for you to create a shortcut for typing that payee's name. Create a shortcut, and type it in any Money 99 text box. The full name appears.

8

- The upper right of the Details screen shows a bar chart of payments to this payee since the beginning of the previous quarter, broken down month by month (see Figure 8.11).

FIGURE 8.11.

The Payee screen bar chart shows how much you've paid to a particular payee over the months.

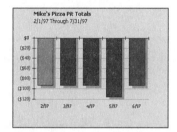

Hold your mouse over any month to see payment details, as shown in this figure.

Right-click the bar chart (see Figure 8.12) to change it to another type of chart, print it, make it into a Favorite place, or change other details of its appearance.

FIGURE 8.12.

A shortcut menu of options is available by right-clicking the Payee bar chart.

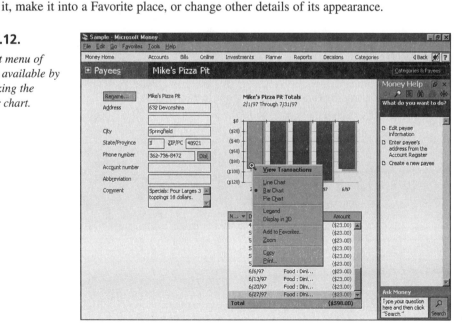

Double-click any chart portion to see the transactions represented by that bar. The View Transactions dialog box appears (see Figure 8.13). From here, you can double-click any single transaction to edit it (such as change the category, check number, date, or amount), or generate a report on that transaction group. When viewing this report, you can click any transaction to edit it.

FIGURE 8.13.

Double-click any chart portion to see details of the transactions it represents.

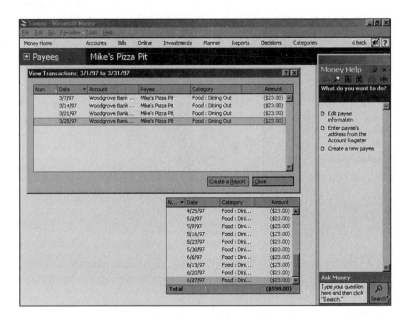

- The bottom right of the Details screen shows a scrollable list of all payments to this payee. The amounts are in parenthesis (and in red) because they are payments, reducing the funds in the account they originate from. The list shows the following details about each transaction:

    Check number

    Date

    Category of the transaction

    Amount

    The sum total of all payments made to that payee (at the bottom right of the list, see Figure 8.14)

FIGURE 8.14.

The Payee Details list tells you quickly how much you've paid a particular payee.

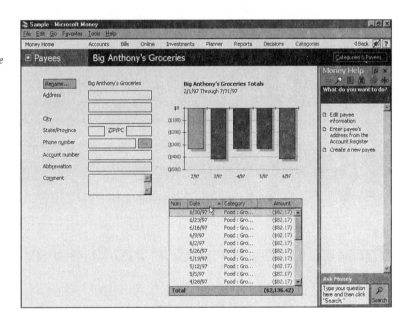

How Transactions Are Listed

By default, each transaction is listed in date order. However, click at the top of any of the four columns (Check number, Category, Amount, and so on) to show the transactions by check number order, payment amount, or alphabetically by Category name (see Figure 8.15).

FIGURE 8.15.

Change the order in which transactions are listed by clicking a column head at the top of the list.

Click at the top of any column to reverse the order. Clicking a second time allows you to see the transactions listed oldest first, or smallest payment amount first, for example. This power to sort transactions can be helpful when you are trying to find one single payment in a long list.

Because the transaction list is not very wide, it isn't possible to fit the entire name of a category on one line. But you can change that: To view an entire category name, drag the spacer between Category and Amount *to the right* (see Figure 8.16), until you can see enough of the Category name to know what it reads completely. To view the amount again, drag the spacer back *to the left* until the transaction Amount appears again.

FIGURE 8.16.

Drag the spacer in between two column heads to make room for Payee's names that do not fit in the space provided.

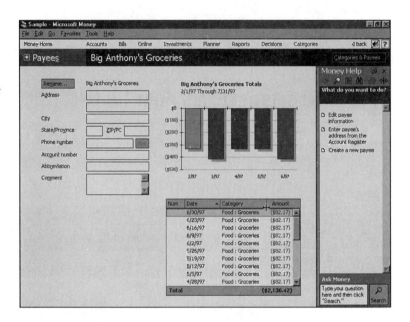

To allow more screen room for the Payee Details screen, close the Money help window by clicking the Close (X) button in the help window's upper-right corner.

Editing Transactions from the Payee Details List

Although this Payee Details list is small, taking up less than a fourth of the screen, it is linked to many features. After learning what you need to know about a group of payments, you can jump right in and edit them if you need to. You can also do the following:

- Double-click any transaction to edit its contents, such as payment amount, category, and check number.
- Right-click any transaction to see a shortcut menu (see Figure 8.17).

FIGURE 8.17.

This menu contains shortcuts for editing a transaction.

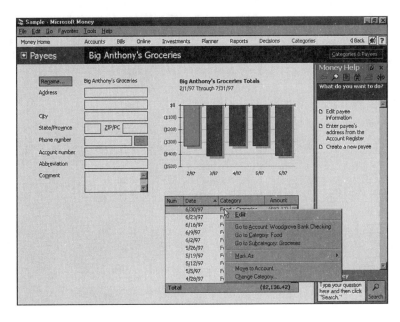

Click an item on the menu to do any of the following:

- Move a transaction to a new account.
- Change its category.
- Mark a transaction as Cleared.
- Open the account or category that the transaction originated in.

Viewing All Payments to a Single Payee

The report that the Payees list automatically creates may not show a large enough date range to suit your needs. For example, if you want to see all the payments you made to this Payee for the entire year, you have to customize the report to show that.

To Do: Changing a Payee Report Date Range

1. After clicking the Create Report button at the bottom of the Payee Details screen, a report appears showing only that month's data. You want to expand this report to include a larger date range.

▼ 2. Click the Customize icon at the bottom of the screen (see Figure 8.18).

FIGURE 8.18.

Customizing a Payee Report to a larger date range.

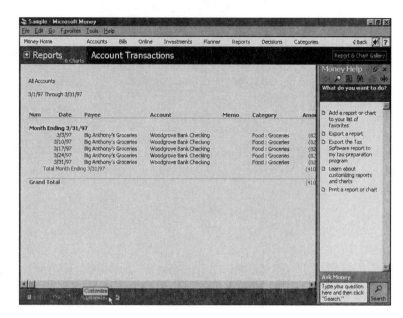

3. Click the Date tab that appears on the Customize Report dialog box.

4. In the Range drop-down list, click and select a new date range, for example Year to Date, or Last Six Months.

5. Click OK, and the report showing the new date range appears.

Reports are covered thoroughly in Hour 16.

Summary

The Payee list provides a convenient and detailed look at all the people to whom you owe money. It helps keep track of payment totals and works hand in hand with categories to see who's getting paid what. You can create detailed reports with the Payees list, revealing all the ups and downs of where your money goes throughout the month or year. In the next hour, you'll learn how Money 99 tracks credit card usage.

Q&A

Q Why would I work individually with a list of Payees?

A The payee list contains contact information about people to whom you owe money. With a quick glance, you can tell how much money you've paid out to one payee in a given time period. You can use the Payee list as a jump-off point to look at related accounts.

Q Why is the Payees list so closely related to the Category list?

A Tracking the reasons why an expense occurs is closely related to whom you pay in regard to that expense. Looking at both categories and payees helps illumine the true nature of many of your expenses.

Q There is a very specific payment that I have to track down. I can't remember too many details about it, but it's important that I locate it in my Money 99 records. Any suggestions?

A Use the Find and Replace tool, found in the Tools menu. Include any details you remember about that payment, using the tabs provided. Money 99 tracks down any payments that meet your criteria.

Q A Payee says I skipped a payment. I have no record that I did so. Where does Money 99 list all payments I made to one specific Payee?

A In the Payee Details screen. From the Payee screen, select a particular payee, and click Details. To the lower right of the screen is a list, showing all the payments Money 99 has recorded for that payee.

8

HOUR 9

Setting Up and Tracking Credit and Debit Cards

In this hour, you'll learn how to manage credit cards in Money 99, as well as how to manage lines of credit and liability accounts. You'll learn how to credit refunds, charges made in error, and cash-back bonuses, and how to "double-track" credit card purchases when you pay your monthly bill from your checking account. You'll also take a glance at how Money 99 manages debt, using the Debt Reduction Planner and Decision Center features. This involves only using credit cards that have been included in your budget as well as your Debt Reduction plan. That way, Money can properly keep track of expenses.

Mortgage, loan, and asset accounts are covered in Hour 10, "Setting Up and Tracking Loans and Mortgages."

Liability accounts are sums of money that you owe from a purchase but do not accrue interest. Examples would be installment payment plans and big screen TVs that you can keep for a year before owing any interest.

How Credit Card Accounts Differ from Other Accounts

A credit card Account Register looks and functions similarly to a checking or savings account. The major difference being that when your credit card account grows, you owe more money. The account balance of a credit card account has an ominously different meaning than a checking account. The bottom line of a credit card shows your credit limit on the left, and how close you are to that limit on the right. The words "You Owe:" appear right before that total (see Figure 9.1).

FIGURE 9.1.

Your account balance appears at the bottom right of your credit card account.

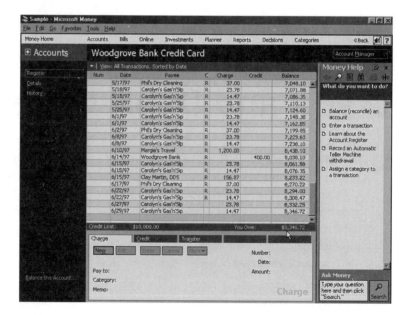

Some other special differences between credit card accounts and checking or saving accounts include:

- The day to day transactions you enter into your credit card account are purchases.
- Instead of check numbers, enter the transaction number that appears on the receipt with each credit card purchase.

- Monthly credit card payments are recorded in your checkbook and applied to the credit card automatically.

How Money 99 Credit Accounts Work

There are special procedures for entering late charges, service fees, cash bonuses, refunds, and partial refunds that only apply to credit card accounts.

When you create a credit card account in Money 99, you do the following:

- Enter the interest rate (including any lower introductory rate information), account number, and the credit limit. (You can easily go back and change these settings.)
- Specify whether you want to track individual purchases you make with this card and whether you intend to pay the entire bill every month.
- Determine whether Money 99 should automatically generate monthly payments toward this account or just remind you when bill-time is approaching.

A Safeguard to Free Credit Card Spending

Money 99 makes it easy to keep track of individual credit card transactions, both when purchases are made and when you pay for them. This is good, because one problem with credit card purchases is that because you are not required to pay the entire balance every month, it's easy to lose track of what was purchased. You end up thinking in terms of "paying off the credit card debt," rather than accounting for individual purchases.

It seems like "double-work," but it's a good idea to account for a credit card purchase *when you pay the bill* as well as when you purchase the item. At bill-time, split your payment across several categories, accounting for each of that month's credit card purchases. This accountability makes you less apt to think of a credit card as "free money." You can easily split a credit card payment, adding only a few minutes to the time it takes to record a payment.

Setting Up a Credit Card Account

Creating a credit card account is similar to setting up a checking or savings account. As long as you know your interest rate, current balance, credit limit, and due date, you have all the information you need to get started.

9

To Do: Creating a Credit Card Account

1. To create a credit card account, right-click Account Manager and select New, or click the New button at the bottom left of the Account Manager screen.

2. The Account Wizard appears and prompts you for new information about this account each time you click the Next button.

3. The questions you are asked depend on the type of account you choose. After naming your credit card's financial institution in the first screen, click Next and you are asked to identify the *type of account* you are creating (see Figure 9.2). Select Credit Card, and click Next.

FIGURE 9.2.

When the Account Wizard asks the type of account you are creating, select Credit Card.

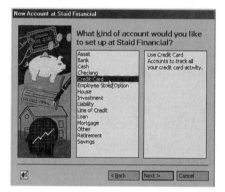

4. The Account Wizard prompts you for the following information, so make sure you have it handy:

   - The name and account number of the account.

   - How much you owe on this account, and whether you intend to pay off the entire balance each month. In this wizard, Money makes a distinction between a credit card and a charge card, in which you pay off the whole balance monthly with no interest rate accrued. Choose which type is yours.

   - The interest rate. If a lower, introductory rate is effective, type that figure in. Then specify how long the lower rate lasts and what it will increase to (see Figure 9.3).

   - The total credit limit. This can be changed easily at any time.

5. Money 99 asks to keep track of each credit card charge rather than just monthly balances. You can choose which option is best for you.

6. You are then asked to put monthly payments for this card on your Bill Calendar and to specify how much you expect to pay each month, when the next bill is due, and which account you want to pay this account *from* (see Figure 9.4).

FIGURE 9.3.

Let the Account Wizard know if your credit card has an introductory rate.

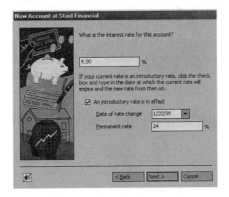

FIGURE 9.4.

The Credit Card Account Wizard offers to automate payments and asks which account you'll be paying the bill from.

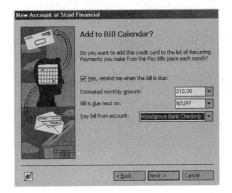

9

7. You are then prompted to set up this account's online options. You learned a little bit about walking through Money 99's Online Setup Wizard in Hour 4, "Setting Up Accounts." Online services are covered in detail in Hour 15, "Money Online." With an Internet connection, you can most likely walk through this setup process in less than 15 minutes. Move through the 5 steps of Money 99's Online Setup for this account, provide password information, and you are ready to go.

Most credit cards also have a Web page with special service offerings for their online customers. After setting up your account, click Contact Information at the left side of the screen. A Web page address for your credit card appears. Click Go To, and investigate what is being offered.

Entering Credit Card Transactions

Try to enter credit card transactions on the same day you incur them. It's easy to forget each time you use your card, and missing transactions can make it hard to balance your account later. So, with your purchase receipts in hand, start Money 99, and do the following:

To Do: Tracking Individual Credit Card Transactions

1. Open your credit card account to the Register View.

2. Click New at the bottom left of the screen. Text boxes appear that should be familiar to you from working with your checking account (see Figure 9.5).

FIGURE 9.5.

Use the Credit Card Register to track individual credit card purchases.

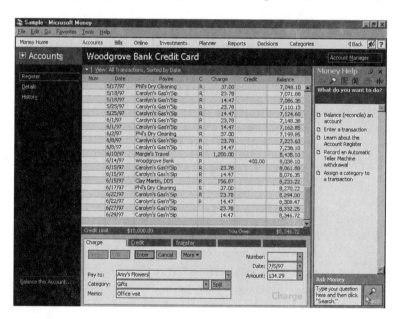

3. In the Pay To text box, type in the name of a retailer, business, or institution you used a credit card to pay. Remember that after typing the name once, it will be in your payee list and automatically appear the next time you begin to type that payee's name.

4. Assign a category to this transaction and a dollar amount.

5. Type in a transaction number. This will be on the credit card receipt you received with your purchase, usually at the bottom near the credit card account number.

6. Make sure the date is accurate. If you are entering receipts from purchases earlier in the month, you'll have to type in a new date in the Date text box, because Money 99 automatically assumes each transaction occurred on the current date.

▼

▲

7. Click Enter. The transaction appears in the Account Register in date order. Notice the account balance rises with each credit card purchase. Although the account balance does not appear as a negative number, remember that this sum is the amount you owe your credit card company, not your remaining available credit.

How to Itemize Credit Card Purchases

Because Money 99 uses detailed category information to project accurate financial forecasts, it's probably a good idea to itemize each purchase in your Money 99 credit card account. That way you can assign each item to its own category. This is better record keeping than simply typing in the full amount for a day's worth of Visa spending. There are two ways to show a breakdown of your credit card purchases:

- Type in a separate transaction for each item purchased. If you happen to have a detailed receipt that shows the cost of each item, then this method works well. Figure 9.6 shows a single $59.34 credit card purchase. It was part of a larger transaction. In Figure 9.7, you'll see all items purchased are broken down according to price and category. The same Transaction Number is applied to the all purchases because all the items were purchased at once on the credit card.

FIGURE 9.6.

This $59.34 credit card purchase, from "Le Great Big Warehouse Store" shows a single transaction, but it was really part of an "spree" of purchases at that same store.

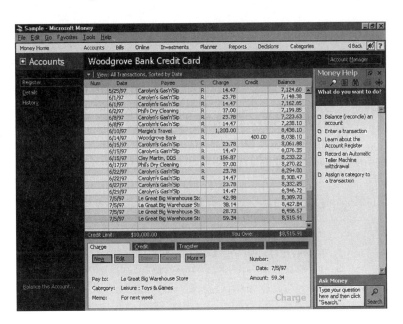

- Enter a single transaction, but split it according to categories. This is good to do if the receipt you were supplied with only shows a grand total. Figure 9.7 shows several credit card transactions with a single total ($211.98), broken into categories

for each item. If you can estimate a cost for each item, that's still a good idea, even
if you are not sure of the exact amount.

FIGURE 9.7.

*A credit card multiple
purchase is broken
down into categories,
but with a single total
price.*

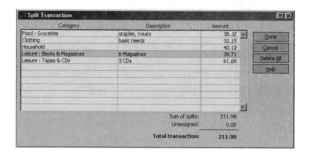

Itemizing credit card purchases makes it easy to obtain accurate refunds
later, should you need to return only a portion of the merchandise or
service.

You cannot tell by looking at the transaction in the normal Register View
that this transaction is split among several categories. To see such transaction details in the Register, change the view to All Transaction Details by
clicking the <u>V</u>iew drop-down list.

Transferring Credit Card Funds to Another Account

Sometimes people use lower interest credit cards to pay off the balance on higher
accounts. To transfer funds from one credit card account to another account of any kind,
do the following:

To Do: Paying Off A High-Interest Account

1. Open the credit card account you want to transfer *from.*

2. Click the Transfer tab at the bottom of the screen. Text boxes appear for specifying the
   target account and dollar amount of the transfer. The From text box is already filled.

3. Type in a dollar amount for your transfer, and a *target account* in the To text box.

4. Type in a specific payee if needed. Most often this is not required for a straight
   fund transfer.

5. Include the date you expect the transfer to be effective, which may not be the current date.

6. Click Enter to finalize the transaction.

▼ Remember that these steps only record this transfer in Money 99. Unless you conducted this online between two accounts at the same institution, the results are far from instantaneous. You will probably still have phone calls to make and forms to fill out and mail in
▲ before the transfer is effective.

Recording a Credit or Refund

You may have to credit your credit card account in the following instances:

- A vendor overcharged you.
- A purchase was returned to the retailer.
- Your credit card issues a credit because you crossed a certain spending threshold. (That means they like you. Spend more.)
- Some vendors or service agencies take back a charge if services are not delivered in a timely manner, such as parcel delivery or repair services.

These refunds or credits can be carried out fairly instantaneously by the agency or retailer, but your account may not show the refund immediately. But how should you record such credits in Money 99?

Refund Considerations

Here are some issues to consider when adding a refund or credit to you credit card account:

- Don't delete the transaction that is being refunded, because you may need a record of it, should there be a problem with the retailer and their agreement to refund the amount. Also, deleting the transaction instantly removes the refunded amount from your credit card account balance. In reality, it may take several days or more for your account to be refunded.

- If an item or service you purchased was refunded in full, you can void the transaction in your credit card account. Doing so removes the sum from your account balance but does not erase the transaction. Having this record on hand is helpful, should you need to pursue the matter further at a later date. (The following To Do section shows you how to void a transaction.)

- If you returned only a portion of a credit card purchase to a retailer or it was determined that you have some sort of discount coming to you that was not applied, then you need to set up a partial refund in Money 99. (The To Do section titled "Crediting a Partial Refund or Return" shows you how to set up a partial refund.)

- If a Credit card company issues you a credit bonus for reaching over a certain spending threshold or for patronizing a favored vendor of theirs, then you may

9

credit your Money 99 credit card account for that amount. This method is also good for recording partial refunds or cash bonuses. To issue a credit to your credit card account, follow the steps in the "To Do: Issuing a Simple Credit to Your Credit Card Account," section later in this chapter.

To Do: Voiding a Credit Card Transaction

1. Right-click the transaction you want to void in the Account Register.

2. Choose Mark As, Void (see Figure 9.8).

3. The word VOID appears in the column where the transaction sum normally appears.

FIGURE 9.8.

Voiding a credit card transaction provides better record keeping than deleting it.

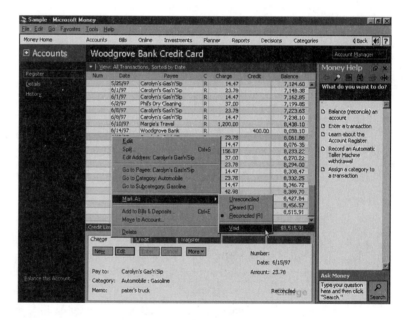

Consider using this method if you've taken something back to the store for a refund or if the entire sum was refunded to you because of poor service.

To Do: Crediting a Partial Refund or Return

1. Click the Credit tab of the credit card account, and select the retailer and original category you chose for this purchase from the drop-down lists.

2. Type in the portion of the original amount you want to assign as credit.

3. Click Enter to finalize the transaction. Figure 9.9 shows an original purchase, with a payee, category, and purchase amount chosen. Figure 9.10 shows a partial refund that applies to that same category and vendor.

FIGURE 9.9.

A credit card purchase.

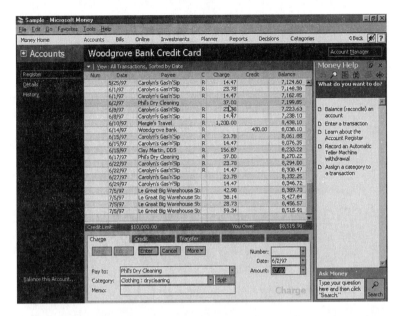

FIGURE 9.10.

This credit card purchase has a partial refund as shown in the Credit column.

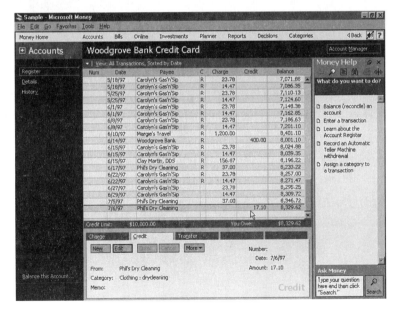

To Do: Issuing a Simple Credit to Your Credit Card Account

1. Open your credit card account and choose the Credit tab.

2. Type in the credit amount and the vendor or agency that is giving you the refund.

3. If this credit is related to a prior purchase, then choose the same category as your original purchase. If not, read the following "Assigning the Right Category to a Credit" section for help.

4. Make sure to include a memo indicating the reason for the credit.

Assigning the Right Category to a Credit

But what category do you assign the credit to? If the credit extended to you is not an increase in your credit limit but a reduction of the balance you owe, then this credit truly is a source of income, not an invitation to go further into debt. Use this categorization if your credit card lender gives you a cash bonus. So when you apply the credit, do the following:

To Do: Categorizing a Credit to Your Credit Card Account

1. Open the account that is granting you the credit, and click the Credit tab.

2. In the From text box, select that same company from the list.

3. Type in the amount and create a new category called Miscellaneous Income. You shouldn't use an income category like Gifts Received, because there can be negative tax consequences if you receive too many cash gifts in a given year (see Figure 9.11).

4. In the Memo text box, type in the circumstances of this credit.

5. Click Enter to apply the transaction.

FIGURE 9.11.

Creating a special category for receiving a credit from a credit card.

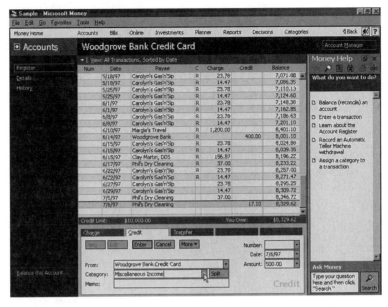

Changing Credit Card Options

Using your credit card account's Details screen, you can change the credit limit, interest rate, estimated monthly payment, and many other specifications.

To Do: Viewing Credit Card Account Details

1. Click Account Manager, and then double-click your credit card account.

2. Choose Details, at the far left of the screen.

   A window showing your account's opening balance, account number and lending bank appears (see Figure 9.12).

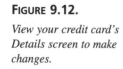

FIGURE 9.12.

View your credit card's Details screen to make changes.

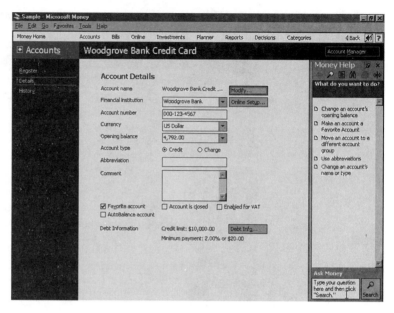

Some of the options you might want to change include the following:

- **Opening Balance**—Changing the opening balance can be helpful if you began making transactions in Money 99's record of this account without really knowing your opening balance. After you get a statement confirming the true opening balance, come to this screen to change it.

- **Account Type**—You may need to change this from credit card to charge card. Charge Cards are usually paid in full every month and do not accrue interest.

- **Abbreviation**—Supply an abbreviation for this account name. (Type the abbreviation in any text box in Money 99, and the full account name appears.)

- **Comment**—Add comments about this account, perhaps the purpose for this card in general.

- **Favorite Account**—A Favorite account appears on the Favorites menu on the menu bar at the top of the screen. Favorite accounts are also at the top of the order in the Accounts drop-down list at the left of the screen.

- **Account Is Closed**— If this is one of those 24% interest monsters, then paying off and closing this account is truly a cause for celebration.

- **AutoBalance Account**—If you don't want to keep track of all credit card transactions, then click the check box **AutoBalance**. You'll learn how to use AutoBalance momentarily, but in a nutshell, when you initiate paying your credit card bill,

Money asks you the amount you owe for that month, interest charges, service charges, and interest rate. After answering these questions, you are done for the month.

- **Modify**—Click the Modify button to change the account name or to turn this credit card account into something entirely different, such as a liability or cash account.

- **Online Setup**—Click this button to return to the five Online Setup steps. This can be helpful if you just received password information from your bank and you can finally get going online.

- **Debt Info**—Click this button to change the credit limit, how much you intend to pay each month, or interest rate (see Figure 9.13).

9

FIGURE 9.13.

Click Debt Info to alter interest rate, credit limit, or payment amounts.

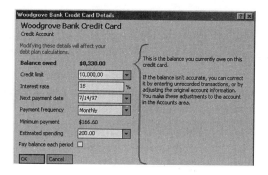

Debt Info lets you instruct Money 99 to pay your account's entire balance each period.

Paying a Monthly Credit Card Bill

You can pay a monthly credit card bill in two ways: the easy, fast way and the long, methodical, thorough way. If you purchased Money 99 in an attempt to wean yourself off the plastic, I recommend the long method for its sheer tedium, an aversion therapy that makes using a credit card not quite so painless.

The short way involves a process called AutoBalance, in which you open your checking account, click the Transfer tab, and fill out a transaction to your credit card account. Money 99 automatically opens a dialog box prompting you for service charge and statement date information. That's all, the thing is done.

The longer method involves opening your Money 99 checkbook with your credit card statement in hand, writing a check to your credit card account, and splitting the transactions amongst that month's payees. This method allows Money's forecasting and budgeting tools to nail your spending habits with frightening accuracy.

Let's look at Using AutoBalance first.

To Do: Paying a Credit Card Bill with AutoBalance

Paying with AutoBalance only requires that you have on hand your statement date, your total balance as of the statement date, and the service/interest charges for that month.

1. Open the account you are going to be paying your credit card with in the Register View.

2. Click the Transfer tab at the bottom of the Register.

3. In the To text box, click to select the lending institution that issued your credit card. The From text box already shows the account you are transferring from.

4. Type in the amount of your payment in the Amount text box.

5. The date text box shows the current date. Type in the date you intend to print and mail the check or transfer the funds online. If you set up the transaction to occur on a later date, money issues reminders for those tasks.

6. Click Enter, and the AutoBalance dialog box appears (see Figure 9.14). Type in the requested information, remembering the relationship between the account balance and the statement date: The balance is only going to reflect charges that vendors have processed before that statement date. In this dialog box, the **Total Amount You Owe this Month** text box refers to the account balance.

FIGURE 9.14.

To see this AutoBalance dialog box, the transaction had to have been started as a transfer.

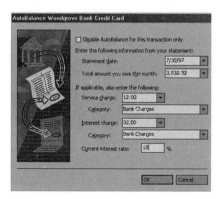

▼

Please note that the Total Amount You Owe this Month is not the same as your minimum payment. You enter your payment for the month when you actually fill out your Money 99 check.

7. If there is a discrepancy between your statement and Money 99's records of this account, then Money automatically creates an adjustment transaction to make up the difference. This is most often not advisable, because such a discrepancy may only mean that a vendor has not sent in the transaction to your bank yet. So you should probably check Disable AutoBalance for this Transaction Only.

8. After verifying the interest rate, amount of this payment, and various service charges by looking at your statement, click OK.

9. In your checking Account Register, you'll see the payment debited from your account. Open your credit card account, and you'll see a payment has been made. If you allowed Money to do an AutoBalance, then you'll see a new transaction that makes up the difference between your Money 99 account record and your bank statement (see Figure 9.15).

9

FIGURE 9.15.

The AutoBalance feature creates an Adjustment Amount transaction in your credit card account.

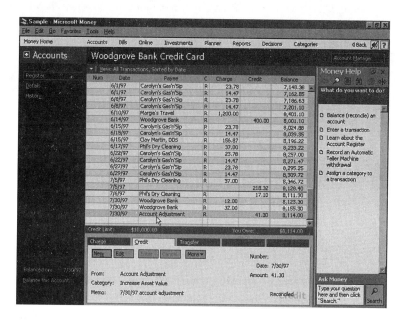

You should only use this AutoBalance feature if you are sure that no amount of going back and checking your math or waiting for tardy vendors to process your purchase can ever rectify this account.

Why Not Disable AutoBalance Permanently?

You *could* disable the AutoBalance feature permanently and not deal with the unneeded adjustment transaction. But if you do, then you won't see this nifty dialog box for reminding you about interest and service charges. To disable AutoBalance permanently, open your credit card account and click Details. Remove the check by AutoBalance Account.

Itemizing Purchase Categories with Your Payment

As mentioned previously, when you pay your credit card bill using a split transaction, you can account for each credit card expense for that month, which provides Money 99 with more fodder for financial reports. You need your credit card statement handy, and be prepared to look over the transactions it contains with at least a glimmer of recognition.

To Do: Paying Your Credit Card Bill with a Split Transaction

In this procedure, you'll be working heavily with the Split Transaction dialog box. The Split Transaction dialog box can hold many transactions, not just two or three, as it is commonly used for.

1. With your credit card statement in hand, open your Money 99 checkbook account to the Register View.

2. Click the Check tab at the lower part of the screen, and click New. Text boxes appear that require your input.

3. In the Payee text box, scroll down and choose your credit card account institution.

4. Type in a total payment Amount, including service and interest charges, which can be gleaned from your statement.

5. Click the Split button, and the Split Transaction dialog box appears (see Figure 9.16).

6. Type in a credit card transaction for each line. Each transaction requires a payment amount and category. If you don't remember exactly how much something costs, come back to that purchase later, before you close this Split Transaction.

7. Enter each purchase for that month, as shown in Figure 9.17.

FIGURE 9.16.

Use the Split Transaction dialog box to assign credit card bill payments to several categories.

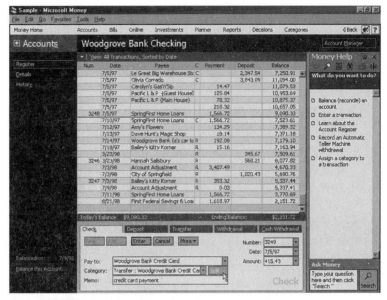

FIGURE 9.17.

Enter each purchase for that month in the Split Transaction dialog box.

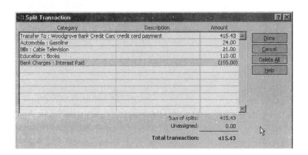

8. If, after entering all the transactions from that month, the sum does not match how much Money 99 says you spent that month with your credit card, click OK. You are shown a few options: You can let Money spread the difference among all the transactions, ignore the discrepancy, or reduce the lower amount to match the higher one. You can also put off thinking about the problem until more purchases come from your account.

9. Probably the best choice is to not allow Money to balance your split transaction right now and perhaps return here with an adjustment later. Click OK to close the Split Transaction dialog box and return to the main checkbook Register.

10. After reviewing the payment again quickly, click OK to finalize the transaction. The payment appears in your credit card account. Your transaction won't appear

▼

▲

different because it is split. You'll see the word Split in the Category text box, but you must edit the transaction and click the Split button to see the breakdown. Or, wait for the Monthly Report to see what kind of light Money 99 shed on your month of credit card activity.

Balancing Your Credit Card Account

When you balance a credit card account in Money 99, you are prompted to type in the current statement date (work from the statement you received in the mail, unless this is an online account) and the current balance of your credit card. Money then assembles a list of all transactions between those dates. Your job is to reconcile each transaction found on your credit card's paper statement that is mailed to you with your Money 99 record of this account. (Balancing an Online Account is covered in Hour 15, "Money Online.")

Two charges will appear on your statement that you did not incur: The bank's service charge and interest charge. Money prompts you to include those in the balancing act, so keep your statement handy and type those in when asked.

Finally, just like balancing your checking account, if all transactions are accounted for, then this task is done. If something doesn't quite count out, you can either postpone balancing, or let Money 99 create an adjustment transactions. Invariably, if your credit card account does not balance, it's best to wait for a vendor to process his charge, and choose Postpone.

If you allow Money 99 to create an Account Adjustment, it will be clearly labeled as such. If it turns out later that you discover the real reason for the discrepancy, delete the Account Adjustment and type in the transaction that makes up the difference.

Remember, when balancing, Money 99 asks for the Total Amount You Owe this Month. This is not the minimum payment due, but the total balance of your account.

To Do: Balancing Your Credit Card Account

1. Wait for your statement to arrive in the mail, or retrieve it online.

2. In Money 99, open the credit card account you want to balance.

3. You will be concerned with the month that falls right in between your *prior* and *current* statement dates. That means transactions that occurred in the last few days may not be relevant here, because there is some lag time between when you buy something, and when that transaction appears on your statement.

4. Take a minute to look over old receipts and see whether there are some credit card transactions you can add to that statement period. In Money 99, it's perfectly OK to enter a transaction and type in an earlier date. Doing so now will make your balancing act less eventful.

5. Click the Balance this Account option at the bottom left of the credit card account screen. The AutoBalance dialog box appears (see Figure 9.18).

FIGURE 9.18.

Use these text boxes to balance your credit card account.

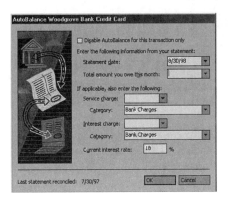

6. Type in the Statement Date and the Total Amount You Owe this Month, and make sure the figure in Total Amount You Owe this Month looks correct.

7. Type in a service charge and interest charge where indicated. Some new credit card accounts may waive interest for the first few months, so this charge may not appear. Note that Money provides categories for these extra charges. This is important, so you can learn later in the year how much you spent on interest and various credit card charges, besides on the purchases themselves.

8. Click Next, and you return to the credit card Account Register. Just as with a checking account, on the left you'll see the Balance Account Worksheet (see Figure 9.19).

FIGURE 9.19.

The left side of the account screen tallies your cleared transactions and keeps track of the total amount as you click the "C" column of each.

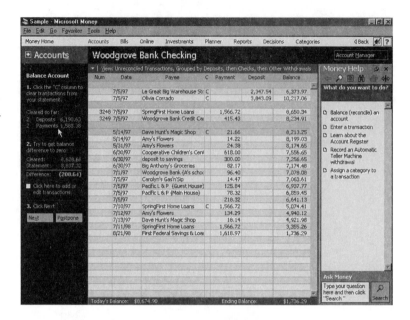

9. Moving back and forth between your paper statement and your Money 99 account, click the "C" column for every transaction that appears in both places (see Figure 9.20). Money 99 is now reconciling transactions that have showed up in both records.

FIGURE 9.20.

Click the "C" column for every cleared transaction.

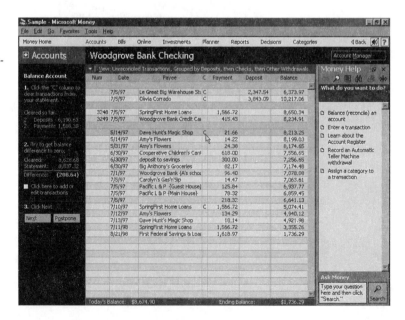

▼ 10. When you are finished matching transactions, note any that appear in your Money 99 account but not on your paper statement. These transactions have probably not yet been sent to the bank by the vendor you made the purchase from.

11. Note transactions that appear in your paper statement but not in Money 99. These are probably purchases that you forgot to record in Money. Wrack your brain and see whether you can recall these purchases. See whether you have misplaced a receipt for them as well.

- If you suddenly remember the purchase, it's not too late to record it in Money to help balance your account. To add the purchase you recalled, click the **Click Here to Add or Edit Transactions** check box.

- If you are relatively sure that this purchase is not yours, then call your credit card company to report a charge made in error.

12. Click Next, and Money tells you that the account is not yet balanced. That's because it requires you to OK the reconciliation resulting from the bank charges before continuing. You are told to either go back and find the missing transactions, use AutoReconcile, or accept the account adjustment proposed by Money (see Figure 9.21). Now even if your account matched perfectly with the statement, you are still going to have to allow Money 99 to do an account adjustment, because of the bank charges. So click the third option: Automatically Adjust the Account Balance. Your account will now be balanced.

FIGURE 9.21.

Even if you've balanced your account, Money still creates an account adjustment to accommodate the service and bank charges.

13. If you have transactions that are unaccounted for, click Go Back to Balancing the Account, and then click the Postpone button, at the lower left of the screen. When you've found the accounting error or the transactions in question finally appear, click Balance this Account again, just as you did at the beginning. You are returned to this same screen, where you can enter the wayward transaction yourself or let Money 99 enter an Account Adjustment transaction. Either way, your account will ▲ finally balance.

Credit Cards and Your Future

Although budgeting and setting financial goals are covered in Hours 13, "Creating a Budget" and 14, "Long-Term Planning and Goals" there are a few factors you should understand now, while setting up a credit card, just so you can see how even occasional use of credit cards can have an effect on good budgeting and goal management. Even before knowing the ins and outs of Money's budgeting tools, it's helpful to develop an idea of how much you'll be using each credit card each month.

To do budgeting and goal planning, Money 99 requires you provide a realistic, if approximate, figure for monthly credit card usage. This is something you can begin to think about now, even before you approach this book's later hours.

To Do: Including a Credit Card in Your Debt Reduction Plan

In a brief preview, the most important debt reduction procedures are the following:

1. Click Planner on the Navigation Bar, then click Debt Reduction Planner (see Figure 9.22). A list of all your debts appears.

FIGURE 9.22.

The Debt Reduction planner includes any debts you specify in its plan.

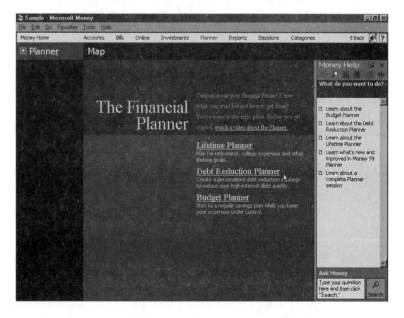

2. The screen that appears is the Include Debt Accounts in Your Page screen. It's divided into debts that are in your plan and those that are not. However, if you've just added a credit card account, you'll find that it isn't in your debt plan yet.

▼   3. Click the credit card in the Debt Accounts Not in Debt Plan list *once* to select it.

4. Then click the Move into Plan button at the bottom of the screen. This instructs Money 99 to include this credit card account when computing how long before all your debts are paid off and how much you'll have to pay.

5. Click Next, at the upper-right of the screen, and you'll see the Define Your Payment Plan screen. This is one of Money's most helpful tools (see Figure 9.23).

FIGURE 9.23.

The Define Your Payment Plan screen gives you information on how much to pay to get out of debt on a certain date.

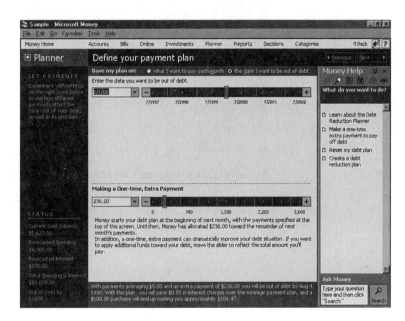

9

Long-term debt like mortgages and college loans are often not included in your Debt Plan.

6. You'll see two sliders with text on the bottom of the screen and on the bottom left, as well. These two text areas contain debt calculations, and they change based on what you do with the sliders:

• The top slider lets you select the date you'd like to be out of debt. (Remember, only credit cards and debts that you included in the plan are included in these calculations.)

• Notice that the calculations on the bottom of the screen and lower left change when you move the slider (see Figure 9.24). These calculations tell you how much you have to pay monthly to be debt free by the date you

▼   choose.

FIGURE 9.24.

Moving the sliders changes the calculations that predict the day you will be debt free.

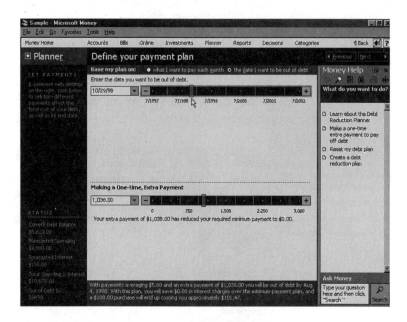

- The bottom slider lets you select an amount for a one-time-only extra payment to get you off to a good debt-reduction start. You'll be amazed at how much difference a one-time only extra payment can make in your debt-reduction plans.

The bottom-left portion of the screen shows your debt status, how much is owed and how deeply your total income is affected by debt. The center bottom shows how much you'll be paying per month to meet your debt-free goal. You'll also learn how much money you'll be saving by debt reduction.

Debt reduction and budgeting are covered thoroughly in Hours 13 and 14.

Summary

Money 99 provides lots of tools for monitoring your credit card expenses. You can change interest rates, credit limits, and any number of credit card account details with a few mouse clicks. Money tracks your credit card account payments easily, and provides tools for keeping your account in balance. In Hour 10, "Tracking Mortgages, Loans and Assets," you'll learn about loans and mortgages, and keeping track of valuable assets.

Q&A

Q What is the main difference between a credit card balance and checking or savings account balances?

A Each purchase you make is recorded in Money 99 as an increase in the amount of money you owe. When your credit card balances rises, you owe more money.

Q How do I pay a credit card's monthly bill?

A As a transfer from your checking account. Money 99 automatically opens a special balancing tool for your credit card account when it sees you making a credit card payment in this way.

Q Why should I go to the trouble of itemizing purchases when I make a credit card payment?

A Because doing so allows Money 99 to accurately understand what you spend your money on, rather than just "credit card."

Q I need to take something back to the store that I bought with a credit card. Can Money 99 handle this type of transaction?

A Yes. Credit card accounts in Money 99 can provide for several recrediting scenarios, such as when you need a partial refund, or when a credit card issues you a cash bonus or gift.

9

HOUR 10

Tracking Mortgages, Loans, and Assets

Money 99 has several tools for managing large sums that you borrow or loan and the assets associated with them. These range from calculators that help you determine how much house or loan you can afford to tools that project what payments will be five or ten years from now. Money 99 also has a Loan Worksheet that does the comparison work when it's time to refinance.

Most loans are associated with assets, so Money 99 provides asset accounts for managing the value of those assets, as well as inventory worksheets for listing the individual items that make up an asset, such as jewelry, expensive furniture, and collectibles. Money also has a New Loan Wizard that sets up your home loan. The New Loan Wizard includes variables for points and insurance, interest rate calculations, and payment scheduling options.

Finally, Money 99's Lifetime Goal Planner helps you set aside finances for long-term goals such as purchasing a home, a second home, or perhaps a small business. The Goal Planner is covered thoroughly in Hour 14, "Long-Term Planning and Goals," but it is briefly discussed in terms of how it helps in managing long-term loans and assets.

Tools for Getting Started

Not all loans are created equal. Even before you take your own financial pulse to determine what you can afford to borrow, first find out what's available to you, and then see the helpful tools Money has provided to figure your own place in these things. First tour Money 99's Decisions pages. The best place to start is to click Decisions on the Navigation Bar, and choose Tools (see Figure 10.1).

FIGURE 10.1.

The tools on the Decisions pages are an invaluable source of clever budget-saving gadgets.

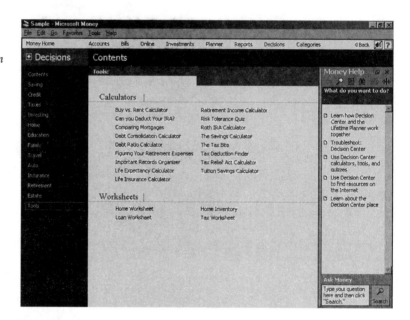

The following are a few of the useful tools you'll find on this page:

- **Buy vs. Rent Calculator**—Use this tool to determine the wisdom of buying a home at this time.

- **Debt Ratio Calculator**—Use this tool to see if you are financially overextended. If action needs to be taken, select Planner on the Navigation Bar, and click Debt Reduction Plan.

- **Compare Mortgages**—Don't forget to come back here later in the process: After you have a few loan quotes, click the Compare Mortgages tool to see what type of loan is best for you.

Now to see what's out there, use Money 99's Marketplace to learn about loan options. For home purchases, auto purchases, and financial information do the following:

- **Home purchase**—With your Internet connection open, choose <u>T</u>ools, Money 99 Marketplace, and then select Home (see Figure 10.2). The Home Advisor directs you towards resources for reading all about various loan options. Also, click Decisions on the Navigation Bar and read some of the articles about home purchasing or taking out big loans.

FIGURE 10.2.

The Home Advisor page keeps you in touch with the latest home-buying news.

10

- **Auto purchase**—Choose <u>T</u>ools, Money 99 Marketplace, and then choose Auto. You are linked to Microsoft Car Point, which tells you everything you need to know before you buy that expensive car.
- **Financial information**—Take the time to read Advisor FYI's Home and Mortgage articles that appear frequently on your Money Home page. Also on the Home Page, Money 99 automatically notifies you if important articles of interest to home buyers appear on the Web.

When to Use the New Loan Wizard

The New Loan Wizard (explored later in this hour) is Money's tool for setting up the details of a loan and scheduling regular payments on your behalf. When you are planning to borrow or loan money, you have some decisions to make. Will this loan be amortized (interest-bearing)? Will there be a balloon payment at the end of the loan? These issues are just as important when you are lending money as they are when you are borrowing it.

Not every instance of borrowing or lending money requires that you use the New Loan Wizard. The previous hour explained liability accounts—when money is borrowed with no interest and the entire loan is due on a certain date. Liability accounts apply to loans for major purchases that do not incur interest every month, or money loaned to or (borrowed from) a friend or relative.

As far as the New Loan Wizard is concerned, the distinction between loans is summed up as this: If a loan accrues interest, use the Loan Wizard to set it up; if the loan does not accrue interest, create a liability account in the Account Manager.

Determining How Much You Can Borrow

Before taking out a loan, either to buy a house or another significant purchase, it's important to know the safe amount to borrow. Money's Home Worksheet looks at your income, debt amount, and loan "extras" to see how much you should borrow at this time. It allows you to play around with a number of options: choosing a smaller down payment for a higher loan amount, choosing less house and a smaller payment, and setting up scenarios for various interest rates. You can also project a higher income than you currently have to see how much you will have to earn to afford that dream house.

> Even though this feature is called the Loan Worksheet, it's a helpful tool in determining the advisability of any major purchase that puts you into debt.

To Do: Learning How Much You Should Borrow

Before opening the Home Worksheet, you should know these things:

- Monthly income.
- A guess at how much monthly payment you think you can handle.
- An idea of how much of a down payment you can swing.
- The current interest rate for the type of loan you are thinking of.
- If you've already been talking to real estate brokers, ask them to suggest a "closing cost factor" because Money 99 does ask for this information. You can leave it blank, if necessary.

1. To open the Home Worksheet, click Decisions on the Navigation Bar, and choose Tools at the lower-left of the screen. In the tools area select Home Worksheet under the Worksheets heading.

▼ 2. The Decisions: Home Ownership screen appears (see Figure 10.3). The Welcome
tab appears with three additional tabs. Read the Welcome screen if you want, and
click the Information tab. The How Much Can I Afford? calculator appears (see
Figure 10.4).

FIGURE 10.3.

*Click Home Worksheet
from the Decisions
page to learn more
about picking the right
mortgage for your
income.*

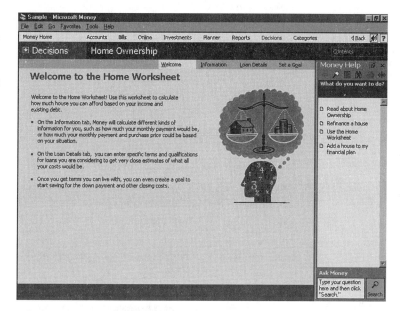

10

FIGURE 10.4.

*Use the How Much
Can I Afford? calcula-
tor to try out various
loan possibilities.*

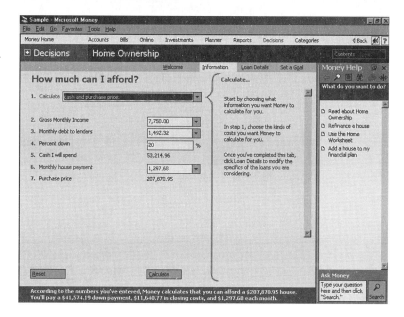

▼

▼ 3. Look at the Calculate drop-down list. This list lets you choose which factors you
want the Home Worksheet to calculate for you. Click the drop-down arrow to see
your choices. You can get Money to look up a number of figures for you, depending on what you already know about your options. Here are some examples:

- If your real estate agent has suggested a particular down payment, and if you
  also have an idea of how much you want to pay monthly, then the Home
  Worksheet will suggest a total house price. To choose this option, select Cash
  and Purchase Price in the Calculate drop-down list.

- If you've got your eyes set on this particular house and you know how much
  per month you think you can handle, then Home Worksheet will calculate
  how much of a down payment you are probably looking at. To get Home
  Worksheet to calculate these numbers for you, click Cash in the Calculate
  list.

- If you are just getting started and don't have many clear ideas about what
  you can do yet, click inside the Percent Down text box, and then click the
  Use Money's default 20% dropdown menu (see Figure 10.5—it's number
  four in the list). Then in the Calculate drop-down list, select the Cash,
  Monthly Payment, and Purchase Price option. The Home Worksheet then calculates an ideal purchase price, monthly payment, and how much money
  you'll have to have up front.

FIGURE 10.5.

*If you know some fig-
ures about the loan
you want, type those
in. Let Money calcu-
late the figures you
don't know.*

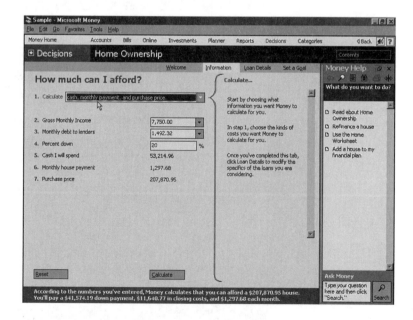

▼

▼ 4. To really begin playing with the How Much Can I Afford? calculator, you may have to provide your own Gross Monthly Income and Monthly Debt to Lenders amounts (see Figure 10.6). Money 99 is supposed to draw these numbers from the Personal Information you provided Money with when you first set up the program. But I've found it sometimes puts in wrong amounts or leaves them out all together. Just type in monthly income figures and an estimate of how much you owe each month into the appropriate text boxes, as shown.

FIGURE 10.6.

Sometimes you have to provide basic data about your income so that the calculator can work correctly.

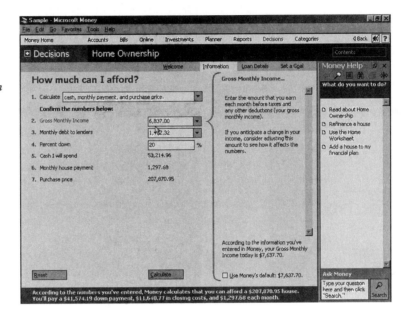

In Hour 13, "Creating a Budget and Savings Goal," you set up a budget based on your income and debt amount. After these are created, Money 99 should instantly determine your income and debt level from those budget figures. Still, when determining how much house you can afford, it's nice to be able to play around with your income and debt numbers to see what the possibilities are if you just changed things a little.

As soon as you select an option in the Calculate drop-down list, some text boxes no longer allow you to put in numbers, while other text boxes that were off-limits suddenly allow your input. That's because Home Worksheet lets you choose which figures it should calculate and which figures you want to provide yourself. Here are

▼ two examples:

▼

- If you know the cost of the house you want, then tell Money to calculate Cash and Monthly Payment (not the house cost, because *you* are providing that).

- If you know your monthly payment limitations, then, in the Calculate list, select Cash and Purchase Price (not monthly payment, because *you* are providing that number).

> If this is your first home and you are new at this game, ask the broker or agent to give you her take on points. *Points* are a percentage of the entire home cost that you pay up front as part of the closing costs (usually 2%). Points add significantly to closing costs but help reduce the loan amount. A real estate agent's knowledge of the market is valuable in determining points that should be paid.

The calculated numbers change as you put in your own data. You don't have to click the Calculate button. Money 99 knows that you've put in new numbers for calculating as soon as you click outside the text box you added numbers to.

At the bottom of the screen, Money explains the significance of these numbers, describing what your options suggest (see Figure 10.7). If you try to suggest a loan amount that is way out of line for your income, Money 99 warns you against this selection.

FIGURE 10.7.

While typing in ideal loan payments or percent down figures, read at the bottom of the screen what Money says about your loan.

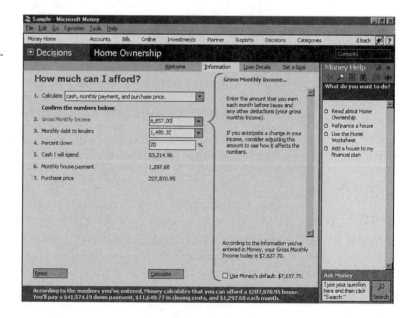

▼

▼   5. To add or alter loan detail information (such as length of the loan, closing costs, points and interest rate options), click the Loan Details tab. The Confirm the Details of the Loan screen appears (see Figure 10.8). Besides adjusting loan specifics, you can also type in a different Debt Ratio or Income Ratio than the one Money uses by default. Choosing new numbers here affects what Home Worksheet determines you can afford at your current income.

FIGURE 10.8.

The Confirm the Details of the Loan screen lets you specify loan figures like points and closing costs.

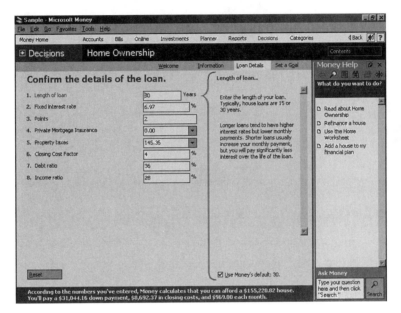

Again, notice at the bottom of the Loan Details screen, that Home Worksheet explains the significance of your choices (see Figure 10.9).

6. To incorporate your new loan plan into the overall goals that Money 99 sets up for you in Goal Planner, click the Set a Goal tab at the upper right. When the Review and Make Changes screen appears, click Set a Goal Now at the bottom left. The

▲   Lifetime Planner opens, which is covered in Hour 14.

FIGURE 10.9.

Whenever you type in new numbers, Money calculates what your choices mean. Read the update at the bottom of the screen.

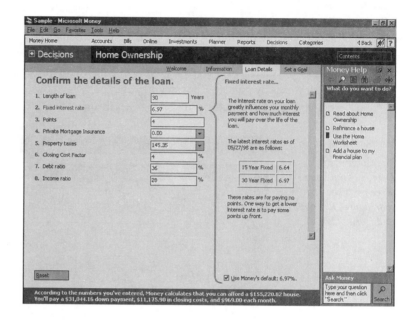

Setting Up a Mortgage Account

Now that you've seen how the Home Worksheet helps determine a good loan, you can set up a mortgage (or interest-bearing) loan in Money 99.

To Do: Creating a Mortgage or Long-Term Loan Account

Although it's easy to change your loan details at any time for various reasons—altering interest rates, balloon payments, and so on—you don't need to set up your mortgage or long-term loan information until after you've received final figures from the bank.

1. In Account Manager, right-click any white space and select New Account. The New Account Wizard appears.

2. If this is the first account you have with the bank you are borrowing from, then type in the name of your lending institution.

3. Click Next to walk through the New Account Wizard, and select Mortgage or Loan when prompted for the type of account you are setting up. The Account Wizard becomes the Loan Wizard after you choose Loan or Mortgage as your account type (see Figure 10.10).

4. Specify whether you are borrowing or lending money. Use this Account Wizard for loaning *only* if you are lending money with interest.

FIGURE 10.10.

The New Loan Wizard helps set up all the parameters of an interest-bearing loan.

5. In the What Would You Like to Name this Loan? screen, type in a name for the loan (this name only serves as identification for your purposes), and again type in the name of the bank you are borrowing from. It won't be listed in the drop-down list if this mortgage or loan is your first account with this bank.

6. You may be asked whether payments have been made previously on this loan. This is important if you are just now letting Money 99 know about a mortgage you've been carrying for awhile. Money offers to record the previous payments for you, or let you start from scratch now.

7. When prompted, specify whether your loan has an adjustable or fixed interest rate. If you choose adjustable rate, then you must provide the date of the next adjustment and period of time between future adjustments (see Figure 10.11).

FIGURE 10.11.

The New Loan Wizard sets up adjustable or fixed-rate interest schedules and amortizes your loan for you.

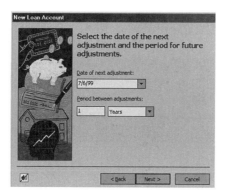

8. The wizard asks you when the next payment is due. If this is a new loan, then this will be the first payment due. (Down payments to obtain the loan are not counted as the first payment.) You are also asked how often payments are made.

▼ 9. Money then asks a tricky question, and you may have to check with your lender to verify the answer: Is calculated interest based on when the payment is due or on when the lender receives the payment (see Figure 10.12).

FIGURE 10.12.

Check with your lender for specifics about how interest is calculated.

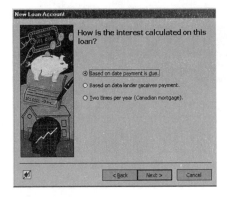

In a series of four screens, you are asked these questions:

- How much remains due on this loan?
- How much is the interest rate?
- Is there a balloon payment due?
- What is the monthly payment including principle and interest?

10. Money can calculate *one* of these equations—any one you choose. Just leave one of the amounts blank and the New Loan Wizard calculates it for you (see Figure 10.13). When you've clicked Next through the last of these four screens, you'll see all the pertinent loan information in one tidy screen (see Figure 10.14).

FIGURE 10.13.

To make the New Loan Wizard calculate a value for a loan, just leave it blank while filling in the other values.

▼

FIGURE 10.14.

The New Loan Wizard displays the final loan numbers.

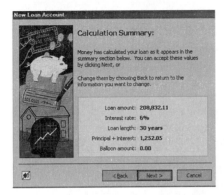

11. Still walking through the New Loan Wizard, Money prompts you to categorize your loan payments, suggesting in the case of a mortgage loan, the category Bills: Loan Interest.

12. You then get a chance to add other Loan Fees to your total loan amount, such as points and closing costs. You can categorize them as you choose. Most often, Bank Charges is an appropriate category.

13. At long last, the New Loan Wizard seeks to automate the payment. You are asked if Bill Reminder should include this bill in its reminders to you. Then confirm the Next Payment Date and specify which account you will most likely use to make this payment. A screen appears confirming all the information you've entered thus far and offering to create an associated asset account for this loan (see Figure 10.15). Associate asset accounts are covered later in this hour.

FIGURE 10.15.

After confirming basic loan information, closing costs, and next payment date, the New Loan Wizard asks to create an associated asset for this account.

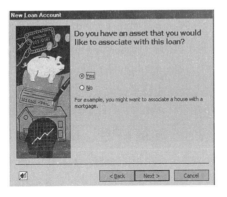

Please note that after you create a mortgage account and an associated asset account (which tracks the rising value of your house, not the loan), you'll have two new account icons in your Account Manager, one representing the loan for the house (mortgage account) and another representing the asset you are paying for (see Figure 10.16).

FIGURE 10.16.

After creating a new loan, you'll see icons in your account manager for the loan and the asset that it's paying for.

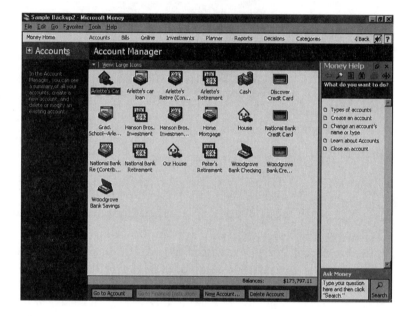

Making Payments on Your Mortgage

After you set up your mortgage loan, you'll rarely have to think about the process of making the actual payment. (Paying bills is covered in the next hour.) For now, it's good to know that when you set up a mortgage or loan payment schedule, Money 99 automatically reminds you of the bill date as it gets closer. Also, a small Bill Reminder icon is placed in your Windows Notification Area (see Figure 10.17). Click it to see upcoming bills.

To pay your mortgage or other loan set up with the New Loan Wizard, don't open the checking account set up to pay that loan. Instead, do the following:

To Do: Paying Your Mortgage or Loan

1. From Account Manager, open the Mortgage account in the Register View.
2. Click New, and a dialog box appears asking if you want to make a regular, or extra loan payment (see Figure 10.18).

FIGURE 10.17.

Look at the bottom right of your Windows screen for reminders of upcoming bills.

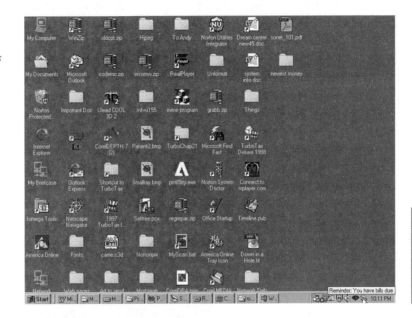

10

FIGURE 10.18.

Determine if you want to make a regular, or extra loan payment.

3. Click Make a Regular Loan Payment, and the Edit Transaction dialog box appears (see Figure 10.19).

FIGURE 10.19.

The Edit Transaction dialog box appears, even when you initiate a regular, monthly loan payment.

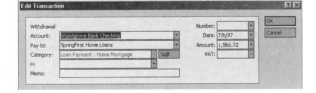

4. Choose an account to pay this loan from (you already have, but Money 99 wants you to confirm it here).

5. In the **Pay To** drop-down list, make sure your lending institution is named. Click OK, and the loan payment appears in the Mortgage Loan Register.

Here's what happens in Money 99 when your loan payment is made:

- The Register records a reduction in the loan principle, showing just how much the loan balance has been reduced.

- If you open the checking account where this payment originated from (remember, this payment occurred without even opening it), you'll find the loan payment transactions in the Register and your checking account balance reduced appropriately.

Automating Your Mortgage or Loan Payment

Rather than be reminded about this payment when it's due, Money 99 can conduct the transaction without your hearing another word about it.

To Do: Automating Your Loan Payment

This process works with any scheduled bill. Mortgages are automatically set up as recurring payments. To make it fully automated takes only one extra step.

1. Click Bills on the Navigator Bar. The Bills & Deposits screen appears.

2. On the far left, click Set Up Bills & Deposits. The Recurring Bills & Deposits screen appears (see Figure 10.20).

FIGURE 10.20.

Use the Recurring Bills & Deposits screen to automate bill payments, including mortgages and loans.

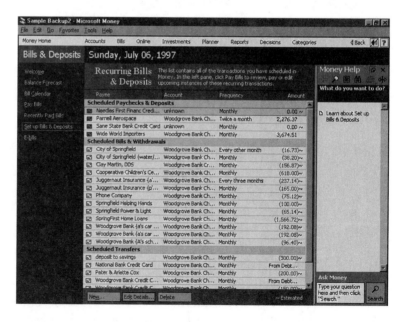

In Hour 11, you'll learn how to set up all your reoccurring bills so they can be paid out conveniently. For now, the only one you may see is the mortgage or loan you created earlier in this hour. You can edit it so Money 99 pays it automatically.

3. Your loan appears in the Scheduled Bills & Withdrawals list Double-click the loan, and the Edit Future Payments dialog box appears.

4. Click Scheduling Options at the lower left of the dialog box. A dialog box appears allowing you to change how often this bill is paid and alter the payment method.

5. Check Enter This into My Account Automatically, and then click OK. Then, click OK again to close the original dialog box behind it.

From now on, Money 99 will automatically pay your mortgage from the designated account on the day it's due. Of course, unless you've set up online payments, you'll still have to print out the check and mail it.

10

> Your home equity can be found at the bottom left of the Register View of the asset account you created at the same time as your loan. On the left is Total Equity, and on the right is Current Value.

Balancing Your Mortgage Account

What Money calls balancing your mortgage account is really just an account adjustment: a way to change the loan total in one step. This is useful if you suddenly discover that you've recorded the wrong loan amount total and you want to change the full amount you owe. What's a bit confusing is that Money suggests assigning this adjustment to a category called "Increase Asset Value." However, this adjustment increases or decreases the amount you owe to the bank, not the value of your home (the real asset).

So to state this properly, *to adjust the value of your loan*, do the following:

To Do: Adjusting the Dollar Value of Your Mortgage Loan

When you are performing this task, make sure you are working with your mortgage account and not the associated asset account, which is the house itself.

1. From the mortgage or loan account Register, click <u>B</u>alance this Account at the bottom left of the screen. The Adjust Loan Balances dialog box appears (see Figure 10.21).

FIGURE 10.21.

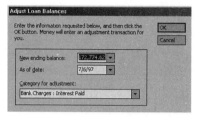

*To register a new value
for your loan, use the
Adjust Loan Balances
dialog box.*

2. You are prompted for a new loan balance, a date that the new balance becomes effective, and a category to assign the difference in value to. Take care in choosing an income or expense category for this adjustment.

> A decrease in the loan amount means you owe less money. Thus, such a transaction should be recorded in an *income category.* Understand, also, that a decrease in how much you owe is called a decrease in the asset value of that loan. To avoid confusion, remember that the asset value referred to here is the value of the loan, not of the house.

3. After filling out the dialog box, click Enter, and an adjustment transaction appears in your Mortgage account for the dollar amount you specified in the dialog box. The distribution of principle and interest from future loan payments will be affected by this Adjustment.

Making an Extra Mortgage Payment

Money 99 makes it almost enjoyable to pay an extra payment, because the Mortgage Account Register shows the principal of the loan being reduced by the entire sum of your extra payment, rather than the usual pittance.

To Do: Making an Extra Mortgage or Loan Payment

1. Open the mortgage account by selecting Accounts on the Navigation Bar and clicking your Mortgage Account Icon. Make sure you're in the Register View.

2. Click the New button at the bottom left of the screen.

3. A dialog box appears asking whether you want to make a regular loan payment or an extra one. Choose Make an Extra Loan Payment.

4. The Edit Transaction dialog box appears. You must fill in the Amount of the payment and the Account you're making the payment from. If you want something to appear in the Payee area of the Mortgage Register, then use the drop-down list to select the name of the mortgage lending institution in the Payee area. Click OK to finalize the transaction.

A payment appears in the mortgage account, and the account providing the funds for this transaction is debited appropriately. Notice that the payment is all principle.

Please note that, unless both these accounts are online, you'll still have to print and mail the check to your mortgage company.

Moving Between Your Related Accounts

Your mortgage account is closely linked with two others, the checking account that pays the mortgage bill each month and the asset account that represents the house itself. Also, the mortgage account is linked to a particular payee: the institution that lent you the mortgage.

To see just how consistent you've been with your payments and to get a summary of your year-to-date payment total, glance at the Payee Details screen of your lender.

10

At times, you'll want to quickly switch between these accounts and views. Here are some examples:

- View how depleted your checking account is after you've paid the mortgage.
- Inspect changes in your home's value as compared to your monthly payment.
- When considering refinancing, you can switch between your mortgage account and asset account to see how different scenarios play out over the long haul.

To Do: Switching Between Loan Account Views

1. First, make sure you're in the Register View of the mortgage account.
2. Right-click any mortgage payment (see Figure 10.22). The shortcut menu appears, offering options that take you to the following related accounts:
    - The account you designated to pay the Mortgage (in this case "Woodgrove Bank Checking")
    - The Payee Details View of the lending bank (see Figure 10.23)
3. To view the *associated asset*—the account that represents the house itself—click Go to Associated Asset at the lower left of the mortgage Account Register.

FIGURE 10.22.

Use the shortcut menu to quickly move between related accounts.

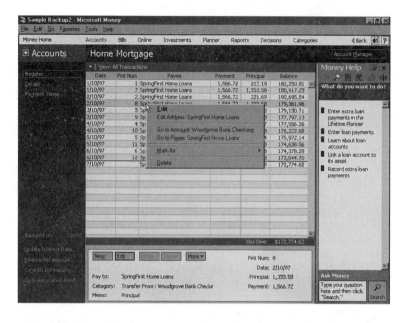

FIGURE 10.23.

Access details about the lending bank by right-clicking any mortgage payment.

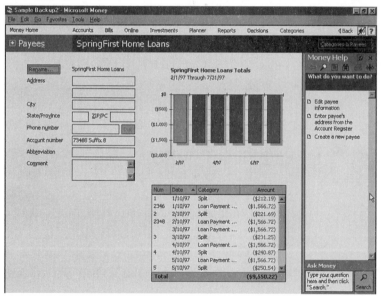

The asset account associated with your mortgage payment is far from static. When you improve your home with repairs and remodeling, these transactions are entered into the asset account and increase its value. When your home rises in value because of market conditions, this, too, requires an adjustment to your asset account. Fire, flood, or earthquake damage similarly decreases its value.

Updating Loan Details

To edit details about your loan, click Details at the left side of the Mortgage Accounts Register View. Open the Details screen to perform these tasks:

- Change or verify your loan account number.
- Make Money 99 aware that this loan is tax deductible.
- Upgrade your mortgage account as a Favorite.
- Type a shortcut abbreviation for this account.
- Link this account to the Goal Planner (see Figure 10.24).

10

FIGURE 10.24.

The Goal Planner helps place this loan in your overall financial strategy.

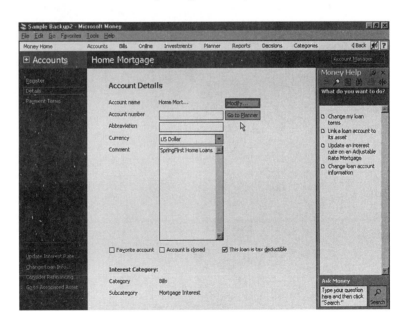

- Change the Account Name (click the Modify button).
- Include comments about this loan in the Comments area.

To close an account, click Account is Closed in the Account Details screen.
You should also use this option when you refinance.

Contact information about the lending institution is not typed in here.
Phone numbers, addresses, Web links, and other contact information for
your lending institution is found on the Payee Details screen of the bank
that loaned you the mortgage.

Changing Specific Loan Information

If you need to enter new fees, such as tax reserves and mandatory insurance, change the
lending institution that receives your payment, or change the way interest is calculated on
your loan, click Change Loan Info at the bottom left of your mortgage account's Register
View (see Figure 10.25). The Change Loan dialog box appears. You can also use this dialog box to enter a new balloon payment, change the number of payments until your loan
is paid off, or type in a new regular mortgage payment amount.

FIGURE 10.25.

*Click Change Loan
Info to edit detailed
loan information.*

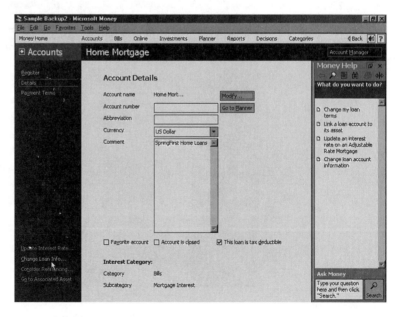

Updating Your Interest Rate

To change the interest rate of your loan, click Update Interest Rate at the bottom left of the Register View of your mortgage account. The Change Loan Wizard appears (see Figure 10.26), prompting you for the following information:

FIGURE 10.26.

The Change Loan Wizard lets you update your interest rate and other loan parameters.

- The new interest rate. The Change Loan Wizard can work with adjustable rates as well.
- When the new interest rate will become effective.
- The new monthly payment.

Please note that the Change Loan Wizard can calculate one of these values. If you know the new interest rate, leave the New Monthly Payment text box blank, allowing Money to calculate the new value. If you know the new monthly payment, leave the Interest Rate text box blank, allowing the new rate to be calculated for you.

Refinancing Your Mortgage or Long-Term Loan

Money 99's Decisions Center has a helpful tool for comparing two loans, the Loan Worksheet. You can compare the true costs of two imaginary loans or see what would happen if you changed gears and refinanced your current loan. You can play around with a new interest rate or a new total sum borrowed (if you wanted to borrow against your current equity so you could remodel your home), or you can check out what would happen if your paid off your balance in 15 years rather than 30.

The Loan Worksheet helps you see what type of deal you are really getting when you receive a refinance offer. To open it, click Consider Refinancing at the bottom left of your mortgage account's Register View. The Loan Planner Worksheet Introduction appears. Read it if you want to. Notice the five tabs across the top: Introduction, Initial Costs, Loan Terms, Variable Rate, and Comparison.

To Do: Exploring Refinancing with the Loan Worksheet

1. Open the Loan Worksheet by clicking Consider Refinancing at the bottom left of your mortgage account, or you can click Decisions on the Navigation Bar, select Tools at the bottom left and choose Loan Worksheet under the Worksheets heading.

2. Click the Initial Costs tab, and under the heading Loan A, click the Use My Loan button at the bottom of the screen (see Figure 10.27). The Loan Selection dialog box appears.

3. Use the drop-down list in the Loan Selection dialog box to choose which existing loan you want to refinance. Those loan specifications will fill the text boxes of the Loan A column. Don't change any of those settings, because those specifications represent the *existing loan* that you want to refinance.

4. Click the Loan Terms tab. Now you can start playing with settings in the Loan B column (see Figure 10.28). This column represents imaginary loan terms and sums that you are considering borrowing. As in the New Loan Wizard, enter the loan information here that you are fairly certain of, and the Loan Worksheet calculates the rest. Use the I Want Money to Calculate drop-down list to determine what the Loan Worksheet should figure out for you.

FIGURE 10.27.

The Loan Worksheet lets you compare the efficacy of two loans.

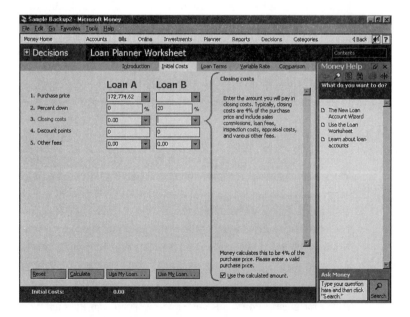

FIGURE 10.28.

The Loan Terms tab lets you adjust variables on your new, as-yet imaginary, loan.

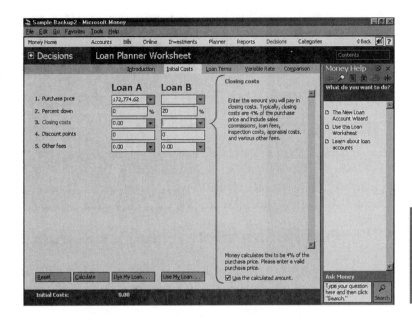

Although the Loan Worksheet is primarily used as a tool for getting a new mortgage, you can also use it to compare "debt consolidation" loans, home-equity-based loans, or any loan possibilities that require close scrutiny before proceeding.

Getting to choose what Money 99 figures out for you can be helpful in the following situations:

- If a refinancing company offers you new terms and a larger total loan, use the Loan Worksheet to calculate the new monthly payment.

- If you are offered "new low payments" with a lower interest rate, enter the new company's figures and let Loan Worksheet calculate the new length of the loan.

- If you have a really ugly balloon payment coming due in a few months and a loan company has offered to refinance the loan, spreading the balloon payment over the life of the whole loan, use the Loan B area to calculate the same loan as Loan A, but without the balloon payment. Just add the balloon payment back into the sum of the entire loan.

5. Finally, if the new loan you are thinking about has a variable interest rate, click the Variable Rate tab to enter when the rate changes, and how often. Then click Comparison to see how Loan Worksheet compares the value of the two loans.

▼   6. After you understand the comparisons, click one of the buttons at the bottom of the
          Comparison tab: Refinance a Loan to refinance your existing loan, or Create a
          Loan to start looking at a new loan without the aid of comparison figures.

Where Do I Put My Loan Company's Contact Information?

You've learned about acquiring a mortgage, checking out terms, refinancing, and making
payments. But what about the company that lends you the money? Where do you make
note of their address, acknowledge the loan officer who's been so near and dear to you
that you want to bake them cookies, and a mark quick link to their Web site?

To Do: Storing Information About Your Loan Company

Keep in mind that if you acquired information about this company online, then Money
99 automatically saves this information in the appropriate location. Remember, your loan
company is a payee, so you'll find them in the Payees List, just like everyone else you
owe money to. Here's how to access this info and update it:

1. In the Register View of your mortgage account, right-click any transaction.

2. Select Go to Payee from the menu that appears.

3. The Payee Details page of the lending institution appears, as shown previously in
   Figure 10.23. If you remember Payee Details from Hour 8, "Tracking Payees," and
   Account and Category Details from Hours 4 "Setting Up Accounts" and 5,
   "Dividing Expenses into Categories," then this arrangement should look fairly
   familiar to you.

   • Contact information about your institution appears on the left, including a
     link to their Web site, if one exists. If there is a special someone, a loan offi-
     cer whom you want to stay in touch with, then type in their personal infor-
     mation as needed.

   • The Bar Chart on the right shows loan payment amounts for the past several
     months.

   • The list on the bottom right shows a total of all payments you've made since
     the beginning of the year.

▲

Asset Accounts

An asset account represents the item you are paying for with your loan. For most of this
hour, the asset being discussed has been a house, but it could be a boat, or a small

business, or a car. An asset account is not a bank account and it is not managed by a lending institution. It's a way for you to manage the value of that asset. For example, most cars diminish in value over time, so you adjust the value of your car asset account by looking up its current blue book value and typing in a new dollar amount in Money 99.

An asset account in Money 99 looks the same as other accounts: it has a Register, and a Details and History page. Use the Details page to type in a new dollar value for that asset, unassociate it with its associated loan (for example, if you refinance, that first loan no longer applies to this account) or change its name. You can also use the Details page to make this account a Favorite or close it.

Recording Changes in an Asset Account's Value

When you remodel your home or add custom parts to a car, you increase its value. To record such changes, create a transaction in the Register of the asset account, making sure you aren't using the *loan associated with* the asset account.

If you are adding value, such as putting in new tiling, then make a *deposit,* or *increase,* to that account, identifying in the transactions how much you spent on the improvement and who did the work (such a transaction also appears in your checking account *as an expense*, having paid the workers to provide and put in the tiles). In the Register of the asset account, you'll see an Increase tab, not a Deposit tab. Be sure to use the memo area to include details about this improvement.

If some event has damaged the asset, such as fire, earthquake, or flood, create a Decrease transaction in the asset account Register. Do this in the same area of the Register where you normally write a check.

The Home Inventory Worksheet

The Home Inventory Worksheet lets you track the value of small components that make up any large asset. The name implies you use it to store information about home articles, use it to track equipment used in a small business or some other asset of value not necessarily related to home. The Home Inventory Worksheet stores information about your items in categories, and these are not changeable, nor can you create new categories. However, even if you are not tracking information about home valuables, you can still use it to record a breakdown of any valuable asset into replaceable components. This is important for insurance and value-tracking purposes, as well as at tax-time.

But there are also other ways to find help while using UnInstaller.
UnInstaller's online Help feature can help you out in any jam. But there are
also other ways to find help while using UnInstaller.

To Do: Tracking Valuables with the Home Inventory Worksheet

The procedure for using the Home Inventory Worksheet is the same if you are tracking
other valuables besides household items, except that you aren't able to use the categories.
All items are stored under the single category "All," in that case.

1. Open the Home Inventory Worksheet by clicking Decisions on the Navigation Bar,
   and choosing Tools on the bottom left.

2. Under the Worksheets heading, select Home Inventory Worksheet (see Figure
   10.29). An empty list appears.

FIGURE 10.29.

*The Home Inventory
Worksheet can track
many types of valu-
ables, not just home
items.*

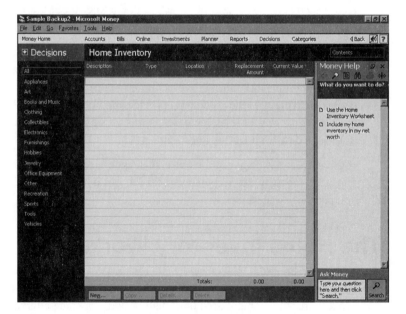

3. Click the New button at the bottom of the page, and a dialog box appears for tracking each item's details (see Figure 10.30). After providing information about your
   item, click Enter, and it will appear in the Home Inventory list. For each item you
   want to track, click New and type in anything you think is warranted. You can
   include, for example, purchase date, purchase price, and helpful identifying notes.

FIGURE 10.30.

Click New at the bottom of the Home Inventory Worksheet to enter details about each item you are tracking.

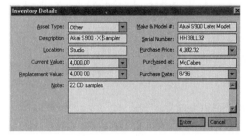

4. Fill the Home Inventory Worksheet with items you hold as valuable. Notice the categories to the left. Each entry on the list appears as a Description, Type, Location, Replacement Amount, and Current Value.

5. To the extent that your valuables fit into these categories, click any of the labels (Appliances, Art, Books and Music, and so on). The labels appear as tabs after you click them.

6. Enter all your books and CDs in "Books and Music," and all your pieces of art in "Art." Click a new tab to reveal a new category for logging in items.

If depreciation is an issue, don't forget that identifying the Date of Purchase is very important.

Creating an Account to Manage Home Inventory Items

Although each home item may not be an asset, their combined value may be considerable. Creating a Home Inventory List lets you track the value of each item and their combined value (listed at the bottom right under Totals), certainly constituting enough value to create an account.

You can have only one Home Inventory Worksheet per Money 99 file.

Money 99 tracks all these assets, creates *Valuable Net Worth* forecasts and uses them to assemble valuable "What I Have" reports. Reports are covered in Hour 16, "Money Reports." To create an account that manages the entire Home Inventory value as a combined asset do the following:

10

To Do: Creating a Home Inventory Asset Account

▼ To Do

1. When you've completed the Home Inventory Worksheet, note the total value. This is going to be the *opening balance* of an asset account you're about to create.

2. Create a new asset account, and name it Home Inventory (or name it after any combined asset value you've used the Worksheet to compile).

3. For the opening balance of this account, type in the total dollar amount from the bottom right of the Home Inventory Worksheet.

4. Click OK, and your new account icon appears with the rest in Account Manager.

5. When you update your Home Inventory Worksheet, make sure you update this account as well.

▲

Summary

Borrowing large amounts of money for a home, car, or other purchase requires a good understanding of how this obligation will affect your finances. Sometimes the effects are not so obvious. Money 99 can help you take a look at your income and decide the type of loan that's best for you. Setting up a long-term loan in Money 99 is a snap. The payments can be automated, and Money 99 shows your progress in whittling down both principle and interest and makes recommendations on how to get the big loan paid off sooner.

Q&A

Q **When should I use the New Loan Wizard and set up a loan account? Whenever I lend or borrow money?**

A Not necessarily. In Money 99, loans require special setup options only when they are interest-bearing. If you borrowed a sum of money from someone without interest, set it up as a liability account, rather than a loan account.

Q **I've never bought a house before. How do I learn what types of loans are available for a borrower like me?**

A Money 99 has many resources for keeping informed on the best mortgage rates, as well as for understanding your rights as a buyer. Read the articles in the Decisions area, choose Tools on the menu bar, and select Money 99 Marketplace.

Q **Can Money 99 help me with refinancing?**

A Yes. Money has tools that calculate the benefits of trading in your loan for a new one. As soon as you find out anything from a potential lender, plug their figures into the Loan Worksheet in the Decisions center, to see how the numbers square up.

Q **How can I keep track of my valuables? I have some things that really qualify as assets. Can Money 99 help?**

A Yes. Money 99 has a Home Inventory Worksheet that categorizes and tracks details about any items you think are of value. The worth of these items are then summarized, and this sum can be saved as an asset account, just like an other Money 99 account.

10

Hour 11

Paychecks, Bills, and Other Recurring Transactions

If having enough money to cover all the bills seems like an endless, cyclical race, Money 99 is good at predicting who the winner will be. In practice, bill-paying and depositing paychecks may seem like a game of hot potato, where *what I have* and *what I owe* get endlessly passed along from month to month. Money can tell you, however, who will be holding the potato at long last: Is there really sufficient funding coming in to cover what must go out?

Money and Planning

In Money, when you schedule a bill to be paid on a regular basis, or a paycheck to be deposited each and every month, Money not only verifies if you've got *this* month adequately covered, but can see how the whole year is shaping up, and makes recommendations on how to create a little comfort zone for your finances. The advice is always savvy and not as obvious as one might think. This hour shows you how to set up paychecks, bills, and any other recurring transactions, some of which are welcome, and some always seem to loom up at the wrong moment. One of Money's greatest tools is this capability to take the surprise factor out of managing expenses from month to month, allowing you to meaningfully plan your finances for the year and beyond.

Up until now, you've seen Money 99 as a series of individual transactions from a checkbook's point of view, or by skimming a list of the people you owe money to, and from the bird's eye view of various accounts. Now you can learn to plan more, see the cycles, and schedule payments and deposits to your own financial advantage.

Not Only Bills

In this hour, you'll be working mostly with the Bills menu (from the Navigation Bar, click Bills), but really, all recurring transactions are scheduled there. When you create a loan, regular payments are automatically scheduled for you, but for other bills and deposits like paychecks and regular income sources, they are scheduled by a trip to Money 99's Bills & Deposits screen.

 When you set up a regular bill or deposit, you don't have to know its exact amount. Type in an estimate, and Money uses that figure for ongoing projections and forecasts, while using the results of previous payments and deposits for monthly and yearly reports.

A Quick Tour of the Bills Screens

When you click Bills from the Navigation Bar, a Welcome screen appears through which you can take a brief video tour explaining how to set up recurring transactions. On the left are controls for opening each Bill & Deposit View (see Figure 11.1).

Each view will be useful to you at one time or another. You'll explore each in detail later, but for now you should see what each of the main views offer:

- **Balance Forecast**—Shows a chart indicating if you are going to have enough money to pay for everything. The chart can focus on one month hence or look ahead for an entire year.
- **Bill Calendar**—Looks like a regular calendar, letting you scroll from month to month. You can see all your pending transactions as far ahead as you want, or scroll backward and see past bills and deposits that have already been paid. Click any day, past or future, to see what is scheduled to occur.

FIGURE 11.1.

To see options for making deposits and paying bills, click Bills on the Navigation Bar.

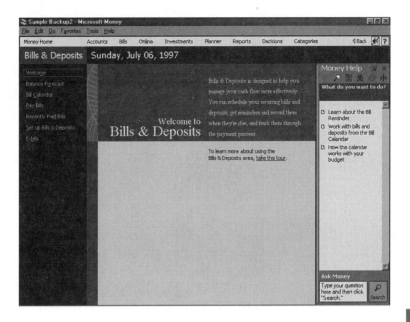

 Use the Bill Calendar view to schedule new recurring transactions. From a Calendar view, it's easy to make sure your deposits are well in place before a round of bill paying begins.

11

- **Pay Bills**—Pay Bills shows a lengthy list of all your upcoming scheduled deposits or bills. The View drop-down list at the upper-left corner lets you determine how far into the future you want to peek (see Figure 11.2).

- **Recently Paid Bills**—Shows a list of all transactions that have occurred in the last 60 days. Please note that deposits are listed here as well, not only bills.

- **Set Up Bills & Deposits**—Use this view to create new recurring transactions, and see a list of all recurring transactions you've set up. This list doesn't show every reoccurrence of a bill or deposit. When you set it up, it appears once here.

 Set Up Bills & Deposits is the only view where you can reschedule a transaction that you previously set up.

- **E-Bills**—To use this, you must have already signed up for an electronic bill paying option using the Online Setup menu.

FIGURE 11.2.

On the Pay Bills screen, click the View menu to specify how far into the future you want to view your obligations.

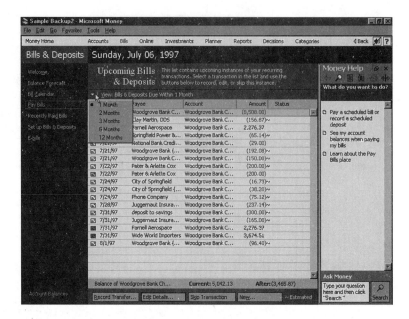

Setting Up an Online Transaction

For this example, Money is informed about regular paychecks you receive. However, the process of setting up a deposit, payment, fund transfer, or investment purchase are all similar.

You begin by clicking Bills on the Navigation Bar, and, when the Bills & Deposits screen appears, selecting Set up Bills & Deposits on the far left. What you see next depends on the following:

- If you are taking a tour at this time, just using the Sample data that comes with Money 99, you'll see some "example bills and deposits," as shown in Figure 11.3.
- If you're building your own Money 99 file from scratch, this list is blank.

To Do: Setting Up a Recurring Deposit or Bill

1. On the Navigation Bar, click Bills. The Recurring Bills & Deposits screen appears (see Figure 11.3).

2. Click Set up Bills & Deposits, at the far left. The Set up Bills & Deposits screen appears.

3. At the bottom left, click the New button. The Create New Scheduled Transaction Wizard appears (see Figure 11.4). This example involves filling out a paycheck deposit. Select Deposit and click Next to continue the wizard walk-through.

FIGURE 11.3.

Set up a recurring bill or deposit on the Recurring Bills & Deposits screen.

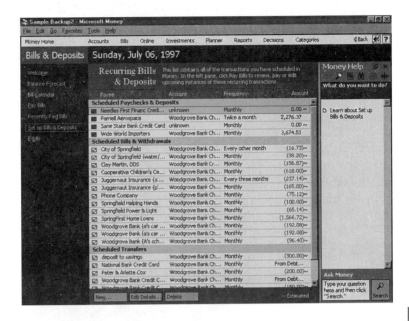

FIGURE 11.4.

From the Create New Scheduled Transaction Wizard, you can create a scheduled bill, deposit, or investment.

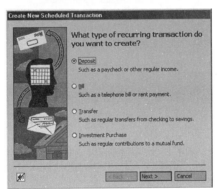

4. The wizard walks you through several screens, asking if this deposit will occur only once or regularly. Indicate how often this transaction will occur, anywhere from once a day to every other year.

When indicating how often a deposit (or any transaction) occurs, notice the subtle differences in the choices provided. You can choose, for example, between "twice a month" and "every other week," or between "monthly"and "every four weeks."

11

▼   5. For this regular transaction, you are prompted to choose between manual, electronic, or direct deposit service. Regarding the last two choices, you must have already arranged these services with your employer and bank, or the bill payee.

6. Money wants to know if this deposit or bill is always the exact same amount or if it varies (see Figure 11.5). Money can work just fine with projected estimated bill amounts and deposits.

FIGURE 11.5.

If you're not sure exactly how much this recurring deposit or bill will be, just make an estimate.

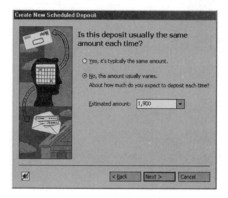

 When viewing any Bill & Deposit screen, an estimated bill or deposit is marked by a wavy, curly symbol, immediately preceding the transaction amount.

7. The Create New Scheduled Deposit screen appears (see Figure 11.6). You see text boxes requiring input from you. Type in the information, or select choices from your existing accounts and payees from the drop-down lists that appear next to each text box.

FIGURE 11.6.

When setting up a new scheduled deposit, you can type in a new payee, or choose from the list.

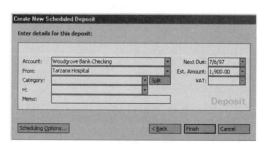

 ▼

▼   When setting up a deposit, you need to fill in these text boxes:

- **Account**—Indicate what account to make this deposit out to.

- **From**—Type in your employer's name, or select your employer from the drop-down list if you've previously entered data about your employer. If this deposit originates from some other source, type that in as well.

> You can type in a totally new account or payee or employer at this time. If you need to fill a text box with a party that does not appear on the drop-down list, just type in the name. If Money 99 and that account or employer have not "met yet," you are asked to answer information about the new item. When you are done with those few questions, Money 99 drops you back in the Set Up Bills & Deposits area, right where you left off.

- **Category**—Be sure to assign a category to this bill or deposit. Feel free to type in a new category if none exists that suits you. When you type in a new category that Money is not aware of, the New Category Wizard appears. When you answer that handful of questions and complete the wizard, Money 99 drops you back where you left off. When you select Paycheck as a category, Money 99 starts the New Paycheck Wizard. If you want to break down portions of your paycheck deposit into specific categories, please see the following section "Itemizing Your Scheduled Paycheck."

> For categorizing paycheck deposits, Money 99 provides three main categories: Gross Pay, Net Pay, and Overtime Pay. You need not use all of these. If you want to track how much you take home every paycheck (Net Pay), choose the Wages & Salary: Net Pay category when asked.

- **Next Due**—Type in the date this deposit is due to occur next. Money doesn't allow you to schedule a deposit or bill that is due today as "Next." You must select a future date. Don't forget to click the drop-down list to use the pop-up calendar. This can save you a lot of time for scheduled transactions.

- **Est. Amount**—Type in a realistic estimated amount for this deposit or bill. You might want to pull out some old deposit slips or invoices to cull a good average.

▼   8. If you want to change Money's schedule for this transaction, or change the amount, click the Scheduling Options button in the Create New Scheduled Deposit dialog box. The Scheduling Options dialog box appears (see Figure 11.7). If this deposit or bill has only a limited amount of cycles remaining (for example, a payment plan spread out for six E-Z payments, or if you are being paid for services rendered in four installments), select the This Deposit Will End at Some Point in Time check box and indicate how many payments or deposits remain. (If you are creating a bill and not a deposit, select the This Payment Will End at Some Point in Time check box.)

FIGURE 11.7.

The Scheduling Options dialog box lets you set up how frequently a transaction should occur.

9. Review your setup of this transaction, making sure you're happy with your choices. Here are some points to check for:

   • If creating a deposit, is your target account named in the Account text box? Is the institution lucky enough to send you money named in the From text box?

   • Is your chosen category truly reflective of the type of transaction? Remember, if you have created a bill for newspaper delivery, it's okay for you to create a new subcategory: Bills: Newspaper, likewise if you receive regular royalties as income. Don't settle for a category that doesn't adequately describe your income source. Create a subcategory called Income: Royalties.

   • Is the amount of your transaction a pretty good estimate of how this payment or income source *averages out* over a year? If the amount fluctuates quite a bit from month to month, look at enough numbers to get a good six-month average to make your guess more accurate.

▼

- If your recurring transaction is a bill, make sure your Due Date coincides nicely with a deposit, insuring adequate funds to cover it.

- If your recurring transaction is a deposit, make sure the Due Date reflects the date that the money *actually clears* the bank, so scheduled bills near that date will be funded.

10. After looking over your scheduled transaction, click Next to finalize it. The transaction appears in the Recurring Bills & Deposits list with the others.

Each transaction has a small "envelope" symbol to its left. Green symbols represent deposits, white symbols represent bills, and yellow symbols are investment purchases like stocks or bonds.

If you ever need to reschedule your transaction, follow these steps: Change the amount or accounts involved, open the Set up Bills & Deposits screen, click the transaction, and choose Edit Details. Then click Scheduling Options.

11

Itemizing Your Scheduled Paycheck

When creating a deposit, you are asked to specify a target account, an amount, and a category. If you select Paycheck as a category, the New Paycheck Wizard appears (see Figure 11.8).

FIGURE 11.8.

The New Paycheck Wizard lets you set up categorizations for your check that more or less mimic how your check is already broken down.

You can choose to track taxes and deductions of all sorts, or track only Net pay. As you click Next, and answer the Paycheck Wizard's questions, here are points to keep in mind:

- You'll be given an opportunity to deposit part of your paycheck into a savings account (see Figure 11.9). It's a bit easier on you if your target savings account has already been created. Then all you'll have to do is select the account from the drop-down list, and type in an amount for the deposit.

FIGURE 11.9.

The New Paycheck Wizard offers to sock away part of your check into a savings account.

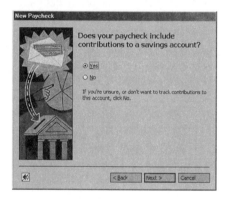

- You can also itemize a 401K (or other pension) deduction, setting aside a regular amount in its own special category. If your deduction is figured as a dollar amount, rather than a percentage of your paycheck, you can tell Money exactly how much is being deducted each pay period. However, if your deduction is figured as a percentage, bear in mind that Money 99 doesn't track deductions based on percentages. In such cases, I'd recommend adjusting your 401K deductions every month, so the amount is accurate.

 Because tax decisions are based on the dollar value of these accounts, it's not advisable to make decisions on 401K accounts based on estimates. Before doing any heavy projecting and planning, call the financial institution that oversees your pension funds to verify the current holdings.

- The New Paycheck Wizard lets you track deductions for each of your paycheck's taxes: federal, state, Medicare, disability, the whole nine yards (see Figure 11.10). Because it's only necessary to know this information at the end of the year, there's not much point in doing all this extra math every month. (You *would* be doing it every month also, because Money 99 only tracks exact dollar amounts you specify. It's not set up to deduct according to tax schedules, so you'd have to specify deduction amounts manually, every check, every month.) You might as well let the government do the math for you.

FIGURE 11.10.

You can recreate your paycheck's tax deductions in Money 99's New Paycheck Wizard. Don't be so quick to undertake all this extra work unless you can think of a really good reason to do so.

To determine whether you are over or under withholding taxes, at any time during the year, run the Tax Worksheet in the Decisions menu.

Special Issues for Scheduling Bills

Scheduling recurring bills is quite simple. With your stack of debts firmly in hand, just start at the top of the pile, entering them one by one. Make sure you are at the Set Up Bills & Deposits screen. Click the New button at the bottom left, and the New Scheduled Transaction Wizard opens. Select Bill, and walk through the wizard as outlined previously. You are prompted for the following information:

- Payee name.
- Name of the account you want to pay *from*.
- Frequency of the transaction (every month, every two months, and so on).
- Estimated (or exact) amount of the bill.
- Bill category and subcategory. Feel free to create new categories as needed.

Notice you are not asked for the bill payee's contact information, such as address and phone numbers. Detailed payee information is entered in the payee's list. (In a moment, you'll learn some shortcuts for navigating between each bill's related accounts, payees, and categories.) Because you are only asked a few questions per bill, building a list of recurring transactions takes little time.

Paying Bills

You've seen how to schedule bills that have to be paid and how to automatically set up payment for them, now you need to learn the actual process of manually paying the bills.

To Do: Paying Bills

1. Click Bills on the Navigation Bar, and the Bills & Deposits screen appears.

   On the left are two views used for showing bills that have yet to be paid, and bills that were recently funded. The two views are

   - **Pay Bills**—The Pay Bills screen shows all the bills that need paying. Click the View icon at the upper right to change the number of months ahead you want to see in this list (refer to Figure 11.2).

   - **Recently Paid Bills**—This list shows all the bills you've paid in the last 60 days.

2. To pay a bill, choose any upcoming bill in the Pay Bills screen, and right-click it.

3. Choose <u>R</u>ecord Payment from the shortcut menu (see Figure 11.11). The Record Payment dialog box appears.

FIGURE 11.11.

To actually pay a bill, right-click and choose Record Payment.

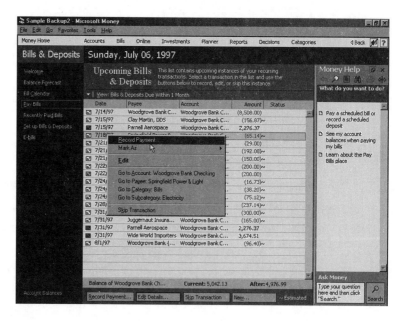

4. Review the details of that bill, and click Record Bill to actually pay it.

5. When you click Record Bill, the account that funds this payment is debited appropriately, and the Recently Paid Bills screen lists your payment.

Remember, you can set up an automatic payment for any bill from the Set Up Bills & Deposits screen, as discussed previously. That way, when the scheduled date arrives, funds from the specified account are spent to pay that bill, and the Recently Paid Bills screen shows it as being paid.

> You can always wait for a particular bill to appear in the Bill Reminder (found at the bottom right of your Windows screen, in the Windows Notification area). This Bill Reminder is operative even when Money is not running. Double-click the icon to see which bills are upcoming. A Start Money button is provided so you can pay the bill right away, if you want to.

Navigating Between Bills, Payees, Categories, and Accounts

Viewing a list of bills is just one part of the puzzle. At times you'll need to take a quick glance at the account that pays that bill, then zip to the payee to remember the address. Or sometimes you'll want to move from bill to category to see how many other similar commitments you are carrying. Money enables you to easily follow a train of thought, then move back to the bill list and continue setting up payments.

To switch between items associated with a particular bill, right-click the bill in the Set Up Bills & Payees list, as shown in Figure 11.12.

The following links appear in the shortcut menu:

- The payee associated with that bill
- The account that pays the bill
- The category and subcategory assigned to that bill
- The next occurrence of that payment

Click any destination to momentarily move there. Even if the destination does not contain an instant link back (for example, right-clicking the account does not take you back to the bill), use the Back arrow on the Navigation Bar to take you back to the Bills & Deposits list.

You can also right-click any transaction in the Paid Bills and Recently Paid Bills list to navigate between related locations.

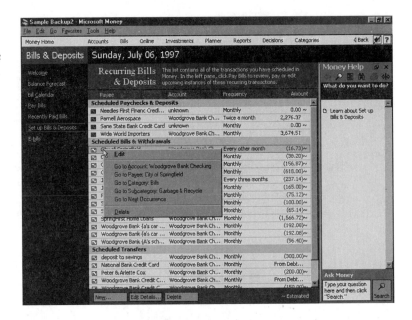

Working with the Bill Calendar

The Bill Calendar is a 12-month calendar allowing access to a day-by-day view of all your scheduled transactions (see Figure 11.13). Using the Bill Calendar to schedule transactions gives you a graphic view of how many transactions occur in a given month, and how ominously the bills crowd around the deposits.

Bill Calendar highlights include the following:

- On your screen a single month is broken into days. If you've scheduled transactions for a particular day, you see them clearly listed on that date in the calendar.

- The basic unit of the Bill Calendar is the day. Browse through the dates to see their scheduled transactions. Click a date to edit a transaction's details, such as its amount, assigned category, or name, as shown in Figure 11.14. Double-click any date to assign a new transaction to it, even if that date is currently empty. (You can only reschedule a recurring transaction from the Set Up Bills & Deposits screen.)

- You can also double-click any date on the Bill Calendar to schedule a new transaction for that date, or record a payment for that date. (Recording a payment manually pays that bill, even if it's prescheduled for another time.)

FIGURE 11.13.

With the Bill Calendar, you can schedule and view recurring transactions.

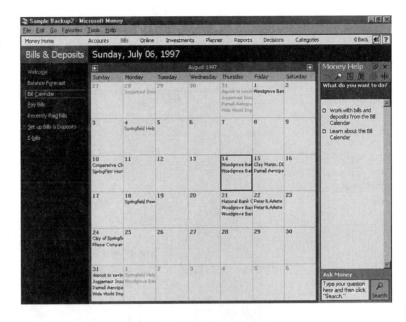

FIGURE 11.14.

Click any transaction in the calendar to alter its details.

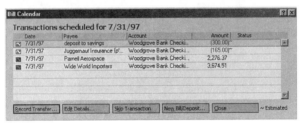

- The Bill Calendar lets you scroll through the months. You can see how they add up a quarter year at a time, or half a year, whatever helps you see the full financial impact of your deposits and bills. To scroll to the next or previous month, click the "forward" or "back" arrow on the same line as the month title.

The Balance Forecast

Conveniently located one click away from any of the bill-paying views is the Balance Forecast (click Balance Forecast, one of the commands in the list to on the left side of any Bill & Deposit screen, as shown in Figure 11.15). Balance Forecast provides a chart that lets you see any account balance. You can see how much money is in any account, as of today, or as of six months from now, and all points in between. This feature lets you stack up your bills next to your ability to pay them. Not only today's bills, but future financial commitments as well. Remember, Money 99 not only tracks recurring bills, but also recurring deposits. If your scheduled transactions are leading to deficit or surplus funding, Balance Forecast tells you about it months before it occurs.

FIGURE 11.15.

In any bill-related screen, click Balance Forecast to view a chart showing how your deposits and bills stack up against each other.

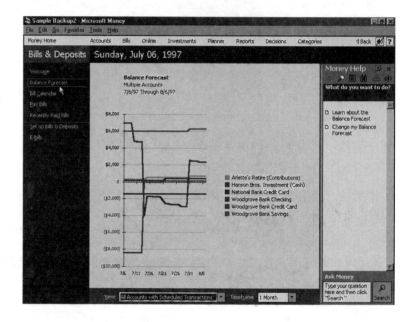

Figure 11.16 shows the Balance Forecast screen. By default, all your spending accounts are shown in this line chart pattern. The account with the lowest balance is shown at the bottom, and your highest funded account appears at the top. The bottom row of the chart shows the *date range* you are viewing. The side column shows the *balance* of each account.

Picking a Balance Forecast Date Range

When you first view Balance Forecast, you are shown what your accounts will look like for the following month. Click the Timeframe drop-down list at the bottom of the screen to change the scope of your forecast (see Figure 11.17). Notice you can view as far as one year ahead. Also, look at the row of dates at the bottom of the forecast. When you are viewing a one-month forecast, the date markers are spaced five days apart. When viewing account balances for an entire year, quarterly date markers are used. The date markers change depending on the scope of your chart at the moment.

FIGURE 11.16.

The Balance Forecast screen shows the current and future balances of all your spending accounts.

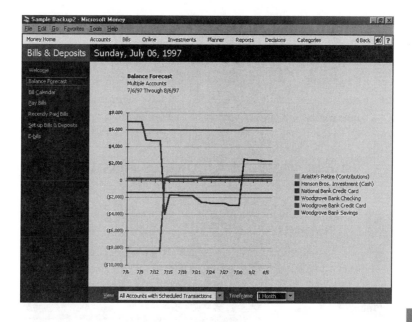

FIGURE 11.17.

Change the date range of your forecast by clicking Timeframe.

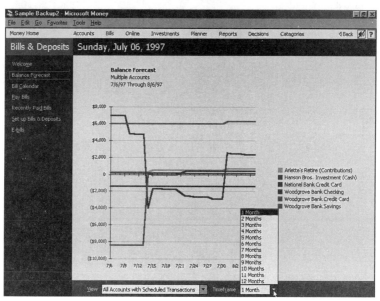

11

Using the Chart to Show Daily Balance Changes

The Balance Forecast charts can show more than general account information. You can use the mouse to help you track even daily alterations in your account balance. This feature can be helpful, if you know that some important transactions took place in a particular time frame, but you are not sure exactly when.

To Do: Viewing Changing Account Balances on a Chart Line

1. Move the mouse cursor over any account line, following it from the beginning to the end.

   Notice when your mouse cursor hovers over a date marker, that account's balance is shown (see Figure 11.18).

FIGURE 11.18.

To see a particular balance, hover the mouse cursor where a date intercepts an account line.

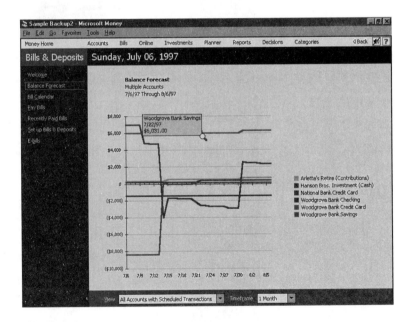

2. Move your mouse more slowly over the same account line. Now notice that, after your mouse cursor "catches" a date marker, you see an updated daily account balance as you slowly move your mouse across that account line.

Selecting Which Account to View in the Forecast

Sometimes it's too confusing to see all spending accounts at once, especially when only one of them is most often used for bill paying. To select one account for the Forecast, click the View drop-down list at the bottom of the screen. Select one account, and it alone will be shown in the Forecast view.

How to Interpret the Forecast

The rising and falling lines represent fluctuations in account balance. If an account shows wild balance swings, it's being used to pay a hefty sum of bills, then replenished again by a deposit of funds. If an account's balance appears low for a while, you lose accrued interest and run the risk of an account overrun. So, when looking over the Balance Forecast, if you notice a prolonged low balance try to find a way to deposit something a bit sooner or spread out bill payments from that account so the levels do not remain low for too long.

Don't forget you can right-click any chart to view it in 3D, print it, or make it a Favorite. This shortcut menu applies to any Budget Forecast chart.

11

Viewing the Budget Forecast

One of the account views in the drop-down list is the Budget Forecast (see Figure 11.19). If you'll remember, some accounts you set up to fund day-to-day activities and others set aside money for occasional expenses.

This forecast shows available funds broken down in those two distinctions. Here's how to interpret its findings:

- The Budget Forecast is a bar chart, each week representing a single bar.
- Each bar of this chart shows total funds available at that particular week, divided into day-to-day accounts at the top in blue, and Occasional Expense Funds at the bottom in yellow.
- Double-click any week, and you can see what money is coming in, and what bills are being paid (see Figure 11.20). Starting and ending account balances for each type of account are shown as well.

FIGURE 11.19

The Budget Forecast compares day-to-day spending with funds set up for Occasional Expenses.

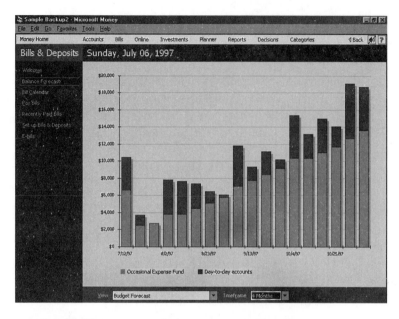

FIGURE 11.20.

After double-clicking a bar in the Budget Forecast chart, you'll see details of that week's transactions. One bar represents one week.

Date	Description	Inflows	Outflows	Balance
Day-to-day accounts				
7/20/97	**STARTING BALANCE**			**1,224.27**
7/21/97	Est. Spending (already in budget): Natio...	100.00		1,324.27
7/21/97	Debt Payment: Arlette's car loan		192.08	1,132.19
7/21/97	Debt Payment: National Bank Credit Card		29.00	1,103.19
7/22/97	Savings deposit to Long-Term Savings		200.00	903.19
7/22/97	Savings deposit to Long-Term Savings		200.00	703.19
7/24/97	Phone Company, Bills : Telephone		75.12	628.07
7/24/97	City of Springfield {water/sewer, Bills : ...		38.20	589.87
7/24/97	City of Springfield, Bills : Garbage & Rec...		16.73	573.14
7/26/97	Projected Transfer from Savings	398.66		971.80
7/26/97	Miscellaneous Expenses		971.80	0.00
7/26/97	**ENDING BALANCE**			**0.00**
Occasional Expense Fund				
7/20/97	**STARTING BALANCE**			**975.98**
7/26/97	Saved leftover income	671.56		1,647.54

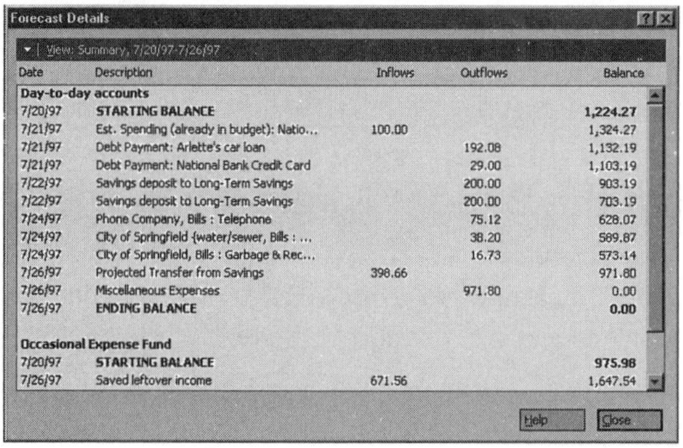

Summary

Money 99 lets you schedule bills and deposits, and gives you lots of tools for knowing the ebb and flow of your funds on hand. You can set automatic payment for a bill from a Calendar view, or by viewing all related bills at once, make sure a deposit is scheduled to adequately cover the payments. Even if you don't know exactly how much a bill or deposit is, you can still set it up to be paid or deposited.

Q&A

Q How can I set up a scheduled bill when I don't know how much it is going to be? Also, my paycheck varies a bit from month to month. What can I do?

A Money 99 lets you input estimates for each bill, and deposit. These estimates help with planning your cash flow situation and give you lots of needed feedback, even if the dollar amount is not 100% correct.

Q What's helpful about the Bills & Deposit screens?

A At a glance, you can see how much you owe, and how much is coming in. You can even see in the coming months if you're likely to have enough to comfortably cover your obligations.

Q Should I itemize the taxes taken out of my paycheck?

A Probably not. If you are concerned that not enough (or too much) is being taken out, run the Tax Worksheet. Looking at the year-to-date totals that are reported on your paycheck, and your W2 at the end of the year will be sufficient.

Q Can I browse through the Bill Calendar and schedule payments right from there?

A Yes, you can. Sometimes viewing a calendar gives you a clear view of when money is likely to get pretty thin. Just pick a date for a particular bill that suits you, and double-click it. You can schedule that bill (and deposit) right then and there.

11

PART III
The Bigger Picture

Hour

12 Printing Checks and Other Forms

13 Creating a Budget

14 Long-term Planning and Goals

15 Money Online

16 Money Reports

17 Charts and the Chart Gallery

18 Money and Taxes

HOUR 12

Printing Checks and Other Forms

In this hour you'll learn how to print your checks onto blank check forms you can purchase from Microsoft. You'll also learn how to print reports, charts, and forecasts. Because printing problems always seem to happen at the worst possible moment, (such as when you need to pay someone quickly) this hour wraps up with some troubleshooting tips for your printer.

Printing Checks

When you actually use Money 99 to print checks, there's one more step to the process that hasn't been covered in previous hours. You've learned about writing checks, setting up checking accounts, and how Money 99 assigns contiguous check numbers from any number you start with. The Check Register advances one digit every time you create a check. However, if you take advantage of Money 99's check-printing feature, there are a few points to remember:

- When you purchase 250 blank checks from Microsoft, the cost is about 20 cents per check. Purchase more at once and the cost diminishes somewhat.

- Money 99 does not print the check number on the check. It's preprinted at Microsoft. So, when assigning check numbers, use the digit printed on your first blank printed check. From then on, Money 99 and the blank printed checks will be in sync.

- When you set up a check to be printed, a reminder appears. It's a little more convenient to print three checks at a time rather than just one.

- You should print a "test check" because alignment problems can be expensive if mistakes are made on real checks.

Ordering Checks from Microsoft

Money 99 requires you to use Microsoft's checks, which you can order by calling 1-800-432-1285. Microsoft will send you free samples, after which you must pony up for the sum quoted previously. You've probably done the math yourself and realized the price of one Microsoft check is more than twice what a normal check costs. You have to weigh the time-saving factor (imagine, never writing another check by hand), against the extra expense.

Microsoft's checks are good all over the world, and you won't have any trouble getting them accepted by your payees. Several styles and designs are available, and, if you run a small business, Microsoft can print a custom logo on your preprinted check for not too much more.

If you have checks from Quicken, those can be used by Money 99 as well. You'll learn how shortly.

You can fill out a Microsoft check by hand if you need to because of convenience. There is no law that says they must be printed out by a computer.

Check Styles

Money 99 sells three styles of checks: Wallet-size, Standard-size, and Voucher. Here are the differences:

- Wallet-size checks are for general consumer use. To accommodate your payees that are scrimping on return postage, Wallet-size checks fit into smaller envelopes, and are convenient for transporting in wallets and evening bags. The memo area on the check is tiny. Each check has a detachable stub. This extra documentation can be helpful at tax-time, because the IRS likes to see paper receipts as well as computerized entries.

- Standard-size checks are larger, and have a large memo area for tracking invoices and other notations. If you're a business owner, consider this check style.

- Voucher checks have lots of room for detail. If you need room for a thorough invoice to make clear exactly what you're paying for (like 25% of a construction job), use voucher checks.

> When ordering Microsoft checks, specify laser, or continuous feed. Laser checks work with inkjet printers as well.

Proceed with Patience

Just a word of warning before you continue. Expect to spend a little time getting the bugs out of your check-printing sessions. Alignment problems are common, and Money 99 includes a check-printing tool that properly centers your check's text just the way it should be. However, there will be some adjusting to do. If you have one of those inkjet printers that have gravity-dependent feeds (you load the paper from up top, and it falls through the printing area), expect extra grief. Practice on normal paper, lining everything up perfect a few times, before you send your expensive checks down the pipe just to see what happens.

12

What Starting Number Should I Pick?

When you order your Money 99 checks on the phone, the nice lady asks you to select a starting number (see Figure 12.1). Yes, you could start at 001, but here is something to keep in mind. *Using Money 99 checks does not mean you ditch your normal checks.* And no, you should not drive yourself crazy trying to match your paper check numbering system with your printed Money 99 checks. (That's all you need, two "check 035s" floating around out there.) So, really, it's best to use a start number for your Microsoft checks that cannot be confused with your paper check numbers. That way, by just glancing at a bank statement, you are able to tell if a certain check was written by hand, or from your printer. So pick a start number that uses an extra digit than your paper checks, so no confusion will ensue. For its part, Money 99 doesn't care what number you start with.

FIGURE 12.1.

When setting up for printed checks, Money asks you what the check number is on your first printed check.

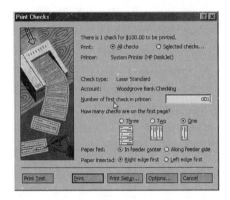

 You can't open the Print Checks dialog box until you've actually set up checks to be printed.

Getting Ready to Print

When your Microsoft checks arrive in the mail, you can get ready to print them right away, or wait until you've got some transactions saved up that need printing. Now you need to know how to set up the checks and your printer.

A Page of Checks

Most often, one page has three checks, and here are three points to remember:

- If you've not yet memorized which way to insert documents in your printer so they are printed right-side-up, you should do so now. You don't want to insert a page of checks and find that the portion you print is all backwards.

- Notice that the check paper is a bit thicker (not wider) than your printer may be used to. Depending on how finely you've adjusted your printer's "page thickness" setting, you may have to reset it, so a page of check's squeezes comfortably through.

- A Page of wallet-sized checks is narrower than a normal page of paper. So, depending on how user-friendly your printer's envelope-printing feature is, you may have better luck running your checks through sideways rather than vertically. If you do feed your checks in vertically, you have to resize the width of your printer's paper tray. If your printers paper tray provides no such option, then try using the "print envelope" feature of your printer.

What Does Money 99 Print on Each Check?

As you can see by looking at your preprinted checks, Microsoft prints your name and address, bank name and address, as well as account number and check number. When you print a check, you provide the following:

- Payee's name
- Amount paid
- Date
- Memo information

On the check stub or voucher area, you can note by hand any relevant information.

Getting Ready to Print Checks

When you are getting ready to print checks, notice the File menu has two commands regarding check printing. The menu option Print Checks is not available unless you've actually created a transaction in one of your accounts that needs to be printed. But to basically set up your printer to accommodate check printing, do the following:

From the File menu, choose Print Setup, and then click Check Setup. The Check Setup dialog box appears (see Figure 12.2).

FIGURE 12.2.

Make sure your sheet of checks is aligned and facing the right way before you print.

12

To Do: Preparing for Check Printing

Most of the settings here need your attention only once, but a couple might need to be adjusted from time to time. To set up a page of checks for printing, do the following:

1. In the Printer panel, select your printer. If no printer is installed, close Money 99, set up your printer for Windows, and return here.

2. In the Check panel, select the *type* of check you ordered in the Type drop-down list. The menu has six check types to choose from:

   - The top three check types are for laser or inkjet printers (Wallet-sized, Standard, or Voucher).

   - The bottom three are for tractor-feed printers (Wallet-sized, Standard, or Voucher).

3. Next, select the paper source from the Source drop-down list. Your choices are Auto Sheet Feeder, or Envelope Manual. If you choose the Envelope Manual setting, the check page must be loaded "just so," according to your printer's instructions. Consult your printer's manual.

4. Most often, make sure the Require Address for Payee When Printing checks box is checked. However, if you have an occasional payee with an uncertain address, go ahead and uncheck it.

5. If you'd like to choose a particular font for your printed checks, click the Font button at the right side of the dialog box. Keep in mind, however, that legibility and a professional-looking check is the number one goal here.

6. Click OK to confirm your check printer settings. Other options are not going to be available until you've specified that checks have to be printed in your Money 99 checking account.

Designating a Check For Printing

By now, you know how to enter a check as a transaction in Money 99. That process designates a payee for your check, deducts the appropriate amount from your checking account, and assigns a category to the transaction. The next step is to get the check from Money 99 to the printer.

To Do: Telling Money 99 You Want to Print a Check

This all happens in your Checking Account Register, so you might want to move over there now.

1. Fill out a check in the Check Register, typing in all the required data, as shown in Figure 12.3.

FIGURE 12.3.

*A check filled out in
the Register. Notice the
command "Print"
shown in the Check
Number drop-down
list.*

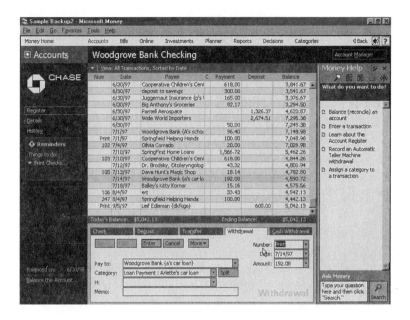

2. Click the Number drop-down list, as shown in that same figure. Select Print this
   Transaction from the options. You'll have no control at this time over the check
   number used by Money 99 for this transaction. You'll set that up momentarily.

3. As soon as you click Enter, a Reminder pops up at the far left of the screen (see
   Figure 12.4). On the reminder is a command that reads "Print Checks."

12

FIGURE 12.4.

*As soon as you set up
even one check for
printing, the Print
Checks reminder
appears.*

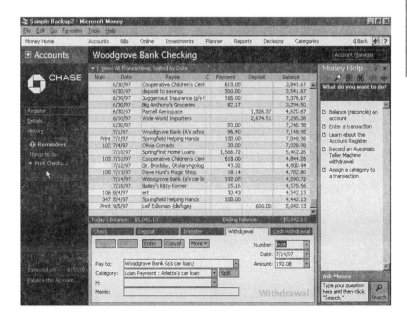

4. After you've designated a few checks to be printed, you can print these checks by clicking that "Print Checks" command, or by choosing File, Print Checks. Printing
▲   checks is covered in the following section.

Printing Checks

When you print checks, you have to position the check sheet just right, and pick the correct check number, so Money 99 can match your paper check's documentation. You also need a copy of a blank page of checks to complete this exercise.

To Do: Printing the Checks

1. Click the Print Checks Reminder at the right of the screen, or choose File, Print Checks. The Print Checks dialog box appears (see Figure 12.5).

FIGURE 12.5.

The Print Checks dialog box enables you to choose which checks to print.

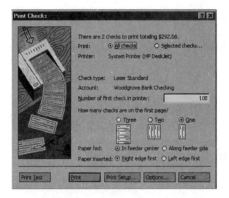

> Unless you specified "No Addresses" in the Options dialog box, you are prompted to add an address for your payee before the check prints.

2. Specify if you want Money 99 to print all checks, or selected ones. If you choose selected checks, a list of all the checks you've set up for printing appears (see Figure 12.6). Click the checks you want to print at this time. In this list, checks
▼   you want printed appear shaded in yellow.

FIGURE 12.6.

This list shows all the checks ready to be printed. Select any or all of them to actually print.

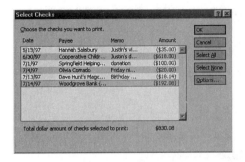

Choose File, Printer Setup to select the actual printer.Click OK.

3. Organize your blank checks so the lowest number is printed first, and type in that starting number in the Number of First Check in Printer text box in the Print Checks dialog box.

4. Look at the How Many Checks Are on the First Page? area. You can insert a page of one, two, or three checks into the print tray. Money accommodates this so you don't have to throw away a page of checks just because you've used the first one. However, look at the check page orientation. Notice that, when you insert a page of *two checks*, Money 99 needs you to put the page in sideways.

Although this check dialog box shows the checks *facing up,* your printer might require you to insert preprinted materials *face down.* Don't let this dialog box fool you.

12

5. Adjust the Paper Fed and Paper Inserted settings to match your printer's mechanics.

6. For practice, place the copy you made of a blank page of checks in your printer, and choose Print Test. If your checks come out aligned and centered properly, then proceed to step 8. If you need to change something, go on to step 7.

7. Check to see if the check sheet is facing the wrong way, flipped around, or out of alignment. If alignment is a problem, click the Options button in the Print Checks dialog box, and make numeric adjustments in the Printing Alignment panel (see Figure 12.7). When your test checks are aligned properly, move on to step 8.

FIGURE 12.7.

If your checks are not centered properly on the page, make adjustments in the Printing Alignment portion of the Options dialog box.

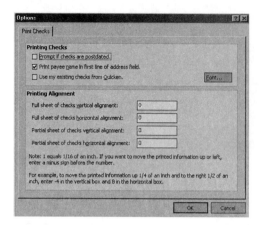

▼

8. Click the Options button, unless the Options dialog box is already open. You'll see options to use Quicken checks, if you have them, and to print the payee's name in the first line of the address text box. Also, you can choose to have Money alert you if you are trying to postdate a check. Click OK to close the Options dialog box, and get ready to print.

9. The Print Checks dialog box reappears. Click the Print button, and your printer begins printing. A confirmation dialog box appears (see Figure 12.8).

FIGURE 12.8.

This box confirms that your checks should be printing. It might take a second for the data to actually reach the printer.

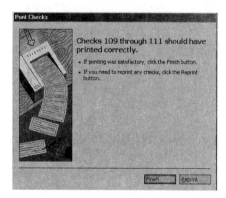

10. If there was yet another problem, you can reprint. Click the Reprint button. Money again asks you to select which checks should be printed. Notice that the check number advances to accommodate the check printed in error (see Figure 12.9).

11. If you did have to print a second time, make sure you go back into your Money 99 Checkbook Register and void the original check printed in error.

▼

FIGURE 12.9.

Money helps you reprint a check printed in error, without messing up your check numbering system.

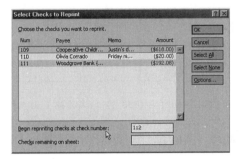

Printing Other Money Documents

Anything you see on your screen in Money 99 is fair game for printing. If you've spent 15 minutes taking one of the Decision Center quizzes, it's interesting to read the results, but wouldn't it be better to have it printed out? After you've answered the questions, and Money runs its analysis, just choose File, Print. Figure 12.10 shows the results screen of the Risk Tolerance quiz (from the Decisions menu). Because this is a lot of data to absorb all at once, you can print it and save it for later.

FIGURE 12.10.

You don't have to absorb all this analysis right now. Print it out and read it later.

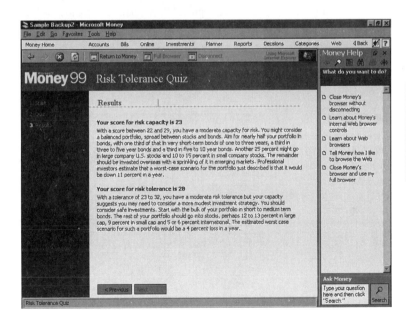

12

Getting Ready to Print Reports

Money 99 Reports have value as paper documents as well. There may be times you'll want to save notarized hard copy for your files, or send a report over to an accountant or a tax firm. Options are available for printing out reports with clarity and flexibility:

- In Money's charts, data is represented by shades of color. If you don't have a color printer, you can't see them. However, if your printer is a dot matrix or black and white, Money can substitute the shading with patterns, such as cross-hatches and rectangles.

- You can export report data to a spreadsheet, allowing you to include Money's data with a broader picture of information.

- When you print a report, you are printing more than is visible on your screen. If there are several screens of data associated with a particular report, all are printed. A monthly report is often more than five pages long.

- Many Money reports draw from other documents. When setting up to print your report, you can specify that these linked documents be printed as well.

- Some of Money's documents, such as articles in the Decisions Center and reports, appear in frames (see Figure 12.11.). Borrowing technology from Web page design, each portion of the screen you see is actually a document unto itself. The left side of the page may be a subarticle, a list of links related to the center screen, or the main page of the article. If you want to print all the frames you can see on the screen, however, Money allows you to do so.

FIGURE 12.11.

This Money 99 screen shows three documents, each in their own frame. Printing right now would only print one of those frames.

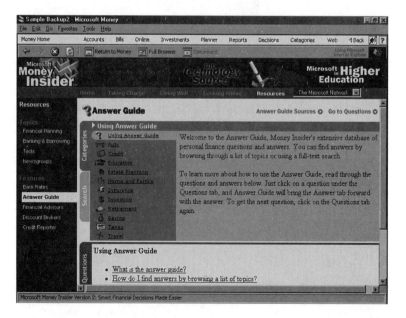

Printing a Report

To print a report, just open the report, and choose File, Print. If you have a black and white or dot matrix printer, before you print, choose Tools, Options, and click the General tab. Make sure Display Charts Using Patterns and Print Charts Using Black and White are selected, as shown in Figure 12.12. After making these adjustments, print the report as you would any other document.

FIGURE 12.12.

To accommodate black and white report printing, click the bottom check boxes in the Display area of the General tab.

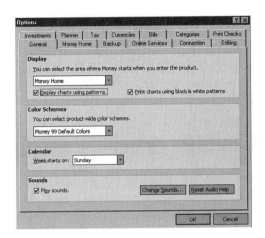

 Reports printed in black ink can't show negative numbers in red, but negative numbers are displayed in parentheses, and thus, are still recognizable.

12

Exporting a Report to a Spreadsheet

At times you may want to include a Money 99 report in a spreadsheet containing other data as well. Money exports your report as a "tab delimited text file." A spreadsheet can open such a file. Each element of the report appears in its own cell. Each number, or each heading for a group of numbers appears in its own cell. To be able to read an entire heading, you have to expand the cell width to accommodate the size of your text heading.

To Do: Exporting a Money Report to a Spreadsheet

When you are finished exporting your report, you'll have a new .txt file that your spreadsheet will be able to open and display.

▼

Your exported spreadsheet file does not affect your Money 99 report or any other Money file.

1. Open the report you want to export, and right-click it. A shortcut menu appears (see Figure 12.13).

FIGURE 12.13.

Right-clicking a report shows menu options for exporting data to open in a spreadsheet.

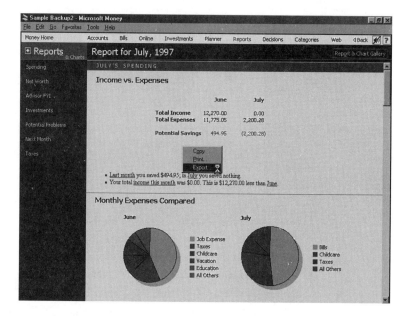

2. Click Export, and a Save menu appears. Choose the folder for saving this file, and name it. Money 99 automatically provides a .txt file extension for the resulting new file.

3. Make a note of this file location because you'll be opening your spreadsheet next and will have to locate it from that program's Open menu. Click OK to finalize saving this new .txt file.

4. Open your spreadsheet and locate the .txt file you just made. Your spreadsheet asks a few questions about how to interpret the data. In answering, keep in mind that Money 99 saved this data as a "tab delimited text file."

5. The spreadsheet opens, and displays the data. However, the cells that contain longer text headings need to be widened, as shown in Figure 12.14.

FIGURE 12.14.

To make room for headings, widen the cells manually.

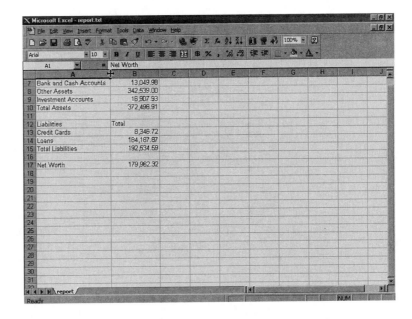

6. Place your mouse cursor at the top of the field marker, as shown in that same figure, and drag to the right. The text that was hidden before now appears.

7. Your Money 99 data is ready to be saved in the native file format of your spreadsheet, and incorporated into a spreadsheet workbook or project.

Printing Documents Linked to an Article

12

Many Money documents, especially reports or articles in the Decision Center, contain links to other documents as well.

To Do: Printing Linked Documents

▼ To Do

1. Open the document you want to print.

2. Choose File, Print. A Print options dialog box appears that looks similar to the one shown in Figure 12.15.

3. Select the Print All Linked Documents check box to print out a copy of every article account record or article related to this current document. This option is only available if the article you're viewing is linked to others, and if your printer supports this function. Some printers do not.

FIGURE 12.15.

Tell Money 99 to print all documents that are linked to the one you are looking at currently.

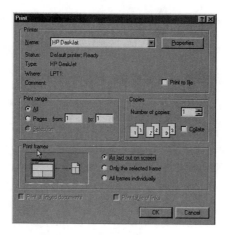

▲

Additionally, many of the articles in the Decisions Center, and some reports, are actually frames. That means your Money 99 screen may be divided into three separate free-scrolling segments.

To Do: Printing Everything on Your Money 99 Screen

1. Open the Money 99 article or report you want to print.

2. Select Print. The Print Setup screen appears, as shown previously in Figure 12.15. Depending on the printer you are using, your dialog box may not look identical to that figure.

3. In the Print Frames area, make sure the As Laid Out on Screen or All Frames Individually button is selected. Again, you'll only see this option if the article you are viewing has frames or if your printer supports this particular function.

▲

Fixing Printer Problems

Printers usually stop working when you need them the most—right before a major deadline or when checks need to be printed. Try the following checklist of problems to look for to get you printing again. The good news is that if something like this happens to you, it's not likely that the printer has broken. There are a handful of steps you can take that will probably have you up and running quickly.

So if you find your printer does not want to print, run through the following checklist:

- Close any programs other than Money 99 before attempting to print.

- A print job needs an amazing amount of free hard drive space. If your hard drive is more than 80% full, erase some files you are not using before continuing.

- A print job not only needs lots of hard drive space, but that free space has to be *contiguous* (all in one big clump, not spread out all over your hard drive). So if freeing hard drive space doesn't work, Defragment your hard drive before continuing. (From the Windows Start menu, click Accessories, then choose System tools, and select Defragment.)

- Try printing one or two checks at a time, rather than several pages worth.

- If none of the previous tips work, then it could be that the small software device that actually operates your printer (called a driver) may not work correctly with Money 99. Log on to one of the following Web pages and download the newest driver for your printer. Make sure you follow the onscreen instructions for installing it.

  `http://www.info-masters.com/drivers/printers.htm`

  `http://www.groupweb.com/printer/drivers.htm`

- Finally, if installing the newest printer driver doesn't help, or if the previous checklist item seems like too much work, you can use *the most simple and basic driver* that your printer company manufactures. This is like buying shoes of a neutral color because they won't clash with anything you wear. They might not be perfect, but at least they'll get you to work. For example:

  If you have a Hewlett Packard Inkjet 870 C printer, then install the driver "Hewlett Packard Ink Jet." Find the driver that has *no letters or numbers* after its name.

  Or if you have an Epson Stylus 1000, then locate the driver called "Epson Stylus." Choose the printer driver with the *fewest parameters* at the end of its name.

What you are doing is installing the simple "plain wrap" driver. Money 99 may be able to work just fine with this less complicated printing device.

12

Summary

Money 99 makes it easy for you to print your own checks by using blanks that you can order from Microsoft. These checks are as accepted as any that you order from your bank. After setting up your printer and perhaps making minor alignment adjustments for each page of checks, it's much more convenient to record that transaction and print the checks in a very few steps.

For printing reports, Money makes it easy to print out anything on your screen, documents that you think need to be shown to an accountant, or archived as hard copy for any reason. You can also export Money 99 data to a spreadsheet format, incorporating Money's reports into a larger spreadsheet workbook project.

Q&A

Q Do I have to use Microsoft checks with Money 99?

A Yes, or you can use Quicken checks.

Q How can I order Microsoft checks and how much do they cost?

A Just call 1-800-432-1285. They'll send you free samples. Bought in quantities of 200, Microsoft checks cost about 20 cents each. They'll cost less if you buy more.

Q So when I get the checks in the mail, I can just put them in my printer and off I go, right?

A Wrong. You'll have to make sure the alignment and paper direction of your printer matches what Money 99 prints. It's best to practice by making a copy of a blank page of checks, experimenting with that first.

Q I only have a black and white printer, and most of Money 99's reports are color-coded. What's the value of printing out a report then?

A In its reports, Money uses colors to show you different types of data but you can substitute patterns instead. You'll see patterns of cross-hatches, rectangles, and other shapes instead of different colors.

HOUR **13**

Creating a Budget

Overview

The first step to creating a budget is the most enjoyable: getting motivated. You need to save for a reason, not just because the school teacher in the back of your mind tells you it's a good idea. It ought to be a pleasurable reason. If budgeting requires that you put off some of the little extras now (it usually does), then there ought to be big extras later.

Motivation

Take some time to think about the things you really want to accomplish in life, prioritize those in a list, and let those become your motivation for budgeting. If you're going to be asking yourself to take fewer trips to the movies, then you ought to be taking one or two trips to Paris at the end of the tunnel. Bottom line: Don't budget and save because you should. Associate the hardship with something fun, at long last.

Information

Secondly, inform yourself: Money 99 can show you how your spending patterns match "the majority" of Americans in your income bracket. Then, find out what you can do differently. There might be some dramatic, initial steps you can take to reduce your spending. If so, getting started with budgeting won't feel like running in place. Initial steps include cutting up high-interest credit cards, refinancing your house, and seeing whether you are getting the best insurance deals available to you.

Examination

Then you can run a critical eye over your current spending and saving pattern just to see where the money goes. This is easier after you've been using Money 99 for a while, because the reports and charts finally start to show a little detail. See if you notice trends or patterns that might be significant, seasonal ups and downs, or some other cause-and-effect relationship.

Creative Change

Finally, while in a positive state of mind, come up with some creative ideas for changing spending patterns, look at day-to-day habits, week-to-week habits, and all the way up to yearly patterns. See where the flexibility is.

Don't worry, Money 99 has tools for guiding you through this entire process and beyond. Let's see how Money can help you with budgeting.

Initial Budgeting Steps

For a nice dose of motivational medicine, at least glance over a few of the articles in the Savings page of the Decisions area (see Figure 13.1). These articles are organized so you can breeze across the main points without getting bogged down in lots of reading. "Strategies to Help You Get Started" includes a handful of pretty painless ways to get a jump-start on saving. Also, "Easy Ways to Pay Yourself First" and "Minimize Your Non-Essential Spending" are worth reading. Both of those articles contain easily digestible budgeting tips that don't condemn you to years of self-enforced poverty.

Then, just so you don't fall into the trap of quantifying your time into some rigid, formulaic dollar value, you might want to look over two articles under the Family tab of the Decisions area (see Figure 13.2), "What's Your Leisure Time Really Worth?" and "Simple Ways to Uncomplicate your Life." These articles encourage you to not think of fiscal expediency as an end in itself.

FIGURE 13.1.

Do a little reading before taking the budgeting plunge.

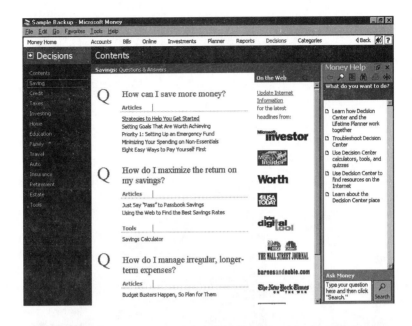

FIGURE 13.2.

Glance over these articles to look beyond the simple money issue.

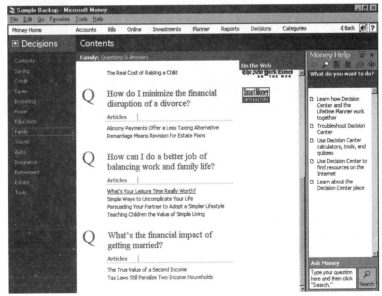

Take Money's Budget Self-Tests

Next up, see where you stand compared to others in your income bracket, take a look at your spending patterns, and administer a couple of Money 99's "self-tests" that clarify your own attitudes about money.

To Do: Compare Your Spending to Others

1. Open an Internet connection and click Savings, on the far left of the Decisions area, near the top.

2. Open the "Minimize Your Spending on Non-Essentials" article, and at the bottom left, under Web Link, click Budget Builder.

3. The Budget Builder Web page appears (see Figure 13.3). Enter your annual preincome tax income where indicated (don't use commas, decimals, or dollar signs).

FIGURE 13.3.

The Budget Builder shows what other people in your income bracket spend their money on.

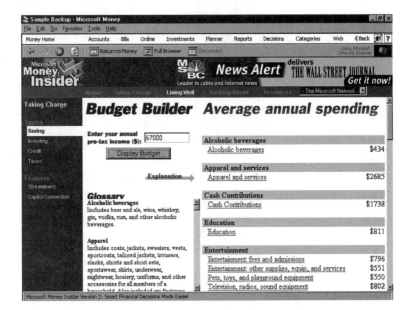

4. Click the Display Budget button.

5. To the right, you'll see a list of basic expenditures and an indication of what "the average American" in your income bracket spends on those expenses.

6. Click any expenditure to see a description of it.

Where I Am and Where I Want to Be

Next, take a look at three key reports:

- **What I Have and What I Owe**—Click Reports on the Navigation Bar, and select either report on the upper left. Then double-click any report option in the main screen as shown in Figure 13.4. These two reports help you take stock and get a good reading of your financial pulse. When you open one of these reports, view the data in different ways by clicking the Chart settings. Viewing your report as a pie, bar, or line chart can point out revealing trends.

FIGURE 13.4.

View your current financial data in report and chart form.

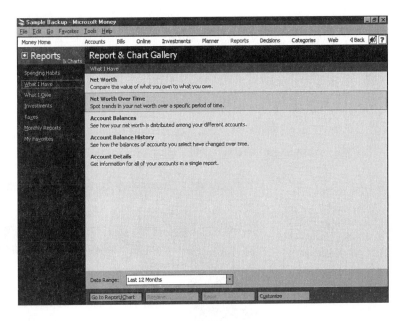

• **Spending Habits**—Click Spending Habits on the Reports drop-down list, and you'll see a list of specific reports for understanding your current financial situation (see Figure 13.5).

FIGURE 13.5.

Read the Spending Habits Reports for some enlightenment about where your money goes.

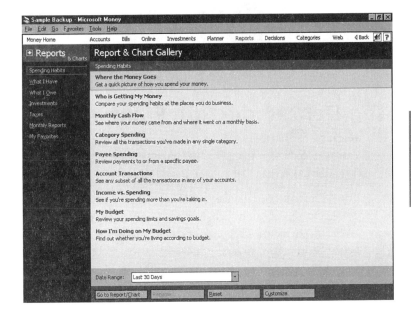

13

You can begin making a plan by using the Savings Calculator. You can set up a savings goal and see what it takes to meet it.

To Do: Starting a Plan with the Savings Calculator

1. From the Decisions Center, click Tools at the bottom of the list of options on the left side of the screen.

2. Under Calculators, click The Savings Calculator.

3. Answer the onscreen questions, as shown in Figure 13.6.

FIGURE 13.6.

The Savings Calculator helps determine how much you can realistically save.

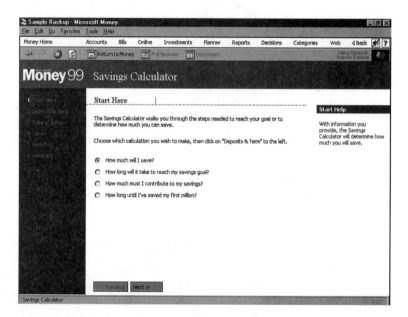

The Debt Reduction Planner

Because the Budget Planner requires data from the Debt Reduction Planner, start with the Debt Reduction Planner. You learned a little bit about it in Hour 9, "Setting Up and Tracking Credit and Debit Cards."

The Debt Reduction Planner's aim is to show you that a debt-free life need not be a pipe dream, but that it can be achieved sooner than you think, with just a little maneuvering and extra payments. The genius behind the Debt Reduction Planner is based on the interaction between two sliders:

- One slider adjusts how much you want to pay every month.

- One slider sets up a one-time-only extra payment to jump-start your Debt-Free Plan.

By manipulating the sliders, you'll see that moving a few dollars in any direction can make such a difference in how soon your debts are paid off.

To Do: Use the Debt Reduction Planner

1. Click Planner on the Navigation Bar, and choose Debt Reduction Planner.
2. A screen appears that is divided in half: The debts that are part of your Debt Reduction Plan are positioned near the top, and the debts you don't want to calculate in this method are below (see Figure 13.7).

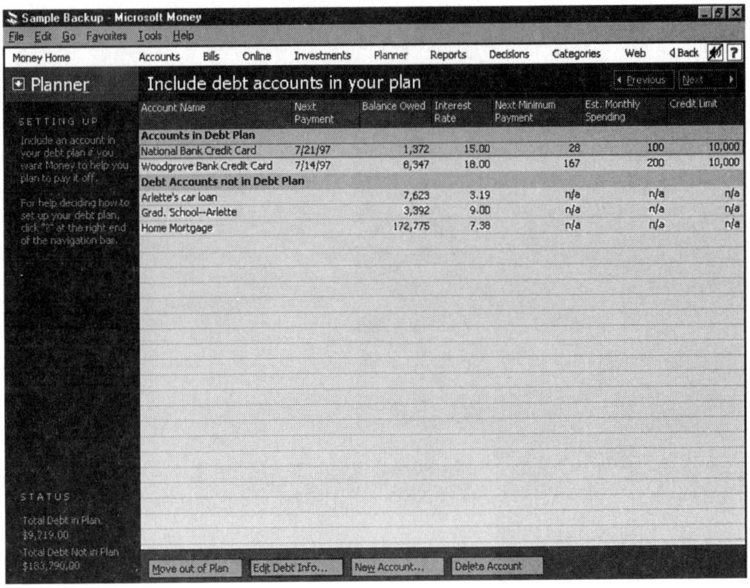

FIGURE 13.7.

Debts included in the Debt Reduction Plan are near the top of the screen. Those outside the plan are beneath.

The Debt Reduction Planner calculates how long it will take you to pay off any set of debts you want to include in the plan. Most often, these would include credit cards and short-term loans. Mortgage and second-trust deed loans are usually not placed in the Debt Reduction Planner unless you want to include them in your plan of being debt-free in the relatively near future.

13

3. To move a debt into the Debt Removal plan, click it in the Debt Accounts Not in Debt Plan area, and then click the Move Into Plan button, at the lower left of the screen.
4. Down near the bottom of the screen, you'll see the Edit Debt Info button for editing existing debt information on any loan (changing its interest rate, payment

▼   amount, or payment schedule) and for removing a debt from the payment plan,
        should you not want to include it in the Debt Reduction Planner's calculations.
        Click this button to make changes to a particular loan or debt.

    5. Click the New Account button to create a new account on the spot, if you need to.

    6. When you've added all the debts to the Debt Reduction Planner that you care to,
       click the Next button, in the upper-right corner. The Define Your Payment Plan
       screen appears (see Figure 13.8).

FIGURE 13.8.

*Using these two slid-
ers, set a regular pay-
ment schedule with a
goal.*

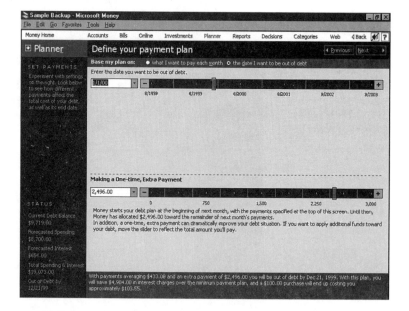

    7. Pick the type of data you want to adjust with the slider. At the very top of the
       screen, you'll see the Base My Plan On area.

        • If you want to move the slider to increase or decrease your monthly pay-
          ments, (and see how the payment amount affects when you'll be debt free)
          then click What I Want to Pay Each Month above the first slider.

        • If you want slider movement to adjust your debt-free date (and by doing so,
          to see what changing the data does to your monthly payment), then click The
          Date I Want to Be Out of Debt.

    8. As you move the slider, keep your eye on the number text box on the left, next to
▼   the slider. It changes with your movements of the slider.

▼ 9. Notice also that you can abandon the slider altogether, and instead type in a payment amount. Click the other button at the top of the screen, and, in the same number text box, type in a debt-free goal date. Keep clicking the buttons back and forth, comparing how changing one value affects the other.

10. At the bottom of the screen, the effects of your changes are reported in a blue box (see Figure 13.9). Notice how moving the slider affects your payment amounts and debt-free date.

FIGURE 13.9.

Adjust the sliders, and the budget calculations below are altered as well.

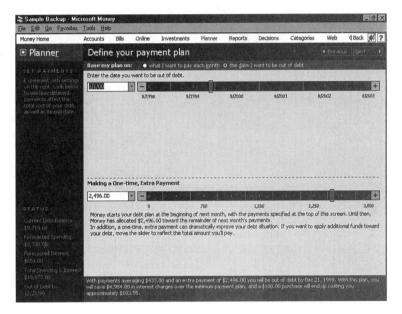

11. The slider at the bottom of the screen adds this factor to the mix: *What would happen if you made a one-time-only extra payment, to jump-start the payoff process?* Use this lower slider to increase or decrease the amount of your extra payment. You'll be amazed at how much this single, one-time extra payment affects your debt-free date.

12. After using the sliders to set your extra payment amounts, click Next to move to the next screen. The View Your Debt Plan chart appears showing the name and amount of each debt in your plan (see Figure 13.10). The chart moves through time from left to right, ending on the day you've mailed in your last credit card payment.

▼ ment.

13

FIGURE 13.10.

This timeline should steadily decrease. It shows your debt level diminishing over time.

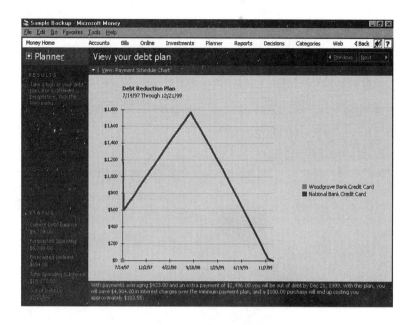

13. Click <u>N</u>ext to see the Goodbye Debt screen, which shows the current status of the debts in your plan.

Because the Budget Planner needs to incorporate your Debt Reduction Plan into the budget, you are now ready to run the Budget Planner.

Making a Budget

To begin making a budget in Money 99, it's a good idea to have an idea of what most of your expenses are on a monthly basis, so you can know what to cut and what to add.

To begin Money's Budget Planner, click Planner on the Navigation Bar and select Budget Planner, near the bottom. Click Income in the options list at the left side of the screen. The Where Does Your Income Come From? page appears (see Figure 13.11).

Including Income Sources in Your Budget

You'll see a list of your regular income sources. Money is ready to process these as part of your budget. In this budget page, you are prompted to list any sources of income you've neglected to tell Money about thus far. That's because Money wants to know all your sources of income to get an accurate picture of your budget. At this page, you can add income you receive regularly or occasionally. Please note as well that you'll be making Money aware of income sources for each income category.

FIGURE 13.11.

*Money's Budget
Planner first looks at
your income sources.*

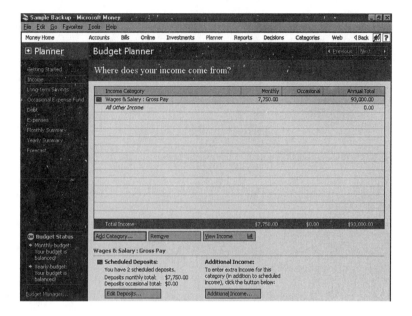

Now if you want to add a new income source that's *part of this category* (in the example shown here, the only category is Wages & Salary: Gross Pay), just click the Additional Income button at the bottom of the screen (see Figure 13.12). Here are two reasons you might need to add a new income source at this time:

- You just remember that you get a bonus from work every Christmas.
- There is a job you expect to have for at least part of this year in addition to your current job that's already listed.

Momentarily, you'll see how to add an income source from different categories, such as stock dividends or royalties.

To see more details about an income source that appears in this Budget list, click once on any income source in your list, and then click the View Income button.

13

FIGURE 13.12.

You have an opportunity to add income to this income category, if you think you've left something out.

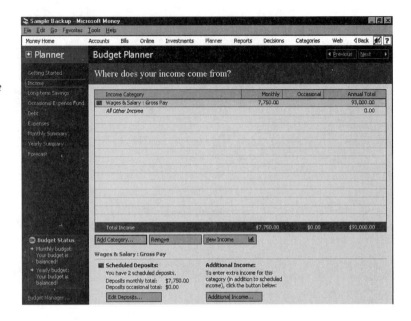

To Do: Including Additional Income in Your Budget

When you click the Additional Income button, you are adding a *dollar amount* to the yearly total that appears in the income list under Annual Total. You won't be prompted to label or identify a source. Money is not now interested in how or when they are dispersed. For the purposes of this budget, only the total amounts are considered.

To add a dollar amount to your yearly income used by your budget, do the following:

1. Click the Additional Income button.. The Customize Income dialog box appears. (see Figure 13.13).

FIGURE 13.13.

If you receive income at times other than once a month, use the Customize Income dialog box to make the Budget Planner aware of these.

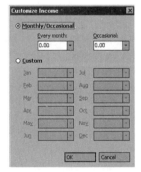

▼   2. If this sum you want to include is monthly, click the Every Month text box, under
      Monthly/Occasional, and type in an amount. Don't forget you can click the down-
      facing arrow to use a calculator.

    3. If this extra sum is occasional, like a bonus or extra job performed, type the sum of
      these occasional earnings in the Occasional text box.

    4. If you receive supplemental income from a job that is regular but not monthly,
      click the Custom button. You'll see 12 text boxes for itemizing how much income
      is added each month (see Figure 13.14).

FIGURE 13.14.

*Use the Custom list for
typing in extra income
sources that change
from month to month.*

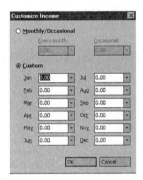

    5. Type in income amounts for any and all months during which this income source is
      received. The sum of all those entries is added to the Annual Total in the main list.

▲   6. Click OK to finalize your additional income adjustment.

> Take care in using the Additional Income button to add income sources.
> Because there is no way to describe details about these extra income
> sources, they won't be categorized well in budget reports.

Adding a Category

13

If an overlooked income category suddenly occurs to you, use the Add Category button
at the lower left of the screen to create a new one. The Category Wizard appears, prompting you to select a category to add to your budget income sources.

However, you won't be taken all the way through the Category Wizard. After selecting a
category, you are returned to the budget screen, and the category you chose to add is
identified at the bottom of the budget screen (see Figure 13.15). In the example shown
here, the category is Investment Income: Interest.

FIGURE 13.15.

Creating a new income category "on-the-fly" during the budget process.

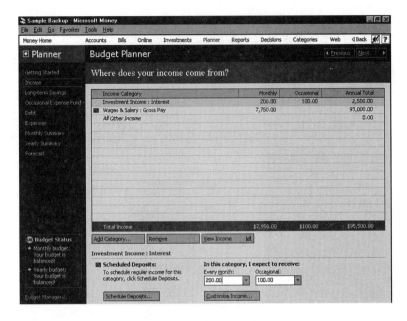

Under your new category title (in this example, Investment Income: Interest), you see four ways to add income from this category to your income:

- **Schedule Deposits**—Click the Schedule Deposits button at the bottom left of the screen to schedule regular deposits from this income source (see Figure 13.16). (You'll be using the same Create New Scheduled Deposit Wizard that was covered in Hour 11, "Paychecks, Bills, and Other Recurring Transactions".) This process adds the new category and deposit to all your regularly scheduled transactions. You'll see it later if you click Bills on the Navigation Bar.

- **In this Category I Expect to Receive: Every Month**—Click the Every Month text box at the bottom of the screen to type in a monthly income amount for this new category. It appears in your budget without further ado.

- **In this Category I Expect to Receive: Occasional**—Click the Occasional text box at the bottom of the screen to type in a non-regular income amount, perhaps something you receive once or twice a year, from this new category you are just creating. Remember, the category is identified right above these two numeric text boxes.

- **Customize Income**—Click the Customize Income button for scheduled (but not monthly) deposits for this income source. You'll see a dialog box allowing you to type in an income amount for each month of the year, as shown previously in Figure 13.14.

FIGURE 13.16.

You can let Budget Planner know about a new scheduled deposit, if you need to.

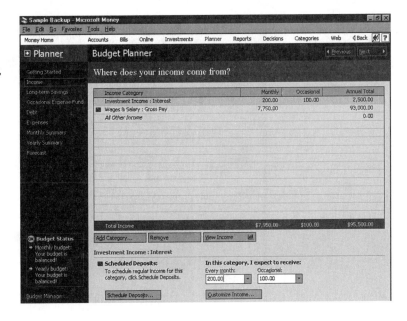

After you click OK to finalize your new income source category, it appears in the Budget Income list with the others. If you want to remove any income source from your budget list, click the Remove button at the center of the Budget screen.

If an income source is "iffy," not certain, don't include it in your budget. A budget is for continuity and reliability. It might be best to err on the side of caution and not include an income source you aren't sure about.

Including Savings in Your Budget Plan

When you've finished including all income sources you want to use with your Money 99 budget, click Next. The What Do You Put into Long-Term Savings? screen appears (see Figure 13.17).

Here you'll see a list of all your contributions to some sort of long-term savings account, including investment and retirement accounts. All the accounts you created to track your pension contributions, mutual funds, and long-term savings should be listed here.

If one is missing, click the New Contribution button, and the New Contribution Wizard appears (see Figure 13.18). This wizard does not create a new account, but rather lets you record a new deduction from your paycheck (or checking account) to a particular long term savings account that *already exists*.

13

FIGURE 13.17.

The Budget Planner calculates all your long-term savings into its recommendations.

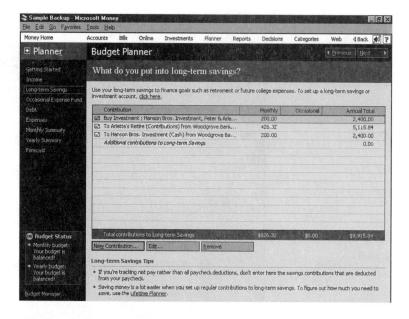

FIGURE 13.18.

Click New Contribution to set aside more savings from an existing account or paycheck.

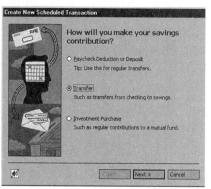

To create a new long-term savings account that would appear on this list, such as a new mutual fund, investment, or pension account, click the phrase "Click Here" at the top of the screen (see Figure 13.19).

FIGURE 13.19.

Click "Click Here" to create a new long-term savings account, rather than set up a new deduction from an existing one.

Click Here ———

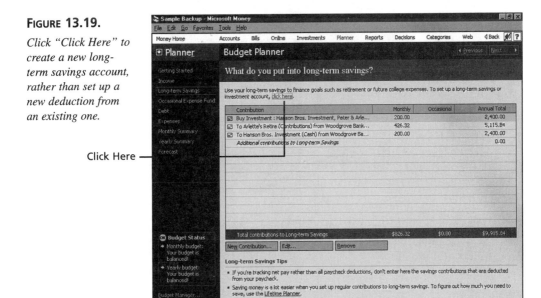

Editing Long-Term Saving Source Accounts

This Contributions list doesn't only show the accounts that *receive* these contributions, but also names the accounts (or paychecks) that the contributions originate *from*, as you can see from this example "from Woodgrove Bank Checking."

To edit the amount of a contribution or change the account that the contribution originates *from,* click the Edit button at the lower part of the screen.

Depending on the type of contribution you are editing, you can change the deduction from your paycheck or change the amount transferred from your checking account to a particular long-term investment account.

Taking the Longer View

To set up a thorough, long-term savings plan that works with life's major events, click Lifetime Planner, at the bottom left of the What Do You Put into Long-Term Savings? screen. You'll see the Lifetime Planner, as shown in Figure 13.20. The Lifetime Planner is covered in Hour 14, "Long-Term Planning and Goals."

13

FIGURE 13.20.

The Budget Planner has a link to the Lifetime Planner.

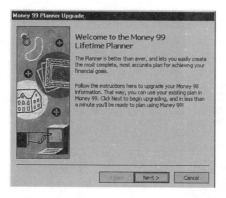

When you are finished finalizing your long-term savings contributions settings, click Next to continue. The What Do You Set Aside for Occasional Expenses? screen appears (see Figure 13.21).

FIGURE 13.21.

The Budget Planner wants you to consider putting more aside for Occasional Expenses.

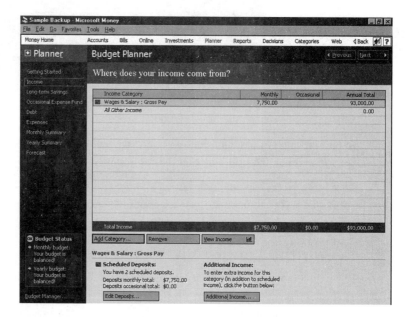

Setting Aside Money for Occasional Expenses

If you'll remember, when you set up an account, you're given an opportunity to specify an account's purpose. One choice is to set aside the money in this account for *Occasional Expenses*. Now any money you've set aside using this option for Occasional Expenses shows up here, in the What Do You Set Aside for Occasional Expenses? List, as shown previously in Figure 13.21.

Add to the amount you set aside for Occasional Expenses by clicking the New Contribution button. Change your contribution in one of two ways:

- *Deduct* an additional amount from your paycheck to an account set aside for Occasional Expenses.
- *Transfer* an amount from your checking account to a special account set aside for Occasional Expenses.

> Occasional Expenses includes events like car or home repairs or semi-regular vacations.

When you are finished reviewing or making changes to your contributions to Occasional Expenses, click Next to move on to the **Review Your Debts and Loans** page, as shown in Figure 13.22.

FIGURE 13.22.

You get one last chance to review your debts and loans for your budget.

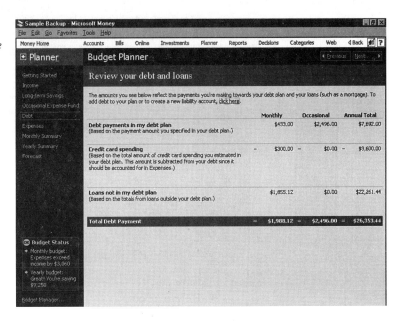

Including Debts and Loans in Your Budget

This page shows monthly, occasional, and annual payments you make to debts that you've included in your debt plan.

Credit card payments are shown broken down the same way, on a separate line.

You'll also see payments made to loans you opted not to include in your payment plan. Most often, only amortized loans such as mortgages and long-term college loans are not included in your debt plan.

If you realize there are certain debts you now want to include in your debt plan, do the following:

To Do: Adding a Debt to Your Budget

1. Click Planner on the Navigation Bar, then select Debt Reduction Planner.

2. Click a debt that is now not included in your plan.

3. Click the Move Into Plan button.

4. Return to your budget by clicking the Back button at the upper right of the screen, and the numbers now show that you've moved that particular debt into your plan.

Viewing Your Expenses

When you're finished adjusting and reviewing your debts and loans, click Next, and you'll see the How Do You Spend Your Money? screen, as shown in Figure 13.23.

FIGURE 13.23.

Before finishing up the budget, you can see all your expenses in one list.

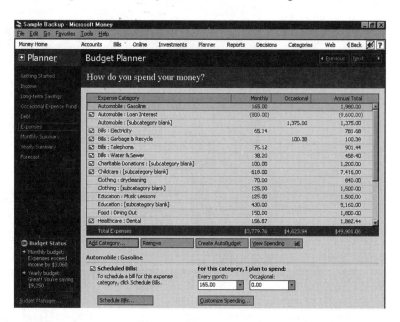

The How Do You Spend Your Money? screen shows all your monthly, occasional and annual expenses broken down into categories, in one big list. You now have one more opportunity to make additional changes to your budget. You'll be using the same tools you learned about during this hour. You can

- Add an expense category.

- Adjust and schedule bill payments (this was covered in Hour 11).

- Add spending amounts by filling in the amount text boxes at the bottom of the screen.

- Click the Customize Spending button at the bottom of the screen to type in a custom spending pattern that changes from month to month or only occurs on certain months of the year.

To see your spending listed in more detail, click the View Spending button at the right of the screen.

Creating an AutoBudget

Still working with the **How Do You Spend Your Money?** screen of the Budget Planner, click the Create AutoBudget button to have Money create a quick budget based on spending categories you've already set up. AutoBudget examines trends in recent expense categories and sets suggested monthly spending amounts for each category.

The AutoBudget list appears. You'll see categories not yet in your budget that Money is now suggesting you move there, complete with suggested monthly spending amounts.

> If this AutoBudget list includes an expense that is not regular, like a one-time car repair, make sure you uncheck that expense, which tells Money *not* to include that irregular expense in your budget. That's because you need not budget for something that will probably only occur once.

Extra Money?

When you are happy with how your spending looks and you feel all categories are accounted for, then click the Next button, and you'll see the Monthly Summary.

Look over the Monthly Summary, especially the heading: Will My Monthly Budget Work? You'll see how much is left over for spending, and notice also that the money you've specified for saving is *not* included in the Total Left Over area (marked with a blue line). One of Money 99's budgeting tricks is to pull money for savings aside, before you begin to think of that sum as spending money.

The Monthly Summary points out how much money per month is *not* designated for expenditures. If non-budgeted income is available, you have two options for how to assign it:

13

- Spend the money (keep it unassigned in your checking account).
- Set it aside in your Occasional Expense account by clicking Save It in My Occasional Expense Fund.

One big advantage of setting up a budget is taking the time to set up an accurate picture of occasional expenses, things that only occur a few times a year. These are easy to leave out of your monthly income and expense cycle.

Adjusting Savings Amounts

As mentioned, Money's trick is to take the extra amount and put it in an Occasional Expense fund. However, if the sum left over appears too large or two small, you have two options:

- If you see you have enough left over to put more into savings, then open your checking account and schedule a heftier transfer of money into savings or have a bigger chunk taken out of your paycheck for savings.
- Likewise, if this budget constraint leaves you a bit too short and you're thinking a bit bigger spending cushion is in order, then open the appropriate accounts and set aside a smaller amount for saving.

When you're finished viewing and adjusting the Monthly Summary, proceed to the Yearly Summary by clicking the Next button.

Your Yearly Summary (see Figure 13.24) tells a different story from the Monthly Summary, because some expenditures are not monthly, but can truly have an impact on your ability to budget. Likewise, income windfalls that occur only a few times per year can change your Yearly Summary drastically. Your budget status is recorded inside a blue line, as highlighted by the mouse in Figure 13.24. If needed, budgeting tips are listed in the lower half of the screen.

Looking Ahead

Finally, to pull more meaning out of this budget, click Next to view the Budget Forecast. Here's what you'll find:

- You'll see a bar chart (see Figure 13.25) representing the balance between your day-to-day account and your Occasional Expense account levels.

FIGURE 13.24.

The Yearly Budget Summary shows a more complete picture than month-to-month, especially if you have expenses and income that do not appear every month.

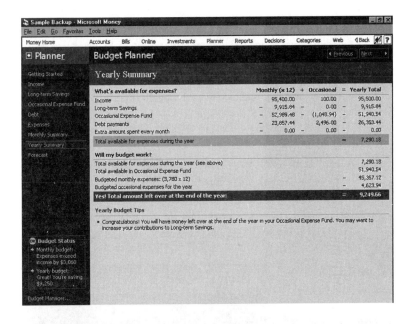

FIGURE 13.25

This bar chart shows day-to-day accounts at the top and Occasional Expense accounts at the bottom.

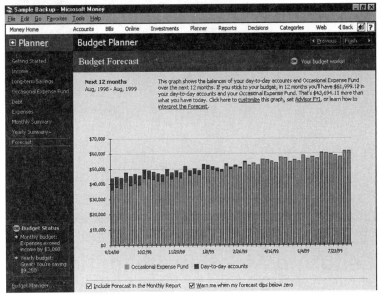

- Each bar on the chart represents one week. Double-click any bar to read details about that period's transactions.
- Above the Forecast chart is a paragraph outlining the next twelve month's financial predictions. Read it to see what's up for your next year.

13

Changing the Chart's Date Range

To change the scope of the chart, click the word Customize in the budget paragraph at the top of the Budget Forecast screen. You'll see the Rows & Columns tab. Click the Show Next drop-down list, and select a different data range for the chart. To change how many days are represented by each bar on the graph, click the Level of Detail drop-down list, which is below Show Next.

Staying Informed

To learn more about what interests you, click Advisor FYI (in that same paragraph where you can click Customize). The Choose Advisor FYI dialog box will appear. Here, you can read financial articles on any area of importance to you (see Figure 13.26), for example Reducing Debt or Budgeting. Now that you've been through the budgeting process, you'll have some idea of what issues are of interest to you.

FIGURE 13.26.

Use the FYI Advisor Alerts to stay informed on financial matters of interest to you.

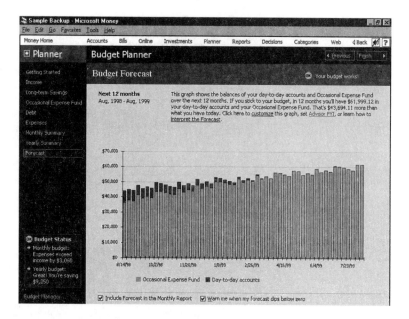

Reducing Monthly Obligations

Now that you've set up a budget with Money 99, it can be a challenge to stay on top of it. However, there are certain steps most people can take to reduce their monthly obligations, and Money has tools in the Decisions Center for helping you research the following:

- Switching high-interest credit cards for lower ones
- Changing auto and life-insurance policies
- Refinancing your mortgage or obtaining a debt-consolidating loan
- Making sure you get the best price and interest rate possible when purchasing a car

Answers to your Financial Questions

You can always obtain up-to-date answers to your financial questions with Ask the Experts.

To Do: Search "Ask The Experts"

1. With your Internet connection open, select Savings from the Decisions Center Welcome screen.

2. Click the Money Insider Web Page icon. The Money Insider Web page provides several financial resources worth exploring.

3. Click Ask The Experts.

4. At the far right, under Resources, click Answer Guide (see Figure 13.27).

FIGURE 13.27.

From the Money Insider Web Page, click Answer Guide, found under Resources.

13

5. Click the Search tab, facing sideways at the middle of the screen (see Figure 13.28).

FIGURE 13.28.

To type in a question or phrase for your search, click the Search Tab, which faces sideways.

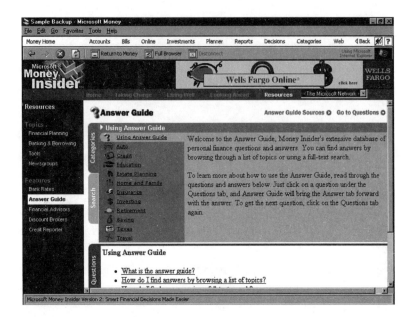

6. In the Search text box that appears, type in a phrase that describes what you want to learn more about.

Summary

Budgeting is more than walking through the Budget Planner. You need to have a goal in mind and a notion of your current financial state. Then you can avail yourself of Money 99's budgeting tools, such as the Savings Calculator, the Debt Reduction Planner and Budget Planner, as well as Money's FYI Advisor Updates.

Q&A

Q Should I just jump in and start walking through the Budget Planner?

A No. Spend some time thinking about goals and looking over your finances first.

Q Does it matter if I run the Budget Planner before I use the Debt Reduction Planner?

A Yes it does. The Budget Planner wants information from the Debt Reduction Planner, so deal with the debts first.

Q What does the Budget Planner really do for you?

A It creates an AutoBudget, which suggests saving and spending amounts, and helps determine if your financial plans are eventually going to place you in the red or the black. It also provides regular updates on how your Budget Plan is being carried out.

Q The Monthly and Yearly Summary Budget Reports pretty much tell you the same thing, right?

A Actually, no. There are expenses and income sources that do not arise every month. Money 99's budget tools take pains to include those sources and calculates them into your yearly budget.

13

HOUR 14

Long-Term Planning and Goals

In this hour, you learn how to use Microsoft Money's Lifetime Planner to create, view, and define strategies for achieving all your long-term financial goals. Use the Lifetime Planner for retirement, vacation budgeting, and child college tuition planning, as well as for any long-term budget planning. The Debt Reduction Planner can help you create a plan to rid yourself of debt, but first let's take a look at how you access the Lifetime Planner.

Viewing the Lifetime Planner

After you have created a plan, Money 99's Planner links all your own accounts together. These include all your savings and debt-reduction plans, budgets, investments, bills, and forecasts. When you make any changes, any accounts that are affected by the changes are automatically updated to keep them as up-to-date as possible. Again, only the data that is affected by your change is updated; no other data is altered in any way unless you modify the data yourself. The Lifetime Planner can do the following for you:

- The Lifetime Planner helps you create plans for buying a home, financing education college plans, and setting retirement goals.

- The Lifetime Planner analyzes all your current financial account information that you input and then creates a plan specific to your own finances. There are certain benchmarks that Money 99 uses when creating your plan, like cost of living increases, for instance.

- The Lifetime Planner makes automatic adjustments. You will always have the most up-to-date information about your finances because when you add or change any financial information, the Lifetime Planner automatically adjusts the information that pertains to your other accounts as well.

How The Lifetime Planner Is Organized

Money 99's Planner is organized into three parts; the Lifetime Planner—to plan for retirement and all other lifetime goals, the Debt Reduction Planner—to create a specific strategy for reducing your high-interest debt, and the Budget Planner—to keep your expenses under control by setting up a budget. You access the Lifetime Planner by selecting the Planner from the Navigation Bar, and then clicking Lifetime Planner (see Figures 14.1 and 14.2).

FIGURE 14.1.

You can access the Lifetime Planner, the Budget Planner, and the Debt Reduction Planner from this Planner screen.

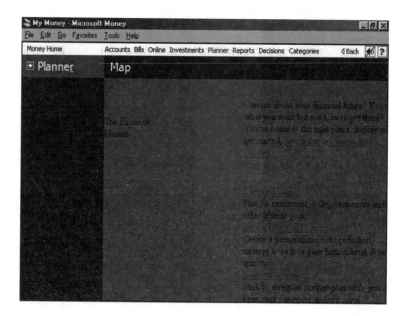

FIGURE 14.2.

The Lifetime Planner screen enables you to create plans for all your long-term goals.

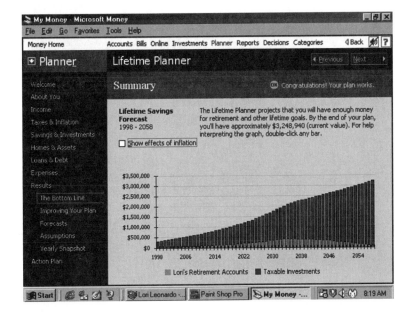

Telling Money About Yourself

To receive personalized financial advice, you need to tell Money 99 some information about yourself. When you start Money 99 for the first time, your Personal Profile appears asking questions for you to answer. You can also access and change your personal information at any time by choosing Tools, Personal Profile (see Figure 14.3).

> The questions include information like your name and age. The more accurately you answer the questions, the more accurately Money 99 is able to create a plan that is personalized to suit you.

When you are done answering the questions in your Personal Profile, click the Done Answering Questions button.

Now you are ready to create a Lifetime plan.

14

FIGURE 14.3.

You access the Personal Profile screen the first time you start Microsoft Money 99.

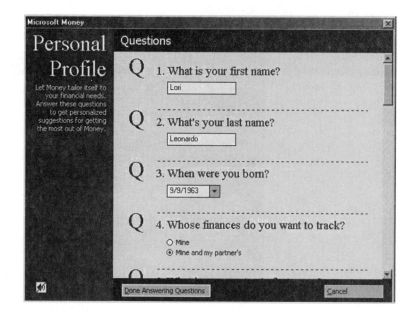

To Do: Create Your Plan for the First Time

▼ To Do

1. Click Planner on the Navigation Bar.

2. Click the Lifetime Planner, located on the right side of the screen.

3. Click Next in the upper-right corner.

4. Follow the instructions on the screen.

5. Then, click Next again, and continue to follow the instructions on the screen. On the last screen, Money 99 displays an Action Plan based on the information you have just entered (see Figure 14.4).

▲

Looking at Savings and Investments

The Planner's Savings and Investments Accounts area is where you enter all your long-term savings and investment accounts.

Let's take a look at how your accounts are grouped by Money 99:

- **Retirement accounts**—Accounts for all your tax-deferred accounts like your 401(k) plan or IRA.

- **Accounts for dependents**—Accounts that are in your dependent's name, such as your child's Education IRA or Education Money Market account.

FIGURE 14.4.

Money uses the Action Plan screen to show a Lifetime plan based on the information it has received from you.

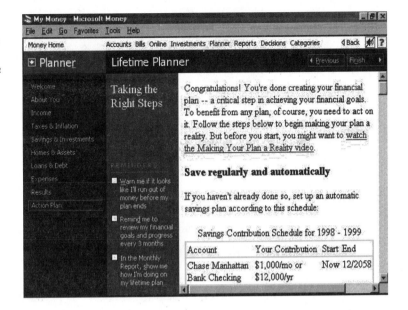

- **Taxable investment accounts**—Accounts for any of your taxable savings or investments.
- **Excluded accounts**—Accounts that you want to exclude from your plan.
- **Employee stock options**—Accounts for ESO grants you may receive from your employer. Any accounts you have already entered in the Account Register are listed here as well. You can also enter your accounts in the planner, and still add or edit your accounts in the Account Register.

Managing Profitable Accounts

Use Expected Returns in the Lifetime planner to plan out the rate of return you forecast for your savings in the future.

Enter both the rate of return you plan to receive before and after you retire.

Money 99 then helps you choose a rate based on these factors and produces a typical model portfolio:

- Highest return in a given year
- Lowest return in a given year
- Average return over investment period
- Typical model portfolio

14

You can pick a rate for before retirement and one for after retirement. You can also get more complicated by picking rates for different account groups for both before and after retirement. This choice is entirely up to you. The following section explains the steps you take to change the rate of return for a group of investments.

Projecting with Various Return Rates

To change the rate of return for a group of investments, you need to access the Expected Return function of the Lifetime Planner.

To Do: Expected Return Function

You can enter the percentage rate of return you expect each year for each account group listed in your Lifetime Planner. This feature is very helpful when you want to show your expected return rates for one or more of your account groups.

1. Click Planner on the Navigation Bar.

2. Click Lifetime Planner, located on the right side of the screen.

3. Click Savings & Investments, located on the left (pane) side of the screen.

4. Click Expected Return and then click Detailed.

5. Enter the percentage rate of return you expect each year for each account group listed (see Figure 14.5).

FIGURE 14.5.

This is the screen where you enter your rate of return that you expect for each account group listed.

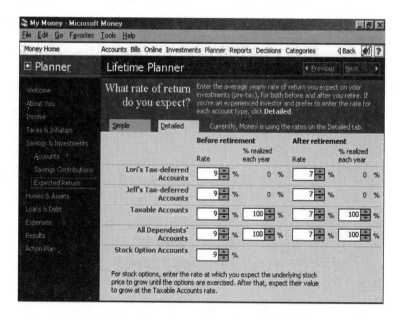

You need to pick rates of return applicable for each account group because you can have different investment time horizons or asset allocations for each of your account groups.

You can't choose different return rates for each account. You can only choose a different return rate for each account *group*, but not for each individual account in each account group.

If you do not know what applicable rate of return to choose, you can select the Simple tab. When you enter a rate, Money 99 displays information about each rate that you choose. Money 99 displays information like risk factors and time horizons, which help you determine an appropriate rate of return (see Figure 14.6).

Even small changes in your rate of return affect your cumulative savings largely due to compounded returns over time.

FIGURE 14.6.

You can try out different rates of return from this screen and see how each one affects your long-range plan.

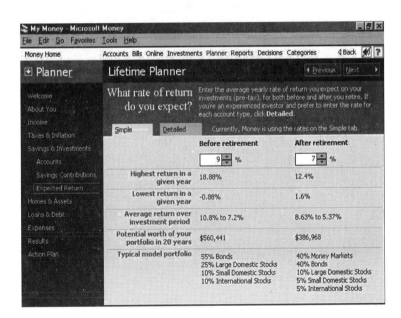

14

Adding a New Investment Account

If you choose to add a new investment account from the Planner, there are four simple steps you take.

To Do: Adding a New Investment Account

1. Select Planner from the Navigation Bar.
2. Click Lifetime Planner on the right side of the screen.
3. Click Savings & Investments, on the left (pane) side of the screen.
4. Click Accounts in the left pane.
5. Click New Account at the bottom of the screen. Now just follow the instructions you see on the screen (see Figure 14.7).

FIGURE 14.7.

Add a new investment account in Money 99's Planner.

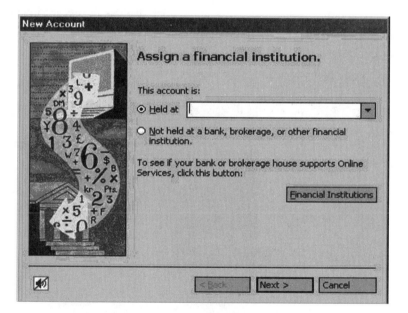

Modifying an Account via the Lifetime Planner

Modifying an account in the Lifetime Planner is similar to adding a brand new account.

For example, if you want to convert your IRA to a Roth IRA, you can modify the type of account at any time. Any information that you modify that affects another area of the plan is modified as well.

Again, select Planner from the Navigation Bar and follow these steps:

To Do: Modifying an Account

1. Click the Lifetime Planner.

2. Click Savings & Investments.

3. Click Accounts located on the left pane.

4. Click the account you want to modify.

5. Click Edit.

6. Select what you want to change from the list that appears.

7. Then, just follow the instructions on the screen (see Figure 14.8).

FIGURE 14.8.

In the Edit Account screen, you modify an existing investment account in Money 99's Planner.

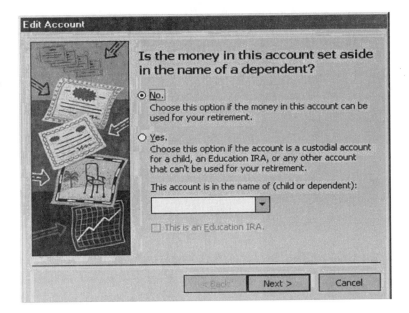

Edit Account

Is the money in this account set aside in the name of a dependent?

○ No.
Choose this option if the money in this account can be used for your retirement.

○ Yes.
Choose this option if the account is a custodial account for a child, an Education IRA, or any other account that can't be used for your retirement.

This account is in the name of (child or dependent):

☐ This is an Education IRA.

< Back   Next >   Cancel

Moving an Account to a New Group

You need to tell Money 99 which accounts are part of your budget and long-term plan, by choosing the appropriate account groups. If you can't find an account group that matches exactly with what you want, you should pick the one that is the closest. Money 99's account groups are

- **Retirement Plans**—This is for tax-deferred accounts, for example, 401 Ks and IRAs.

14

- **Long-Term Savings and Investments**—This is for major purchases in one or more years in the future, for example, a down payment for a home or a new car.
- **Short-Term Savings**—This is for bills and purchases that will happen within a year, for example, car insurance and your savings of three to six months living expenses.
- **Spending Money**—This is for daily expenses, which is your primary checking account. Of course, you can have as many Spending Money accounts as you want.
- **Exclude from Savings Plan**—This is for money that will not be used to finance your personal goals, for example, a donation to a charity.

Now that you know about Money 99's account groups, how do you move an account from one group to another? Here is an example of how to move one account into the Retirement Account group.

To Do: Moving an Account to Another Account Group

1. Click Planner on the Navigation Bar.
2. Click The Lifetime Planner.
3. Click Savings & Investments.
4. Click Accounts.
5. Click the investment account you want to move.
6. Right-click the account, and then click Go To Details.
7. Select Retirement account. You can check the account in the Savings & Investments area of the Lifetime Planner. You should now see it listed under the Retirement Accounts group.

You place your account in the Retirement Accounts group if you plan to use this money in retirement only and not for other plans.

You can only move tax-deferred investment accounts to Retirement Accounts. That means you can't move any checking or savings accounts.

Planning a Long Range Goal

Money 99's Financial Planner enables you to actually plan for long-range goals. You can use Money 99 not only to keep track of your current finances, but to help you forecast future plans as well.

The Lifetime Planner

After you create your plan, the Lifetime Planner lets you know what you need to do now to begin your long-range plan. As long as you keep your accounts up-to-date, the Lifetime Planner will forecast your plan accurately and will take your plan effectively into the future.

> You should think about checking your plan every three months or so just to make sure you are right on track. Of course when something changes in your financial picture, you should update your plan as necessary.
>
> You can always check results from a big event in your Lifetime Planner to see how it affects your financial outlook. You can always choose to exclude it from your plan until a later time as well.

Using the Lifetime Planner to Create "What Ifs?"

What Ifs are beneficial to use for long-range projections like taking vacations or planning for your child's college education without affecting your real long-range plans. You use What Ifs when you just want to take a look at long-range projections that you may be thinking about and want to see how they affect your plan.

To use Planner's What Ifs, you need to access the Lifetime Planner, which is again found under the Planner menu on the Navigation Bar.

To Do: Using Planner's What Ifs

1. Click the Lifetime Planner.
2. Click the name of the place or event that you want to modify. You'll find this on the left (pane) side of the screen.
3. Now you can enter the information you want to try out. You can see if you can afford to take a European vacation by clicking on Expenses in the left pane (see Figure 14.9).

14

FIGURE 14.9.

Enter and try out expenses to see how they affect your long-range plan.

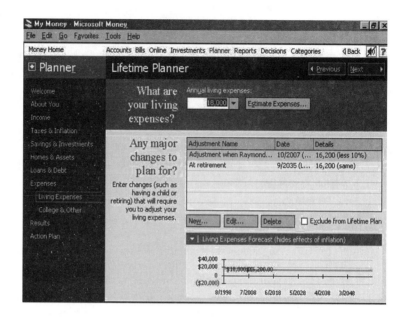

4. Just click College & Other and enter your vacation expense (see Figure 14.10).

FIGURE 14.10.

Enter your expense event here.

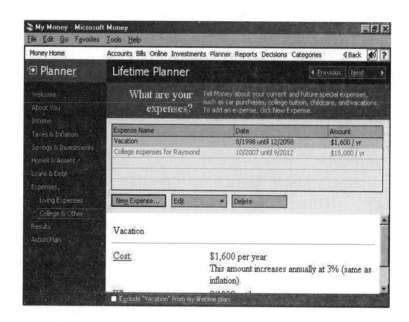

5. Click Results on the left (pane) side of the screen. Money 99 shows you the results (see Figure 14.11).

FIGURE 14.11.

Money 99 displays your results from adding a new expense to your plan.

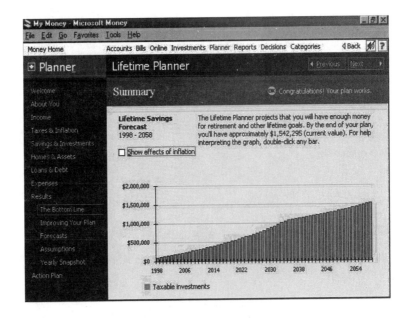

6. Return to step 4 where you added your expense and highlight the event you just added, then check E<u>x</u>clude from My Lifetime Plan.

7. Click Results again and notice the differences in your plan with and without the added expense (see Figure 14.12).

FIGURE 14.12.

Money 99 displays your results from excluding this new expense to your plan.

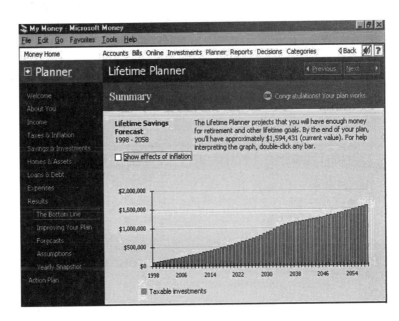

14

▼ If you don't like the result with your added expense, but still want to take a vacation, Money 99 gives you ideas on how to adjust other areas of your long-range plan. You just need to click Action Plan in the left (pane) side of the screen (see Figure 14.13).

FIGURE 14.13.

Money 99 gives you ideas on how to adjust other areas of your long-range plan.

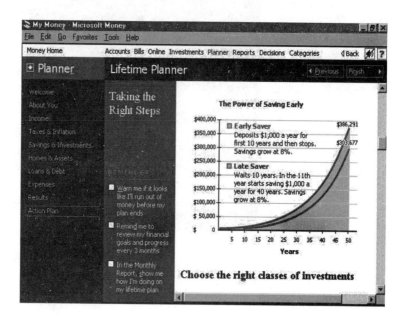

You can leave events that you excluded from your lifetime plan as they are, and then decide to incorporate the event into your plan. Just return to step 4 and uncheck that
▲ option to include the event in your long-range plan.

More Ways to Learn About Your Plan

After you have entered all your financial information in Money 99, you can find out ways to learn more about your financial picture.

Identifying Problems in Your Plan

The Improving Your Plan area in the Lifetime Planner is where you can find out about ways to improve your plan. When you use this area, you can view an analysis of your plan. You can read about ways to learn about any problems in your plan. Money 99 also has many links related to financial areas that might affect your plan.

To Do: Access the Improving Your Plan Area

1. Select Planner from the Navigation Bar.
2. Click the Lifetime Planner.

3. Click Results.

4. Click Improving Your Plan.

5. Just follow the onscreen instructions (see Figure 14.14).

> Suggestions that you find in Improving Your Plan are automatically adjusted anytime you make any additions or modifications to your plan.

FIGURE 14.14.

Money 99 gives you ideas on how to improve your long-range plans.

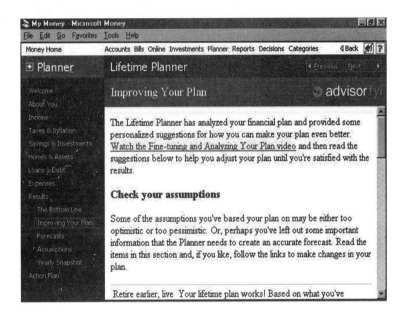

> You don't need to be exact when entering all the details. If you don't know something, you can estimate as best as you can, Your forecasts will give you a general idea, and then you can always go back later and fill in more details.

The Bottom Line

The Bottom Line Results area shows you if you have enough savings to achieve all the goals in your financial plan.

Money 99 and the Lifetime Planner integrate everything in your forecast, so as you update your accounts, your forecast is then updated automatically.

14

To view your bottom-line forecast, go to the Lifetime Planner (by now you should know it is off the Planner menu in the Navigation Bar).

To Do: Viewing Your Bottom-Line Forecast

1. When you are in the Lifetime Planner, click Results.
2. Then click Forecasts.
3. Select Will I Have Enough Money for Retirement?
4. Follow the onscreen information (see Figure 14.15).

If for any reason your chart is in the negative, check out the Improve Your Plan area that was discussed in the previous section.

It is normal for the values to be small the further away you are from retirement. The values will, of course, increase the closer you are to retirement.

Check the Bottom Line area often to see if you are still staying on track to achieving your long-range goals.

FIGURE 14.15.

The Bottom Line area allows you to check to see if are staying on track with your long-range plans.

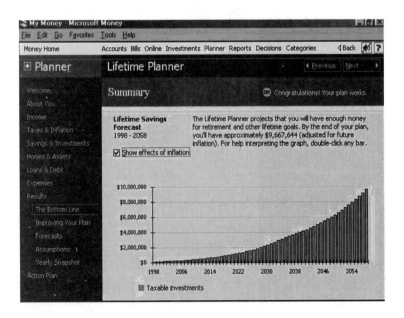

Assumptions

In the Assumptions area, you can see about items you entered when you created a Lifetime Plan for the first time. It shows you the assumptions about you that make up the basis for your plan.

This area is updated automatically as you change any of your input variables and details. You can check that all the assumptions about you are accurate assumptions, and that they are as complete as possible.

Anything you have entered in the Lifetime Planner can be changed by going to the appropriate area in the Lifetime Planner. If you want, for example, you can change the age at which you will retire.

To Do: Changing Your Retirement Age

1. Go to the Lifetime Planner.

2. Click Assumptions.

3. Select About You to change your retirement age (see Figure 14.16).

Money 99 makes assumptions that you do not input yourself. To learn more information about these assumptions, choose Tools from the menu bar and click Microsoft on the Web, then select the Microsoft Money Home Page.

FIGURE 14.16.

You can check that all the assumptions about you in the Lifetime Planner are accurate assumptions.

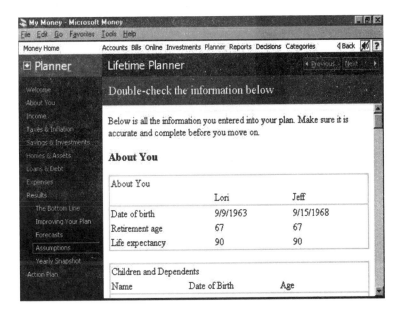

14

Snapshots

In the Yearly Snapshot area, you analyze your plan just for one year. You can see the whole picture for an upcoming year or for one particular part of your plan. Again, with Money 99 your accounts are automatically updated when your make any additions or changes in your plan. The Yearly Snapshot always reflects these changes in your plan as well.

You should be getting the hang of this by now, just go to the Planner and follow these steps.

To Do: Viewing my Yearly Snapshot

1. Click the Lifetime Planner.

2. Click Results.

3. Select Yearly Snapshot.

4. Choose the year that you would like information on at the top of the screen (see Figure 14.17).

> To see the details of a particular part of a graph, double-click that part of a graph.

FIGURE 14.17.

In the Yearly Snapshot screen, you analyze your plan just for one year at a time.

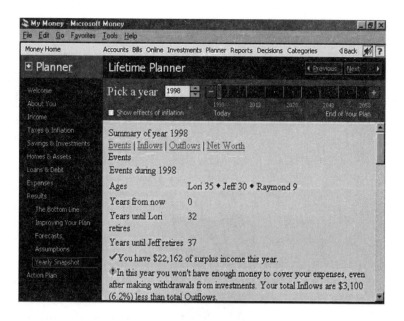

The Action Plan

You have already seen how the Action Plan works in other sections of this chapter. The Action Plan helps you begin your new long-range plan. Again, Money 99 automatically updates your Action Plan as you make any additions or changes to your plan. This keeps you right on track with your long-term goals. Use this area to see Money 99's ideas for achieving all your financial goals (refer to Figures 14.4 and 14.13).

Viewing Forecasts that Include Your Goals

Viewing Forecasts in the Lifetime Planner enables you to see any forecasted events that you select. Events like forecasted future salary and forecasted future income. These forecasts are used in the following examples.

To Do: Viewing Forecasts

1. Click the Lifetime Planner.
2. Click Results.
3. Click Forecasts.
4. Select How Will My Salary Change over Time? (see Figure 14.18).

You can forecast how your yearly raises and inflation will change your forecasted future salary earnings throughout your life.

After you retire, any salary you have entered from a part-time job is not included here. It is included, however, in your total retirement income.

Another example of forecasting future events is to forecast your future income.

To Do: Forecasting Your Future Income

1. Click the Lifetime Planner.
2. Click Results.
3. Click Forecasts.
4. Select What Income Will I Receive? (see Figure 14.19).

14

FIGURE **14.18.**

In the Forecasts screen, you can forecast future events like future salary.

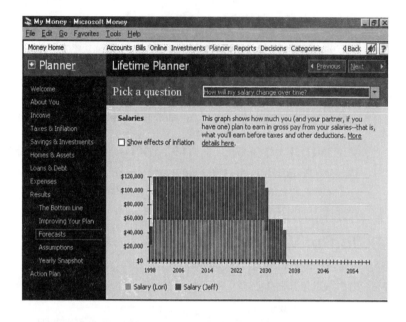

FIGURE **14.19.**

You can forecast future events like future income in the Forecasts screen.

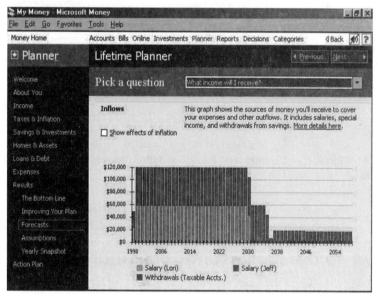

You can also print a complete financial plan at this time from the Lifetime Planner.

To Do: Printing Your Complete Financial Plan

1. Go to the Lifetime Planner.

2. Choose File, Print.

3. Click the Complete Financial Plan option.

4. Click OK.

HIDE OR SHOW INFLATION?

Throughout the Financial Planner, you will find charts that let you see your finances in two different ways: Hide the effects of inflation and Show the effects of inflation. The differences between them and how they affect your plan include:

Hide the effects of inflation—This reflects the current actual value of an item. This number is helpful when looking at the values of similar items in your financial plan that occur in different years. This is how you view the real cost of an item.

Show the effects of inflation—This reflects an annual 3 1/2% inflation in addition to the actual value of an item. Use this view to see how your budgeted figures will be changed by inflation. If you change the estimated annual inflation rate in the Lifetime Planner's Taxes & Inflation area, this view will reflect that new rate of inflation.

Using the Decision Centers

Money 99's Decision Center gives you good advice on financial management planning. The Decision Center, with hundreds of articles, is a good place to go when finding out about all your basic information on saving and planning for the future, investing, buying a home, financing your car, retirement planning, and so on.

The Decision Center and the Lifetime Planner work together by offering the latest advice and helping you make the estimates in your Lifetime Planner much more accurate.

14

The Decision Center tools help you calculate financial estimates which you will see later in this section. You can also use the Decision Center tools to perform similar calculations to the Lifetime Planner that are short-term, like seeing how long it would take you to save $5,000. There are many areas in the Decision Center that you can look at, but for now check out Saving, Auto, and Tools.

Savings

You can use Money 99's Decision Center to check out articles and tools that could help you save more money and make more informed financial decisions.

To Do: Opening the Savings Area of the Decision Center

1. Click Decisions from the Navigation Bar.
2. Select Saving on the left pane (see Figure 14.20).

FIGURE 14.20.

You use Money 99's Decision Center to check out articles and tools that could help you save more money.

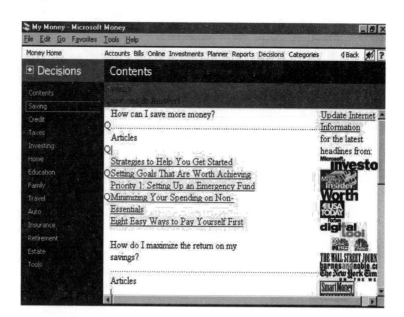

Articles on how to save more money are underlined in blue. Just click the specific link to read that article. For example, Figure 14.21 shows Eight Easy Ways to Pay Yourself First.

Automobile

How do you find the right car? The Automobile area of the Decision Center can answer that question for you. You can find out about new or used vehicles as well as learn some good test driving tips. This section also helps you in deciding whether you should lease or buy a car. To access the Auto section of the Decision Center, just go to the Decision Center area and click Auto.

Calculator Tools and Worksheets

The calculators in the Decision Center really help you make specific financial decisions.

FIGURE 14.21.

The Decision Center screen contains articles like this one: Eight Easy Ways to Pay Yourself First.

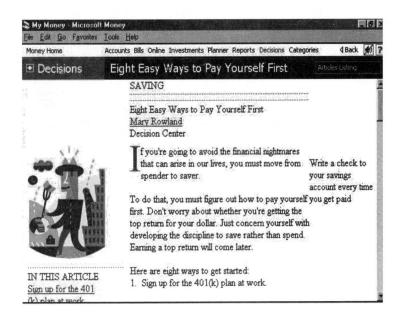

To Do: Viewing Money 99's Calculators

1. Click Decisions from the Navigation Bar.
2. Click Tools in the left (pane) side of the screen.

   Now you should see a list of calculators beginning with the Buy vs. Rent Calculator.

14

3. For now, click the Retirement Income Calculator.

4. Then click Retirement Years. You can choose and compare how your retirement would look if you retire at 70 instead of 65. Compare the difference.

> By now you have noticed items in blue and gray text. Gray items have been selected by you to exclude from your lifetime plan. Blue items have an end date that has passed already.

Summary

In this past hour, you learned about how to use Microsoft Money's Lifetime Planner to create, view, and define strategies for achieving all your long-term financial goals. You can use the Lifetime Planner for college tuition planning, retirement planning, vacation budgeting, and for any long-range financial planning. After you have created a plan, Money 99's Planner links all your accounts together. These include all your savings and debt-reduction plans, budgets, investments, bills, and forecasts. When you make any changes, all your accounts are automatically updated to keep them as up-to-date as possible.

Q&A

Q Why would I want to exclude an account in my plan?

A You should exclude any accounts that do not directly affect your financial plans. For example, you may have accounts you want to set up that keep track of charitable trusts, or someone else's funds that do not affect your financial plans directly.

Q How are my Lifetime Planner accounts related to my other accounts in Money?

A Your Lifetime Planner accounts and your other accounts in Money 99 are one and the same. Keep in mind, however, that you can only enter estimated values and create future forecasts in the Lifetime Planner.

Q What if I don't track my investments very well?

A You can still have a valid financial plan without having to balance all your accounts. Enter estimated values for your account balances. Be sure to update your estimates from time to time.

Q What if my kids have money in a UTMA or Education IRA?

A You can earmark the funds to show that your children own them by changing the owner of an account. Funds that are earmarked in this way are not available for your plan other than for college expenses.

14

HOUR 15

Money Online

In this hour, you will learn about Money 99's online banking services and features. Use Money 99 Online Services to pay bills online, download current bank statements, transfer money between accounts online, and, of course, balance your checkbook online as well. Let's first look at how to set up and configure Money 99's online services.

Getting Online

All it takes to get online with Money 99 is a modem and a phone line. If you want to browse the Web, you need an Internet account from an Internet provider as well. You can also browse the Web using Money 99's own internal browser, which you'll learn about later in this chapter. First take a look at the types of online services Money 99 offers:

- Web banking offers you the ability to update your bank accounts and balances electronically and pay bills from your financial institution's own Web site.

- Paying bills online allows you to pay bills electronically from any U.S. checking account.

- Direct statements allow you to electronically update your banking records and account balances and let you transfer money between accounts.

- Online quotes allow you to electronically download the latest stock quotes for tracking your investments.

Installing Explorer

When you install Microsoft Money 99, Internet Explorer 4.01 is installed as well. However, when you access the Internet while you are in Money 99, you can access Web pages using Money 99's own internal Web browser. This browser opens in Money only and allows you to browse Web pages without having to leave the Money 99 application.

You browse Web pages by clicking a hyperlink. A *hyperlink* can be text (usually underlined in blue), a picture, a 3D image, or an imagemap. When you move your mouse cursor over a link, your cursor changes into a hand. Clicking a hyperlink takes you to the Web page to which the link refers.

Choosing an Internet Connection

To fully access and use Money 99's features and services, you need a modem and an Internet service provider (ISP). Your Internet service provider enables you to connect to the Internet through a phone number you dial using your modem.

If you are already connected to the Internet, Money 99 uses that particular configuration to connect you to the Web.

Configuring Money 99 for the Internet

Follow the directions given here to configure Money 99 to connect to the Internet. (Follow these steps ONLY if your computer IS NOT configured to use the Internet.)

To Do: Configuring Money 99 to Connect to the Internet

1. Choose Tools, Connection Settings from the menu bar.

2. Click the Connection tab.

3. Click the Connect button.

4. Follow the instructions that you see on the screen to configure your computer to the Internet (see Figure 15.1).

FIGURE 15.1.

The Connect screen settings enables Money 99 to work with your Internet Connection.

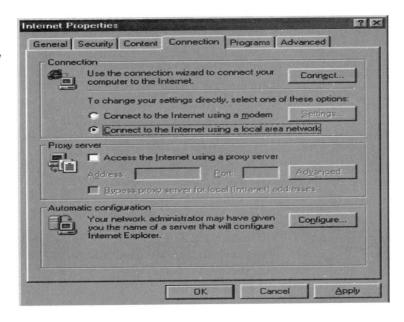

Using AOL with Money 99

If you use America Online as your Internet service provider, you need to make additional changes to Money 99 settings to connect to the Internet through Money.

AOL doesn't use the standard dial-up networking connection method that other ISP's use when connecting you to the Internet. When using Money 99 with AOL, you need to start your AOL connection first before Money 99 can connect.

The following steps show you how to use AOL with Money 99. After you make the necessary settings changes, Money 99 prompts you to start your AOL connection when Money needs to connect to the Internet.

To Do: Configuring Money 99 to Work with AOL

1. Choose Tools, Options.

2. Click the Connection tab.

3. In the Internet Connection section, make sure the Prompt Me When an Internet Connection Is Required… option is checked (see Figure 15.2).

4. Click the Connection Settings button and the Internet Properties dialog box appears.

5. Click the Connection tab.

FIGURE 15.2.

Select the Prompt Me When an Internet Connection Is Required... option.

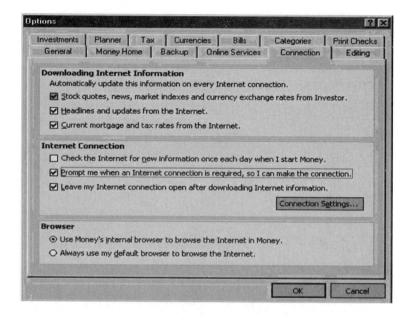

6. Click Connect to the Internet Using a Local Area Network (see Figure 15.3).

A local area network (LAN) is usually only used when you have a direct connection to the Internet and do not dial in using a modem. However, if you use AOL, you need to configure Money 99 in this way to properly connect.

After Money 99 is properly configured to use the Internet, you can browse the Web from inside Money, or you can use Internet Explorer, or you can use any other default browser.

Electronic Payments, Transfers, Automatic Payments, Electronic Bills

Electronic payments *(Epays)* are used for paying regular bills online. Each Epay is a one-time transaction. Epays can be set up in three places in Money 99: the Account Register, Bills & Deposits, or the Connect place in the Online Banking area.

FIGURE 15.3.

Select the Connect to the Internet Using a Local Area Network option.

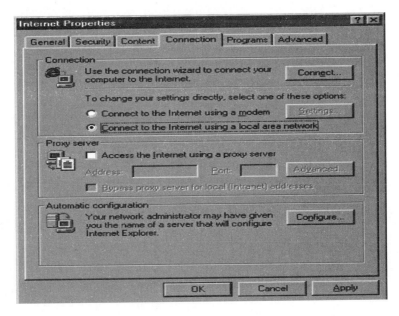

Electronic transfers can be used to electronically transfer funds between two accounts if the accounts are both with the same bank or financial institution. Both accounts also need to be set up for Direct Statements. The Direct Statements service allows you to download online bank statements. You can set up this service directly with your bank or financial institution.

Automatic payments *(Apays)* are used to send regular payments for bills that have a fixed amount and due date. After you set up an Apay one time, money from your account is automatically sent to your payee at regular intervals that you set up. You can set up an Apay on a weekly, monthly, quarterly, or yearly schedule. Apays can be set up in the Bills & Deposits Area.

Electronic bills *(E-Bills)* are bills you actually receive and pay online directly over the Internet. E-Bills are sent to you over a secured Web site server where you can display them as well as pay them. E-Bills are not considered part of Money 99's Online Services. You can sign up for them, however, through the Bills & Deposits area in Money 99.

Choosing a Bank with Online Services

Before you can pay bills online electronically, you must configure and set up Money 99's online services.

To Do: Setting Up Money 99's Online Services

1. Click Online on the Navigation Bar.

2. Double-click the name of your financial institution or bank account with which you want to set up online access.

3. Click Online Setup from the left pane.

4. Select Investigate Offerings.

5. This connects you to the Internet through a toll-free number (if you do not already have Internet access). Money then downloads any information pertaining to your financial institution and what online services it offers and any fees it charges for these services.

6. If your financial institution offers Direct Financial Services, Money 99 asks if you want to take a look at their online service options.

7. If you want to review these options, select Review Service Details.

8. Select Read Signup Info to read about information including fees for signing up with online services through your financial institution.

9. If you choose to go ahead and set up online services, select Set Up Direct Services and follow the instructions on the screen (see Figure 15.4).

If your financial institution offers Web financial services, the services are set up automatically by Money 99. However, you still need to go to your financial institution's Web site to sign up. It usually takes a day or two for your financial institution to sign you up for online banking services.

Paying Bills Online

You can pay bills directly online providing you have a U.S. checking account and you have set it up for Direct bill Payment. Direct Bill Payment allows you to pay bills directly from your computer.

After you set up Direct Bill Payment at your financial institution, you can have your payment sent electronically from your checking account to your designated payee. You enter your payment as you normally would in your Account Register.

FIGURE 15.4.

Find information about services and fees associated with your financial institution's online services.

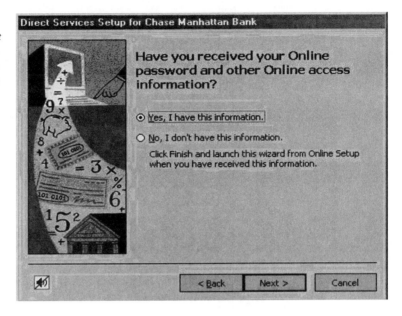

15

To Do: Entering an Epay in Your Account Register

1. Enter your payment in the Account Register as you normally would when writing a check.

2. Click Epay in the Number text box and the due date in the Due Date text box. (Money 99 may ask you to accept a later date if your financial institution can't process your payment by the due date.)

3. Select Online from the Navigation Bar.

4. Double-click the bank or financial institution that is involved with the transfer.

5. Click Connect in the left pane.

6. Check to see that the Epay appears in the list of transactions displayed (see Figure 15.5).

7. Click the Send Payments button that is on the bottom of the screen.

8. Follow the onscreen instructions. Money 99 displays a summary of the information transferred during the call (see Figure 15.6).

FIGURE 15.5.

The Transaction Box screen provides a list of Epay transactions.

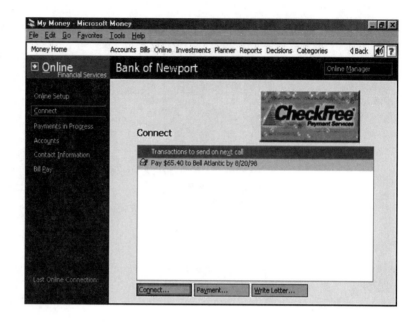

 You can save the call summary by selecting Save As.

FIGURE 15.6.

Money 99 displays information about your Epay call transfer.

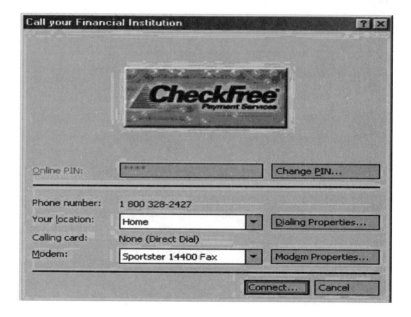

15

If you see a list showing your Epay transaction, your financial institution is most likely only set up for Web Financial Services. You must check with your financial institution and have it set up for Direct Financial Services to pay bills electronically through Epay.

Notice that the first time you enter a Payee for an Epay, you are asked all important payee information such as name, address, and account number. Make sure this information is correct, otherwise, your Epay may not go through properly.

SENDING EPAYS

If you have entered a list of Epays to send but want to wait before actually sending some of them through, you can right-click the mouse button in the transaction list on the ones you don't want to send and select Don't Send On Next Call. This excludes those transactions from being processed on the current call.

When you are ready to send them, select those same transactions, right-click the mouse button and select Send On Next Call.

Updating Your Balance Online

Money 99 allows you to update your balance online. Specific services depend, however, on your bank or financial institution. Online statements are available for both Direct Banking and Web Banking.

Direct Statements

Before you can update your statement, you need to download it electronically first.

To Do: Downloading a Direct Statement

1. Select Online from the Navigation Bar.
2. Double-click the bank or financial institution from which you want to download the statement.
3. Click Connect in the left pane.
4. Click the Get Statement button at the bottom of the screen and follow the onscreen instructions.
5. After the connection has ended, you can click Close to end the download.

Web Statements

Your bank or financial institution may allow you to access your statement from their Web site. The instructions are a little different from downloading Direct Statements.

To Do: Accessing Statements from the Web

1. Select Online from the Navigation Bar.
2. Double-click the bank or financial institution from which you want to download the statement.
3. Click Connect in the left pane.
4. Select the Get Statement button and log on to your financial institution's Web site.
5. If you use Money 99's own internal browser, click Statement to Download located on the Web bar. (If you use your default browser, find and click the appropriate icon to download your statement on your financial institutions Web site.)

> You do not need to update your Account Register right after you download your bank statement. You can always do this at a later time at your convenience.

Reading Your Statements

After you have downloaded your bank statement from your financial institution, you are ready to update your Account Register electronically with this new information.

To Do: Updating Your Account Register

1. Select Online from the Navigation Bar.
2. Double-click the bank or financial institution from which you downloaded your bank statement.
3. Click Statement & Balances in the left pane.
4. Select the account with the statement from the account list that is displayed.
5. Select Read Statement and follow the onscreen instructions.
6. Click Skip to skip over any transaction in your statement. You can click Postpone to end the session entirely. Any transactions you choose not to update will remain on your statement, allowing you to update at a later time.

> After you have updated your Account Register electronically with your last statement, all electronic transactions show as an "E" (for electronic) instead of "C" (cleared manually) in the Cleared text box of the Account Register.

Transferring Money Between Accounts Online

Money 99 allows you to transfer money electronically between accounts providing you have signed up for direct banking service with your bank or financial institution.

You may be able to transfer money between your bank, investment institutions, and credit card accounts. However, the type of services that are provided to you depends entirely on your financial institution.

The first step is to go to the Account Register for the account you want to transfer money *from*.

To Do: Transferring Money Between Accounts

1. Select Accounts from the Navigation Bar.
2. Look to the left pane and click the down arrow to select the account to which you want to transfer funds.

> If you don't see the account that you want listed, check for it under Closed Accounts or Other Open Accounts.

3. Click the Transfer tab at the bottom of the screen.
4. In the Number list select Electronic Transfer (Xfer), fill in all the appropriate transfer information, and then click Enter (see Figure 15.7).

FIGURE 15.7.

You can transfer money from one account to another.

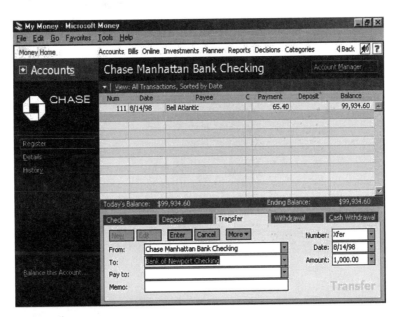

▼ After the transactions have been marked as transfers, you will notice in the Account Register that a lightning bolt and an open envelope appear in the Number text box right ▲ next to the word "Xfer."

After you have marked accounts for transfer, you still need to send the transfer electronically online.

To Do: Sending the Transfer Electronically

1. Select Online from the Navigation Bar.
2. Double-click the bank with which you are electronically transferring.
3. Click Connect in the left pane of the screen.
4. Click the Send Payments button and follow the onscreen instructions (see Figure 15.8).

> If your financial institution or bank does not provide direct banking services, you can still transfer money between accounts. You can make payments from one account to another account using Epay.

FIGURE 15.8.

Send your electronic transactions, such as payments or transfers.

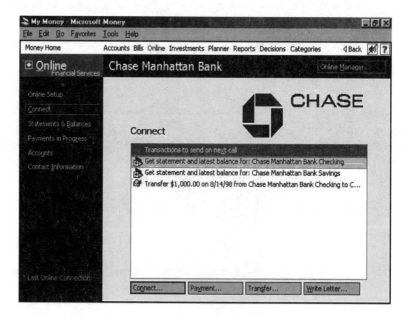

Emailing Your Bank

Again, you can email your bank or financial institution if you are set up for direct banking services. You can request information about your account, order more checks, or any other information you want to obtain from your bank or financial institution.

To Do: Emailing Your Bank

1. Select Online from the Navigation Bar.
2. Double-click the bank or financial institution to which you want to send email.
3. Click Connect and then select Write Letter in the left pane.
4. Choose the type of letter you want to send and then click Continue.
5. Follow the onscreen instructions (see Figure 15.9).

FIGURE 15.9.

Write an online letter (email) to your bank or financial institution.

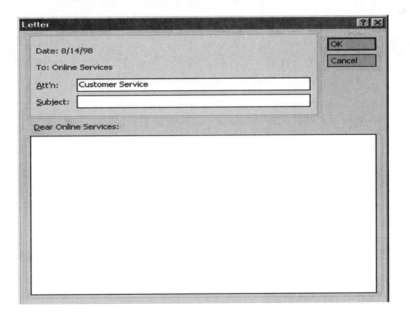

Your letter is now added to the transactions list in the Connect place screen. The Connect place screen appears when you transmit or send any transactions electronically. When you connect to your bank or financial institution for Direct Statements (downloading bank statements), to transfer money, or to send Epays, you will see your letter listed in the Transactions to send on next call list. Just send your online letter as you would all other electronic transactions. Money 99 sends your letter to the appropriate person or

 department.

You can also double-click the letter in the Transactions to Send on Next Call list, if you need to make any changes or additions to the letter before you actually send it. You need to connect again to check for a response from your bank or financial institution.

> If you aren't sure whether your bank or financial institution offers direct banking services and you want to contact them by phone, select Online from Money 99's Navigation Bar and click Contact Information in the left pane of the screen.

You only have access to the Write Letter button if your bank or financial institution is set up for direct banking services like Direct Statements or Direct Bill Payment (Epays).

Statements & Balances Area

If you are set up for direct banking services or have downloaded an online bank statement from your financial institution's Web site, you can access the Statements & Balances area from your Online Financial Services screen.

Money 99 allows you to access information about your online bank statements, transactions, and account balances as shown in Figure 15.10.

- You can access and read any online statements you may have for various accounts.
- You can find out how many transactions appear on each online bank statement.
- You can find out your online account balances for all online accounts that have been set up for direct banking services. Note that the balance reflects transactions that have cleared your financial institution up until the point that you download your bank statements.

To Do: Opening the Statements & Balances Area

1. Select Online from the Navigation Bar.
2. Select Statements & Balances in the left pane of the screen.

Payments in Progress

The Payments in Progress screen lists all your electronic payments (Epays) sent out to your Direct Bill Payment service. The list displays all Epays sent in the last 60 days. You can see the payee, as well as the date the payment should be sent. You can also view the status of a payment, such as whether it has cleared your account or not. For your records, a confirmation number also is assigned by your bank or financial institution for use in tracking the transaction.

FIGURE 15.10.

You can read and access your online bank statements on the Statements & Balances screen.

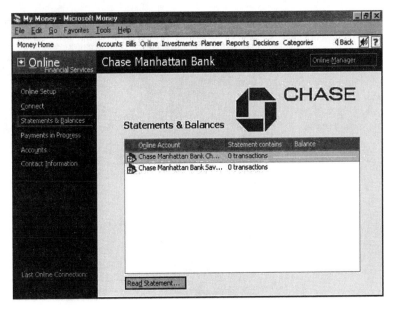

You can only access the Payments in Progress area of your Online Financial Services screen if your bank or financial institution has been set up for Direct Bill Payment (see Figure 15.11).

To Do: Payments in Progress

1. Select Online from the Navigation Bar.
2. Select Payments in Progress in the left pane of the screen. The Payments in Progress screen appears as shown in Figure 15.11.

> The Payments in Progress screen does not list any Web payments you may have made directly to your financial institution through their own Web site. Only Epays that require Direct Bill Payment are listed.
>
> Although you cannot track specific Web payments like you can Epays, you can see if the transaction has cleared by downloading and reading your online bank statement.

FIGURE 15.11.

The Payments in Progress screen lists all the online electronic transactions (Epays) that have been sent to your Direct Bill Payment service.

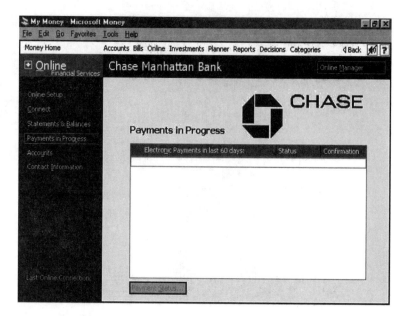

Bill Paying Information

Even if you have accounts at several banks or financial institutions, you can still use Money 99's Online Services. For Direct Bill Payment, you can sign up for the service through any participating institution. For Direct Statements (to download your bank statements and transfer funds), you can also sign up with all your banks or financial institutions that provide this service to you. For Web Financial Services, you can access your accounts through a financial institution's Web site providing they offer this service to you.

Standing Orders

A Standing Order is a type of sell order you can place with your brokerage firm to sell a certain number of investment shares at a set price. If you set up this service with your brokerage firm, they enter your order for you, and if it is the right time to sell your shares, they automatically sell them for you. If the price does not reach the one *you* set, they continue to hold the shares. Any money you receive from selling these shares is automatically deposited (credited) to your account. Any fees your brokerage firm may charge you for this service are automatically deducted (debited) from your account. This service is set up entirely with your brokerage firm and not with Money 99's Online Services.

You can add any Automatic Transaction to your Account Register by down-loading and reading your online bank statement from the bank or financial institution with which you have an Automatic Transaction account. Money 99 takes the information you downloaded and enters it into your Account Register so you don't have to.

If Your Bank Does Not Offer Online Service

You can use Direct Bill Payment even if your bank or financial institution is not online by signing up for this service through a third-party provider.

 ## To Do: Third-Party Providers

1. Select Online from the Navigation Bar.

2. Double-click your account in the Online Financial Services Manager.

3. Click Online Setup in the left pane of the screen.

4. Click Investigate Offerings to see what third-party providers are available to you (see Figure 15.12).

FIGURE 15.12.

Choose your Online Services provider.

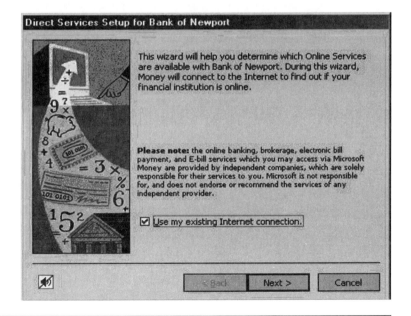

 If you formerly used Quicken for your online banking but want to switch to Money 99, you have to cancel your Quicken Online Banking Service first. Then you can sign up for Online Banking in Money 99.

Special Online Situations

Each time you enter an Electronic Payment (Epay) to a specific payee, you have set up an instruction that is pending until you send it during an online connection. There may be a situations in which you want to cancel a transaction online or to check the status of a transaction.

Canceling a Transaction Online

If you haven't actually sent the transaction electronically yet, you can delete the Epay entry from your Account Register. Go to your Account Register and find the Epay transaction (there should be an Epay in the Number text box). Select the transaction by clicking it and pressing the Delete key on your keyboard.

If you already sent your payment electronically, but it has not gone to the payee yet, follow these steps:

To Do: Canceling a Transaction

1. Go to the Account Register that has the Epay you want to cancel listed.
2. Select Accounts from the Navigation Bar.
3. Click the down arrow at the top of the left pane, and select the account that has the transaction to cancel.
4. Right-click the Epay you want.

> You can tell whether the electronic transaction has not been cleared by your financial institution by the lighting bolt and envelope image that is displayed before the check number.

5. Select Void from the Mark As menu.
6. Money 99 then asks you whether you want to send an instruction to your financial institution to cancel the transaction. Answer Yes to cancel this payment.

Money 99 displays "**VOID**" in the Register's Balance text box and a lighting bolt and an open envelope in the Number text box that indicates the transaction to cancel (see Figure 15.13).

FIGURE 15.13.

*Note the transaction selected to cancel is marked as "**VOID**".*

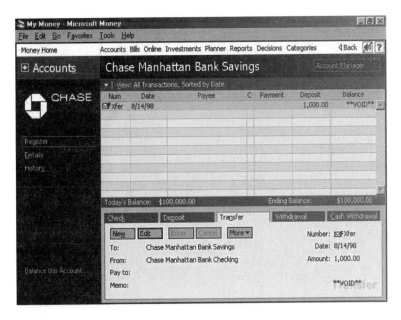

Now that you have selected a transaction to cancel, you still will need to send this instruction through to Money 99.

To Do: Sending a Cancel Instruction to Money

1. Select Online from the Navigation Bar.
2. Double-click the financial institution with the Epay you want to cancel.
3. Click Connect in the left pane of the screen.
4. Click the Connect button and follow the onscreen instructions (see Figure 15.14).

If the Epay you want to cancel has already been sent to the payee, you need to get a Stop Payment order from your bank or financial institution.

Following Up on an Online Payment

You can check the status of an Online Payment to see whether the electronic payment has cleared your account.

*You send online trans-
actions and instruc-
tions to your financial
institution through the
Connect screen.*

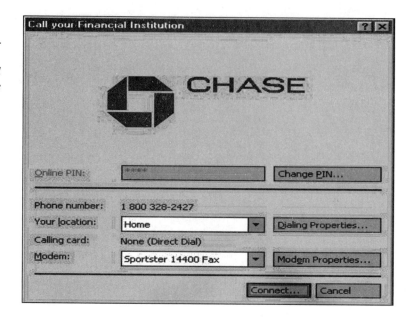

To Do: Checking the Status of an Online Payment

1. Select Online from the Navigation Bar.
2. Double-click the financial institution with the Epay you want to check the status of.
3. Click Payments in Progress in the left pane of the screen.
4. Select the transaction you want to check from the transaction list.
5. Click Payment Status.

A Payment Status dialog box appears. Now you can see whether the payment was transmitted and if and when it cleared your bank account.

Canceling an Online Automatic Payment

You can permanently cancel an online Automatic Payment (Apay) or cancel just one occurrence of an Apay as well.

To Do: Cancel an Apay Permanently

You can delete a recurring Apay in Money 99 and create an instruction to permanently cancel the Apay at your bank or financial institution.

1. Select Bills from the Navigation Bar.
2. Click Set Up Bills & Deposits in the left pane of the screen.

15

3. From the list that appears, select the recurring bill you want to cancel.

4. Click Delete.

5. Money asks whether you are sure you want to delete this bill; click Yes.

Now that you have selected an Apay for cancellation, you must send this instruction through Money 99's Connect area.

6. Select Online from the Navigation Bar.

7. Double-click the account that has this Apay.

8. Click Connect in the left pane of the screen.

9. Click the Send Payments button and follow the onscreen instructions.

To Do: Cancel Only One Apay Occurrence

You can also delete just one occurrence of an Apay in Money 99 and create an instruction to cancel just this one occurrence of the Apay at your bank or financial institution.

1. Select Accounts on the Navigation Bar.

2. Click the down-arrow next to the word Accounts in the left pane of the screen.

3. Click the account containing the Apay transaction you want to cancel.

4. Click Register in the left pane of the screen.

5. Right-click the transaction you want to cancel.

6. From the shortcut menu that appears, select Mark As, Void.

Money 99 displays "**VOID**" in the Register's Balance text box and a lighting bolt and an open envelope in the Number text box that indicates the transaction to cancel.

Now that you have selected an Apay occurrence for cancellation, you need to send this instruction through Money 99's Connect area (just as you did in the previous section).

> The previous steps cancel only one occurrence of an Apay or one payment only. All other Apays continue to be paid unless you permanently cancel them by deleting the recurring transaction.

Canceling Your Online Banking

If you want to cancel your Online Banking service, you need to call your bank or financial institution directly.

You can find your financial institution's contact information by going to the Contact Information area in Money 99.

To Do: Canceling Your Online Banking

1. Select Online from the Navigation Bar.

2. Double-click the financial institution with which you want to cancel your online services.

3. Click Online Setup in the left pane of the screen.

4. Click Change Direct Services.

5. In the Direct Services Setup Wizard, click Modify Online Services for an Account.

6. Select the account for which you want to cancel services.

7. Uncheck the Direct Bill Payment and/or Direct Statements check boxes.

8. A warning message appears; click Yes.

9. If this is the only account you want to cancel for online services, click No, I'm Finished and follow the onscreen instructions.

> If you have multiple accounts that have been set up for Direct Financial Services at one financial institution, you must make sure you cancel services for each account following the steps listed here.

Cancel Web Financial Services

The Web Financial Services are provided to you by your bank or financial institution. You never need to cancel it in Money 99 unless your bank or financial institution is charging you a fee for its service.

If a fee is involved, you should call your bank or financial institution and cancel your service with them directly. If you need to locate their contact number, select Online from Money 99's Navigation Bar, double-click the bank's name, and click Contact
▲ Information in the left pane of the screen.

What If I Change Banks

All accounts at your old bank that are set up for Direct Financial Services need to be canceled if you change banks.

To Do: Changing Banks

1. Set up new accounts first in Money 99 for your new bank.

2. Close all your old accounts in Money 99.

3. If your new bank or financial institution offers Online Services that you want to set up, you need to set them up with your financial institution.

> You must notify your old bank or financial institution that you want to cancel their Online Services you had set up to keep from being billed and having electronic payments (Epays) or automatic payments (Apays) sent from your old accounts.

15

Summary

In this hour, you've learned that Web banking enables you to electronically update your bank accounts and balances and topay bills from your financial institution's own Web site. Paying bills online allows you to pay bills electronically from any U.S. checking account. Direct statements allows you to electronically update your banking records and account balances, and lets you transfer money between accounts. Online quotes allows you to electronically download the latest stock quotes for tracking your investments.

Q&A

Q Why is it important to investigate online banking services with my financial institution?

A Your financial institution may offer many different online services at different costs. It's important to check out what they offer and the cost before you sign up for any online banking services.

Q Are there any special requirements for Direct Bill Payment (Epays)?

A You need to make sure you set up Direct Bill Payment at your financial institution. Also, the checking account you set up for direct payment must be a U.S. checking account.

Q At what point can I update my accounts electronically?

A After you have downloaded an online bank statement, you can electronically update your Account Register with the new information. Bank statements are available through both Web and direct online banking in Money 99.

Q Why download my bank statement online?

A Money 99 takes the information you downloaded and enters it into your Account Register so you don't have to. Money 99 also matches your statement transactions with your manual transactions that you have entered. You can see what transactions have cleared, and get an accurate account balance at any time.

HOUR 16

Money Reports

In this hour, you will learn how Money 99 can display your financial information through Reports and Charts. After you have entered your financial information in Money 99, you can use Money 99's reports and charts to better understand and evaluate your finances. Money 99 uses the category information that you enter in your Account Register for most of its reports and charts. The any features of Money 99's reports and charts include:

- **You can customize reports and charts**—Money 99 allows you to customize reports and charts by selecting the information you want to appear.
- **Save your customized reports and charts**—Money 99 allows you to save your customized reports or charts. You can save your report or chart to the My Favorites list as well.
- **Money 99's monthly reports**—Money 99 takes a snapshot of your current monthly finances and assimilates them in various monthly reports.

Where Money Gets Its Data

Most of the data Money 99 uses for its reports comes from the category information you enter for each transaction in your Account Register. If you haven't been entering categories yet, it would be beneficial to you to do so if you want to use Money 99's report information.

Adding Helpful Data

You can use the category label to track your income and expense patterns in Money 99's reports.

Using categories and subcategories in your Account Register helps you keep track of your financial picture.

Paying Attention to the Scope of the Report

You can limit which transactions Money 99 displays in a report. You can set up criteria like date range, category, account, and payee. You can also display different transactions and account information in Money 99's reports.

Choosing a Date Range

You can customize reports to display your financial information through a date range. For instance, you may want to run a report that displays your financial information by month, quarter, or year.

How Reports Work

Money 99 gives you many standard reports you can run to better evaluate your online financial picture.

Take a look at where your money is going and compare your income and expenses. Track tax-related income and expenses as well.

Harnessing Helpful Information

To see a list of Money 99's standard reports and charts, follow these steps:

To Do: Viewing Money 99's Reports and Charts

1. Select Reports from the Navigation bar.
2. Click a group to see the list of reports and charts for that particular group (see Figures 16.1 and 16.2).

FIGURE 16.1.

Choose from many of Money 99's reports and charts.

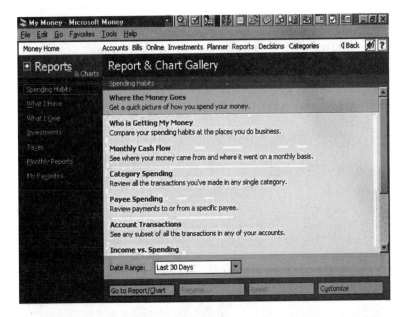

16

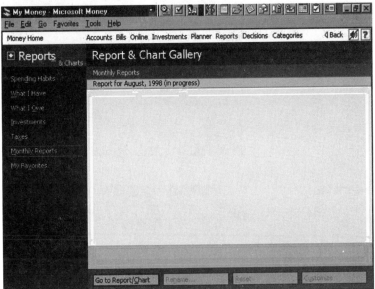

FIGURE 16.2.

The Monthly Reports screen allows you to run Money 99's Monthly Reports.

Navigation Through a Report

You can navigate through the report by clicking entries that appear in the left pane of the screen. If you see a magnifying glass with a plus sign when you move your cursor over a figure amount in a report, you can double-click it to see a list of transactions that support that amount.

For an example, let's take a look at a Money 99 report.

To Do: Opening Money 99's Spending Habits Report

1. Select Reports from the Navigation bar.

2. Click the Spending Habits group in the left pane of the screen.

3. Money 99 displays the reports and charts this group contains.

4. Double-click the Report you want to view (see Figure 16.3).

5. Click any amount to see a list of transactions that support it (see Figure 16.4).

FIGURE 16.3.

The Spending Habits report is one of the many reports Money 99 displays.

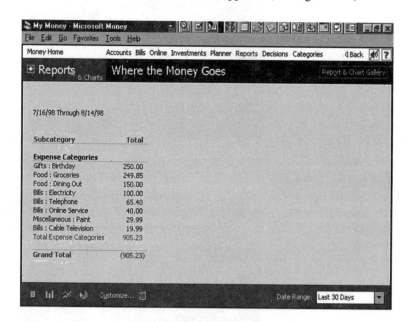

FIGURE 16.4.

Money 99 displays the transactions that support a figure amount listed in the report in the Transactions list.

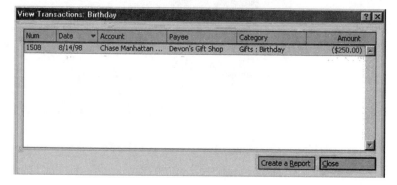

Making a Report a Favorite

After you have viewed a report, you can add it to your own personal list of favorites.

To Do: Add to Favorites

1. View the report that you want to add to your list of favorites.
2. Right-click the report and select Add to Favorites from the shortcut menu that appears (see Figure 16.5).
3. Enter the name you want to give the report.
4. Click OK to add the report to the My Favorites area.

16

FIGURE 16.5.

Right-click the report to open the shortcut menu.

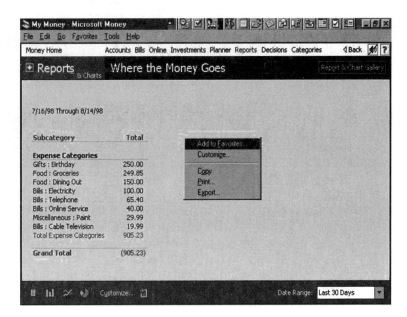

Exporting Reports

After you have viewed a report, you can also export your report to another format like Microsoft Excel.

To Do: Exporting a Report

1. View the report you want to export.
2. Right-click the report and select Export from the shortcut menu. Money 99 displays an Export Report dialog box.
3. Follow the onscreen instructions (see Figure 16.6).

FIGURE 16.6.

*You can export a
report in several
types of formats.*

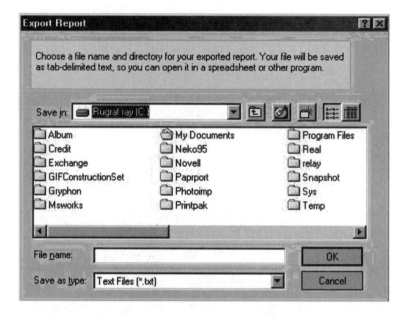

WORKING WITH AN EXPORTED FILE

When you export a file, you can work with it in a word processor, spreadsheet, or tax-preparation software program.

When you export a file in Money 99, it is saved as a tab-delimited text file with the extension .TXT. The tab-delimited format enables your data to be exported into columns and rows, the way it is displayed in Money 99.

If you are using a tax-preparation software program that opens files exported from Money 99, however, you save the file as a Tax Exchange Format with a .TXF extension.

A helpful report to export is the Tax Software Report. You can export this report and save it in the Tax Exchange Format (.TXF). Most current tax-preparation software can import .TXF files. This report keeps you from having to enter your repetitive information when preparing your taxes.

See the following steps to export the Tax Software Report, but refer also to your tax-preparation software instructions for importing the file you have saved in Money 99.

To Do: Exporting the Tax Software Report

1. Select Reports from the Navigation bar.
2. Click Taxes on the left pane of the screen.
3. Double-click the Tax Software Report.

4. Right-click the report and select E<u>x</u>port from the shortcut menu that appears.

5. Follow the onscreen instructions that appear in the Export Report dialog box (see Figure 16.7).

The information is now ready for you to import into your tax-preparation software program.

Before you export the Tax Software Report, you should assign a tax form line to each tax-related category or subcategory in the Categories & Payees area.

16

FIGURE 16.7.

You can export your Tax Software Report to be used in a tax-preparation software program.

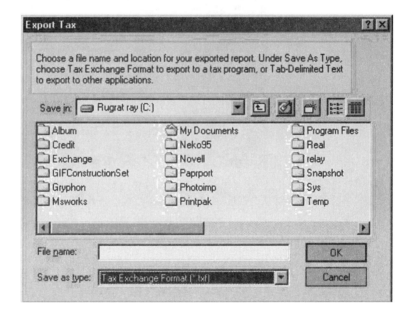

A Report Versus a Chart

We have been discussing Money 99's reports throughout this hour. Money 99 also allows you to display your financial information in the form of a chart.

Knowing the Most Helpful Way to View Information

A chart is a good way to get a quick snapshot of your financial picture. You can view a chart the same way you view a report in Money 99.

To Do: Viewing a Chart in Money 99

1. Select Reports from the Navigation bar.

2. Click the type of chart you want in the left pane of the screen (see Figure 16.8).

FIGURE 16.8.

Choose the type of chart you want to view.

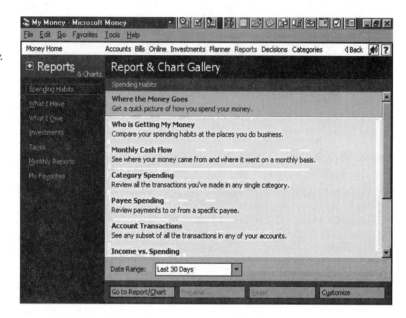

3. The Report & Chart Gallery is displayed; click the chart you want to view.

4. Use the text boxes at the bottom of the screen to modify all the common specifications of your chart.

 5. Click Go to Report/Chart to view your chart (see Figure 16.9).

Switching Between Reports and Charts

Many of your reports can be viewed as charts. You may want to switch between viewing a report and a chart. Not all reports, however, can be viewed in all types of chart formats. If a chart type is not available for that particular report, the option button appears grayed out.

FIGURE 16.9.

The chart is displayed on the screen. You can choose to customize or print your chart.

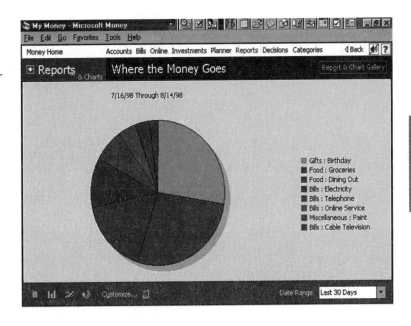

16

To Do: Switching Between the Report and Chart

1. Select Reports from the Navigation bar.

2. Click a group in the left pane of the screen to see what reports and charts it displays.

3. Double-click the report that you want to view.

4. Click one of the four buttons located at the bottom of the screen that represent the types of reports and charts available (see Figure 16.10). The four button choices are

   - Report
   - Bar Chart
   - Line Chart
   - Pie Chart

5. Now your report or chart is displayed in the format you selected (see Figure 16.11).

FIGURE 16.10.

You can switch between viewing a report or a chart and choose which kind of chart you want by clicking one of these buttons.

FIGURE 16.11.

This is an example of a Money 99 bar chart.

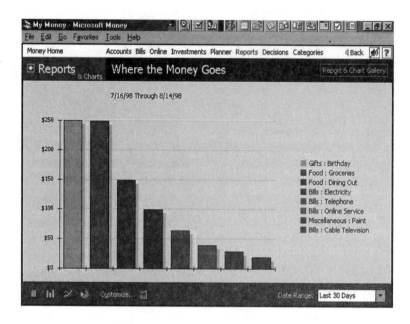

Editing a Chart in a Report

You can customize or edit your report or chart even after you are viewing it. You can change certain detail information for a report or chart. Information that you can change, such as Date Range, Accounts, or Categories is displayed at the bottom of each report or chart you view from Money 99's Report & Chart Gallery.

To Do: Editing Your Report or Chart

1. Select Reports from the Navigation bar.
2. Click a group to see the reports and charts that it displays.
3. Click the report or chart you want to view.
4. You can edit text boxes like Accounts, Date Range, or Categories that are located at the bottom of this screen.

> If you do not see any text boxes at the bottom of the screen, this report or chart cannot be modified in this way.

5. Click the detail you want to include or modify from the drop-down list that appears.

Opening a Report

Money 99's Report and Chart Gallery displays reports and charts by group. For example, if you want to view the Spending Habits group, follow these steps:

To Do: Viewing the Spending Habits Group

1. Select Reports from the Navigation bar.
2. Click the Spending Habits group located in the left pane of the screen.
3. A list of reports and charts relating to this group appears.
4. Select the report or chart you want to view.
5. Click Go to Report/Chart at the bottom of the screen (see Figure 16.12).

FIGURE 16.12.

The Spending Habits Report is generated from Money 99's Report & Chart Gallery.

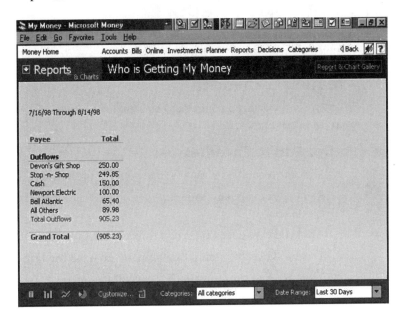

You can double-click the report or chart you want to view or you can click Go to Report/Chart to view it as well.

Loan Reports

You can create two types of loan reports in Money 99:

- **Loan Amortization Report**—This report shows how your future loan payments will be broken down into principal and interest. It is based on the loan information you entered into Money 99 and not on loan payments you have made in the past. However, you can customize the report to include your past payments.

- **Loan Terms Report**—This report summarizes all your loans and their terms. If you need more detailed information, you can customize the report to include additional loan details.

> Like all other reports in Money 99, loan reports can be viewed in Money 99's Report & Chart Gallery.

Working with Reports

You can modify Money 99's reports and charts to better help you get an accurate and complete representation of your finances.

Creating a Favorite

When you are viewing a report that you want to save and run again, you can add it to your list of favorites.

To Do: Add to Favorites

1. View the report you want to add to your list of favorites.
2. Right-click the report, and select Add to Favorites from the shortcut menu that appears.

   After you have added the report to your list of favorites, you can view it again.
3. To view the report again, select Reports from the Navigation bar.
4. Click My Favorites from the left pane of the screen.
5. You should see a list of your favorite reports.
6. Just double-click the favorite report you want to view.

> After you add a report to your list of favorites, you can also rename or delete it.

To Do: Renaming a Report or Chart

1. Click on the report or chart you want to rename from the My Favorites list.
2. Click Rename, located at the bottom of the screen, and enter a new name.

To Do: Deleting a Report or Chart

1. Click on the report or chart you want to delete from the My Favorites list.
2. Click Delete, located at the bottom of the screen.

   Your report has now been deleted from your list of favorites.

16

Customizing Reports

You can customize Money 99's reports and charts to fit your own needs. The specific changes you can make depend on the report or chart you want to change:

- **Limit transactions**—You can limit which transactions appear in your report or chart. You can choose the date, category, account, and payee that you want to view.

- **You can add more**—You can add additional information such as payment number and transaction status to your report. You can group the report into accounts or date range or by category.

- **Switch between reports and charts**—You can display charts as reports and reports as charts.

- **Change fonts**—You can change fonts and report column widths, as well as chart options such as legends and gridlines.

- **Easily customize reports and charts**—In most report windows, you will find text boxes that you can modify, like Accounts, Date Range, or Category.

Printing a Report

Before you actually print a report, you should set up your printer to print Money 99's reports and charts.

To Do: Setting up your Printer

1. Choose File, Print Setup.
2. Click Report and Chart Setup.
3. Select your printer in the Printer list box.

You only need to do this once, unless you plan to use another printer.

Now you are ready to send a report or chart to your printer.

To Do: Printing Your Report or Chart

1. View the report or chart you want to print.

2. Choose File, Print.

3. Select your print options from the Print Report dialog box that appears and then click OK.

> If you are printing to a color printer, Money 99 prints the report in color. Otherwise, Money 99 prints your reports and charts in gray tones.

Resetting Reports You've Customized

You may want to change your customized report back to the original way Money 99 displayed it.

Money 99 allows you to reset a customized report to its original format. You may want to save your customized report to your list of favorites, however, in case you change your mind.

To Do: Resetting a Customized Report

1. View the customized report that you want to reset.

2. Click Customize at the bottom of the screen.

3. Click Reset in the Customize Report dialog box that appears (see Figure 16.13).

The Monthly Report

The Monthly Report summarizes your financial information for the end of every month. The main Money 99 Home Screen notifies you at the end of each month that the report is now ready to be run.

The Report Categories

The Monthly Report is broken down into seven categories.

- **Spending**—Looks at your spending habits over the past two months.
- **Net Worth**—Looks at how this month compares to your long-term goals.
- **Advisor FYI**—Lists any advice that Money 99 has given you over the past month.
- **Investment Performance**—Gives you a summary of all your investment gains and losses over the past month.

- **Potential Problems with Your Account**—Lets you know whether there are any problems with your account like missing or inaccurate information in Money 99.
- **Upcoming Financial Events**—Lists all non-monthly schedules expenses such as birthday or holiday gifts.
- **Income Tax**—Lets you know whether any taxes are due for the month.

FIGURE 16.13.

You can reset your customized report to the original format from this screen.

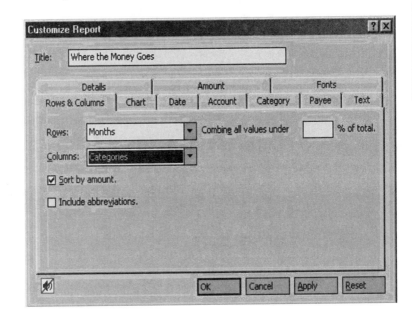

16

How to Use the Information

You view the Monthly Report the same way you view any other Money 99 reports.

To Do: Viewing Money 99's Monthly Report

1. Select Reports from the Navigation bar.
2. Click Monthly Reports in the left pane of the screen.
3. The Report & Chart Gallery appears. Select the Monthly Report you want to view (see Figure 16.14).

FIGURE 16.14.

Select the Monthly Report you want to view from the Report & Chart Gallery screen.

You can navigate through the report by clicking the entries that are displayed in the left pane (see Figure 16.15).

FIGURE 16.15.

This is an example of Money 99's Monthly Report.

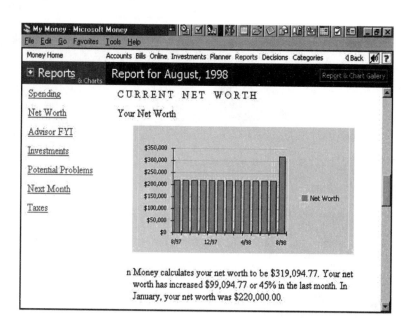

Viewing Transactions

When you move your cursor over any amount in the Monthly Report, the cursor changes into a magnifying glass with a plus sign in it. This means that Money 99 can enable you to see a list of transactions that were used by Money 99 to support that figure amount. Just double-click the figure amount. Withdrawals, deposits, transfers, and all other transactions will be displayed if those transactions support the figure amount in the report (see Figure 16.16).

FIGURE 16.16.

Money 99 displays a list of transactions that support the figure amount in the report.

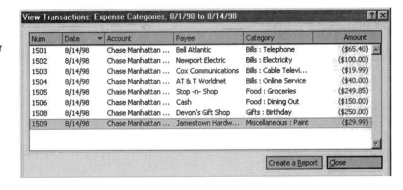

Summary

Money 99 can display all your financial information through reports and charts. After you have entered your financial information in Money 99, you can use Money 99's reports and charts to better understand and evaluate your finances. Money 99 uses the category information that you enter in your Account Register for most of its reports and charts.

Money 99 allows you to customize reports and charts by selecting the information you want to appear on the report or chart. You can save your customized reports for charts. You can save your report or chart to the My Favorites list as well. Money 99 also takes a snapshot of your current monthly finances and assimilates them in various monthly reports.

Q&A

Q What can I do with an exported file?

A You can work with an exported file in most word processors, spreadsheets, or tax-preparation software programs.

Q Can you export a chart to another program as well?

A You cannot export a chart to another program the way you can export a report. However, when you are viewing the chart, you can copy it and paste it into another program such as a word processing or spreadsheet software program.

Q When I create a favorite report, what happens to the original?

A The original report remains unchanged when you create a favorite report.

HOUR 17

Charts and the Chart Gallery

Money 99 allows you to view your financial picture in a variety of graphic charts. These charts help you spot trends and compare different categories. For example, you can use a chart to view the trend in your expense spending. Has it increased or decreased over the last six months?

Money provides you with a gallery of dozens of charts, and an options box full of different ways to display your financial data.

Tracking Your Money with Charts

Charts compress data. If you want a detailed breakdown of your checking account payments, look in the Account view, not a chart. But if you want to see which expenses take up the biggest piece of the pie each month, a chart is a valuable way to see that information.

Many books have been written on how to most effectively display data in charts. In short, they can be summarized as:

- Line charts display trends well.
- Pie charts display comparisons, but not trends.
- Bar charts display trends and comparisons.

Not all reports can be displayed in every graph type. If a graph type is not available, the icon for that chart will be grayed out.

Selecting the Chart of the Day

A good place to begin exploring the usefulness of charts is to explore your *Chart of the Day*. The Chart of the Day appears on your Financial Home Page.

Money rotates up to five different charts as Charts of the Day. You can select which charts to display.

To Do: Define Chart of the Day Display

1. View the Financial Home Page in Money 99.
2. Click the Personalize Your Financial Page link on the left side of the Financial Home Page.
3. In the Options dialog box that appears, make sure the Chart of the Day check box is selected.
4. Again, in the Options dialog box, click the Chart of the Day button.
5. Select all five check boxes in the Select Chart of the Day dialog box, as shown in Figure 17.1. By selecting all five charts, you're telling Money to rotate five different charts—a different one each working day of the week.

FIGURE 17.1.

You can display up to five different charts on your Financial Home Page.

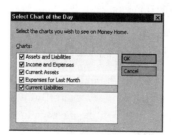

▼   6. Click the OK button in both dialog boxes to close them, and scroll down your
         Financial Home Page to see your Chart of the Day. Figure 17.2 shows the Assets
         and Liabilities chart, but yours may be different. You can move your mouse over
         one part of the chart (without clicking) to see a value for that chart item.

FIGURE 17.2.

*Scroll down your
Financial Home Page
to view the Chart of the
Day.*

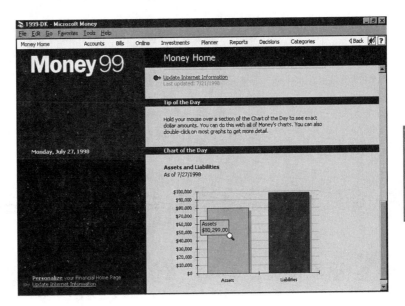

▲

Changing Chart Display

You can view your Chart of the Day as a bar chart, a line chart, or a pie chart. You can
also assign a *legend*, and/or a 3D View to your Chart of the Day.

If you see some valuable information in a Chart of the Day, you can customize that chart
and save it as a favorite.

To Do: Customize Your Chart of the Day and Make It a Favorite

1. Right-click your chart, and select Pie Chart from the context menu.

2. Right-click your chart again, and select Legend. Right-click again and add 3D
   View.

3. Right-click the chart one more time, and select Add to Favorites from the context
   menu. In the Add to Favorites dialog box, name your chart (you can accept the
   default name, but you might want to add the word "Chart" at the end). Figure 17.3

▼

▼

shows a chart being named "Assets and Liabilities Pie Chart." After you name your chart, click the OK button in the Add to Favorites dialog box.

4. After you define a favorite chart, you can see it at any time. Just click the Favorites menu, and select your chart from the list of favorite views.

FIGURE 17.3.

Part of creating a favorite chart is giving it a name.

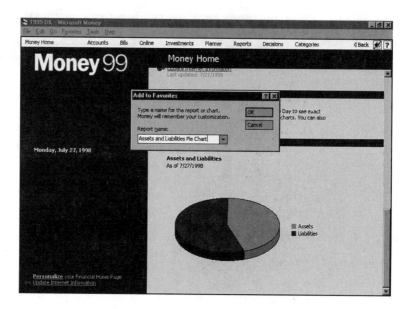

▲

Locating and Opening Charts

You just explored your Chart of the Day. You saw that information about your accounts can be summarized and displayed graphically to give you a big picture of your financial state.

Many of the reports available in Money 99 can also be viewed as charts. In the previous hour, you learned to view and customize reports. Now you'll see how you can view these reports as graphs.

To Do: View a Report as a Chart

1. Click the Reports link in the Navigation Bar.
2. From the list of Report categories on the left side of the view, click What I Have, and click Net Worth in the list of reports on the right side of the window.
3. Click the Go to Report/Chart button at the bottom of the window.
4. Click the Bar Chart icon to see this report as a bar chart, as shown in Figure 17.4.
5. By moving your cursor over a bar in the chart, you can see the value of that category.

▼

▼ **FIGURE 17.4.**

You can view a report as a bar chart.

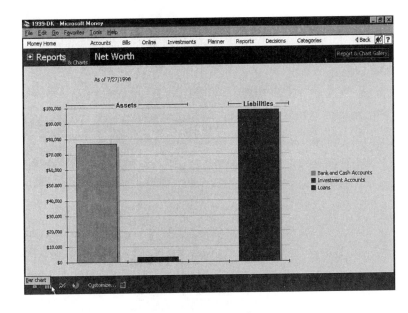

▲

Opening a Transaction from a Chart

If a chart segment is associated with a transaction, you can open that transaction directly from your chart.

To Do: Open a Transaction from a Chart

1. In the Reports View, select the Spending Habits category (on the left) and the Monthly Cash Flow report (on the right). Then click the Go To Report/Chart button at the bottom of the window.

2. Click the Bar Chart icon at the bottom of the view to see this report in bar chart form.

3. Move your cursor over different bars in the chart. Those bars that are associated with transactions display a "+" sign in the magnifying glass icon, as shown in Figure 17.5.

4. Right-click a bar that displays a "+" symbol, and choose View Transaction from the context menu. A View Transactions window opens displaying the transaction, as shown in Figure 17.6.

> Not all chart elements can be viewed as transactions. For example, an investment account balance is not a transaction.

17

▼   5. You can right-click any line in the View Transactions window and select Edit to edit that item. You can also go to associated accounts by right-clicking an item in the View Transactions window.

FIGURE 17.5.

Chart segments associated with a transaction display a "+" symbol.

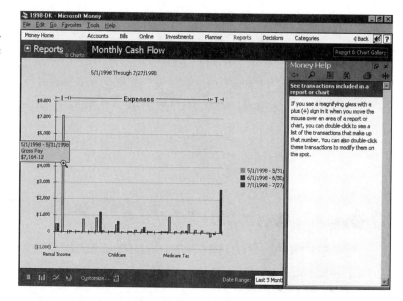

FIGURE 17.6.

You can view a transaction from a chart.

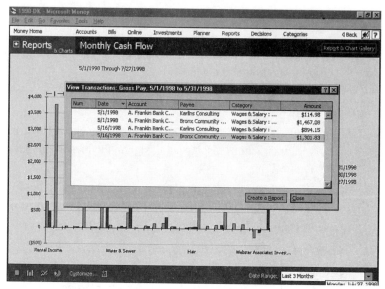

▲

Customizing Charts

Because most of Money's dozens of reports can be graphed, there are many ways you can look at your financial picture graphically. Each chart has its own set of options, and it will take a bit of experimenting to produce a chart that is tailored to focus on the exact trends, relationships, and comparisons you are interested in.

You can access an entire range of customizing features for your chart by clicking the Customize icon at the bottom of the window. When you click the Customize button, the Customize Report dialog box opens. This is the same dialog box you used to customize reports in the previous hour in this book. But there are additional options here that are available for charts. When you view your report as a bar, line, or pie chart, you can modify many of the attributes of that chart in the Chart tab of the Customize Report dialog box.

In the Chart tab, you can change the type of chart by selecting one of the option buttons in the View As area. You can assign labels to a pie chart by selecting the None, Percents, or Dollar Amounts option buttons in the Pie Labels area.

You can use the Show Legend drop-down list to select from three legend options: None, At Bottom of Chart, or To Right of Chart.

The Show in 3D check box assigns 3D effects to your chart. The Show Gridlines check box adds horizontal lines across a bar or line chart, making it easier for you to estimate numbers associated with lines and bars.

Finally, if you are charting a budget report, the Chart tab in the Customize Report dialog box includes three check boxes in the Chart Amounts For area. The Actual check box displays your actual spending and income. The Budget check box displays your budgeted amounts for income and expenses. The Difference check box displays the discrepancy between your budget and your real income and expenses.

In the next section of this hour, you'll learn to customize a monthly cash flow chart. The customizing features you learn here can be applied to other charts as well.

Changing Date Ranges

Every chart that displays a data with time values allows you to filter the graphed data by date. For example, the chart in Figure 17.7 displays cash flow for all dates. This chart provides a far-reaching overview of cash flow, but it isn't very useful for focusing on details.

FIGURE 17.7.

Charting for all dates provides a long range view.

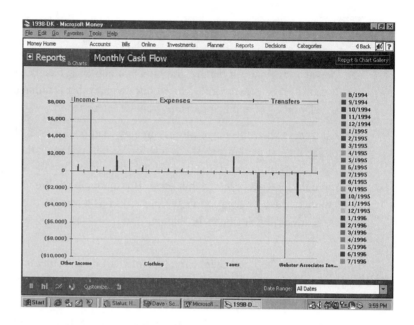

To change the date range, click the Date Range drop-down list arrow in the lower-right of the chart window, and select a range.

Figure 17.8 shows the same cash flow chart as Figure 17.7, but this time for the current month only. It's easier to see specific expense and income categories in this view.

FIGURE 17.8.

You can zoom in on this month's cash flow.

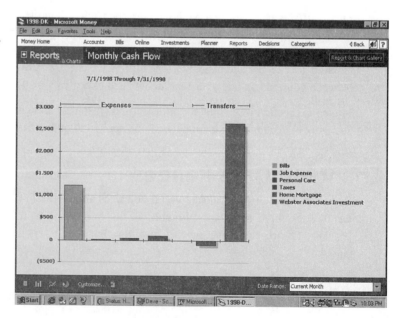

Switching Between Chart Types

You can toggle between viewing your data as bar, line, or pie charts by clicking the different icons in the lower-left corner of the window.

You can view your data as a report by clicking the Report icon in the lower-left corner of the Report window.

Renaming a Chart

At the top of the Customize Report dialog box (which you open by clicking the Customize button below a chart), you can change the chart title.

Type a new title in the chart to describe your graph, as shown in Figure 17.9.

FIGURE 17.9.

Rename your chart in the Customize Report dialog box.

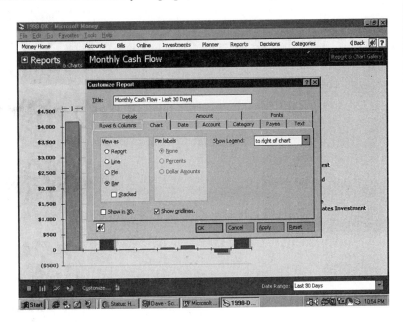

Your new chart name becomes part of the chart. A bit later in this hour you'll learn how to save custom configured charts (including titles) as favorites.

In the previous hour, you learned to define reports by selecting certain accounts and date ranges to filter reports. You can use all these filtering features with graphs as well. Report options also exist that are specific to graphs. In the Chart tab of the Customize Report dialog box, you can define:

- Chart type.
- 3D display.

- Special features for pie or bar charts.
- Gridline display.
- Legend display.
- Rows and columns by defining what information is displayed on the chart's X (horizontal) and Y (vertical) axes.

Defining Chart Display

You can select chart type and display options by opening a chart and making changes in the Customize Report dialog box.

To Do: Define Chart Options

1. In the Report and Chart Gallery, view the Who is Getting My Money report. Click the Customize button at the bottom of the window.

2. Click the Date tab in the Customize Report dialog box, and choose Last 6 Months from the Range drop-down list.

3. Click in the Chart tab and click the Pie option button.

4. Click the Percents option button in the Pie Labels area of the dialog box. Click the Apply button in the dialog box to see how your chart will look. Then click and drag on the title bar of the Customize Report dialog box to move it out of the way, as shown in Figure 17.10.

FIGURE 17.10.

Choose options to define a pie chart.

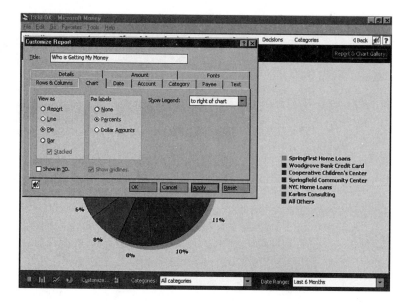

▼ 5. Change the chart to a line chart by clicking the **Line** option button. Click the **Apply** button in the Customize Report dialog box again to see the new chart format.

6. Click the **Bar** option button, and the Show in 3D check box, and then click the OK button to view your chart as a 3D bar graph.

Different information is best displayed with different chart types. Experiment to find a format that gives you a good look at the information you need.

Defining Rows Versus Columns

Some charts can display two different series of values. For example, you might want to take a look at where your money is going in two ways:

- Where have you been spending money over the last six months?
- Over the last six months, which months have been the ones in which you spent the most money?

These two questions both require the same data to answer, but you can display that information differently depending on what you are trying to summarize.

You can change what information is charted in the Rows and Columns tab of the Customize Report dialog box.

> Data display is organized in the Rows and Columns tab because here you can elect to chart information by row (the horizontal rows that store information in a report) or by column (the vertical columns that intersect with rows in the report). It actually isn't necessary for you to think of your chart in terms of rows and columns, although if you're familiar with charting spreadsheets, you might find this helpful. All you really need to worry about is selecting what information you want in your chart—regardless of whether that information is organized in rows or columns. You'll see how to do that in the following To Do exercise.

▲

To Do: Define Row and Column Options

1. In the Report and Chart Gallery, view the Who is Getting My Money report.

2. Click the Customize button at the bottom of the report window. Click the Date tab and select Last 6 Months from the Range drop-down list.

3. Click the Rows and Columns tab in the Customize Report dialog box.

4. Pull down the Rows drop-down list and select Categories. Pull down the Columns drop-down list and select Months. Click the Apply button to see how your chart looks.

▼   5. If you have many spending categories, your information will be a little overwhelming in a bar chart. You can consolidate bars by using a stacked bar chart. Click the Chart tab, select Bar as the chart type, and select the Stacked check box.

6. Click the OK button to view your stacked bar chart. Not all bars have legends in the X axis (at the bottom of the chart), but you can identify any bar by pointing to it. Figure 17.11 shows the content of one of the chart bars.

NEW TERM   **X axis and Y axis**—The horizontal line across the bottom of a chart is referred to as the X axis, and the vertical line along the left edge of a chart is called the Y axis.

FIGURE 17.11.

You can interpret chart data by pointing to a bar.

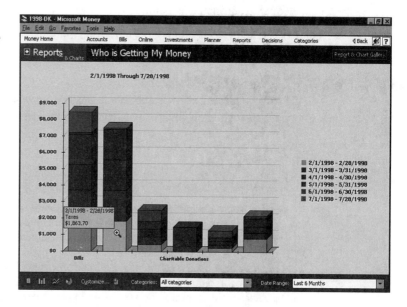

The way the data is organized makes it easy to identify which are your largest expense categories. But it is difficult to get a clear idea of which months had the highest expenses. The next step refocuses the chart to illustrate monthly expenses.

7. Now display this same data in a way that focuses on expenses by month: Click the Customize button in the chart view, and click the Rows and Columns tab in the dialog box. Select Months in the **Rows** drop-down list, and Categories in the **Columns** drop-down list. Deselect the **Sort** by Amount check box. Your dialog box
▼   should look like Figure 17.12.

▼ **Figure 17.12.**

You can organize chart data by Month.

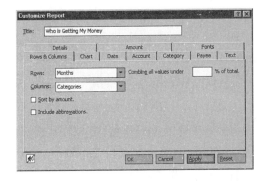

8. Click the OK button in the Customize Report dialog box. The resulting chart is shown in Figure 17.13. Each column in the chart represents a month. Each segment of a bar represents an expense category. The legend below identifies each expense category.

Figure 17.13.

You can view a bar chart with a time period graphed as rows.

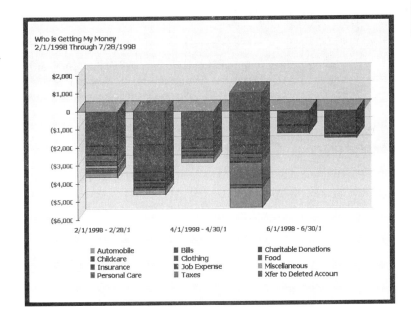

▲

The X axis (bottom of the chart) in Figure 17.13 identifies months. The X axis labels are not as helpful as they could be, because some of the dates are not completely displayed and other months are not identified at all. However, if you point to a column on the chart with your cursor, the month is identified.

When you print your graph, the X axis labels are a little more helpful (you'll learn how to do that a little later in this hour, in the section "Printing a Chart").

Creating a Favorite Chart

After you spend time defining a chart that you will want to see again, you can save it as a favorite. Just select the Favorites menu and choose Add to Favorites.

You are prompted with the Add to Favorites dialog box. Enter a name for your chart and click the OK button.

Now, you can see this chart (updated with new data) by clicking the Favorites menu and selecting your charts.

Resetting Customized Charts

If you want to return to the default settings for a report (which means viewing it as a report, not a chart), you can do that by clicking the Reset button in the Customize Report dialog box.

The Reset button is not active (available) if you just saved a custom report as your favorite. But it is available in the Report and Chart Gallery.

> Resetting report defaults removes *all* the custom attributes you've assigned. Don't reset the defaults unless you want to lose your custom chart. If you created a custom chart you want to keep, save it as a favorite.

Printing a Chart

Printing your chart is easy. The hardest part is to first define the chart itself. Then view the chart before you print it.

With your chart in view, you should define your printer setup to print landscape pages (sideways, so they are wider than they are long). To do this, select File, Print Setup, Report and Chart Setup from the main Money 99 menu bar. Then, click the Landscape option button in your printer's setup dialog box, and click the OK button.

With your printer set to print landscape (for charts and reports), select File, Print from the menu bar and click OK in the Print Chart dialog box.

If your printer is black and white, colors are converted to black-and-white shading when you print your chart.

Exporting a Chart

You can copy your chart to another Windows application by right-clicking the chart and selecting Copy from the context menu. Then open another application (like Word, or PowerPoint for example), right-click a page or slide, and select Paste from the context menu.

Figure 17.14 shows a Money 99 chart displayed in a PowerPoint slideshow.

FIGURE 17.14.

You can even view a Money 99 chart in a PowerPoint slideshow.

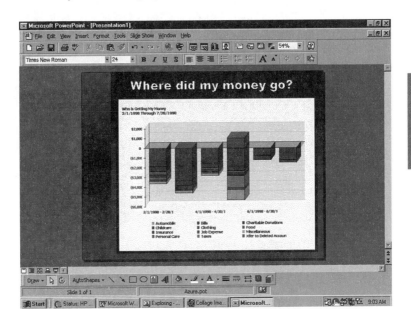

Summary

Charts allow you to visualize your financial picture. A chart summarizes large amounts of data to let you step back and get an overview of your accounts.

You can zoom in on chart information by moving your cursor over any part of a chart. You can also open accounts by double-clicking segments of charts.

Q&A

Q Can I graph any combination in Money 99?

A Money 99 has a large gallery of charts. However, Money 99 is not a charting or graphing program like Excel and does not have as many formatting or graphing options.

Q Can charts be saved in different file formats?

A No, charts created in Money are saved as part of your Money files. You can, however, copy your Money 99 charts to other applications and save them there as graphic image files.

HOUR 18

Money and Taxes

Money 99 makes tax time easier to handle. In Hour 5, "Dividing Expenses into Categories," you learned to divide different expenses into specific categories. These categories will help you organize your expenses when you prepare your taxes.

For example, one of Money's standard categories is Healthcare. You may be able to deduct some of your healthcare expenses, and Money makes it easy to itemize that expense. If you kept (didn't add to or modify) Money's standard categories, tax information is associated with that category for you. You can print a report that breaks down your tax-related income and expenses.

Money 99 is not a tax preparation package. But Money can convert your files to a format that can be imported into tax-preparation software.

How Money Helps You with Your Taxes

Money 99 helps with your taxes in two ways:

- During the year, money organizes your expenses and helps you project your expected tax bill.

- At tax time, Money prepares information to help complete your tax forms.

Most of the work of preparing for tax time is done by Money automatically. As you'll see in this hour, each time you associate a category with an expense or income transaction, Money organizes that information into tax-related categories.

Preparing for Taxes

The main thing you need to do to get help from Money at tax time is to make sure that your records are up-to-date and accurate. Hour 21, "Regular Tasks" has some suggestions for regular account maintenance, including periodically double-checking to make sure that your accounts reflect all your transactions.

Before you use Money to help prepare your taxes, answer these questions:

- Are your Money 99 accounts completely current?
- Have you associated every transaction with a Category?

> You'll get more for your money if you stick with the program's pre-defined income and expense categories. These standard categories are already associated with tax-related information. You'll find it much easier to prepare tax records if you are vigilant about assigning a category to each transaction.

If your Money accounts are accurate and up-to-date, you've done most of the work of preparing your taxes.

Viewing Categories with Tax-Associated Information

All the standard Money categories have tax information associated with them. You can view, add to, or modify these associations.

To Do: Viewing and Modifying Category Tax Information

1. Select the Categories View in the Navigation Bar.
2. Click the Views triangle at the top of the window to pull down the list of views, and select Categories, Subcategories, and Tax Information. The new view includes a column that associates tax-related categories with income tax schedules and form lines. Figure 18.1 shows healthcare expenses and their associated tax information.

FIGURE 18.1.

You can view tax-related information for categories.

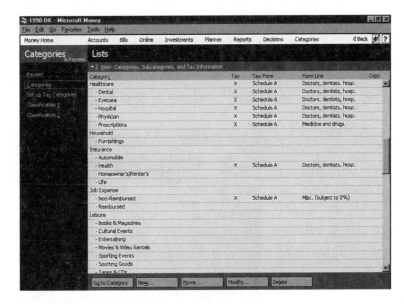

3. If you scroll down the list of categories to the Income items, you'll see associated tax information for income as well as expenses.

Assigning Tax-Related Information to Categories

You just saw that Money 99 has already assigned tax information to standard categories. You might want to add your own tax information because you added an additional category, or because categories that are not normally deductible are, in your case, tax deductions.

For example, Homeowner's Association dues may not be deductible for your residence, but might be for rental property. In that case, you could change the tax status for the standard Bill category to "Homeowner's Dues."

> Remember, neither this author nor Money 99 are tax advisors! For advice on deductible expenses, consult a tax authority.

To Do: Adding a Tax-Associated Category

1. To add a tax-associated category, click the Set up Tax Categories link in the left side of the Categories View.

2. Click the expense (or income) category in the list.

▼   3. Select the Include in Tax Reports check box in the form at the bottom of the list.

4. Pull down the Tax Form drop-down list, and select a tax form with which this category is associated.

5. Pull down the Form Line drop-down list, and select a line on the tax form to which you want to associate this item, as shown in Figure 18.2.

FIGURE 18.2.

Link an expense category to a tax item.

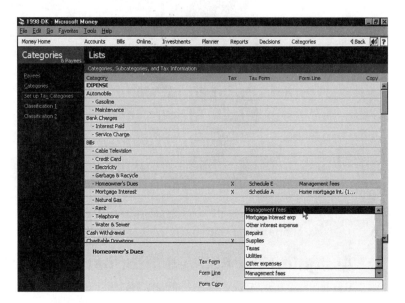

6. Complete the form by entering 1 in the Form Copy text box (or a higher number for additional copies). If you only need one copy of a tax form, select 1.

▲

You can enter or modify associated tax information for any category this way.

Reviewing Money Insider's "Taxes" Articles

Money isn't a tax preparation program, nor does it offer legal or tax advice. But there are several useful articles on preparing your taxes available in Money 99.

To read articles on preparing your taxes, click the Decisions on the Navigation Bar. In the Decisions View, select Taxes from the Decisions list on the left side of the window.

You can read any of Money's tax advise articles by clicking the link to them (see in Figure 18.3).

You can also update your tax article list by clicking the Update Internet Information link on the right side of the window.

FIGURE 18.3.

Select one of Money's tax articles.

Filling Out the Tax Worksheet

18

Money 99's Tax Worksheet can be used at any time of the year to analyze how your tax picture is shaping up. The Tax Worksheet does not fill out your taxes for you, nor it is something to use at the end of the year.

The Tax Worksheet monitors your tax deductions, payroll deductions, and the latest tax rules. The analysis it provides will help you prepare for tax time.

To Do: Filling Out the Tax Worksheet

1. Go to the Decisions View by clicking Decisions in the Navigation Bar.

2. In the left side of the Decisions View, click the Tools link. On the right side of the Tools View, click the Tax Worksheet link. There are five tabs in the Tax Estimator. The Overview, Income, Adjustments, and Deductions tabs collect information about your income and deductions.

3. Some of the text boxes in the first four tabs of the Tax Worksheet are filled in with information you've already told Money. But you should go through each text box in each tab, check the information there, and edit it as necessary. When you click in a tab, you'll see an explanation of it on the right side of the window as shown in Figure 18.4.

▼ FIGURE 18.4.

You can get help with a
Tax Worksheet text box.

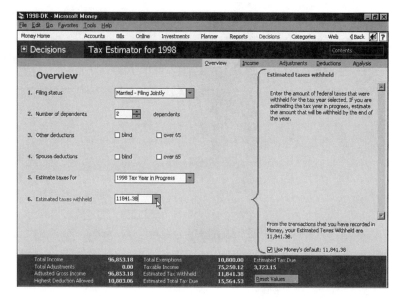

4. After you have completed filling in all the text boxes in the Tax worksheet, click
   the Analysis tab in the worksheet to see a summary of your tax status and to get
   advice. Figure 18.5 shows the results of a tax analysis.

FIGURE 18.5.

The results of the tax
analysis are shown
here.

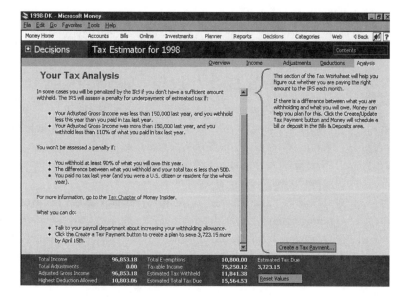

The tax calculations that the Tax Worksheet uses are downloaded from the Internet whenever you log on. If you don't log on to the Internet, you can enter your own updated tax information.

To update the tax information that Money 99 uses to calculate your tax analysis manually, select Tools, Options and choose the Tax tab. Choose Custom from the Show Rates For Filing Status drop-down list, and enter new tax information. Figure 18.6 shows tax information that was updated manually.

FIGURE 18.6.

Enter custom tax calculation data.

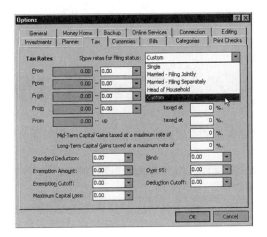

Remember that the analysis you get from the Tax Worksheet is not legal tax advice, but it will help you plan ahead and make sure that you have enough money set aside to pay your taxes.

Preparing Tax Forms

Money can prepare four tax-related reports for you:

- The *Tax Related Transactions Report* itemizes every tax-related transaction in your accounts. This report provides you with a detailed breakdown that you can use to prepare your taxes.
- The *Capital Gains Report* is shown in Figure 18.7. This report itemizes gains and losses for each of your investments.
- The *Loan Interest Report*, shown in Figure 18.8, itemizes your loan payments. This report breaks down your payments into principal and interest, making it easy for you to total your interest payments, which may be tax deductible.

FIGURE 18.7.

You can itemize capital gains for tax time.

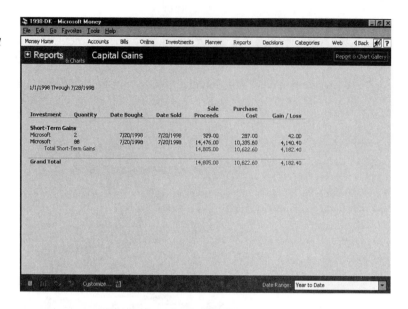

FIGURE 18.8.

You can calculate loan interest payments.

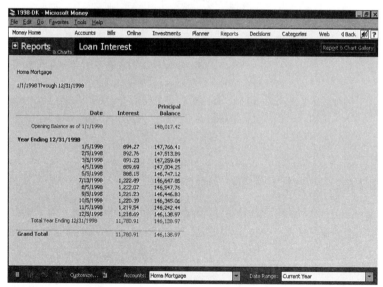

- The *Tax Software Report*, shown in Figure 18.9, provides a summary of tax form totals.

FIGURE 18.9.

The Tax Software Report gives you tax form information.

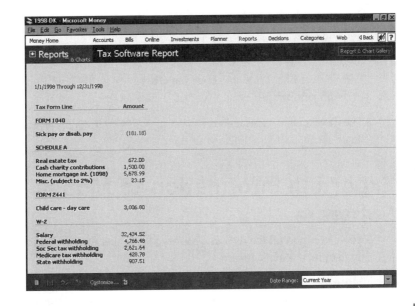

To Do: Printing a Tax-Related Transactions Report

1. Click Reports in the Navigation Bar.

2. Select Taxes from the list of links on the left side of the Reports View.

3. From the list of four tax reports that appears in the center of the window, click Tax-Related Transactions, as shown in Figure 18.10.

18

FIGURE 18.10.

You can prepare a Tax-Related Transactions report.

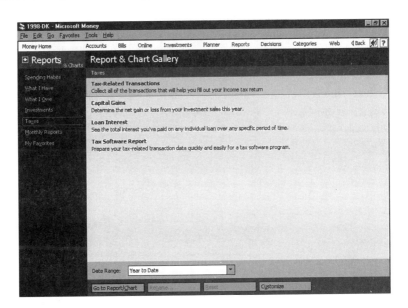

4. Select Year to Date from the Date Range drop-down list at the bottom of the window.

5. Click the Go to Report/Chart button at the bottom of the window.

6. Select File, Print, and click the OK button in the Print Report dialog box to print an itemized list of all tax-related transactions.

The Tax-Related Transactions Report provides your tax preparer with all the information he or she needs to complete your taxes.

Exporting Information to Money and Tax Software

You can export all the data in a Money 99 file in a format that is universally recognized by tax preparation software.

Money 99 offers two export formats, Tax Exchange Format (*.txf) and Tab Delimited Text (*.txt). Tab delimited text files can also be opened by other software packages, including spreadsheets and database programs.

To Do: Exporting Money 99 Files to *txf Format

1. Select File, Export to Tax Software from the Money 99 menu.

2. In the Export Tax dialog box, enter a filename for your new file in the File Name area.

3. Select the *.txf file format from the Save as Type drop-down list.

4. When you have completed the Export Tax dialog box, as shown in Figure 18.11, click the OK button.

FIGURE 18.11.

You can export Money files to tax preparation software.

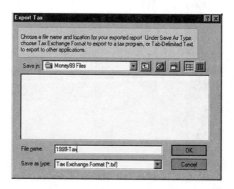

You can import the *.txf file you created in your tax software program.

Summary

Money helps you prepare for tax time by organizing your transactions into tax-form related categories. Also, during the year you can use the Tax Worksheet to see how your taxes are shaping up, and to assess whether or not you are deducting enough from your payroll taxes or setting aside enough savings to pay your taxes.

Money automatically updates the tax rates used in the Tax Worksheet whenever you log on to the Internet.

At tax time, Money has four reports that provide the information you or your tax preparation expert needs to file your taxes.

Q&A

Q Will Money 99 calculate how much interest was paid on a home loan?

A Yes, Money's Loan Interest Report calculates interest payments.

Q Is Money 99 a tax preparation program like Turbo Tax?

A No, but Money 99 files can be exported into a file format that can be imported into tax preparation software.

18

PART IV
Advanced Tools

Hour

19 Money as an Investment Tool

20 Money and Your Small Business

21 Regular Tasks

22 Backing Up and Archiving Your Data

23 Customizing Money

24 Converting from Quicken

HOUR 19

Money as an Investment Tool

You can use Money 99 to track your investment portfolio. In this hour, you'll learn to set up separate accounts for each of your investments and to track and manage these accounts.

Of course, the first step in managing your investments in Money is to pull together your existing records. If they are in paper form, start by gathering them together and organizing them. As you've seen in previous hours, the very process of entering your account information into Money is an organizing tool that helps you sort out your investments.

In this hour, you'll also learn to use Microsoft Investor online to track your investments. Investor is available to users of MS Money, and works hand in glove with Money 99 to provide you with current information on your investments.

Defining Your Investments for Money

The first step in enabling Money to help manage your investments is to create a separate investment account for each of your investments.

There are basically two types of accounts that you can set up:

- An *investment account* is used to track more than one investment included in a single statement.

- An *investment* is a single investment, like a stock or mutual fund.

> The wording of the two types of investment accounts is a little confusing, because Money 99 calls almost everything you track an "account." To understand how Money keeps track of investments, we'll use the word "account" to mean something different—an "investment account" is a special type of account that tracks more than one investment, although an "investment" is a single investment. The difference between an investment account and an investment is that an investment account tracks several different investments that are included in the same statement, although an investment is just one investment.

In this hour, you'll learn to manage both investments and investment accounts in Money 99.

Setting Up an Investment Account

Before you can track and manage your investments in Money, you must set up both of these types of accounts. Do you have your investment information handy? If so, you're ready to start.

To Do: Create a New Investment Account

1. Select the Investments View in the Navigation Bar, and click the New button at the bottom of the Investments View.

2. Select A New Investment Account in the New dialog box, as shown in Figure 19.1. Then click the Next button.

3. In the next dialog box, enter the name of the institution that is managing your investment. For example, in Figure 19.2, Webster Associates has been entered. (If you are not using a financial institution to manage this investment account, you should skip ahead to the next "To Do" section where you'll learn to track single investments.) Then click the Next button again.

19

FIGURE 19.1.

Set up an account to track several investments covered by a single statement.

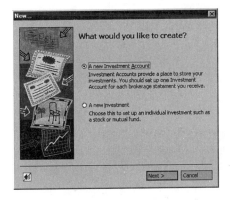

If your financial institution supports online investing with Money 99, you can click the Financial Institutions button in the dialog box and select your investor from the list as shown in Figure 19.2.

FIGURE 19.2.

Dozens of financial institutions allow you to manage your investments online with MS Money.

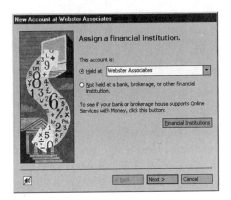

4. The next dialog box asks you what *kind* of account you want to set up. You have three choices: Employee Stock Options, Investments, or Retirement Account. The selection you make helps Money present you with a coherent picture of your finances, including your retirement picture. After you have selected an investment type, click the Next button.

5. The following dialog box suggests an account name—this is for identification purposes in your Money 99 records. You can accept the suggested name or type a new one. Then click the Next button.

6. In the next dialog box, tell Money whether your investment is tax-deferred by selecting either the No or Yes option buttons. Then click the Next button.

▼ 7. In the subsequent dialog box, enter the value of *investments* in your account in the text box at thetop of the dialog box. (Remember, you can always click the down arrow next to a box like this and use the calculator to enter values, as shown in Figure 19.3.) Do *not* enter the balance in any associated cash account in this box. Instead, if you have an associated cash account, click the <u>Y</u>es option button. Then click the Next button.

FIGURE 19.3.

Money needs to know the estimated value of investments in your account.

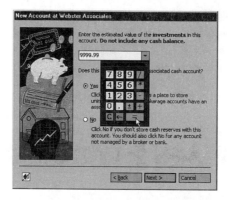

8. If you selected the <u>Y</u>es option button in the previous dialog box, you are prompted to enter the balance in your associated cash account in the next dialog box. You can add to or change this information later if you need to, but if you have your cash balance handy, enter it now. You can also select a currency from the drop-down list in this dialog box. Then click the Next button.

9. The final dialog box in this wizard informs you that you've finished setting up your investment account. Soon you'll be managing your investments in the Accounts View. There is one more step, however, before you can do that—you

▲ need to define the specific investments that you'll be managing in this account.

Associating Securities with an Account and Getting Online Quotes from Investor

Now that you've defined an investment account, it's time to tell Money what investments you will be managing in that account.

To Do: Assign Individual Investments to an Account

1. Select the Account Manager View, and in the list on the left side of the window, click the investment account you just defined.

If you don't see your account in the Account Manager, or you want to change the way you are viewing your accounts list, you can click the down arrow in the upper-left corner of the Account Manager, and select from many different ways to view your accounts. Figure 19.4 shows the accounts in Large Icon View.

FIGURE 19.4.

Pick an Account Manager View that will help you keep your accounts organized.

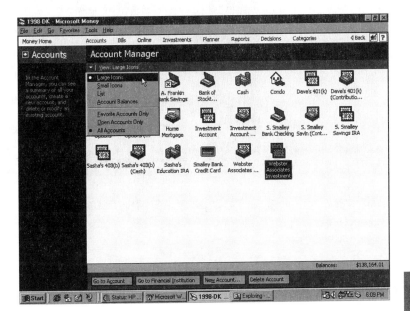

2. It's easier to enter an investment transaction by using the form. You can enter transactions in forms by clicking the down arrow in the upper-left corner of the Account window and selecting Use Forms to Enter Transactions, as shown in Figure 19.5.

3. Click the New button in the investment form. Type the name of the investment in the Investment box and click the Enter button. The Create New Investment dialog box appears, as shown in Figure 19.6. Select one (you must choose *only* one) of the option buttons to define the type of investment this is: Mutual Fund, Stock, CD, and so on. Then click the Next button.

Remember, right now you are defining a specific investment that is *part of* a larger account. If you want to set up a *specific account* dedicated to a *single investment*, you should consult the section "Setting Up an Account for a Single Investment" later in this hour.

FIGURE 19.5.

*Entering investment
transactions is easier
in a form.*

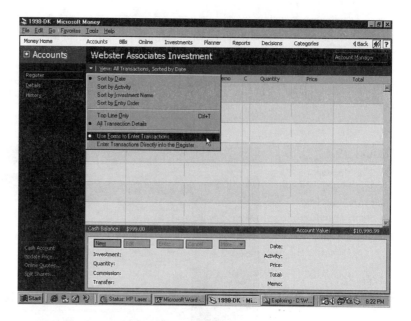

FIGURE 19.6.

*Money prompts you to
define new investments.*

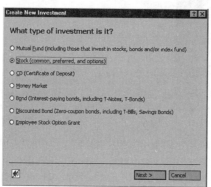

4. The next New Stock dialog box prompts you to enter information about your
   investment. If you entered a stock, you can look up the symbol for your stock by
   clicking the Find Symbol button. Clicking this button launches Microsoft Investor,
   and connects to the page in Investor with information on your stock. Figure 19.7
   shows that Microsoft Investor was used to find the symbol for Microsoft
   Corporation.

5. If you looked up your stock in Investor, you can also find out the latest quote on
   your investment! Investor tracks information on thousands of stocks. You just saw
   how you can use Microsoft Investor to supply you with other online information
   about your investments. You can click the stock symbol and find out at what price

▼   your stock is selling. Figure 19.8 shows the process of getting a current quote on Microsoft stock.

FIGURE 19.7.

You can look up a Stock Symbol in Investor.

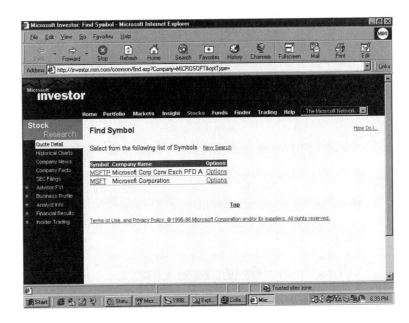

FIGURE 19.8.

Investor provides updated stock quotes online.

19

▼

6. Click the Finish button to finish defining your investment. Then select Buy, Sell, or Other Activity from the Activity drop-down list. Money can keep more accurate track of your investments if you use Buy instead of Add for purchasing stocks.

7. In the Price text box enter the price you paid for your stocks or other investment. If you just looked up the price online with Investor, you know exactly what you paid.

8. Finish entering information on your investment. The Date text box has today's date by default, and the Total text box is calculated automatically. When you have finished defining your investment in the form, click the Enter button to place the transaction in the Account ledger.

Setting Up an Account for a Single Investment

If you are tracking a single investment, you can define that investment in the Investment View. From the Investment Portfolio, click the New button at the bottom of the window. In the first dialog box, select the option button titled A New Investment (not the A new Investment Account button). Then click Next and use the wizard to define your investment.

Working with Mutual Funds

If one or more of the investments you are tracking in Money is a Mutual Fund, you can tell Money how you want to calculate the cost basis for your fund. The cost basis is the total price you paid for your investment, used for calculating profit and loss for taxes. Money tracks that value in one of three ways:

- Actual Cost Basis
- Average Cost Basis (single category)
- Average Cost Basis (double category)

Actual Cost Basis uses the actual price you paid for a fund to calculate cost basis. *Average Cost Basis (single category)* calculates capital gains based on the *average* price you paid for a fund over time. *Average Cost Basis (double category)* is the same as Average Cost Basis (single category) except that cost basis is figured differently depending on whether your investment pays off in long-term or short-term gains.

To keep your tax records consistent, you should use the same cost basis in every account in which you hold a given mutual fund.

To Do: Define Average Cost Basis for a Mutual Fund

1. Click Investments in the Navigation Bar.

2. Click the mutual fund for which you will define a cost basis, then right-click and select Go to Details from the context menu.

3. Select a method of calculating cost basis from the Cost Basis drop-down list.

Maintaining Investment Accounts

After you have defined your investment account and each individual investment, it's easy to enter additional transactions for that account.

Simply go to the Accounts View (using the Navigation Bar), and double-click the investment account in which you will be buying or selling stocks or bonds.

Tracking Stock Prices

After you have defined a stock, you can quickly view its current price in the Investment Portfolio. Click the Online Quotes button and you are prompted with a list of your stocks. Select the check box(es) for those stocks whose price you want to check.

If you are not connected to the Internet, you are prompted to activate your Internet connection. After you download the latest quotes, you can view a price history of your stock by double-clicking it.

Buying Additional Stocks

Click the New button in the investment form at the bottom of the window to enter additional transactions. If you are buying or selling stocks that you have already defined, you can select them from the New drop-down list, as shown in Figure 19.9.

FIGURE 19.9.

After you define a stock, you can make additional purchases.

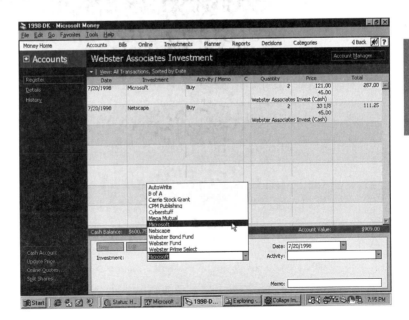

19

Selling Stocks

Selling stocks works just like buying stocks, at least as far as Money is concerned. You can sell a stock by selecting the stock from the Investment drop-down list and choosing Sell from the Activity drop-down list. Enter the number of stocks, the price, a date (if other than today's), and your broker's commission (again, Money calculates the totals for you).

If you sell shares of a stock that you have purchased in more than one lot, you'll see the What Shares Should I Use? dialog box. You have the option of accepting the default—to sell shares FIFO (First in, first out)—or to sell lots in some other order.

As you enter various stock purchases, each separate purchase is considered a lot, or block. When you sell, Money assumes "FIFO," (First in, First out), and calculates profit and loss based on figuring that you are selling the first lots of stock first, and the last ones last.

If you elect to sell shares in an order other than that in which you bought them, the wizard prompts you for information on how you want to sell your shares.

After you finish defining which shares to sell (if that is necessary) click the Enter button to enter the transaction in your ledger.

Transfer Money to an Investment Account

You can transfer money into an investment account from any other account (including a different investment account). For example, you might want to transfer money from a checking account to one of your investment accounts.

To Do: Transfer Funds from a Checking Account to an Investment Account

1. Click Accounts in the Navigation Bar to see a list of your accounts.
2. Double-click the account *from which you will be transferring funds.*
3. Click the Transfer button in the form at the bottom of the window.
4. The current account appears in the From text box. In the To text box, use the drop-down list to select the investment account to which you are transferring funds.
5. Enter the amount that you want to transfer and enter a check number (or select Print or epay).
6. When you have defined your transfer, click the Enter button in the form. The transfer is logged in your checking account ledger as well as your investment account.

Viewing Investment Information

After you set up investment accounts in Money, you can instantly monitor the status and performance of your entire portfolio or individual accounts.

In the remainder of this hour, you'll learn to use Money and Investor to zoom in on a particular stock or step back and appraise your financial status.

Total Portfolio Value

The Account Manager is a quick way to get an overview of all your investment accounts. To see a list of all your investments with balances, click Accounts in the Navigation Bar. In Accounts View, select the Account Manager as shown in Figure 19.10.

FIGURE 19.10.

After you define a stock, you can make additional purchases.

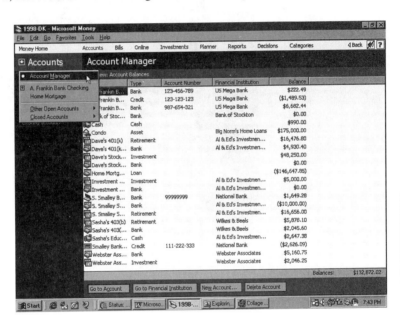

From the Accounts View, click the down arrow at the top of the Accounts Manager, and select Account Balances. Each account's current balance is displayed, with a total balance in the bar at the bottom of the list.

Viewing Investment Account Details

You can view and change information about any particular investment account in Details View. To see an investment's details, click Investment View in the Navigation Bar, and double-click the investment in the Details link on the left side of the window.

The resulting Account Details screen tells you how you've defined your account and allows you to enter information like account number and contact information for your investment counselor.

This screen also has check boxes that let you define tax status. In Figure 19.11, the IRA account has tax-deferred tax status assigned. If you wanted to convert this IRA to a retirement account (with no tax due until retirement withdrawals), you could select the Retirement Account check box.

FIGURE 19.11.

Accounts can be tax deferred on retirement accounts with no taxes due until retirement.

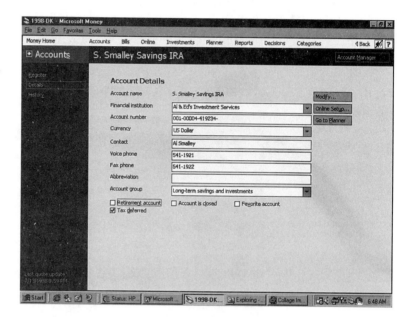

Retirement Planning

Money 99 incorporates your investment portfolio into the planner. When you use the planner to project your retirement scenarios, there are different ways you can handle tax-deferred investments.

When you create a retirement account, or convert an existing account to a retirement account the balance is integrated into the Savings & Investments area in the Lifetime Planner.

Viewing Investments in Graphs

The Reports View has six reports to help you track your investments. Five of these reports can be viewed as graphs to provide a summary picture of your investments.

To see an investment report, select the Reports View and choose Investments from the list of links on the left side of the window.

You can see any report by double-clicking it in the right side of the view. You can then see a report in chart form by clicking one of the three chart icons (bar, line, or pie) at the bottom of the window.

Not all chart types are available for all reports. Chart types that are not available will be grayed out.

The five (graphable) reports are

- **Portfolio Value by Investment Account**—This report can generate graphs that display the relative value of different investments.

  Figure 19.12 displays a bar chart generated from the Portfolio Value by Investment account report to compare the values of several accounts.

FIGURE 19.12.

Compare the value of accounts with a chart.

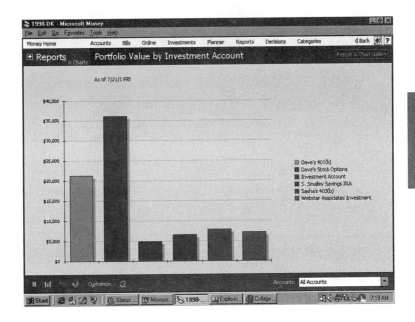

- **Portfolio Value by Investment Type**—Lets you compare the value of different types of investments like stocks, bonds, funds, and so on. This is similar to the previous chart, except that it compares the value of different *types* of investments.

- **Performance by Investment Account**—Useful for comparing growth rates of account values.

- **Performance by Investment Type**—Compares growth rates for types of investments in your portfolio.

- **Price History**—Tracks value of selected stocks. In Figure 19.13, the performance of a big investment in a favorite stock is compared to the performance of the Standard and Poor's 500.

FIGURE 19.13.

Ouch! This stock doesn't look too good compared to the Standard and Poor's 500.

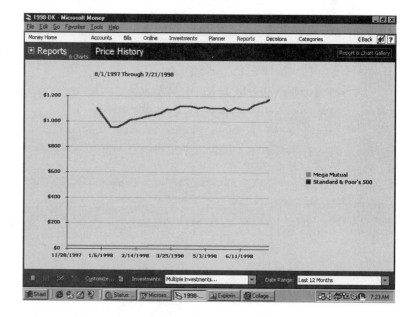

 The Investment Transactions report keeps track of too much information to be graphed effectively, so no graph is available for this report.

Each investment report in graph form is a powerful tool for visualizing your investment status. The following "To Do" exercises show you how to create one of these graphs—the Portfolio Value by Investment Account Graph. You can use these basic steps to create graphs from other Investment reports.

To Do: Create a Portfolio Value by Investment Account Graph

▼ To Do

1. Select the Reports View and click the Investments link in the list of report categories on the left side of the window.

2. Double-click the Portfolio Value by Investment Account report on the right side of the window.

3. Click the bar chart icon underneath the report.

4. Click the Customize button. In the Chart tab of the Customize Report dialog box, select legend location from the Show Legend drop-down list.

5. Select chart type. In Figure 19.14, a 3D non-stacked bar chart is defined with gridlines.

FIGURE 19.14.

A 3D bar chart is defined.

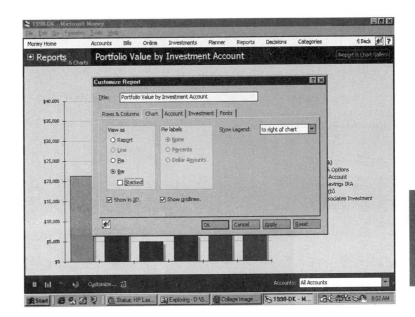

6. Click the Account tab in the Customize Report dialog box and select the accounts that you want to include in the chart by clicking the check boxes next to them.

▲ 7. Click OK in the Customize Report dialog box and view your chart.

For a more detailed discussion of charts, see Hour 17, "Charts and the Chart Gallery."

Summary

Money 99 lets you define and track many types of investments. You can organize your investments into accounts or track them as individual investments. You can also distinguish between tax-deferred, retirement, and taxable investments.

Money is closely integrated with Microsoft Investor, allowing you to check the status of a stock instantly online.

Money's reports and graphs allow you to view the status of your investment accounts quickly.

Q&A

Q Can Money 99 track investments online?

A Yes, and it's easy to do.

Q Can Money 99 track tax free investments?

A Yes, retirement accounts are treated as tax free investments.

HOUR **20**

Money and Your Small Business

Money 99 has all the personal finance planning tools you'll need, unless your financial picture is in the Bill Gates ballpark. Money is not a business accounting program, and if you are going to be running a large business, you should explore financial packages dedicated to just that.

On the other hand, if you have a side business, if you're self-employed, or if you hire a couple of assistants, Money 99 probably has everything you need to track your business accounts.

Running your small business with Money requires some customizing of accounts and how they work. In this hour, you'll learn to adapt Money to running your small business.

Starting Your Business

The first step in setting up a small business in Money is to create a new account. If your nonsalary income is inconsequential, there's probably no need to create a separate small business account. But if you will be issuing dozens of invoices, incurring dozens of business expenses, or issuing payroll checks, you'll probably want to create a new Money 99 file dedicated exclusively to your business accounts.

In Figure 20.1, a new file is being designed that will be used to track a Lawn and Gardening service.

FIGURE 20.1.

Small businesses are easier to manage with separate Money 99 files.

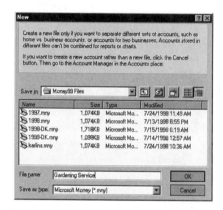

To Do: Create a New Small Business Account

1. With Money 99 open, select File, New from the menu bar.

2. Assign a name for your business file and click the OK button in the New dialog box.

3. You'll be prompted with the Personal Profile form—fill it out, selecting the Self Employed option button near the end of the form, and then click Done Answering Questions.

▲

How Money Can Help Your Business

In many ways, you will organize your small business accounts and transactions the same way you set up your personal accounts. As you set up your new Money 99 file, go to the Accounts View, and define the accounts you will use for your business. If you are not using separate checking, savings, or credit accounts for your small business, you might want to consider just tracking your small business expenses in your personal Money 99 file.

In Figure 20.2, three accounts have been set up to begin tracking a small business:

- Cash Account
- Checking Account
- Credit Card Account

FIGURE 20.2.

Start your small business file by defining dedicated business accounts.

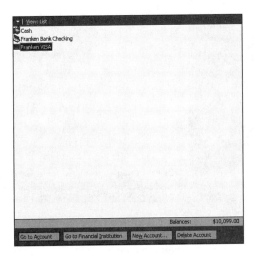

Of course, you can add more accounts as you develop your business file, but this basic list gets you started. You should use your checking, cash, and credit accounts to pay all your bills. Deposit income to those accounts as well.

With these accounts set up (and balances entered), you can begin to create additional accounts to manage your business.

Tracking Expenses and Liabilities

The easiest way to track your expenses and liabilities is to issue checks or make cash or credit payments, and record these payments as transactions. By keeping your small business transactions in a separate file, you can monitor your business debts and expenses.

The main thing you need to do to prepare to manage your business expenses and liabilities is to create new categories to which you will assign business expenses.

In Figure 20.3, a few expense categories have been set up to organize business expenses.

20

FIGURE 20.3.

You should delete existing categories and create new ones for your business.

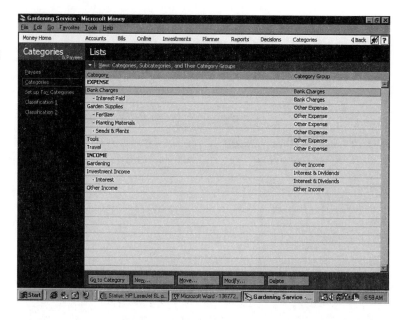

Before you go through the tedious process of deleting all existing categories by hand, you can automate the process. Select Tools, Options and click the Categories tab. Use the Remove Unused Categories button as shown in Figure 20.4. Then click the OK button in the dialog box to remove categories not in use.

Monitoring Large Numbers of Transactions

With your accounts and categories set up for your small business, you can begin to enter income and expense transactions, just as you would for personal accounts.

You can define recurring transactions to track regular income and bills that are owed each month.

To Do: Enter a Recurring Income Transaction

1. In the Bills area, click New at the bottom of the window.

2. Click the Deposit button in the Create a New Scheduled Transaction dialog box and click Next.

3. Select the More Than Once… option button in the next wizard dialog box, and choose Monthly from the Frequency drop-down list. Click the Next button again in the wizard dialog box.

FIGURE 20.4.

You can quickly wipe out Money's personal-based categories in the Options dialog box.

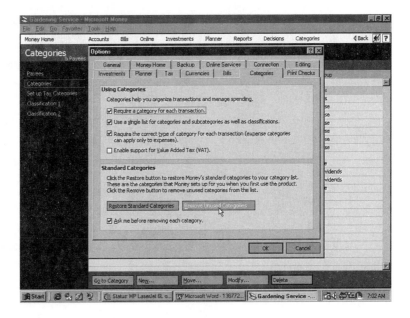

4. Enter deposit details in the next dialog box, including the account to which the income will be deposited, the payee (in the From text box), and the amount. Click the Next button again.

5. Choose a Payment Method from the drop-down list. If you will be depositing the income in the account yourself, choose Manual, and then click Next.

6. Use the remaining wizard dialog boxes to define the amount of the regular income, and whether to enter the first payment.

After you define a regular source of income, that transaction is automatically recorded each month. When you open your small business file, you'll see a list of outstanding invoices or other income. For example, in Figure 20.5, the home page shows that the Joneses owe $100. This particular bill didn't have to be entered manually for this month, because it's a regular, recurring business transaction, and is automatically posted.

You can define regularly occurring *expenses* the same way you defined regular income. For example, if you have expenses like office rent that are the same each month, you can automatically post those to your Accounts View.

After you define recurring income and expense, you can update your accounts by right-clicking a posted income or expense transaction, and updating it from the context menu. For example, when a bill is due, you can right-click it, select Record Payment from the context menu, and select Record Payment. Or, if the amount of the bill or income is the same each month, you can select Mark As, Received, as shown in Figure 20.6.

20

FIGURE 20.5.

Regularly scheduled income is automatically posted, and overdue bills are displayed at the Money Home Page.

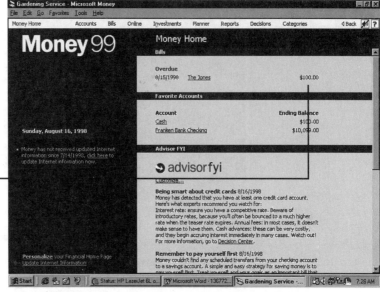

Current bills and payments

FIGURE 20.6.

Automating your regularly scheduled income and expense postings makes entering payments as easy as a mouse click.

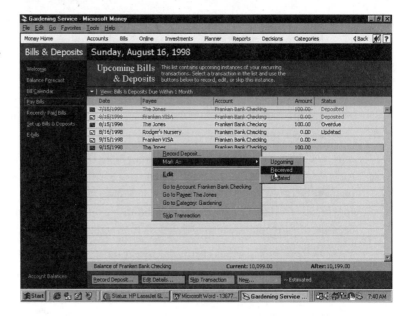

Tracking Expenses

If you set up a separate file for your business accounts, you can monitor your business income by using many of the reports that are normally used for tracking personal finances.

You can see a list of available chart and report categories by clicking Reports in the Navigation Bar. In Figure 20.7, the Income vs. Spending chart is used to see how the bottom line is shaping up.

FIGURE 20.7.

Money's personal finance reports and graphs can also track business accounts.

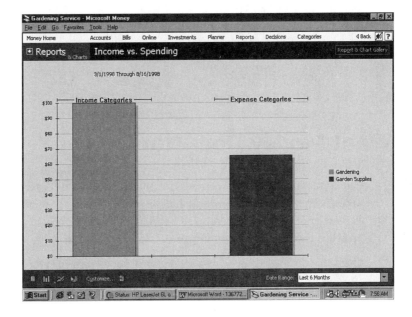

Not all of Money's reports and charts are specifically useful for monitoring your small business, but many are. Table 20.1 lists some reports and graphs that you might find particularly useful for tracking the status of your business.

TABLE 20.1. REPORTS AND CHARTS FOR SMALL BUSINESS MANAGEMENT.

Report or Chart	Found in Category	Useful For
Income vs. Spending	Spending Habits	View your net income
Monthly Cash Flow	Spending Habits	View long term income versus expenses
Category Spending	Spending Habits	Break down spending by category to monitor expenses
Payee Spending	Spending Habits	Review income by source
Upcoming Bills	What I Owe	Anticipate upcoming expenses
Current Month Report	Monthly Reports	An overall summary of your business activity for the month

20

Keeping Up-to-Date

As you have already seen in this hour, Money reminds you of unpaid (due) bills, and owed income. A list of overdue bills and income appears on the Money Home Page. You'll also see a breakdown of due bills and income in the Bills View. You can look ahead to see scheduled bills (and income) using the Bill Calendar.

To Do: View Upcoming Bills and Income

1. Select the Bills View from the Navigation Bar.
2. Click the Bill Calendar link on the left side of the window.

What Money Does Not Do

So far this hour, you've seen that Money's structure for tracking your personal finances can be adapted to a small business. You may have noticed that there are some business procedures that Money does not handle. Money 99 will not produce invoices for you, nor is there any way to link invoices to accounts. However, you can create invoices manually, and then enter the invoice information into Money's Bills View as income.

One thing that Money is not particularly well set up for is handling paychecks as expenses. But this can be done, and in the remainder of this hour, you'll explore how to record payroll expenses in Money.

Managing Payroll

Tracking payroll stretches the framework of what's possible with Money 99, but it can be done. If your small business employs dozens of employees, you'll probably want to use a business-sized accounting program, or use a bookkeeping or accounting agency.

If you are issuing paychecks to a small number of people, you can use Money to keep track of your payroll. There are no built-in payroll accounts in Money, so you'll have to define your own.

When you write payroll checks, you are required to deduct and keep track of several categories of taxes, including Federal and State taxes, Social Security taxes, as well as other taxes and deductions such as retirement accounts or medical insurance.

Creating Special Payroll Accounts

The first step in preparing to write paychecks is to define a Payroll expense category. After you create a Payroll category, you'll create additional subcategories to break down payroll expenses and itemize deductions for each check.

To Do: Create a Payroll Category

1. Select the Category View from the Navigation Bar
2. Click the New button at the bottom of the window.
3. Select the Create a New Category option button and click Next.
4. Select the Expense option button in the Category Type area, and enter Payroll in the Name text box, then click Next again.
5. Select Other Expense from the list of existing groups, and click the Finish button.

Creating Subcategories for Deductions and Contributions

Before you can assign payroll expenses, you need to create subcategories for each deduction. In this way, you'll keep track of Social Security, federal and state taxes, and so on.

To Do: Create a Subcategory for Federal Income Tax

1. With the Payroll category selected in the Categories View, click the New button at the bottom of the window. In the first New Category dialog box, select the Add a Subcategory to Payroll? option button, and click the Next button.
2. In the next New Category dialog box, enter Federal Income Tax in the Name box.
3. Click the Next, and then Finish buttons in the dialog boxes to complete the New Category Wizard. Your new subcategory should appear under Payroll in the Categories list.

You will probably also want to create deduction subcategories for:

- Social Security tax
- Medicare tax
- State income tax

You might also need to create subcategories for expenses such as:

- State SUI/SDI taxes
- Retirement accounts
- Medical insurance deductions

20

Creating a Subcategory for Net Income

In addition to creating subcategories for income *deductions*, you should create an additional subcategory under Payroll for net income. This way, you can track (and even calculate) net income after payroll deductions.

To Do: Create a Subcategory for Net Income

1. With the Payroll category selected in the Categories View, click the New button at the bottom of the window. In the first New Category dialog box, select the Add a Subcategory to Payroll? option button, and click the Next button.

2. In the next New Category dialog box, enter Net Income in the Name box, as shown in Figure 20.8.

FIGURE 20.8.

Along with entering payroll deductions, a net income subcategory is helpful when you issue paychecks.

3. Click the Next, and then Finish buttons in the dialog boxes to complete the New Category Wizard. Your new subcategory should appear under Payroll in the Categories list.

Issuing Paychecks

If you have created a Payroll category, and subcategories for all your deductions, you're ready to issue payroll checks.

Money won't calculate deductions for you. Money does not provide advice on how much of a deduction is required for each category. Tax information is available from the IRS or your state (or province) tax folks.

Assuming that you have obtained this information, and calculated how much you need to deduct for each category, you're ready to generate a paycheck.

As you enter payroll information, Money 99 can calculate net pay, after you enter gross pay and deductions.

To Do: Generate a Paycheck

1. Go to the Bills View, and click the New button at the bottom of the window.

2. In the Enter Payment Details area of the dialog box, select an account from which to generate a check, and enter the payee name in the Pay To area.

3. Still in the same dialog box, enter a total (gross) pay amount in the Amount area. In Figure 20.9, a paycheck is being generated for $750 *gross pay*.

FIGURE 20.9.

Enter gross pay as an expense.

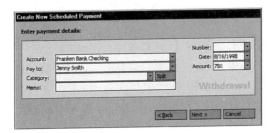

4. Click the Split button next to the Category text box, and select the first of your payroll deductions. In Figure 20.10, a deduction is entered for Federal Income Tax.

FIGURE 20.10.

Payroll deductions can be recorded as split categories.

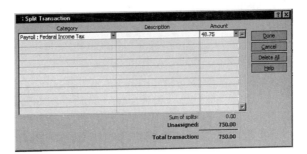

5. After you enter your first deduction in the Split transaction dialog box, press the Tab key to move to the next line and enter another deduction.

6. After you have entered all your deductions, enter Net Income as your last subcategory. Don't enter an amount for this subcategory. Instead, right-click the row and select Add Unassigned Amount Here from the context menu, as shown in Figure 20.11.

7. After you enter all subcategories, the Unassigned amount at the bottom of the dialog box should be 0.00. Click the Done button. Click the Next and Finish buttons, and record your payment.

20

FIGURE 20.11.

Money calculates the remaining amounts in a split category.

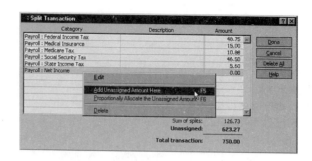

Information for Tax Forms

If you break down each payroll check into subcategories, you can easily access the information you need for making tax payments. You can also print the information you need for employee tax forms such as W2 forms. You can create a report with all the tax numbers you need. This report subtotals all deductions for each employee for a year.

To Do: Generate an Annual Report of All Payroll Deductions for One Employee

1. Click Reports in the Navigator, and click the Spending Habits link in the list of Reports on the left side of the window.

2. Click the Category Spending report on the right side of the Reports View window, and select Payroll from the Categories drop-down list.

3. Click the Customize button at the bottom of the Reports View window. From the Subtotal By drop-down list, select Subcategories as shown in Figure 20.12.

FIGURE 20.12.

Money's expense reports can be subtotaled by category.

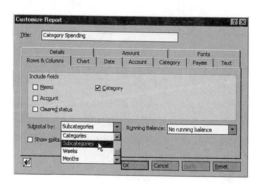

4. Click the Payee tab in the Customize Report dialog box, and select the check box for the single employee for whom you want to generate a year-end tax report. Then click OK.

▼ 5. Your report will show all subcategories for the selected employee—this will show you subtotals for each income tax deduction. Figure 20.13 shows a report for one employee. You can generate as many tax reports as you need by changing the selected employee in the Payee tab of the Customize Report dialog box.

FIGURE 20.13.

You can create a year-end employee tax record.

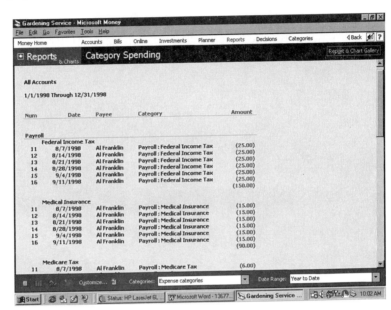

▲

Summary

Money 99 is a personal, not a business financial package. But there are two good reasons to use it to manage your small business: Money is powerful enough to handle small business records and many folks include small business income and expenses as part of their personal finances.

In general, you should create a new, separate Money 99 file to track your business records. That way, your business records are easy to isolate and compile.

20

Q&A

Q Can you write payroll checks with Money?

A You can write *any* check with Money. If you set up a Payroll category and appropriate subcategories, you can generate tax reports when you need them.

Q Does Money generate invoices or track my sales contacts?

A No.

HOUR 21

Regular Tasks

Using Microsoft Money helps you structure your financial management into regularly scheduled activities. When you set up your Money accounts, you entered scheduled payments and income. As you've already seen, Money prompts you to pay due (and overdue) bills.

At the same time, Money works best and helps you the most if you set up a regular schedule of entering transactions and checking on your financial status. You've heard the old saying "garbage in, garbage out." If you neglect to enter payments or keep your data current, Money won't be worth much to you. Or, to put it in a more positive light, if you regularly maintain your Money 99 files, you'll have an accurate picture of your finances. Either way you look at it, it's important to maintain a regular schedule.

To keep your Money accounts accurate, you should establish a regular pattern of maintaining your records. In this hour, you'll explore methods for organizing your data entry and updating into daily, weekly, monthly, quarterly, and annual activities. Work your way through the procedures in this hour, to prepare yourself to organize your own file maintenance schedule. For example, if you only pay a few bills a week, you could organize a neat stack on your desk, and enter them regularly each Friday. The important thing is that you establish a regular routine so all the financial events that occur in the real world get reflected in your Money 99 accounts.

You might also want to develop a daily, weekly, and/or monthly routine for checking up on your investments online, and monitoring the status of your financial health. You'll learn to do that in this hour as well.

Daily Chores

When you pay bills by check, or with your credit card, you can either enter the bills in Money as you pay them, or you can wait until you get your monthly statement or bill and record them at that point. I do both. This has a number of advantages:

- By entering your bills as you pay them, you have a more current, accurate picture of your balances.

- If you enter bills as you pay them, you can use your monthly statement to double-check your account.

- By entering each payment as you make it, you can check your monthly statement and make sure you weren't billed or debited incorrectly by your bank.

> Of course you are also probably saving hard copy receipts. Receipts are your ultimate backup, and they also can serve as an additional way to double-check the accuracy of your expense records at the end of a week, month, or year.

Keeping Track of Receipts

Scenario: Today you paid eleven bills by check. A pile of receipts is lying on your desk. Instead of throwing them in your monthly receipts file, and waiting for your bank statement, you can enter your payments right away.

Here, we'll explore the process of making payments on irregular, one-time only bills, the kind that are not tracked in Money or paid automatically.

To Do: Make a One Time Only Payment

▼ To Do

1. With your Money file open, select the Bills area.

2. Click the New button at the bottom of the Bills area, and in the Create a Scheduled Transaction dialog box, click the Bill option button. Click the Next button in the wizard.

▼   3. Because you are entering a one-time only bill here, click the Only once option but-
          ton as shown in Figure 21.1, then click the Next button in the wizard.

FIGURE 21.1.

*Some bills don't fit into
your regularly sched-
uled payments list—set
up a frequent schedule
to enter them manually
in Money.*

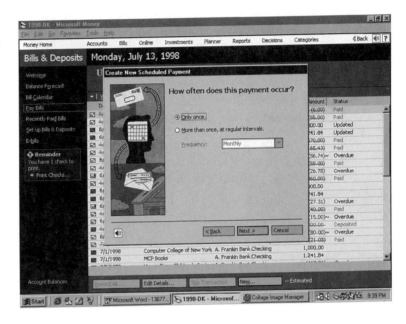

▲   4. Enter the details in the Create a New Scheduled Payment dialog box, and record
          the payment.

> If you make small, irregular payments from cash, you should set up a cash
> account. You can initiate and replenish a cash account by transferring
> money from a checking account or other account. You can review the
> process of creating new accounts in Hour 4, "Setting Up Accounts."

Recording Credit Card Transactions as They Are Made

The same approach you just learned for entering irregular payments on a daily basis can
be used to enter payments from a cash account, your checking account, or your credit
card.

Again, the point to keep in mind is to set up a regular routine, and record payments
before you get your statement.

21

Thinking "Category"

Perhaps you've got the mind of an accountant—each time you grab a pack of gum at the airport gift shop you mentally assign it to an expense category. Let's see, would that be medical preventive care (to prevent ear popping), food, entertainment... For the rest of us, it requires conscious organizing and discipline to maintain expense categories for the money we spend. As you enter irregular payments, you'll be tempted to let your well-structured category list go to pieces. There is going to be a pull to do that, because in the real world, it is sometimes difficult to figure out where to assign expenses like haircuts, tai chi lessons, developing photos, and so on.

Each time you enter a new expense or new income, you are prompted to enter a category. The first step, always, is to click the Category drop-down list and carefully examine your existing categories. Then, if you really need to, you can create a new category.

To review the principles involved in adding new categories (and when not to), look back at Hour 5, "Dividing Expenses into Categories."

What's New at Money's Home Page?

There are many reasons to check in at the Money 99 home page regularly. A quick stop at the page each day lets you see a graph of the day, as well as a tip of the day.

Wherever you are in Money, you can jump to the Home Page View by clicking the Money Home link in the upper-left corner of the window (under the main Money menu bar). The tip of the day is actually worth the time to check out. When you start working with Money 99, you should focus on exactly what you need to get your accounts set up and functioning. But as you use Money day in and day out, you can learn tips that will save you time and let you get more out of Money.

You can choose from a variety of graphs to display daily by clicking the Personalize link at your home page. That opens an Options dialog box where you can define the contents of your home page. In Figure 21.2, a Chart of the Day is being added to a home page.

The Chart of the Day button in the Options dialog box lets you choose from any or all of five different charts that can be displayed on your home page. These charts are

- Assets and Liabilities
- Income and Expenses
- Current Assets
- Expenses for Last Month
- Current Liabilities

FIGURE 21.2.

You can customize your home page by adding a Chart of the Day.

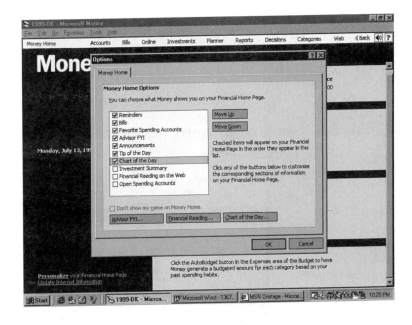

If you review each of these charts every day, you'll have a very complete picture of your financial situation.

Figure 21.3 shows a breakdown of some rather modest assets.

FIGURE 21.3.

The Money Home Page can provide advice on how to use Money as well as updates on your financial situation.

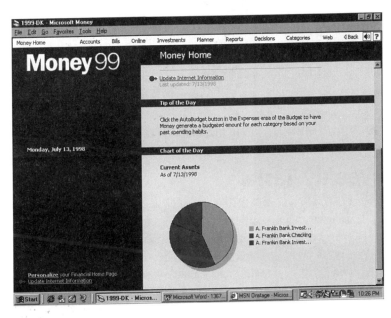

21

You can also update your Internet reading and get up-to-date information from Microsoft Investor in the Investments area of Money. Investor periodically offers free trials, or you can become a paid subscriber. When you do, you can access comprehensive information about your investments, as well as timely articles on financial issues.

Connecting to investment information online is easy if you have an Internet connection.

To Do: Get Investment Information Online

1. Click the Investments link.
2. In the Investments area, click the Refresh this Page link, as shown in Figure 21.4.

FIGURE 21.4.

One click in the Investments area connects you to current online financial information.

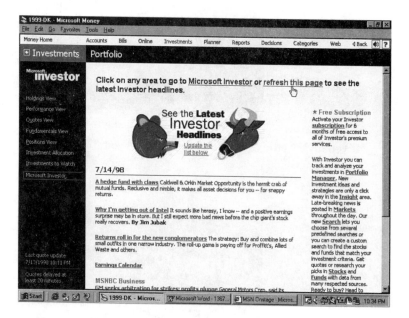

▲ 3. Follow links from Investor to access current online financial data.

Weekly Tasks

Obviously, you will define your own schedule for checking up on, and maintaining, your accounts. All the activity you explored in the previous section can be done weekly (or even monthly) instead of daily if you want. Miscellaneous bills can be paid every three days or every day. Investments can be tracked daily, weekly, or monthly. The important thing is to set a routine and maintain it so you really take advantage of what Money can do for you.

You might want to make a habit of checking on various reports on a weekly basis. For instance, one good routine to schedule is entering upcoming bills. This gives you a more accurate picture of your finances, and reminds you to make payments.

Here is a suggested checklist of things you might want to add to your weekly routine:

- Check in at the Money Home Page, update Internet information and see what new articles will help your financial planning.
- Enter new bills that will be due in the coming week to remind yourself to pay them.
- Back up your Money files (see Hour 22, "Backing Up and Archiving Your Data" for a complete discussion of manually backing up files).
- Review your accounts for overdue bills.

Monthly Tasks

In Hour 16, "Money Reports," you learned to generate and use Money reports, and in Hour 17, "Charts and the Chart Gallery," you learned to view your financial status in chart form. Having mastered these skills, you might want to build into your routine a regular review of this information. Tasks like this can be done monthly to provide you with an overview of your finances.

It is also important to reconcile your Money accounts with your paper statements. This ensures that what you see in your Money reports is accurate.

Your monthly "to do" list might include the following:

- Delete regular bills you no longer pay. Did you cancel premium cable? Decide to drop your subscription to the 80's Retro CD of the Week club? You should include some housekeeping in your list of monthly tasks to clear these bills from your schedule.
- Organize your tax records. Go through your expenses and make sure that all tax deductible expense are organized and documented in case the IRS wants to see them.
- Review your Monthly Reports.
- In the What I Owe category of the Reports View, take a look at your Upcoming Bills and Deposits This Month report to plan ahead for coming income and expenses.
- Reconcile your paper records with your Bills and Deposits.

21

Create and Back Up a Money Archive

In the next hour, you'll learn to create archive files. These files store old records. Depending on the size of your accounts and the volume of your transactions, you might want to back up weekly, monthly, or annually.

Delete Regular Bills that No Longer Apply

At some regularly scheduled point, you should review your scheduled bills, and delete ones you no longer pay.

To Do: Delete Inactive Bills

1. Go to the Bills area.

2. Click the Set up Bills & Deposits link in the left side of the Bills area.

3. Click the transaction that you want to remove from your list of regular transactions, then click the Delete button. In Figure 21.5, haircuts is being removed from a regular list.

FIGURE 21.5.

Not all payments need to be on your regularly scheduled list; you can avoid clutter by deleting irregular expenses.

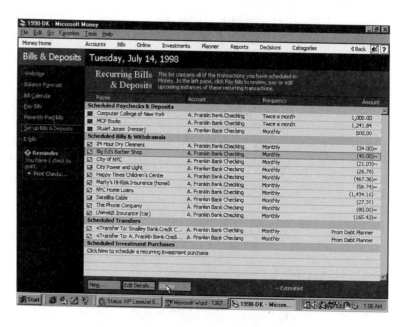

Deleting Outdated Payees

In the same way you just learned to delete a regularly scheduled payment, you can also delete the following types of regularly scheduled transactions:

- Deposits
- Transfers
- Investment Purchases

Once a month is a good time to review whether you want Money to continue to make these transactions automatically.

Closing or Deleting Old Accounts

You can also keep your Money accounts lean and mean, neat and trim by deleting or closing accounts you no longer use. What's the difference between closing and deleting an account? If you close an account, it no longer shows up in your account lists, but you can still see transactions that took place with this account. If you delete an account, you remove all transactions associated with that account. In general, it's more prudent to close accounts instead of deleting them.

To Do: Close or Delete an Account

1. View the Accounts area.
2. Right-click the account you want to close.
3. From the context menu, select Account is Closed or Delete. In Figure 21.6, the A. Franklin Bank Savings Account is being closed.

FIGURE 21.6.

Closed accounts can still be viewed, and opened again.

21

There are two big advantages to closing an account rather than deleting it: you can still view old transactions in closed accounts, and you can reopen them by right-clicking them in the Accounts area and selecting This Account is Open from the context menu.

Quarterly Tasks

Particularly if you are running a small business, the end of each quarter is a time to review your tax records. In Hour 18, "Money and Taxes" you learned to use Money to help calculate your taxes, and to integrate tax records into your accounts.

Here are some projects you might want to consider at the end of each tax quarter:

- Create a "How Am I Doing?" chart for the quarter (see Hour 17 for a reminder of how to create charts).
- Assess the state of your tax records.
- Decide if you are withholding too much or too little

Near the End of the Tax Year

In Hour 18, you learned to create tax reports to help you prepare for filing your annual income tax returns. Here's where all the hard, diligent work you did maintaining your Money Accounts really pays off. Four reports are available in the Reports area by clicking the Taxes category on the left side of the window.

Summary

A big part of making Money do its job is establishing regular "to do" lists for the end of each day, week, month, quarter, and year. Each person, and small business, will have different requirements for these lists. In general, the more intensively you use Money, the more transactions you have, the more frequently you should maintain your accounts.

Q&A

Q How can I really be sure that my Money 99 accounts are accurate?

A Your accounts will be accurate if you make complete and regular entries, and if you implement regularly scheduled procedures for reconciling your Money account and your paper records (receipts, deposits, and so on).

Q How many income and expense categories should I maintain?

A In general, you want to keep your categories list small. Before adding a category for a payment or income, carefully review your existing categories and see if you can squeeze the transaction into one of them. Keeping the number of categories small makes tax records easier to organize, and helps you chart your finances.

21

Hour **22**

Backing Up and Archiving Your Data

Your Money files can become corrupted—in other words, they can go bad due to system problems with your computer or your software. And, files can be deleted accidentally, from within Money or from Windows' file management utilities. For all these reasons, you should frequently back up your files. How often is frequently? If you enter a dozen or so transactions a day, you should back up every day.

When you back up your files to your hard drive, you create safe copies of your files that can be restored if your current working files are corrupted or accidentally deleted. However, these backup files are only as safe as your hard drive, and hard drives crash. For that reason, you should also back up your files to an alternate media, like a zip drive, a tape drive, or floppy disks.

In this hour, you'll learn how to carefully back up your files, and restore them if necessary.

Archiving is another way to protect your files. However, archived files are *moved out* of your file, and into a separate archive file. That file can be opened at any time, so you can view old transactions. Think of archiving as Money's way of taking old files up to the attic for storage. They're not cluttering up your files, but they're available if you need them.

Backing Up Your Money File

When you install Microsoft Money 99, the program default settings back up your files on your hard drive each time you exit a session. In addition, every 14 days, Money 99 prompts you to back up your files on floppy disks.

You can also back up files while you are in a Money 99 session. In the rest of this hour, you'll learn to manage these backup options to keep your hard-earned Money files safe and sound.

If something goes wrong with your original Money files, you can restore them from backup files.

Backing Up Files Manually

Scenario: You've just entered 400 important transactions. Rather than wait until you exit Money, you'd like to back up your files right away. You can back up your files during a Money 99 session to either your hard drive, or to floppy disks (or another media).

To Do: Back Up Your File

1. Select File, Backup from the main Money menu bar.

2. Use one of the two option buttons to select your hard drive, or floppy disks (or other media, like a tape drive). In Figure 22.1, the files are backed up to floppy disks.

3. Click OK in the Backup dialog box. The Backup to Floppy dialog box appears next. Here you can just click the Backup Now button to confirm that you want to make a copy of your files on your floppy disk(s). (The Options button opens up the Backup tab of the Options dialog box, which you'll explore later in this hour.)

4. If necessary, Money prompts you to remove your floppy disk, and insert another one, until all your files are backed up.

FIGURE 22.1.

You can back up your files to a floppy disk at any time.

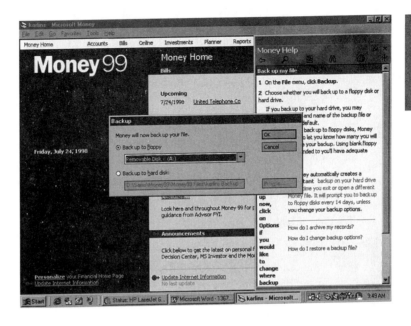

22

It's a good idea to store your backup floppy disks at a separate site than where your computer is located. This way, you are protected against fire or other damage.

Other Ways to Back Up Your Files

If your files are relatively small, you can back up to floppy disks. If you maintain many accounts, and manage complex personal finances with Money 99, you might consider a backup option such as a tape backup machine, a zip drive, read/write CDs, or an online backup service.

Backing up to a tape drive, a zip drive, or a read/write CD (CDRs or CDRWs) is just like backing up to floppy disks. The only difference is you select your tape drive from the drop-down list in the Backup dialog box.

If you contract with an online backup service, you'll get instructions on how to transfer your backup files over the Internet to your storage server.

Changing Backup Preferences

You can customize the way Money backs up your files in several ways. Backup features are defined in the Options dialog box. You can:

- Elect not to automatically back up your files. This is *not a good idea*—backing up files is important in case something goes wrong with your originals.

- View a prompt before Money automatically backs up your files. This is a helpful option—not so you can avoid backing up, but so you get reassurance that Money is backing up your files.

- Compress your backup files to save disk space.

- Define a target alternate media (besides your hard drive) to which your files will be backed up.

- Decide how often to make backup files on your alternate media (for example, floppy disks or a tape drive).

To Do: Change Backup Options

1. Select Tools, Options from the main Money menu bar and click the Backup tab.

2. You can deselect either of the two check boxes in the dialog box to disable automatic backup.

> Disabling automatic backup is not a good idea. These files are your precious financial records, and even if you have hard copy backup in the form of bills and checks, restoring your records by hand is much more of a hassle than letting Money automatically back up your files.

3. You can use the Save In text box to define a new file folder or filename for your hard drive backup files.

4. The Prompt Me... check box displays a dialog box that you can click OK in to start automatic backup. The Make My File Small... check box uses compression software to reduce the file size of your backup files. Compressed files are generally reliable, but not as safe as noncompressed files. If you are combining hard disk backups with frequent backups to your floppy disk, compression is a fairly safe option.

5. The number in the Automatically Back Up to Floppy... text box defines how often your work will be backed up to floppy disks or other media. You should back up every day if you enter more than six transactions in a day.

6. You can define a backup target other than your floppy disk drive by clicking the Save In drop-down list. If you have a tape drive on your system, it displays as an option here.

7. You can use the Make My File Small... check box in the Floppy area of the dialog box to compress your backup files. Again, compressing files can reduce file size by

▼

▲

more than half, but it makes your backup system slightly less reliable. It is a good idea to use compression for only one of your two backup files (either hard drive or floppy disks).

22

Of course, you can just confirm the default backup options if you want. But you should back up to floppy disk (or a tape drive) daily if you do significant work with Money 99.

Restoring Files from a Backup

If for any reason you need to restore a backup file, follow these steps:

To Do: Restore a Backed Up File

1. Select File, Restore Backup from the Money menu bar.

2. In the Restore Confirmation dialog box, click the Restore from a Backup File option button, and click the Next button in the dialog box.

3. Your most recent backup file is listed in the Restore Backup dialog box. If you have several backup files and want to choose between them (for example, if you back up to both a tape drive and floppy disks), you can click the Open a Different Backup File option button. If you choose this option, you'll see a list of available backup files, like the list in Figure 22.2.

FIGURE 22.2.

Money gives you the option of restoring any backup file you create.

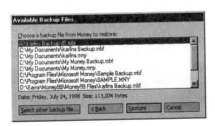

4. After you select a file to restore, click the Restore button. You'll be prompted with a Restore Target, as shown in Figure 22.3. You can accept the default, or define a new target folder or filename. Then click the Restore button in the Restore Target dialog box. That's it—your backup files have been restored.

▲

FIGURE 22.3.

You can change the folder or filename of a file created from backup files.

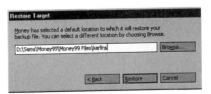

Archiving Your Data

Archiving is different than backing up files. Backup files contain all the information in your current Money accounts. The purpose of a backup file is to duplicate your files in case something goes wrong and files are corrupted or destroyed.

Archiving, on the other hand, is used to store old records. In the remainder of this hour, you'll learn how and why you might want to archive some of your transactions.

Basically, an archive is a file where you store old records. Frequent archiving keeps your files free of old, out-of-date records.

Archiving Strategies

Archiving keeps your file size down and your ledgers manageable. The number of records you may want to send to an archive file will be based on how many transactions you handle. If you create dozens of transactions a day, and hundreds each month, you may want to archive at the end of each month. That way, you create monthly records that you can open any time you want.

Or, if you create only a few dozen transactions each month, you may elect to archive once a year, creating archive files for each year's worth of transactions.

How to Archive Your Money Accounts

Before you begin to archive your file, decide which files to archive. For example, once a year you could archive your checking account file, moving all your previous year's records to an archive file:

To Do: Archive Old Records

1. Begin by opening the file from which you will archive records. Then select File, Archive from the main Money 99 menu. You'll see the Archive dialog box.

2. In the Remove Transactions... text box, enter a cutoff date. Records before this date will be moved to a new (archive) file. In Figure 22.4, all records with transaction dates of 1/1/99 or earlier have been moved.

FIGURE 22.4.

Archived records are selected by date of transaction.

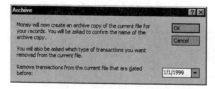

> The date you enter in the Remove Transactions... text box must be equal to or earlier than your current system date.

3. Click OK in the Archive dialog box. You will see another Archive dialog box, as shown in Figure 22.5. Here, you can select a folder from the Save In drop-down list, and enter a filename in the File Name box. One easy file-naming strategy is to use the time period for the archive, for example, "May 98," "1st Qtr 98," or "1998."

FIGURE 22.5.

Create a New (Archive) file to hold old checks.

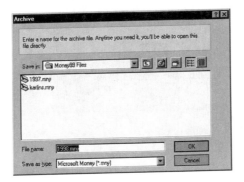

4. Click OK in this Archive dialog box. If you are archiving a checking account, you'll see the Archive Checking dialog box shown in Figure 22.6. Here you decide whether or not to Remove (move) all transactions, only cleared and reconciled transactions, only reconciled transactions, or no transactions. If you want all checks that have not yet cleared or been reconciled to *stay in your current* file and not be archived, choose the second option button, as shown in Figure 22.6. Finally, click the OK button in the Archive Checking dialog box. Your selected records are copied to a new file.

FIGURE 22.6.

This example archived only checks that have cleared and transactions that have been reconciled.

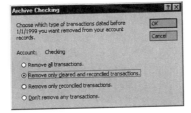

Opening an Archive File

Unlike backup files, which must be restored to be used, archive files can be opened like any other Money 99 file. If, for example, you use archiving to move your annual records to separate files, you'll have the option of opening your files for any particular year.

In Figure 22.7, records from 1997 are being opened.

FIGURE 22.7.

Archived files can be opened just like any Money 99 file.

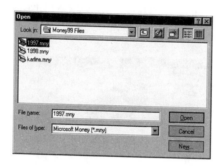

Opening an archived file is as simple as selecting File, Open, and double-clicking the file in the Open dialog box.

Summary

Backing up your files is a way to protect yourself against having files accidentally destroyed or corrupted. Your financial records are valuable, and would be tedious (if not impossible) to restore. The short time it takes you to back up your files is worth it.

Money 99 makes backing up files easy. If you don't change the program defaults, your files will be backed up to a hard drive file each time you close a file.

You can adjust Money's default backup procedures from the Backup tab in the Options dialog box.

Archiving is a way to create new files from selected (old) records. Archived files can be opened just like any other Money file.

Q&A

Q What's the easiest, most reliable way to back up files each day?

A One easy, safe strategy is to archive your files to both your hard drive and to floppy disks at the end of each session.

Q Where are archive files kept?

A You assign a folder and filename to an archive file when you create it. You can open these files just like any other Money file.

HOUR 23

Customizing Money

You can choose from many approaches and systems for keeping track of
your money. Money 99 is a flexible program that encompasses most of those
approaches to money tracking and management. By adjusting the Money
environment, you can customize the program to match your needs.

Customizing at a Glance

In this hour, you'll explore ways you can customize Money, including:

- Turning auto-entry options on or off.
- Defining how the Planner will project your budget.
- Deciding how Money will handle income and expense categories.
- Updating currency exchange rates so you can convert currencies as
  you enter transactions.
- Specifying how checks are printed.
- Customizing tax estimate criteria.

Many of the customizing options found in Money 99 are located in the
Options dialog box, which you can get to by selecting Tools, Options from

the main Money menu bar. You'll be spending a good part of this hour exploring all kinds of cool features hidden in that underrated dialog box.

Changing Billing Options

Money helps you remember when you have bills to pay. When you open a Microsoft Money file, the Money 99 Home Page reminds you which payments are due.

You can customize this feature to tell Money how (and if) you want to be reminded of unpaid bills.

You can also have Money prompt you to define recurring bills. If you pay a bill twice, Money can be programmed to suggest that you enter that bill to your bill calendar.

To Do: Customize Bill Reminder Features

1. Select Tools, Options from the menu bar, and click the Bills tab in the Options dialog box.

2. Click the Use Bill Reminder check box to display reminders for when bills are due on your Money Home Page. To turn off this feature, deselect the check box.

3. In the Remind Me… text box, enter the number of days that you want for advance warning of a bill. For example, if you want to be reminded a week in advance for due bills, enter 7 in the text box. Then click OK in the Options dialog box.

You learned to add regularly occurring bills to the Bill Calendar in Hour 11, "Paychecks, Bills, and other Recurring Transactions." You can also program Money to suggest that recurring bills be entered in the Bill Calendar.

To Do: Tell Money to Suggest Adding Recurring Bills to the Bill Calendar

1. Select Tools, Options from the menu bar, and click the Bills tab in the Options dialog box.

2. Click the Watch My Transactions for Recurring Payments check box to tell Money to notify you when you make a second payment to a payee. Click OK in the Options dialog box.

Now when you make a second monthly utility bill payment, for example, Money will suggest that you add that payment to your Bill Calendar.

Automating Data Entry

Money comes with a number of features that speed up data entry. For example, in Figure 23.1, the letter U has been typed in the Pay To text box of the Create New Scheduled

Payment dialog box. Because the United Telephone Company is the only company start-ing with the letter "U" to which a check has been written, Money has supplied the rest of the payee name.

FIGURE 23.1.

Let Money do the typing!

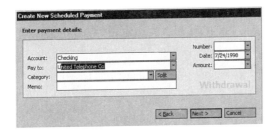

23

Other auto-entry features include letting Money hit the period for you to insert a decimal point, and features that help you avoid errors like entering a check twice.

All these handy auto-entry shortcuts can be turned on and off by selecting Tools, Options from the main Money menu bar, and clicking the Editing tab. Clicking in a check box turns a feature on (or off, if a check is already in the check box).

Figure 23.2 shows the Editing tab of the Options dialog box with every auto-entry feature selected. You might be a bit more selective, but most of these features save time and help cut down on entry errors.

FIGURE 23.2.

Entry and confirmation option settings for those of us who hate to type and make a lot of mistakes.

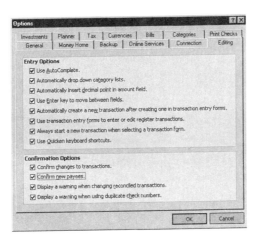

You can access any of Money's auto-editing features by selecting Tools, Options from the Money menu bar, and clicking the Editing tab. Clicking a check box next to an editing feature turns that feature on. Deselecting a check box turns the feature off.

Table 23.1 gives a rundown of what the Editing Option features do, and why you might want to use them.

TABLE 23.1. EDITING OPTIONS.

Feature	What It Does/Why Use It?
Use AutoComplete	You start typing, and Money guesses at the rest (based on your previous entries). A great time-saver that cuts down on typos.
Automatically Drop Down Category Lists	Lets you pick existing categories from drop-down lists.
Automatically Insert Decimal Point in Amount Field	Most folks will want this—you type 14645 and you get 146.45.
Use Enter Key to Move Between Fields	Pressing the Enter key on your keyboard moves you to the next text box. Most people find this the intuitive way to enter data.
Automatically Create a New Transaction...	If you enter a lot of transactions at once, this will save you time by opening a new transaction after you enter one.
Use Transaction Entry Forms...	Opens a transaction form for you to edit, rather than just letting you edit directly in a ledger.
Always Start a New Transaction...	When you finish a transaction, Money opens a new form.
Use Quicken Keyboard Shortcuts	Activates dozens of shortcut keys that match those used in Quicken.
Confirm Changes to Transactions	Prompts you to accept or cancel a transaction before it is entered—good for folks who make typing mistakes and need to review what they've entered.
Confirm New Payees	A handy way to avoid entering John Smith, Jon Smith, and Jon Smithe for the same payee.
Display a Warning When Changing Reconciled Transactions	Warns you if you try to change a transaction already reconciled in your account.
Display a Warning When Using Duplicate Check Numbers	Use this unless you're operating an elaborate scam where you want to write lots of checks with the same check number.

Almost all the options in the Editing tab of the Options dialog box are helpful. You might start by selecting them all, and turning off ones that get in your way.

Choosing How Aggressively the Planner Tracks Income

In Hour 14, "Long-term Planning and Goals," you learned to use Money to help plan your long-term financial goals using the Goal Planner. You learned to use the Planner to define your goals, and then Money provided you with advice on meeting those goals. But how does Money decide things like how much money you should be socking away for discretionary expenses, or how much money you need in IRAs? Money comes with default settings that determine the advice provided by the Goal Planner. But those criteria can be changed.

The forecasts and decisions generated by the Planner depend on options chosen in the Planner tab of the Options dialog box. Those options break down into three areas:

- **Discretionary Expenses**—By how much do you want to reduce your spending?
- **Contribution Limits**—After you have put the maximum tax-deductible amount into an IRA, do you want to continue saving?
- **Sweep**—How much surplus income do you want to invest, if any?

All these options can be defined by selecting Tools, Options from the main Money menu bar, and then clicking the Planner tab.

In the Discretionary Expenses area, use the spin box to enter an amount in the percent by which you want to reduce your spending. Figure 23.3 shows expenses cut by 5%.

FIGURE 23.3.

Decisions entered in the Planner tab are implemented when you use the Planning Wizard.

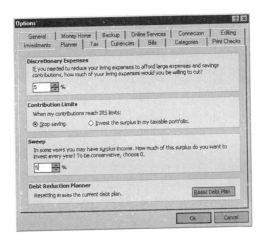

In the Contribution Limits area of the dialog box, you decide whether to continue to invest in a retirement account after you've reached the limit of your deductible contributions. For example, Figure 23.3 shows an election to stop saving after paying the maximum allowed into an IRA account.

In the Sweep area, you can define how much of your surplus income you want to invest. Figure 23.3 shows a decision to invest 5% of surplus income. When you've defined your planning priorities, click OK and these decisions are implemented in the Planning Wizard.

Changing Categories, Investment Options, and Currencies

Expense and income categories play a critical role in how you organize your finances. One of the great things about Money is that it organizes your expenses into categories, making it easy to track where your money has gone, and prepare for tax time.

If you want to track your stock and bond investments in Money, there are several options available. If your income or expenses involve more than one currency, you can update currency exchange rates and let Money incorporate current rates in calculating your accounts.

Defining Expense Category Rules

You need to make two basic decisions about how you handle expense categories:

- Do you want to define rules forcing you to assign categories to expenses and sources of income?
- Do you want to define your own custom categories or use those provided by Money?

With your strategy in mind, you can apply these rules to how you work in Money. To define category rules, select Tools, Options and click the Categories tab in the Options dialog box.

To constrict all your transactions to defined categories, click the Require a Category for Each Transaction check box in the dialog box. To restrict your expenses and income sources to a single list of categories, click the Use a Single List for Categories… check box. To keep yourself from mixing up income and expense categories, click the Require the Correct Type of Category for Each Transaction… check box. Use the Enable Support for Value Added Tax (VAT) check box to allow for Value Added Tax (VAT) in transactions. In Figure 24.4, all four of these categories are selected to provide maximum supervision from Money, helping make sure all transactions are assigned to appropriate categories.

FIGURE 23.4.

Money can enforce certain rules when it comes to assigning transactions to categories.

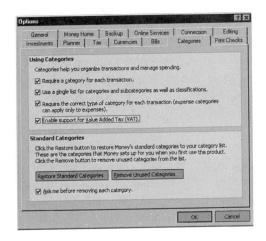

You can also use the two buttons at the bottom of the Categories tab to organize your categories list. The R<u>e</u>store Standard Categories button restores the default list of categories that come with Money.

If you use the R<u>e</u>store Standard Categories button, make sure the <u>A</u>sk Me Before Removing Each Category check box is selected so you can confirm before any of your existing categories are deleted.

The <u>R</u>emove Unused Categories button cleans up your categories list by removing those categories that don't have any transactions assigned to them. This cleans up your ledgers for summaries, and for tax time.

Defining Investment Tracking and Currency Rates

If you are using Money to track your investments, you can use the Options dialog box to define how Money treats your investments.

You can define investment options in the Investments tab of the Options dialog box. To get to those choices, select Tools, Options, and click the Investments tab in the dialog box.

Table 23.2 gives a rundown of the Editing Option features available for investments and why you might want to use them.

TABLE 23.2. EDITING OPTIONS.

Option	What It Does / Why Use It?
Treat Bond Prices As a Percentage	Displays bond prices as percentages of par value instead of dollars (or other currency).
Require a Transfer Account	Money forces you to assign a transfer account so liquidated investments are sent to another account.
Track All Investments As FIFO	Investments are tracked as "first in, first out."
Calculate Investment Gains	Three option buttons allow you to calculate investment gains year to date, over the last 52 weeks, or all (entries) to date. The Capital Gains button allows you to set the schedule Money will use to calculate capital gains.
The Investment Categories Button	Allows you to assign income from investments to income categories. For example, income from an employee stock option plan could be automatically assigned to the Bonus income category.
Employee Stock Options	The two option buttons allow you to calculate these stocks based on total shares or vested shares.

In this global economy, more and more people are getting paid or making payments in other currencies. Even small businesses and home finances might involve payments in dollars and yen, pesos, or baht (the currency in Thailand).

You can enter current exchange rates by selecting Tools, Options and selecting the Currency tab. The first step in this dialog box is to select the currency that you mainly use, and click the Set As Base Currency button. Then, click a second currency, and define an exchange rate in the Exchange rate box. This rate is applied when you enter transactions in the second currency.

If you have other options to define, select a different tab. As with all the option tabs, after you have finished defining options, click OK.

Specifying How Checks Are Printed

You define how you want to print checks in two places: the Check Setup dialog box and the Options dialog box. The Check Setup dialog box lets you print to one of the available pre-printed check forms. If you want to customize those forms to match your printer, or use Quicken checks, you can fine-tune these features in the Options dialog box.

To Do: Define a Check Form

1. Select File, Print Setup, Check Setup.

2. In the Check Setup dialog box, select a printer from the Printer drop-down list.

3. In the Check area of the dialog box, select a check form from the Type drop-down list, and a paper bin if necessary from the Source drop-down list. In Figure 23.5, Wallet-style checks are selected.

23

FIGURE 23.5.

Choose from a variety of check forms for your Money printed checks.

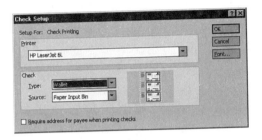

In the Print Checks tab of the Options dialog box, you can use three check boxes to define your checks:

- Prompt If Checks Are Postdated warns you if you try to print a postdated check. You'll be given the option of changing the date to the current date.

- Print Payee Name in the First Line of the Address Field places the name of the company or person getting the check on the check.

- The Use My Existing Checks from Quicken option is discussed in detail in the section "Special Assistance for Quicken Users," in Hour 24, "Converting from Quicken."

The Printing Alignment options allow you to adjust how much of a margin is placed around your checks by your printer.

Setting Up Internet Connection Preferences

A complete discussion of Internet connections and downloading financial data is beyond the scope of this book. But you can find a number of options in the Connection tab in the Options dialog box that allow Money to automatically check the Internet for information relevant to your finances. The check boxes in the dialog box are easy to follow, and if you select them, Money automatically logs you on to the Internet and downloads the information you want for your accounts.

Money has its own internal Web browser, which meshes well with the data downloaded to Money. You should leave the option button for this option checked.

Specifying Tax Filing Status and Rates

The Tax tab in the Options dialog box allows you to define your tax status. The default settings in this dialog box provide a good approximation of tax rates in the United States. You can leave these default settings alone, or customize them for other countries or tax statuses.

To customize the tax settings, click the Show Rates for Filing Status drop-down list and select Custom. Then enter your customized tax rates. Figure 23.6 displays a custom tax rate.

FIGURE 23.6.

If a custom tax option is what you've select-ed, use caution to ensure the Mid-Term and Long-Term rates are set correctly (if applicable).

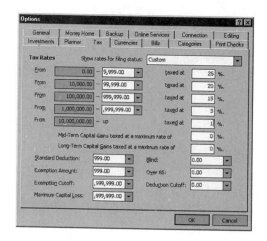

Setting Options for Downloaded Statements

If you elected to sign up for online banking, the Online Services tab in the Options dia-log box allows you to control how transactions get posted to your online account.

The Display Each Downloaded Transaction check box prompts you to approve each time you download a transaction. This adds time to your online banking, but it's worth it to make sure every online transaction is correct.

The Add Description to Memo Field check box enters information like the posting date, the ATM location, or bank fee in the Memo text box of your transaction. Your bank decides how much of this information, if any, they will provide.

The Look for Matching Transactions check box helps you locate duplicate payments.

Finally, use the Match Transactions check box to decide how frequently to look for duplicates. If you pay bills once a month, you might want to set this to 30 or 31 days to flag duplicate payments within that span of time.

Summary

Money can be transformed into a program specially tuned to your own accounting and budgeting needs. Many of these options are found in the many tabs in the Options dialog box. In this hour, you explored options that allow you to define such diverse features as auto-entry, criteria used by the Planner, and rules for using income and expense categories, entering currency exchange rates, and defining check layout.

23

Q&A

Q **I get paid in yen and renmimbi and pay my bills in Hong Kong dollars and Mexican pesos. Can Money convert all this to U.S. dollars?**

A Sure, just enter exchange rates in the Currency tab of the Options dialog box.

Q **I didn't like the way the Planner projected my budget. How do I control that?**

A The Planner uses criteria that are defined in the Planner tab of the Options dialog box.

HOUR 24

Converting from Quicken

Quicken and Microsoft Money have a similar set of features. Both programs are easy to use and convenient, and they both allow you to manage your personal finances. Some folks prefer Quicken, some prefer Money. But the main reason people choose to switch from Quicken to Money is that the online features provided by their bank are compatible with Money.

If your mega-bank just merged with an ever bigger giga-bank, your online banking may now be compatible with Money. Quicken has a larger installed user base, but according to the most recent articles I've read, Money already has more banks that support it.

Others may have elected to switch to Money 99 for offline reasons. But whatever your reasons for converting from Quicken to Money, welcome. You'll find that the interface and features in Money 99 are very compatible with those you used in Quicken. You'll find that converting your Quicken files to Money is a breeze.

Allowing Money to Convert Your Quicken Files

Microsoft Money 99 provides an easy-to-use wizard that handles all the work of converting your Quicken file to Money. You tell Money where to find your Quicken File, and then kick back, answer some questions, assign a name to your file, and back it up.

All you need to know to get started is

- The name of your Quicken file
- The new name you want to assign to the file in Money 99

> The following steps work if your Quicken files were created with version 3 or later.
>
> If you created your Quicken accounts with older versions, skip ahead to the section "Importing Other Quicken Files."

To Do: Import Quicken Files

1. If you just finished the tour of Money, or just started up Money straight out of the box, you may be prompted to specify a file you want to convert from Quicken. If you don't see a prompt, just select File, Convert Quicken File from the Money 99 menu bar as shown in Figure 24.1.

2. From the Convert Quicken File dialog box that appears, navigate to your Quicken file. In Figure 24.2, you'll see an old Quicken file—karlins.QDF. Of course, your file will have a different name.

3. When you locate your Quicken file, click the Convert button in the dialog box. If you had a password assigned to your Quicken file, you are prompted to enter it.

4. Next, you are prompted to enter a new name for your Money file. You can accept the default filename and folder suggested by Money, or you can navigate to a new folder or enter a new filename. Then click the Next button in the Converter Wizard.

5. When Money finishes converting your Quicken file (and it might take a few minutes), you'll see a Summary of the Conversion, as shown in Figure 24.3. Your old Quicken balance is shown along with the new Microsoft Money Balance. After you've admired your account balance, click the Finish button to end the Conversion Wizard.

FIGURE 24.1.

The Convert Quicken File option is right near the top of the Money File menu.

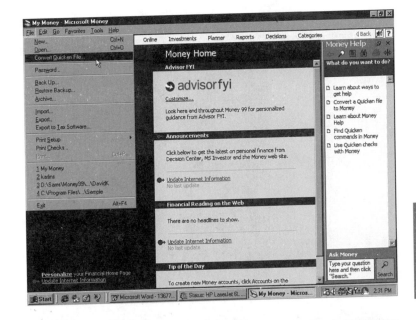

FIGURE 24.2.

The first—and hardest—step in converting your Quicken files is to find them.

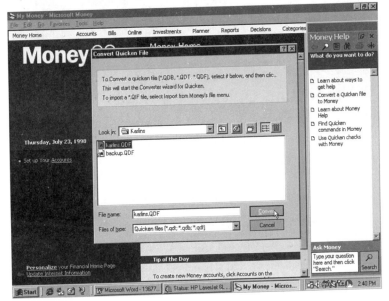

24

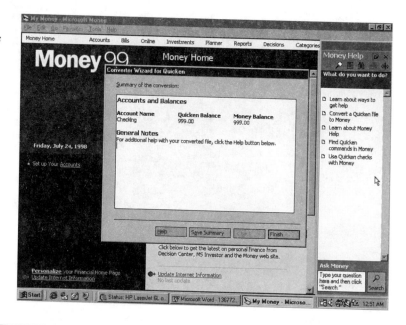

FIGURE 24.3.

After Money converts your Quicken files, your balance is displayed.

In most cases, your Quicken and Money balances will match. If they don't, see the section "Resolving Account Balance Differences" later in this hour.

Importing Quicken Data After Installation

In the example just discussed, you imported Quicken data. This procedure works for any file created by Quicken For Windows (versions 3 or later). If you are using an older version of Quicken, or the Macintosh version, you can't use this procedure. You should look over the discussion in the next section of this hour, "Importing other Quicken Files."

A few things to keep in mind when you convert your Quicken accounts:

- Make sure Quicken is closed when you do the conversion to Money.
- Select File, Convert Quicken File from the menu.
- Follow the wizard steps, as discussed earlier in this hour.

Importing Other Quicken Files

Money's easy-to-use Conversion Wizard works if your Quicken files were created in version 3.0 or later created using the Windows version of Quicken.

Mac users are unfortunately out of luck. However, if your files were created in an early version of Quicken, you can covert them to Money 99 by saving them as .qif files. You can then import those files into Money. This same technique works with other financial packages that support exporting to Quicken's *.gif file format.

To Do: Import Files into Money

1. Select File, Import from the Money 99 menu.

2. Hold down the Shift key, and click all the *.qif files that you want to import, as shown in Figure 24.4.

FIGURE 24.4.

You can use the QIF file format to import files not supported by the Conversion Wizard.

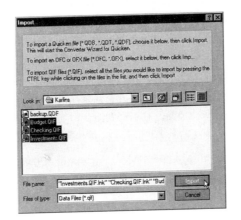

▲   3. Click the Import button in the Import dialog box.

Quicken Elements Lost in Conversion

In general, the more complex your Quicken accounts, the greater potential for problems in converting them to Money 99. Here are a few tips to help avoid loss of data or disrupting your accounts:

- Just use one budget in Quicken. If you have several different budgets that you used in Quicken, delete all but one before you convert. If you have more than one budget in your Quicken account, Money converts the most recent. Older budgets are archived.

- Quicken supports multiple levels of subcategories; for example, you might have an expense category of Education: Tuition: Summer School. Money supports only one level of subcategories, so when your Quicken file is converted, the example above would become a subcategory called Tuition-Summer School and the expense would be listed as a subcategory of Education.

- Your password converts, but if you defined passwords for transactions, those do not import.

If you are converting a complex Quicken file to track short sells in investment accounts or other complex investment activities, you should study the Topic "Learn How Quicken File Elements Convert in Money," found in the Help menu.

Special Assistance for Quicken Users

The folks at Microsoft know that many of you converted from Quicken to Money 99, and they want you to like it here. You'll recognize many elements of the interface, and overall Money looks and works much like Quicken.

Some of the differences between Money and Quicken were listed in the previous discussion of converting files. Microsoft has an entire, easy to find section of the Help window dedicated to Quicken users. Just select Help, Help for Quicken Users from the main Money 99 menu and you'll see a clickable list of helpful articles.

One of the most considerate things about Money is that it allows you to use your Quicken checks, so if you just got in 144,000 Quicken checks, there's no need to send them back.

To Do: Print Quicken Checks with Money 99

1. Select Tools, Options from the Money 99 main menu.
2. Click the Print Checks tab in the Options dialog box.
3. Select the Use My Existing Checks from Quicken check box.
4. Click OK in the Options dialog box.
5. From the main Money 99 menu, select File, Print Setup, Check Setup.
6. Choose a check type from the drop-down list and click OK in the Check Setup dialog box.

Now when you print a check, you can use your old Quicken checks.

Resolving Account Balance Differences

If you have a complex Quicken account, you may have to do some troubleshooting to resolve account balance differences. After conversion, the Conversion Summary dialog box alerts you if there is a discrepancy in balances.

Here's a checklist to review if your balances do not match:

- If you set up Quicken to automatically make loan payments, Money may count those payments twice. Go to the Bills area in Money and check to see if payments are counted twice.

- Money and Quicken handle scheduled transactions differently. Money will not import or convert Scheduled Transaction in Quicken transaction groups. You need to add these manually in the Account Register.

- Money does not import data from a Quicken Debt Reduction Plan.

- If you neglected to save and close Quicken before converting, not all your data will be imported into Money 99.

- Differences in investment account figures can be caused by the fact that Money does not import CD interest the same way Quicken does. Check your CD balances if your Quicken and Money balances do not match.

Noting Similar Commands

Dozens of Quicken shortcut keys have been incorporated into Money 99.

To Do: Use Quicken Shortcut Keys in Money

1. Select Tools, Options from the main Money 99 menu bar.
2. Click the Editing tab in the Options dialog box.
3. Select the Use Quicken Keyboard Shortcuts check box and click OK.

After you turn on the Quicken shortcut keys, you can experiment by using your old Quicken keys to make sure they work. Where Money is different from Quicken, the shortcut keys will make adjustments for you. For example, Ctrl+A in Quicken opens the Account List, although in Money it opens the Account Manager. Other frequently used shortcut keys work exactly the same: Ctrl+P opens the Print dialog box, Ctrl+S splits a transaction, and Ctrl+O opens a file.

Summary

It's easy to convert Quicken files to Microsoft Money. And after you convert them, the transition to Money 99 is made smoother by the option of using dozens of your old Quicken keyboard shortcuts. Where Money and Quicken diverge, the Quicken shortcuts in Money help you find your way to the area or feature you are looking for.

With complex Quicken accounts, you may experience a discrepancy in your Quicken balance and your new Money 99 balance after conversion. If that happens, you have to review each area of your Money files to locate the problem, but you can start with the most common conversion problems listed in this hour under "Resolving Account Balance Differences."

Q&A

Q **Which is better, Money or Quicken?**

A Both Money and Quicken have similar features and are easy to use. The determining factor might be which program is supported by your bank's online banking system. More banks currently use Microsoft Money.

Q **How much of a hassle is it to switch from Quicken to Money?**

A Microsoft Money comes with an easy-to-use wizard that converts your Quicken files to Money's format. Special help menus make the transition a breeze.

INDEX

Symbols

3D, viewing charts in, 247

A

Abbreviation option (Details screen), credit card accounts, 182
accessing
  Account Register, 133
  accounts, 74
  computer system information, 56
  Decisions pages, 198
  Lifetime Planner, 300
  Web statements, 334
account balances
  negative, 69
  troubleshooting, 148
Account Created! dialog box, 77
account groups, 307-308
Account Is Closed option (Details screen), credit card accounts, 182
Account Manager
  New Account icon, 61
  total portfolio value, viewing, 407

transactions, editing, 72-73
viewing all accounts, 67
writing checks, 115
Account Register, 170
  Check tab, 117-119
  Deposit tab, 125
  opening to write checks, 116
  Transfer tab, 127
  uses of, 62
Account Type option (Details screen), credit card accounts, 182
Account Wizard for creating credit card accounts, 172
accounts
  accessing quickly, 74
  asset, 222-223
  Balance Forecast, selecting, 247
  balances, understanding, 67
  balancing
    asset accounts, 149
    Balancing Wizard, 144-147
    mortgage accounts, 213-214
  closing, 73, 218, 435
  creating, *see* creating, accounts

credit card, *see* credit card accounts
deleting, 73, 218, 435
depositing funds, 125
description of, 10-11
determining purpose of, 61
expenses and liabilities for small businesses, 415-418
Favorites, creating, 74
investment, *see* investments, accounts
mortgage, creating, 206-210
moving between, 215
navigating, 67
online, 75-79
opening to write checks, 115
organizing
  account checklists, 65-66
  tracking for small businesses, 414-415
overview of, 59
payroll, 420-422
quick access to, 74
reconciling, 123
resolving differences when converting from Quicken, 466
start dates, 80-81

transactions, editing, 72
transferring funds between, 126-128, 335-336
types of, 60-61
unpaid bills, viewing, 420
viewing, 67-71
Accounts area, Money Home screen, 27
Accounts button, Navigation bar, 38
Action Plan area, Lifetime Planner, 317
active features, description of, 47
Actual Cost Basis and mutual funds, 404
Add Category button, Budget Planner, 283-284
Add Classification dialog box, 110
Add to Favorites command (Favorites menu), 380
Add to Favorites dialog box, Chart of the Day, 369
adding
investment accounts, Lifetime Planner, 306
payees, 155
reports to favorites, 353, 360
Additional Income button, Budget Planner, 282-283
Adjust Loan Balances dialog box, 213
adjusting
start dates for accounts, 80-81
value of mortgage loans, 213
Advisor FYI
budget information, 294
Home and Mortgage articles, 199
Money Home screen, 30
All Transaction Details command (View menu), 134
America Online (AOL), configuring Money to use, 327-328
applying
classifications to transactions, 108-109, 112
subitems to transactions, 112

Archive command (File menu), 444
Archive dialog box, 445
archiving files
opening archive files, 446
overview of, 440
strategies for, 444
articles
Money Home screen, 30-31
on taxes, accessing, 386
Ask the Experts Web page, 295
asset accounts, 60
balancing, 149
creating for home inventories, 226
overview of, 197, 222
recording changes in value of, 223
assets
description of, 8
Home Inventory Worksheet, using, 223-225
preparing list of, 8
assigning
categories
credits, 180
groups of transactions, 102-104
paycheck deposits, 235
transactions, 95-97
tax-related information to categories, 385
transactions to new categories, 102
associated asset account, description of, 215
Assumptions area, Lifetime Planner, 315
ATM cash withdrawals, tracking, 142-143
AutoBalance Account option (Details screen), credit card accounts, 182
AutoBalance feature, 184-186
automatic fill-in feature and writing checks, 120
automatic payments (Apays), description of, 329
automating
bill payment of mortgage, 212-213
data entry, 450-452
Automobile area, Decision Center, 321

Automobile category, viewing, 88-89
Average Cost Basis (double category), description of, 404
Average Cost Basis (single category), description of, 404

B

Back button, 10, 43
Back feature, Navigation bar, 39
backing up files
upon closing, 34
manually, 440
options, 441
Options dialog box preferences, 441-442
overview of, 439-440
restoring files, 443
Backup command (File menu), 440
Balance Forecast view, 230
accounts, selecting, 247
charts, using, 246
date range, selecting, 244
interpreting, 247
overview of, 243
balancing accounts
asset, 149
Balancing Wizard, 144-147
credit card, 188-189, 191
mortgage, 213-214
troubleshooting, 148
banks
emailing, 337
online services
changing, and, 346
multiple financial institutions, 340
bar charts, description of, 368
bar graphs, Category, 101
Bill & Deposit views, 230-231
Bill Calendar view, 230, 242
bill paying online, 75, 79
Bill Reminder feature, 241, 450
bills
automating payments for mortgage, 212-213
deleting inactive, 434

making extra payments for mortgage, 214

navigating between related items, 241

paying, *see* paying bills scheduling recurring, 239

Bills area, Money Home screen, 26

Bills button, Navigation bar, 38, 230

Bills tab, Options dialog box, 450

borrowing money, 200-205

Bottom Line Results area, Lifetime Planner, 313-314

brokerage firms, Standing Orders, 340

browsers
Internet activity and, 16
Money's internal Web browser, 326

Budget Builder Web page, 274

Budget button, Category Detail screen, 101

Budget Forecast view
Budget Planner, 292, 294
interpreting, 247

Budget Planner
Add Category button, 283-284
Additional Income button, 282-283
Budget Forecast, 292, 294
Create AutoBudget button, 291
debt and loan payments, 289-290
Edit button, 287
expenses, viewing, 290
income sources, 280
Lifetime Planner and, 287
Monthly Summary, 291-292
occasional expenses, 288
savings information, 285
Yearly Summary, 292

Budget/Actuals report, 6

budgeting
Advisor FYI, 294
Budget Builder Web page, 274
changing patterns, 272
credit cards and, 192-194
Debt Reduction Planner, 276-280

Decisions area, 272
examining patterns, 272
motivation for, 271
reports, 274-275
Savings Calculator, using, 276
self-tests, 273
see also Budget Planner

Buy vs. Rent Calculator tool, Decisions pages, 198

buying stocks, 405

C

calculator tools, Decision Center, 321

calling Microsoft technical support, 56

canceling
online services, 345-346
payments with online services, 344-345
transactions with online services, 342-343

Capital Gains report, 389

cash accounts, 60, 66, 141-144

cash withdrawals, tracking, 141-143

categories
adding information to for tax preparations, 385
advantages of, 88, 94
assigning
to credits, 180
to groups of transactions, 102-104
paycheck deposits to, 235
transactions to, 102
Automobile, viewing, 88-89
creating, 87, 90-93, 98
deleting, 87, 93
description of, 11
entering, 430
expenses, dividing into, 85
modifying, 87
relationship to reports, 350
renaming, 87
restoring standard, 94
tax information, tracking with, 104
transactions 95-98
viewing for tax preparations, 384

Categories & Payees screen, 86-87

Categories button, Navigation bar, 86

Categories tab, Options dialog box, 454-455

Category bar graph, 101

Category Details screen, viewing and editing, 99-101

Category Transaction list, 101

category types and writing checks, 120

CD-ROM
installing Money, 12
Online Banking Tour, 75

Change Category dialog box, 104

Change Loan dialog box, 218

Change Loan Wizard, 219

changing
banks and online services, 346
Money Home screen, 28

channel guides, 10, 41

charitable contribution records, gathering, 7

chart display, defining, 376-377

Chart of the Day, 430
Financial Home Page, 368-369
Money Home screen, 28, 30

Chart tab, Customize Report dialog box, 373, 375

charts
Balance Forecast, using, 246
customized, resetting, 380
customizing, 361-362, 373
date ranges, changing, 373
deleting from My Favorites list, 361
displaying
data, 367
rows versus columns, defining, 377-379
editing, 358
exporting, 381
favorites, saving as, 380
features of, 349
overview of, 367
printing, 362, 380
renaming, 361, 375
reports, viewing as, 370

switching
between types, 375
to reports, 356-357
transactions, opening from, 371-372
viewing, 350, 355-356
by group, 359
in 3D, 247
Check Free's Online Bill Paying service, 79
check numbers, specifying, 118
Check Register, reconciling accounts, 123
Check Setup dialog box, 257, 456-457
Check tab, Account Register, 117-119
checking accounts, 60, 64, 66
checklists, organizing accounts with, 65-66
checks
editing, 122
ordering from Microsoft, 254-255
printing, *see* printing, checks
restoring voided, 125
voiding and deleting, 124-125
writing, *see* writing checks
classifications
advantages of, 105
applying, 108-109
creating, 105-106, 110
creating second, 112
organization of, 106-107
overview of, 88
renaming, 106
subitems, creating, 108
transactions
applying to, 112
viewing in, 109
closing
accounts, 73, 218, 435
Money, 33
commands
Favorites menu, Add to Favorites, 380
File menu
Archive, 444
Backup, 440
Check Setup, 457
Convert Quicken File, 462

Export to Tax Software, 392
Import, 465
Print, 380
Print Checks, 260
Print Setup, 257
Restore Backup, 443
View menu
All Transaction Details, 134
Enter Transactions Directly, 135
Comment option (Details screen), credit card accounts, 182
Compare Mortgages tool, Decisions pages, 198
computer system information, locating, 56
configuring
Money, 326-328
online services, 329-330
printers, reports and charts, 361
Connect feature, financial institution, 79
Connection tab, Options dialog box, 457
contact information, storing, 222
context-sensitive help from Help system, 51-53
Conversion Wizard, importing Quicken files, 464-465
Convert Quicken File command (File menu), 462
converting from Quicken
comparing features, 466
importing files, 462-465
lost data, avoiding, 465
overview of, 461
Quicken shortcut keys, using, 467
resolving account balance differences, 466
wizard, using, 462
Create AutoBudget button, Budget Planner, 291
Create New Investment dialog box, 401
Create New Payee dialog box, 155
Create New Scheduled Deposit screen, 234-237

Create New Scheduled Transaction Wizard, 232
creating
account checklists, 66
accounts, 61, 63
cash, 141, 143-144
checking or savings, 64
credit card, 65-66, 171-172
home inventory, 225-226
investment, 65
mortgage, 206-210
tracking value of homes, 64
categories, 87, 90-93, 98
classifications, 105-107, 110
desktop shortcuts, 20
files, 22-23
Lifetime Plan, 301
multiple Money files, 24
second classifications, 112
split transactions, 137-140
subcategories, 87, 98
subitems for transactions, 111
transactions, dates and, 70
credit card accounts, 60
Account Register, 170
balancing, 188-189, 191
budgeting and, 192-194
creating, 65-66, 171-172
credits, issuing to, 180
funds, transferring, 176
overview of, 170
partial refunds or credits, recording, 178
paying bills, 183-187
purchases, itemizing, 175-176
refunds or credits, recording, 177
transactions
recording, 429
tracking, 171, 174-175
voiding, 178
viewing in Details screen, 181-183
credits
categories, assigning to, 180
issuing for credit card accounts, 180
currency rates, tracking, 456
Currency tab, Options dialog box, 456
cursors, changing icon, 46

Customize Income dialog box, 282
Customize Report dialog box
  chart display, defining, 376-377
  Chart tab, 373, 375
  Reset button, 380
  Rows and Columns tab, 377-379
customizing
  bill reminder features, 450
  Chart of the Day, 369
  charts, 373
  overview of, 449
  reports and charts, 361-362
  tax calculations, 389

D

daily tasks, 428-432
data entry, automating, 450-452
date of transaction and writing checks, 118
date ranges
  Budget Forecast
    changing, 294
    selecting, 244
  charts, changing, 373
  Payee report, changing, 165
  Payees list, 154
  reports, 350
dates for transactions, creating, 70
Debt Info option (Details screen), credit card accounts, 183
debt payments and Budget Planner, 290
Debt Ratio Calculator tool, Decisions pages, 198
Debt Reduction Planner
  budgeting, 276-280
  credit cards and, 192-193
Decision Center
  Automobile area, 321
  calculator tools, 321
  Family tab, 272
  Lifetime Planner and, 319
  Money Home screen, 31
  reducing monthly obligations, 294
  Savings area, 272, 320

Decisions link, Navigation bar, 38
Decisions pages, 198
deductions and contributions categories, creating for small businesses, 421
default reports, resetting, 380
Define Your Payment Plan screen, 193
Delete Category dialog box, 93
deleting
  accounts, 73, 435
  categories, 87, 93
  checks, 124-125
  inactive bills, 434
  outdated payees, 434
  reports and charts from My Favorites list, 361
Deposit tab, Account Register, 125
depositing funds, 125
  categories, assigning, 235
  itemizing, 237-238
desktop shortcuts, creating, 20
Details screen, 70-71
  Automobile category, 88
  editing, 217
  investment accounts, 407
  viewing, 181-183
dialog boxes
  Account Created!, 77
  Add Classification, 110
  Add to Favorites, 369
  Adjust Loan Balances, 213
  Archive, 445
  AutoBalance, 184
  Change Category, 104
  Change Loan, 218
  Check Setup, 257, 456-457
  Create New Investment, 401
  Create New Payee, 155
  Customize Income, 282
  Customize Report, 373-380
  Delete Category, 93
  Direct Services Setup For, 77
  Edit Transaction, 98, 101, 211
  Export Report, 353
  File Required, 21
  Find and Replace, 158-160
  New, 398
  New Account At, 77

New Category, 422
Open, 23
Options, see Options dialog box
Print Checks, 260, 262
Record Payment, 240
Scheduling Options, 236
Select Chart of the Day, 368
Split Transaction, 186
Direct Services Setup For dialog box, 77
direct statements from online services, 333
disabling AutoBalance feature, 186
displaying
  charts, 377-379
  data in charts, 367
documentation required to set up, 4, 7
documents, printing, 263, 267
donation records, gathering, 7
double-clicking, opening with, 47
downloaded statements, customizing, 458
downloading direct statements, 333
drivers for printers Web sites, 269
drop-down lists, overview, 44

E

E-Bills view, 231
Edit button, Budget Planner, 287
Edit menu, overview of, 39
Edit Transaction dialog box, 98, 101, 211
editing
  Category Details, 99-101
  checks, 122
  Details screen, 217
  payee information, 160-162
  reports and charts, 358
  transactions, 121
    after entering, 72-73
    in categories, 98
    from Payee Details list, 164
    reconciled and cleared, 123

Editing tab, Options dialog box, 450-452

electronic bills (E-Bills), description of, 329

electronic payments (Epays)
choosing when to send, 333
description of, 328
Register, entering in, 331-333

electronic transactions
canceling payments, 344-345
canceling transactions, 342-343
checking status of payments, 343-344

electronic transfers, description of, 329

emailing banks, 337

employees, generating tax information for, 424-425

end of tax year tasks, 436

Enter Transactions Directly command (View menu), 135

estimating transaction amounts, 234, 236

Exclude from Savings Plan account group, 308

exiting Money, 33

Expected Return function, Lifetime Planner, 304-305

Expected Returns, Lifetime Planner, 303

expense categories, 454-455

expense records, gathering, 7

expenses
Budget Planner, viewing, 290
categories, dividing into, 85
tracking for small businesses, 415-418

Explorer-based features, 10

Export Report dialog box, 353

Export to Tax Software command (File menu), 392

exported files, working with, 354

exporting
charts, 381
files, 392
reports, 353
to spreadsheets, 265-266
Tax Software Report, 354

F

Family tab, Decisions area, 272

FAQs (Frequently Asked Questions), 54

Favorite Account option (Details screen),credit card accounts, 182

favorites
accounts, creating, 74
reports
adding to, 360
making, 353

Favorites list, 10

Favorites menu commands, 39, 380

File menu commands, 39
Archive, 444
Backup, 440
Check Setup, 457
Convert Quicken File, 462
Export to Tax Software, 392
Import, 465
Print, 380
Print Checks, 260
Print Setup, 257
Restore Backup, 443

File Required dialog box, 21

files
archiving
opening archive files, 446
overview of, 440
strategies for, 444
backing up, see backing up files
creating, 22-23
exported, working with, 354
exporting, 392
importing from Quicken, 462, 464-465
Money, 24
opening, 22

Financial Home Page and Chart of the Day, 368-369

Financial Institutions button and online investing, 399

Financial Planner, 319

financial planning and Decision Center, 319-321

financial records checklist, 7

financial self-portrait, creating, 4-6

Find and Replace dialog box, 158-160

finding banks supporting online accounts, 76

floppy disks, storing backup files on, 441

Forecasts, Lifetime Planner, 317

frames, printing documents in, 264

Frequently Asked Questions (FAQs), help options, 54

funds, transferring, 176

G-H

Go menu, overview of, 39

Goal Planner, 453

goals
credit cards and, 192-194
Lifetime Planner and, 309-310, 312

graphs for small business management, 419

Help system
context-sensitive help, 51-53
Help Topics Channel Bar, 48-50
keyword searches, 50-51
online help, 53-55
overview of, 48
Tooltips, 48, 52

hiding information on payee line, 156-157

History view, 70

Home Advisor page, 199

Home button, 10

home buying and points, 204

Home Inventory Worksheet, 223-226

home page, checking, 430-432

Home screen, overview, 9-10

Home Worksheet, 200-205

hyperlinks, description, 326

I-J

Import command (File menu), 465

importing Quicken files, 462
after installation, 464
comparing features, 466
Conversion Wizard,
464-465
lost data, avoiding, 465
resolving account balance
differences, 466
shortcut keys, using, 467
**Improving Your Plan area,
Lifetime Planner, 312**
**Include on Tax Reports check
box, Category Details
screen, 101**
income categories, 454
income records, gathering, 7
**income sources and Budget
Planner, 280**
**inflation and Financial
Planner, 319**
initiating Money, 19
installing Money, 12-14
**Internet, configuring Money
for, 326**
Internet connection, 15-16
**Internet connection
preferences, Options dialog
box, 457**
Internet Explorer 4.1, 12, 16
**Internet resources for
loans, 199**
**Internet service providers
(ISPs), selecting, 326**
**Internet-based help options,
53-55**
**interpreting Balance and
Budget Forecasts, 247**
**investment information,
accessing online, 432**
**investment tracking, defining,
455-456**
investments
accounts, 60
adding to Lifetime
Planner, 306
assigning to,
400-401, 404
buying stocks, 405
creating, 65-66,
398-400, 404
definition of, 398
maintaining, 405
modifying in Lifetime
Planner, 306-307
mutual funds, 404

selling stocks, 406
tracking stock
prices, 405
transferring funds
to, 406
definition of, 398
retirement planning and,
408-411
total portfolio value,
viewing, 407
tracking, overview of, 397
viewing information in
Details view, 407
**Investments tab, Options
dialog box, 455-456**
Investor, 402
invoices, 420
**ISPs (Internet service
providers), selecting, 326**
**issuing credits for credit card
accounts, 180**
itemizing
paycheck deposits, 237-238
purchases by credit card,
175-176

K-L

**keyword searches, Help
system, 50-51**

liability accounts, 61, 170
**Lifetime Goal Planner,
overview of, 197**
Lifetime Plan, creating, 301
Lifetime Planner
accessing, 300
Action Plan area, 317
Assumptions area, 315
Bottom Line Results area,
313-314
Budget Planner and, 287
Decision Center and, 319
Expected Return function,
304-305
Expected Returns, 303
features of, 299
Forecasts, viewing, 317
Improving Your Plan
area, 312
investment accounts,
306-307
long-range goals and,
309-310, 312

Savings and Investments
Accounts area, 302
Yearly Snapshot area, 316
limiting scope of reports, 350
line charts
description of, 368
History view as, 70
**linked documents,
printing, 267**
links
Help Topics, 49-50
Money Home screen, 31-32
Navigation bar, description
of, 38
listing transactions, 163
loan accounts, 61
updating information, 218
updating interest rates, 219
**Loan Amortization
report, 359**
Loan Interest report, 389
loan payments
automating, 212-213
Budget Planner and,
289-290
making extra, 214
Loan Terms report, 360
Loan Wizard, 65
Loan Worksheet, 219-221
loans
asset accounts, 222-223
Decisions pages, 198
determining amount to
borrow, 200-205
Marketplace, 198
refinancing, 219-221
reports, types of, 359
locating payees, 157
long-range goals, 309-310, 312
**long-term loan accounts,
creating, 206-210**
**Long-Term Savings and
Investments account
group, 308**

M

**maintaining investment
accounts, 405-406**
making deposits, 125
managing investments, *see*
investments
**manually paying bills,
240-241**

Marketplace, 198
Memo area and writing
    checks, 118
memo feature and writing
    checks, 121
menu bar, 39-40
Microsoft
    ordering checks from,
        254-255
    support Web sites, 14
    technical support,
        calling, 56
Microsoft Car Point, 199
Microsoft Investor, 402
Microsoft Money Home Page,
    help options, 54
Microsoft Online Help
    database, help options, 55
Modify button (Category
    Details screen), 100
Modify option (Details
    screen), credit card
    accounts, 183
modifying
    categories, 87
    investment accounts,
        306-307
Money
    advantages of, 4
    files, 24
    installing, 12-14
    screen, channel guides, 41
    uninstalling and
        reinstalling, 14
Money 99 Investor Web page,
    links to, 32
Money Home link, Navigation
    bar, 38
Money Home screen, 24, 41
    Accounts area, 27
    articles, 30-31
    Bills area, 26
    changing display, 28
    chart of the day, 28, 30
    links, 31-32
    monthly report, 27
    overview of, 25-26
    updating, 32-33
Money Insider Web site, links
    to, 31
Monthly Report
    categories of, 362
    Money Home screen, 27
    transactions, viewing, 364
    viewing, 363

Monthly Summary, 291-292
monthly tasks, 433-435
mortgage accounts
    balancing, 213-214
    creating, 66, 206-210
    editing in Details
        screen, 217
    updating, 218-219
mortgage payments
    automating, 212-213
    making, 210-214
mortgages, refinancing,
    219-221
moving
    accounts from one group to
        another, 308
    between accounts, 215
multiple Money files,
    creating, 24
multiple payees at one
    company, 155-157
mutual funds, 404

N

natural-language questions,
    description of, 50
navigating
    accounts, 67
    bill related items, 241
    reports, 351
Navigation bar, 10
    help tool, 53
    links, 38
    overview of, 37
negative account balances, 69
net income categories,
    creating for small
    businesses, 421-422
New Account At dialog
    box, 77
New Account icon, Account
    Manager, 61
New Account Wizard, 63-65
New button, Category Details
    screen, 100
New Category dialog box, 422
New Category Wizard, 90-93
New Contribution
    Wizard, 285
New dialog box, 398
New Loan Wizard, 197-199,
    206-210
New Paycheck Wizard,
    237-238

O

occasional expenses and
    Budget Planner, 288
one-time-only payments, 428
Online Banking area,
    Navigation bar, 76
Online Banking screen, 75
Online Banking Wizard, 77
Online Financial Services
    screen, Statements &
    Balances area, 338
online help system, 53-55
online options
    browsers and, 16
    installing and setting up, 13
    Internet connection,
        setting up, 15
Online Registration,
    selecting, 13
online services
    accounts, 75-79
    banking features, 325, 328
    bill paying, 75, 79
    canceling, 345-346
    changing banks, 346
    configuring, 329-330
    direct statements, 333
    emailing banks, 337
    multiple financial
        institutions, 340
    Online Financial Services
        screen, Statements &
        Balances area, 338
    paying bills, 330-331, 333
    payments, canceling,
        344-345
    Payments in Progress
        screen, 338-339
    Standing Orders, 340
    third-party providers, 341
    transactions
        canceling, 342-343
        checking status of,
            343-344
        setting up, 232-237
        transferring funds, 335-336
    Web statements,
        accessing, 334
Online Services tab, Options
    dialog box, 458
Online Setup option (Details
    screen), credit card
    accounts, 183
Open dialog box, 23

opening
  archive files, 446
  double-clicking, using, 47
  files, 22
  Money, 19
  Payee Details screen,
    160-162
  Payees list, 152
  reports, Spending
    Habits, 352
  transactions from charts,
    371-372
**Opening Balance option
  (Details screen), credit card
  accounts, 182**
**options, right-clicking to
  access, 44**
**Options command (Tools
  menu), 94**
Options dialog box
  backup preferences,
    changing, 442
  Connection tab, 457
  customizing features, 449
    adding recurring bills to
      Bill Calendar, 450
    bill reminder, 450
    Bills tab, 450
    Categories tab, 454-455
    Currency tab, 456
    Editing tab, 450-452
    Investments tab,
      455-456
    Planner tab, 453
  Online Services tab, 458
  Print Checks tab, 457
  Remove Unused Categories
    button, 416
  Tax tab, 458
**ordering checks from
  Microsoft, 254-255**
organizing accounts, 65-66

P

Pay Bills view, 231, 240
paychecks
  depositing, 235-238
  issuing for small businesses,
    422-423
**Payee Details list, editing
  transactions from, 164**
**Payee Details screen, opening,
  160-162**

**Payee report, changing date
  range, 165**
payees
  adding, 155
  deleting outdated, 434
  locating and replacing, 157
  multiple at one company,
    155-157
  overview of, 90
  viewing and editing
    information, 160-162
Payees list
  date range, 154
  opening, 152
  overview of, 151
  screen overview, 153
  storing contact
    information, 222
  working with, 154
paying bills
  credit card accounts,
    183-187
  manually, 240-241
  mortgage, 210, 212
  online services, 330-333
payments
  canceling for online
    services, 344-345
  one-time-only, 428
**Payments in Progress screen,
  338-339**
payroll for small businesses
  accounts, creating, 420-421
  checks, issuing, 422-423
  managing, 420
  subcategories, creating,
    421-422
  tax information, generating,
    424-425
**Performance by Investment
  Account report, 410**
**Performance by Investment
  Type report, 410**
Personal Profile
  overview of, 21
  updating information
    in, 301
pie charts, description of, 368
Planner, Navigation bar, 38
**Planner tab, Options dialog
  box, 453**
planning, overview of, 229
**points (for home buying),
  description of, 204**
**Portfolio Value by Investment
  Account report, 409, 411**

**Portfolio Value by Investment
  Type report, 409**
preparing for taxes, 384
  adding information to
    categories, 385
  reports, 389-390
  printing, 391
  Tax Worksheet, 387-388
  viewing categories, 384
Price History report, 410
**Print Checks command (File
  menu), 260**
**Print Checks dialog box,
  260, 262**
**Print Checks tab, Options
  dialog box, 457**
**Print Setup command (File
  menu), 257**
**printers, configuring for
  reports and charts, 361**
printing
  charts, 380
  checks, 253
    Check Setup dialog box,
      456-457
    information on each, 257
    Options dialog box, 457
    practicing, 255
    preparation, 256-257
    selecting transaction,
      258, 260
    setup options, 258
    steps for, 260-262
  Complete Financial
    Plan, 319
  documents, 263
  linked documents, 267
  Quicken checks, 466
  reports, 264, 362
    preparing for taxes, 391
    steps for, 265
  screens, 268
  troubleshooting, 268-269
Product Tour screen, 21
purchases, itemizing, 175-176

Q-R

quarterly tasks, 436
Quicken
  help options, 55
  printing checks, 466
  see also converting from
    Quicken

quick access to accounts, 74

rate of return on investments,
  304-305
reading articles on taxes, 386
Recently Paid Bills view,
  231, 240
reconciling accounts, 123, 466
Record Payment dialog
  box, 240
recording
  credit card transactions, 429
  credits or refunds to credit
    card accounts, 177-178
Recurring Bills & Deposits
  screen, 212, 232, 234
recurring bills,
  scheduling, 239
recurring transactions,
  232-237, 416-417
refinancing mortgages or
  loans, 219-221
refunds to credit card
  accounts, 177-178
Register, 68-69
  accessing, 133
  activities options, 136-137
  credit card, 170
  entering electronic
    payments, 331, 333
  overview of, 133
  transaction area, editing
    transactions, 72
  updating electronic
    transactions, 334
  updating mortgage
    accounts, 218-219
regular tasks, see tasks
reinstalling Money, 14
Remove Unused Categories
  button, Options dialog box,
  416, 455
renaming
  categories, 87
  charts, 375
  classifications, 106
  reports and charts, 361
replacing payees, 157
Report & Chart Gallery
  screen, 363
reports
  Budget/Actuals, 6
  budgeting, 274-275
  categories and, 350
  customizing, 361-362

date ranges, 350
deleting from My Favorites
  list, 361
editing, 358
exporting, 265-266, 353-354
favorites
  adding to, 360
  making, 353
features of, 349
investment, graphable,
  408-411
limiting scope, 350
loans, types of, 359
monthly, Money Home
  screen, 27
navigating, 351
opening, Spending
  Habits, 352
Payee, changing date
  range, 165
printing, 264-265, 362
renaming, 361
small business
  management, 419
switching to charts, 356-357
taxes, 389-391
viewing, 350
  as charts, 370
  by group, 359
Where the Money Goes, 4
Reprint button (Print Checks
  dialog box), 262
Reset button (Customize
  Report dialog box), 380
resetting
  customized charts, 380
  customized reports, 362
Restore Backup command
  (File menu), 443
Restore Standard Categories
  button (Options dialog
  box), 455
restoring
  files from backups, 443
  standard categories, 94
  voided checks, 125
retirement accounts, 61, 66
retirement planning, 408-411
Retirement Plans account
  group, 307
right-clicking, accessing
  options, 44
Rows and Columns tab
  (Customize Report dialog
  box), 377-379

S

saving charts as favorites, 380
savings accounts, 60, 64, 66
Savings and Investments
  Accounts area, Lifetime
  Planner, 302
Savings area, Decision
  Center, 320
Savings Calculator, using for
  budgeting, 276
savings goals, creating, 67
savings information and
  Budget Planner, 285
Savings page, Decisions
  area, 272
scheduling recurring
  bills, 239
Scheduling Options dialog
  box, 236
screens
  Payees list, 153
  printing, 268
second classifications,
  creating, 112
Select Chart of the Day dialog
  box, 368
selecting
  single-clicking, using, 47
  start date, 5-6
  transactions, 47
self-tests, budgeting, 273-274
selling stocks, 406
sending funds electronically,
  336
Set Up Bills & Deposits
  view, 231
setting up
  online accounts, 75-79
  online transactions, 232,
    234-237
  recurring deposits or bills,
    232-237
Short-Term Savings account
  group, 308
shortcut keys from Quicken,
  using, 467
shortcuts, creating on
  desktop, 20
single-clicking, selecting
  with, 47
small businesses
  accounts, creating, 413-414
  expenses and liabilities,
    tracking, 415-418

organizing and tracking, 414-415
payroll, managing, 420-425
running with, 413
unpaid bills, viewing, 420
Spending Habits report, 275, 352
Spending Money account group, 308
Split Transaction dialog box, 186
Split Transaction feature and writing checks, 118
split transactions
creating, 137-140
examples of, 138
paying credit card bills with, 186-187
spreadsheets, exporting reports to, 265-266
standard-size checks, 255
Standing Orders, online services, 340
start dates
accounts, 80-81
benefits of, 6
description of, 4
selecting, 5
starting Money, 19
statements, downloading, 458
Statements & Balances area (Online Financial Services screen), 338
stocks
buying, 405
prices, tracking, 405
selling, 406
storing
backup floppy disks, 441
contact information, 222
subcategories, 87, 90-93, 98
Subitem Details screen, 109
subitems
classifications, 108, 110
transactions, 111-112
switching between
bill related items, 241
chart types, 375
reports and charts, 356-357
views, 215

T

tasks
daily, 428-432
monthly, 433-435
near end of tax year, 436
overview of, 427-428
quarterly, 436
weekly, 432
tax information
categories, tracking with, 104
generating for small businesses, 424-425
tax lines, description of, 40
Tax Related Transactions report, 389
tax settings, customizing, 458
Tax Software report, 354, 390
Tax tab, Options dialog box, 458
Tax Worksheet, filling out, 387-388
taxes
overview of, 383
preparing for
adding information to categories, 385
reports, 389-391
Tax Worksheet, 387-388
viewing categories, 384
reviewing articles on, 386
third-party providers of online services, 341
Tools menu commands, 40, 94
Tooltips
description of, 48
Help system, 52
total portfolio value, viewing, 407
tracking
cash withdrawals, 141-143
expenses and liabilities for small businesses, 415-418
investments
overview of, 397
stock prices, 405
tax information, 104
transactions for credit card, 171, 174-175
transaction area, Registry view, 69
transaction dates, writing checks, 118

transactions
applying classifications to, 112
assigning categories to groups of, 102-104
assigning to new categories, 102
canceling online services, 342-343
categories, 95-98
Category Transaction list, 101
checking status of, 343-344
classifications, applying to existing, 109
creating, dates and, 70
definition of, 3
editing, 121
after entering, 72-73
from Payee Details list, 164
reconciled and cleared, 123
electronic
types of, 328
updating Register with, 334
estimating amounts, 234, 236
finding in large lists, 158-160
listing, 163
locating and replacing, 157
online, setting up, 232-237
opening from charts, 371-372
recurring, 232-237, 416-417
selecting, 47
split
creating, 137-140
paying credit card bills with, 186-187
subcategories, creating, 98
subitems, creating, 111
tracking for credit cards, 171, 174-175
viewing, 109, 134-135, 364
voiding for credit card accounts, 178
Transfer tab, Account Register, 127
transferring funds, 126-128
credit card, 176
into investment accounts, 406
online services, 335-336

troubleshooting
    account balances, 148
    installation, 14
    printing, 268-269

U-V

uninstalling Money, 14
unpaid bills, viewing, 420
Update button, 10
updating
    Money Home screen, 32-33
    mortgage accounts, 218-219
    Personal Profile
        information, 301
    Register, electronic
        transactions, 334
    tax information, 389

video tour of Money, 21
View menu commands,
    134-135
View Transactions
    window, 371
viewing
    accounts, 67-71
    Automobile category, 88-89
    categories
        in transactions, 95-96
        tax preparations, 384
    Category properties, 100
    Category Details, 99, 101
    charts, 247, 355-356
    Details screen, 181-183
    Forecasts, Lifetime
        Planner, 317
    investment accounts,
        407-411

Monthly Report, 363
payee information, 160-162
reports, 350, 359, 370
transactions, 134-135, 364
    in categories, 98
    in classifications, 109
unpaid bills, 420
views
    Bill & Deposit, 230-231
    Budget, 101
    switching between, 215
voiding
    checks, 124-125
    transactions, 178
voucher checks, 255

W

wallet-size checks, 255
Web browsers, 16, 326
Web Financial Services,
    canceling, 346
Web sites
    Ask the Experts, 295
    Budget Builder, 274
    Microsoft support, 14
    Money 99 Investor, 32
    Money Insider, 31
    printer drivers, 269
Web statements,
    accessing, 334
weekly tasks, 432
What I Have, and What I
    Owe reports, 274
What Ifs, Lifetime Planner,
    309-310, 312
What's This?, Help
    system, 52

Where the Money Goes
    report, 4
wizards
    Account, 172
    Balancing, 144-147
    Change Loan, 219
    Create New Scheduled
        Transaction, 232
    Loan, 65
    New Account, 63-65
    New Category, 90-91, 93
    New Contribution, 285
    New Loan, 197, 199,
        206-210
    New Paycheck, 237-238
    Online Banking, 77
    overview of, 43
writing checks
    Account Register, 116-119
    automatic fill-in
        feature, 120
    category types, 120
    memo feature, 121
    opening accounts, 115
    overview of, 115

X-Z

X axis, definition of, 378

Y axis, definition of, 378
Yearly Snapshot area,
    Lifetime Planner, 316
Yearly Summary, Budget
    Planner, 292